POSTHUMOUS LIVES

POSTHUMOUS LIVES

WORLD WAR I AND THE
CULTURE OF MEMORY

BETTE LONDON

CORNELL UNIVERSITY PRESS
Ithaca and London

Copyright © 2022 by Cornell University

All rights reserved. Except for brief quotations in a review, this book, or parts thereof, must not be reproduced in any form without permission in writing from the publisher. For information, address Cornell University Press, Sage House, 512 East State Street, Ithaca, New York 14850. Visit our website at cornellpress.cornell.edu.

First published 2022 by Cornell University Press

Library of Congress Cataloging-in-Publication Data

Names: London, Bette, author.
Title: Posthumous lives : World War I and the culture of memory / Bette London.
Description: Ithaca [New York] : Cornell University Press, 2022. | Includes bibliographical references and index.
Identifiers: LCCN 2021020709 (print) | LCCN 2021020710 (ebook) | ISBN 9781501762352 (hardcover) | ISBN 9781501762376 (pdf) | ISBN 9781501762369 (epub)
Subjects: LCSH: World War, 1914–1918—Influence—Great Britain. | Memorialization—Great Britain. | Memory.
Classification: LCC DA577 .L58 2022 (print) | LCC DA577 (ebook) | DDC 940.4/60941—dc23
LC record available at https://lccn.loc.gov/2021020709
LC ebook record available at https://lccn.loc.gov/2021020710

In memory
Robin London
Oscar London
Clara London

CONTENTS

List of Illustrations   ix

Preface   xi

Acknowledgments   xv

Introduction: The Afterlife of
Commemoration   1

1. Material Boys: Lives of the Dead
   and the Objects of Biography   33

2. Sorley's Travels: The Afterlife of a
   World War I Poet   72

3. Posthumous Was a Woman: War
   Memorials and Woolf's Dead Poets
   Society   120

4. Absent from Memory: Shot at Dawn
   and the Spectacle of Belated
   Remembrance   158

Notes   195

Bibliography   243

Index   257

Illustrations

I.1. Tower of London Poppies	2
I.2. The unveiling of the Cenotaph at Whitehall	3
I.3. The Cenotaph at Whitehall	3
I.4. Poppies at Tower of London, *Weeping Window*	5
I.5. Judenplatz Holocaust Memorial, Vienna, Austria	8
I.6. Poppies: *Weeping Window*, St. Magnus Cathedral, Kirkwall	13
I.7. Chloe Dewe Mathews, *Shot at Dawn* (1)	15
I.8. Shot at Dawn Memorial, National Arboretum, Staffordshire	16
I.9. Chloe Dewe Mathews, *Shot at Dawn* (2)	18
1.1. Frontispiece and title page from *Edward Wyndham Tennant* (1919)	34
1.2. Frontispiece and title page from *Christopher: A Study in Human Personality* (1918)	45
1.3. Julian and Billy Grenfell as pages	49
1.4. Front cover of *The Book of Bentley* (1918)	53
1.5. Facsimile copy of poem written by Edward Wyndham Tennant	58
1.6. Frontispiece and title page from *A Soldier of England* (1920)	61
2.1. Frontispiece photograph from *The Letters of Charles Sorley, with a Chapter of Biography* (1919)	79
2.2. Book jacket, John Press, *Charles Hamilton Sorley* (2006)	86
2.3. Royal Mail commemorative stamp, "All the Hills and Vales Along, CH Sorley" (2015)	95
2.4. Sorley's Signpost dedication	103
2.5. Book jacket, *The Poems and Selected Letters of Charles Hamilton Sorley* (1978)	107
2.6. Book jacket, *The Collected Poems of Charles Hamilton Sorley* (1985)	108
2.7. Sorley's Signpost in winter	112
2.8. Plaque commemorating Charles Hamilton Sorley, Aberdeen	115
3.1. Edith Cavell Memorial, St. Martin's Place, London	141
3.2. Edith Cavell funeral service in Westminster Abbey, *Daily Mirror* (1919)	143
3.3. Edith Cavell enlistment poster	146

x   ILLUSTRATIONS

3.4. Conscientious Objectors' Commemorative Stone, Tavistock
Square, London   157
4.1. Grave of Private Albert Ingham, Bailleulmont Communal
Cemetery, in Pas-de-Calais, France   159
4.2. Pinewood stake with metal plaque, from Shot at Dawn Memorial   178
4.3. Shot at Dawn Memorial, National Arboretum, Staffordshire   186

Preface

I come to this book from a place of forgetting. Although World War I has always seemed to exercise a peculiar hold on the British public, in the United States, despite the obligatory injunctions to remember, it remains our "forgotten war," an event even celebrated as such. The fervor around the war's centenary that was so striking in the United Kingdom did not extend with like intensity to the United States, where commemoration of the war was considerably more muted. The presumed showpiece of the US World War I centennial project, the National World War I Memorial in Washington, DC, did not open until April 2021, and the memorial remains unfinished; its centerpiece—a fifty-eight-foot-long, twelve-foot-tall bronze bas relief sculpture—is projected to be installed in 2024. What Gail Braybon describes as typically British behavior finds no echo in the United States: "People will tell you they *know* about this war—even though they are unlikely to claim much knowledge of many other historical events."[1] As Dan Todman notes, "They hold to their beliefs about these events with a fierceness that suggests personal experience."[2] Perhaps not surprisingly, then, I was never particularly engaged by World War I until I found myself in the middle of writing a book about it. As a scholar of twentieth-century British literature, I could, of course, reel off a number of accepted tropes about the war's influence on modern consciousness and the development of literary modernism—truisms I might now be more inclined to question. But unlike the British scholars I read as I researched this book, who so frequently dedicated their own books to relatives who had fought and sometimes died in the war, I recognized no immediate personal connection to it. Geoff Dyer opens *The Missing of the Somme*, his meditation on British remembrance, with a quote from Yvan Goll's "Requiem for the Dead of Europe": "*On every mantelpiece stand photographs wreathed with ivy, smiling, true to the past.*" "Dusty, bulging, old: they are all the same, these albums," Dyer goes on. "The same faces, the same photos. Every family was touched by the war and every family has an album like this."[3]

My family has no such album. And the overdetermined affective response to the war that Dyer assumes, and around which he launches his reflective

xi

xii   **PREFACE**

travelogue, has no real equivalent in the United States. But precisely for this reason, I have been fascinated by the British obsession with the Great War's remembrance. It was only late into this book that one of my cousins reminded me that our grandfather, on my mother's side, fought in the war—for the Austro-Hungarian army. Bernhard Gruen, who became Benny Green when he emigrated to the United States in 1921, lived in Radomyl Wielki, Poland, an Austrian province of Galicia; family lore has it that he joined the army so as to be allowed to leave the country. Had he not succeeded, he and his family would most likely have been exterminated during World War II, along with all the other Jewish residents of his village. Like other Jews who fought for Austria and Germany, his war service was doubly, or even triply, forgotten: by the state, by himself, and by his family. In Austrian (and Polish) memory of the war, where a national narrative was slow to emerge, Jews were marginalized, while in Jewish memory, especially after the Holocaust, there was no place to claim this experience. No stories of my grandfather's war circulated in our family, and remembrance was not part of my family's American narrative. Of my paternal grandfather, who emigrated to the United States in 1907, I realize only now I know nothing about his war service; had he remained longer in Russia, he might have been a member of the forces that took my other grandfather prisoner. What I do know about Benjamin London, né Pinchas Ladyzhinsky, is that his first wife died in 1918 in the influenza epidemic that followed the war, which is how he came to marry my grandmother. My family, then, has not been untouched by the war, even if we do not share the same remembrance rituals.

In my case, I came to the war somewhat circuitously, having studied practices of mediumship and automatic writing in the early twentieth century in my previous research—a subject that continued to nag at me, coloring the way I thought about other literary productions of this period. Both spiritualism and psychical research experienced a surge in response to the war's devastating losses, and while the influence of the war and the negotiation of grief and bereavement were only subtexts in my earlier work, their presence became increasingly important to my newer thinking about writing modern deaths and sustaining remembrance of the individual. The writing of this book was also punctuated by deaths that touched me closely—that of my sister near the beginning of my work on the book, her life abruptly foreshortened, and that of my father near the end of it, his life prolonged long after his brain was ravaged by the erasure of memory. In an uncanny echo of the war's tragic coda, after the book was completed and under review, my mother also died, one of the many victims of the COVID-19 pandemic. The tropes this book explores, then, and the remembrance practices it interrogates are not merely academic.

For both personal and professional reasons, speaking with the dead—giving posthumous life and voice to them—was unfinished business for me.

This book has been a long time in the making, its writing shadowed by the wars in Iraq and Afghanistan—conflicts that, to some extent, had their roots in the aftermath of World War I. The rituals of remembrance around these wars reflect another kind of inheritance. During the book's composition, *PBS NewsHour*'s weekly tribute, in silence, to the soldiers killed in Iraq and Afghanistan (including photographs, name, rank, and hometown for each individual) formed a steady backdrop, while the *New York Times* launched its "Faces of the Dead" and the *Washington Post* its "Faces of the Fallen" projects. As I read through the memorial volumes produced by families struggling to create narratives out of the too-short lives of now long-dead soldiers, I was listening to radio portraits on NPR of the current wars' casualties, young people widely separated by class, education, and national identity from the ones I discuss in chapter 1 of this book, but whose unnaturally brief lives posed similar memorial problems. At the same time, the 9/11 Memorial controversies played out in the background, rendering the issues I grappled with in the commemoration of World War I newly pertinent. Just as I was finishing an early draft of the manuscript, and again several years later in the wake of the Black Lives Matter movement, controversies over monuments, Confederate and otherwise, surged into the spotlight, yet another reminder of the way the questions of how, why, and what we remember, so prominently highlighted by the remembrance of World War I, continue to speak to the present. Indeed, the afterlife of its contested practices of commemoration may be one of the Great War's greatest legacies.

Acknowledgments

An undertaking of this nature and duration has many claims on memory. At the University of Rochester I have been gifted with wonderful colleagues both in and outside the Department of English. Their knowledge, engagement, and intellectual camaraderie have been of immense benefit to me. Special thanks to Tanya Bakhmetyeva, Morris Eaves, James Longenbach, Jean Pedersen, and Stewart Weaver. John Michael and Sharon Willis did more than anyone could ask for, reading the entire manuscript in an earlier iteration and providing incisive commentary and much-needed support at a critical moment; throughout, they have been ideal interlocutors. I have been lucky to have the backing of enlightened department chairs over the course of this book's long evolution. Rosemary Kegl, Katherine Mannheimer, and John Michael all encouraged me in my work on the book in many direct and indirect ways, including providing support for leave applications. The University of Rochester provided financial support toward the production costs of the book, for which I am grateful to Gloria Culver, the dean of the College of Arts and Sciences, and to the English Department.

I am also grateful to the University of Rochester for an opportunely timed Bridging Fellowship to our Humanities Center, where I enjoyed a semester's release from teaching and a year of stimulating interdisciplinary discussions on the theme of "Memory and Forgetting," just as the final stages of the book were coming together. Joan Rubin, the Humanities Center's director, deserves special thanks for her support in this endeavor and for arranging, through the center, multiple forums for me to present my work on the war's memory to both academic and nonacademic audiences. I am also grateful to the center's visiting fellows Benjamin Nienass and Daniel Blim for directing me to new sources and theoretical perspectives on memory and memorialization. My students at Rochester in multiple undergraduate courses and graduate seminars have repeatedly restored my faith in this book and helped me to refine my thinking on the subject. I am grateful to them for their intelligent engagement.

Over the years I have presented material from this book at multiple conferences, including meetings of the Modernist Studies Association, the International

xvi **ACKNOWLEDGMENTS**

Conference on Narrative, the Space Between Society, the International Virginia Woolf Conference, and the Northeast Modern Language Association, where I was a featured speaker for the British and Anglophone Division, and more specialized conferences such as the "Death and Representation" conference sponsored by the University of Rochester's English department, the "Great War from Memory to History" conference at Western Ontario University, and the English Association's "British Poetry of the First World War" conference at Oxford University, and as part of the Juxtapositions lecture series at the University at Buffalo and the Phelps Colloquium at the University of Rochester. My book has been enriched by the feedback I received on these occasions and by the intellectual contacts they fostered. Among those deserving special notice for arranging panels and other venues for presentation are Stacy Hubbard, Suha Kudsieh, Holly Laird, Elizabeth Outka, and Melissa Zeiger.

I am grateful to my editor at Cornell University Press, Mahinder Kingra, for ably shepherding the manuscript from review to production—and for the enthusiasm with which he greeted the book from the beginning. And I am grateful to the anonymous readers for the Press for their intelligent and thoughtful commentary and helpful suggestions for revision. Matthew Skwiat has been a tireless research assistant; I am indebted to him for his help in searching out images and obtaining image permissions, as well as contributing two images he personally photographed. Jennifer Thompson Stone ably assisted with proofreading and other editorial matters in a late stage of production. Melissa Mead, the University of Rochester archivist, provided invaluable assistance scanning images; I do not know what I would have done without her. Grainne Lenehan, the college archivist at Marlborough College, searched out information on Marlborough College's commemoration of Charles Sorley. Julian Putkowski has kept me alerted to new creative and critical sources on the shot-at-dawn soldiers. Jean Moorcroft Wilson generously granted permission to reproduce images of the book jackets for two Cecil Woolf publications.

These acknowledgments would not be complete without mention of the friends and family who have sustained me. Morris and Georgia Eaves and John Michael and Sharon Willis have been my bedrock, providing emotional support and inspired meals and conversation. Through illness and loss, they have been my second family. I am grateful as well to my actual family—including those who did not live to see the book's completion: my sister Robin, who believed in this book before I even knew it was one, and my parents, whose support for me was always unwavering. As ever, I am grateful to Jonathan Hahn, Geoffrey Hahn, and Francesca Luciani Hahn for being part of my life—and to Olivia and Marcus Hahn for reminding me of what matters. Joel and Amy London have provided stalwart support, and Liz and Stephanie London, in their unfolding lives, are creating new London family memories. Barry Green reminded me of my own family's connection to the war, and Jenny Altschuler, with her genealogical expertise, helped me fill in some of the details. Finally, my debt to Tom Hahn cannot be measured. He has read every word of this book—too many times to enumerate—and his voice is inevitably intertwined with mine. For too many years now he has put up with my World War I obsession. His love and support have seen me through both the best and the worst of times.

Several sections of this book have been previously published. Parts of chapter 1, in a somewhat different framework, appeared as "Writing Modern Deaths: Women, War, and the View from the Home Front," in *The History of British Women's Writing, 1880–1920*, vol. 7, ed. Holly Laird (London: Palgrave Macmillan, 2016), 284–297. A version of chapter 3 was published as "Posthumous Was a Woman: World War I Memorials and Woolf's Dead Poet's Society," *Woolf Studies Annual* 16 (2010): 45–69 (copyright © 2010 by Pace University Press), and a version of chapter 4 as "The Names of the Dead: 'Shot at Dawn' and the Politics of Remembrance," in *The Great War: From Memory to History*, ed. Kellen Kurschinski et al. (Waterloo, ON: Wilfrid Laurier University Press, 2015), 171–192. I am grateful to Palgrave Macmillan, Pace University Press, and Wilfrid Laurier University Press for permission to republish these works.

POSTHUMOUS LIVES

Introduction

The Afterlife of Commemoration

From July to November 2014, in what has been called "the defining image of the 2014–1914 commemorations," the "most visited and talked about public art installation for a generation," the Tower of London became a staging ground for the Great War's centenary celebration.[1] During the four months of The Poppies installation, formally titled "Blood Swept Lands and Seas of Red," 888,246 ceramic poppies were "planted" in the Tower moat and cascaded from its window—one poppy for each British and colonial soldier killed during the war. The effect was stunning. For a brief moment, this corner of London was transformed into a virtual trench, a theater of war, a field of memory—an embodiment of the installation's title (figure I.1). Conceived by Paul Cummins, a ceramic artist, and executed by Tom Piper, a freelance set designer, the installation was in fact envisaged theatrically—as an immersive experience. But to revise my previous statement, it was a theater not so much of war as of the war's memorialization; as the ever-present poppies signaled, it was a site of remembrance of the war's commemoration. Indeed, the Tower of London poppies installation recalls, in spectacular fashion, the memorial frenzy of the 1920s—one reason I have chosen it as my starting point for this book. As Alex King observes, "The commemoration of the dead of the First World War was probably the largest and most popular movement for the erection of public monuments ever known in Western society."[2]

INTRODUCTION

FIGURE I.1. Tower of London poppies. "Blood Swept Lands and Seas of Red," July 28–November 11, 2014. Photo credit: Rick Ligthelm, https://creativecommons.org/licenses/by/2.0/deed.en

For the four months the Tower was occupied in 2014, an estimated five million people visited the installation—the closest thing perhaps to the crowds that thronged the unveiling of the permanent Cenotaph and the burial of the Unknown Warrior in November 1920 (according to some reports, a million in one week alone), which was replicated on a smaller scale in tens of thousands of memorial unveilings across the nation (figure I.2). Each night of The Poppies installation saw the reenactment of other established memorial rituals: the reading of names from the Roll of Honour, the playing of "Last Post" at sunset. And just as the public clamored in 1919 to make the original Cenotaph—a wood and plaster edifice hastily constructed for the Peace Day celebration of July 1919—a permanent memorial in the heart of London, public calls to extend the life of The Poppies began almost the moment the exhibition opened.

In both cases, the intensity of the popular response exceeded all expectations. Indeed, in the case of the Cenotaph—an empty tomb—many were skeptical of the public embracing such an abstract, geometric, and minimalist formation: no sculpted figures, no flowery words, no ornate decoration, and, most controversial at the time, perhaps, no Christian symbolism (figure I.3). Nor did it include what would become one of the defining features of later World War I memorials: the listing of name upon name of the fallen. Instead,

FIGURE I.2. The unveiling of the Cenotaph at Whitehall (1920). Photo credit: Horace Nicholls © Imperial War Museum (Q 31513)

FIGURE I.3. The Cenotaph at Whitehall (2018). Photo credit: Matthew Skwiat

4   INTRODUCTION

it offered only the dates of the conflict and the terse inscription "The Glorious Dead." Reporting on responses to the proposed design for the original monument, Lord Curzon, the chair of the War Cabinet Committee on Peace Celebrations, enumerated the objections: "that it was foreign to the temper and custom of the nation; that it might not be easy for the public to assume a properly reverential attitude."[3] In the event, however, so powerful was the emotion the Cenotaph generated and so reverential the attitude of the public that no changes in design were allowed when the memorial was made permanent, despite the efforts of some powerful special interests; the *Church Times* even went so far as to blast the public response as "cenotapholatry."[4]

Imagining the Great War in the Age of Postmemory

If the Cenotaph's stark white stone and understated presentation contrast sharply with The Poppies' overflowing Technicolor declaration, both structures served similar functions for their respective audiences, carving out of busy London a space of private reckoning with the monumental reality of death in war. And both offered this space for private contemplation amid a crowd of others. The conditions, however, that produced these temporally distant memorial moments were dramatically different. While memorials like the Cenotaph were erected to meet the needs of a grief-stricken nation—to provide a locus for still-overwhelming emotion—The Poppies spoke to those without living memory of the war or, in many instances, even living memory of those who lived through it. In this sense, the installation was literally postmemory. As its reception suggests, however, it also spoke to a more particular understanding of the term—to a desire to experience the deep and affective relationship to the past that Marianne Hirsch has described as "postmemory," to the longing for personal connection to what many perceived to be the shaping event of the century. For Hirsch, writing in the context of the Holocaust, "postmemory" references the affective burden of "inherited memories" for "the second generation," the children of Holocaust victims and survivors. It "describes the relationship that the 'generation after' bears to the personal, collective, and cultural trauma of those who came before—to experiences they 'remember' only by means of stories, images, and behaviors among which they grew up. But these experiences were transmitted to them so deeply and affectively as to *seem* to constitute memories in their own right."[5] The audience for The Poppies, however, almost all at least two generations removed from the Great War's trauma, was, one might argue, in search of this burden.

FIGURE I.4.   Poppies at Tower of London. *Weeping Window*. Photo credit: iStock.com/asmithers

Consequently, affect, like the poppies themselves, had to be manufactured. The scale of the installation and the labor required to realize it—888,246 handmade poppies, each requiring three days' work from skilled potters; the thirty thousand volunteers recruited to execute the planting; the feats of engineering to create the scaffolding structures (figure I.4)—all worked to visibly convey the magnitude of the human tragedy that was gradually unfolding (at 80,000 "lives/poppies" per week) in the installation's compressed time frame. In this, The Poppies recalled the massive efforts to construct the military cemeteries and the Great War's memorials to the missing—structures that also innovatively dealt with the problem of visualizing death on such a large scale; although the exhibition's designer insisted that he "had always hoped to create something very different" from the "ordered formality" of the "Flanders Field memorials," the echoes nonetheless persisted.[6]

By all accounts, the installation was wildly successful in producing what participants reported as a profoundly moving experience—an opportunity, in a highly personalized way, to touch and be touched by the human toll of this catastrophic occurrence of a hundred years ago. As Tom Piper remarked, "Everybody felt they could own it," much the way contemporary audiences responded to the burial of the Unknown Warrior in 1920; in the case of The Poppies, some did so quite literally—through the postinstallation purchase of individual poppies (twenty-five pounds each, with proceeds distributed to six

6   **INTRODUCTION**

charities).[7] The installation, however, was not without its detractors, most notably Jonathan Jones, the art critic for the *Guardian*, who attacked it on grounds both political and aesthetic. "It is deeply disturbing," he wrote, "that a hundred years on from 1914, we can only mark this terrible war as a national tragedy"— that we "still narrowly remember our own dead" but do not mourn any of the other victims, a practice, in fact, at odds with centennial commemorations on the Continent. Echoing century-old complaints about the burial of the Unknown Warrior as "an orgy of sentimentalism," he attacked the installation as "a deeply aestheticised, prettified and toothless war memorial," suggesting that it would have been more fitting to fill the Tower moat with bones and barbed wire.[8] Even more interesting than the critique, however, was the vehemence of the pushback against it. The *Daily Mail* shot back with the headline "Why DO the Left Despise Patriotism?" (October 29, 2014). And Prime Minister Cameron intervened to defend The Poppies, calling it a "stunning display" and "extremely poignant."[9] The artists who designed the installation were quick to cast the controversy in terms of an out-of-touch art establishment at odds with the powerful forces of a grassroots populism: Turner Prize elitism versus art for the people. Indeed, they were quick to advertise their likely snub by the Turner Prize committee; one leading figure in the art world was reported as saying that if The Poppies had been signed by one of the darlings of the avant-garde like Rachel Whiteread or Jeremy Deller (both of whom later went on to produce their own centenary installations), it would surely have snagged a nomination.[10] Piper went even further, suggesting that if the installation had been done by anyone else—anyone, that is, other than a Derby-based ceramics artist and a stage designer—it would have been duly recognized by the arbiters of culture.

The situation, of course, was somewhat more complicated, in part, at least, a conflict between competing culture industries. For the populism of The Poppies was a populism aligned with state-sponsored institutions. Indeed, the parade of dignitaries photographed paying their respects—the prime minister, for example, and members of the royal family—was reminiscent of the processional march associated with Armistice Day ceremonies at the Cenotaph, if not quite as scripted. And while defenders of The Poppies pushed back against Jones's accusation of a United Kingdom Independence Party fingerprint, Nigel Farage, the party's leader, exploited the occasion to have himself prominently photographed wiping a tear at the memorial. Only days after the artists announced that they would be overlooked for the Turner, it was disclosed that they were to receive one of the highest Order of the British Empire awards, the MBE, in the queen's New Year Honours List, to be inducted as Members of the Most Excellent Order of the British Empire. As the Tower of London location signals, moreover, the installation marks (and exploits) an intersection of commemoration, British tourism, and the heritage industry—one of whose arms, Historic Royal Palaces, sponsored it.[11]

Turner bashing, I should point out, has its own long history, a popular British sport since the prize's inception in 1984. In 1993, for example, the K Foundation established an anti-Turner prize, at twice the monetary value, for the worst artist of the year, shortlisting precisely the same artists as the Turner Prize did. Rachel Whiteread, singled out for comparison in The Poppies controversy, had the dubious distinction of winning both prizes simultaneously in 1994, of being declared both the best and the worst visual artist of the year.[12] She was also, incidentally, the first woman to win the Turner. I mention this here because Whiteread's many credentials include the design of the Judenplatz Holocaust Memorial in Vienna, unveiled in 2000—a memorial to the sixty-five thousand Austrian Jews who perished during the war. Also known as the "Nameless Library," the memorial is a concrete structure whose walls are covered in rows and rows of books, the spines turned inward, so that only the edges of the cover and the closed pages are visible. The door is locked, offering no access (figure I.5). When Whiteread offered her own more modest contribution to the First World War Centenary commemorations in October 2018, she created a similarly closed-off, inside-out structure in Dalby Forest, Yorkshire: a concrete casting of the interior of a Nissen hut, a prefab military structure invented during the war and used by the military as barracks and hospital units, as well as prisoner-of-war and reforestation labor camps. In contrast to the hypervisibility of The Poppies, the Nissen hut formed a part of Whiteread's "Shy Sculpture Series," a succession of casts of small buildings sited in unexpected, out-of-the-way places.[13] Both the British and the Austrian constructions, then, represent a very different understanding of the work a war memorial might do from the Tower of London poppies, rendering unthinkable the idea that The Poppies was an artwork that could have been produced by her. As Simon Wiesenthal declared at the unveiling of the Judenplatz memorial, "This monument shouldn't be beautiful, it must hurt."[14] He might have added, it must be difficult, baffling. By contrast, the creators of The Poppies lauded its accessibility and transparency. "It was so simple and beautiful," Piper claimed, requiring no "intellectual comment"; "It's not pretentious, and what you see is what you get," Cummins corroborated.[15]

One can hear in these remarks echoes of the debates that surrounded the postwar memorial project—a project whose iterations I take up in subsequent chapters—and the same rejection, by and large, of modernist art in favor of traditional motifs and forms as an appropriate language for bereavement. This, in fact, is the gist of Jay Winter's argument in *Sites of Memory, Sites of Mourning*:

FIGURE I.5. Judenplatz Holocaust Memorial, Vienna, Austria. Photo credit: Yair Haklai, https://creativecommons.org/licenses/by-sa/3.0/deed.en

"The Great War, the most 'modern' of wars, triggered an avalanche of the 'unmodern.'"[16] Indeed, despite the potentially modernist features of the Cenotaph, it was not embraced by modernists, and as Jenny Edkins argues, over the years it has been increasingly appropriated by state-sponsored rituals and ceremonies that "re-introduce the elements of myth and glory that the monument itself so carefully side-stepped."[17] By the time of The Poppies installation, however, the conceptual terrain of memorial-making had decisively shifted in the direction of minimalism and abstraction, as evidenced by the Vietnam Veterans Memorial in Washington, DC, as well as major Holocaust memorials throughout Europe. Reviving the postwar antimodernist debates, as The Poppies controversy did so many years later, thus threatened to cast the installation as a throwback. But if The Poppies' reception invoked these earlier debates, it did so as a postmemory occurrence—without any acknowledged sense of the history it was repeating.

The Poppies was undoubtedly a phenomenon—a national event, much like the Cenotaph and the Tomb of the Unknown Warrior had been, and a global visitor attraction. It captured the imagination of the public in ways even its originators could not have dreamed possible. "The whole country has been struck by the power of this work," David Cameron proclaimed, an assessment

THE AFTERLIFE OF COMMEMORATION

confirmed in media coverage.[18] This formulation, however, leaves no space for possible dissension. Indeed, the rush with which any critique was silenced made proper affective response to the installation a mark of citizenship, homogenizing remembrance in the presumption of a single, unified, and unifying experience. As Winter argues, such an attitude defined the very nature of remembrance from the war's inception: "After August 1914, commemoration was an act of citizenship. To remember was to affirm community, to assert its moral character, and to exclude from it those values, groups, or individuals that placed it under threat."[19] Virginia Woolf, as I will discuss in chapter 3, recoiled from this enforced unity and the compulsion to perform an affective response that was prescripted, and she was not alone in expressing such sentiments. In her diary entry for December 12, 1920, Woolf decried the spectacle of "women crying Remember the Glorious Dead, & holding out chrysanthemums" on the night of the Cenotaph's unveiling. "A ghastly procession of people in their sleep," she called the evening's outpouring.[20] D. H. Lawrence, as Marlene Briggs documents, was even more vocal in his attack on the entire "iconography of remembrance," disparaging two of its centerpieces: the Tomb of the Unknown Warrior (1920) and the Haig Fund poppy appeal (1921). For Lawrence, identification with the tomb was, in Briggs's words, "a species of idolatry when veterans can neither feed nor clothe themselves without begging"—a sentiment shared by many veterans.[21] As early as November 11, 1921, the Cenotaph had become a site of protest in what was called "a pilgrimage of the unemployed," with ex-servicemen distributing handbills reading, "BUT DON'T FORGET THE UNKNOWN WARRIORS LIVING."[22]

Indeed, as recent scholarship has demonstrated, within the United Kingdom, and across the British Empire more generally, the war was experienced and remembered differently among different national, regional, gender, and class constituencies, differences masked by the uniformity The Poppies so strikingly figured. The installation, in fact, suppresses all particularities of the soldiers represented, including that of the soldier whose words—the "blood swept lands and seas of red"—ostensibly inspired it: a soldier, according to Cummins, "who was actually female, posing as a man so she might fight."[23] Gender, however, was only one of the differences The Poppies glossed over. A growing body of scholarship, for example, has explored the conflicted subject of Irish memory, while Anzac memory has emerged as its own complex and distinct entity in Australia and New Zealand. For colonial soldiers, the gap in remembrance practices is even greater. As Santanu Das reminds us, "Just because Britain is obsessed with the war does not mean it is regarded as being equally significant or holds the same meaning in the former colonies."[24] Claire Buck has illuminated the British wartime "fascination with the cultural and racial

10   INTRODUCTION

otherness" of Indian and other non-European soldiers and "the strangeness of their presence on the home ground of the British isles," when, for example, they were sent to recuperate in English military hospitals; her research prompts the question of how we might *now* read the symbolic presence of these soldiers on British home soil in The Poppies exhibition.[25] Visitor responses to the installation suggest that they simply did not register them.[26] The specificity of the number—888,246 poppies—moreover, suggests a comprehensiveness in the body count far from assured, especially in the case of colonial soldiers, as Michèle Barrett's work on differential burial practices indicates.[27] Nor does it speak to the many lives lost that remain, in Judith Butler's term, ungrievable within the terms of the memorial: those who cooked, transported, and labored; those who died after the war from war-related physical and psychic injuries; nurses, munitions workers, ambulance drivers; conscientious objectors; civilian casualties.[28] There is also the even more fundamental question of the underlying assumption, enforced by the cult of the dead and its long legacy, that the dead are the only figures to be memorialized and the primary way we measure the war's impact.

One of the great ironies of The Poppies installation was the ability of fake poppies to inspire authentic emotion—much as they did when the British Legion first established Poppy Day in 1921, and the Remembrance Poppy "stormed public sentiment." Within a year, demand for the silk poppies had tripled, and the poppies acquired added pathos with the decision to have them manufactured by disabled veterans.[29] But in 2014 the choice of poppies as the vehicle for the centenary commemoration was overdetermined and, for some, at least, coercive. For others, the emotion generated was short-lived, if not spurious, as evidenced by the opportunistic sale of previously purchased poppies on online auction sites after the exhibition was dismantled. If, as a member of the Women's Co-operative Guild remembered, "between the wars it was absolutely unthinkable not to wear a red poppy on 11 November,"[30] in the years leading up to the centennial, poppy wearing had become increasingly politicized. A number of right-wing groups amped up the celebration of the poppy as the embodiment of national identity, while some on the left, decrying "poppy fascism," even went so far as to organize poppy burnings.[31]

Such contentiousness, however, was not an entirely new phenomenon. By the mid-1920s the poppy was already embroiled in controversy, with the No More War Movement protesting its ties to military culture; in 1933 the Women's Co-operative Guild began producing and selling white poppies as a symbol for peace—a practice that continues to the present under the auspices of the Peace Pledge Union, where it has become a symbol of "alternative Armistice Day" celebrations. Pointedly, "the white poppy signified all the dead of the war, military, civilian, allied and enemy."[32] Since 2000, supporters of the soldiers shot at dawn for desertion and cowardice have worn poppies with the centers painted white to remember the way these men died—with a white cloth pinned over their hearts as they faced the firing squad. In Ireland, the poppy has long been considered a divisive symbol because of its association with the British Armed Forces, so much so that when a portion of The Poppies was exhibited in Northern Ireland in 2017, the contentiousness of the symbol was the first thing the local sponsors had to plan for.[33] The poppies, then, that made up the "seas of red" in the Tower of London exhibition were not necessarily neutral symbols, despite efforts to align the installation with contemporary peace movements and despite the designer's insistence that he approached the project from the perspective of a pacifist.

The poppy, of course, was also challenged for being too predictable—a stand-in for a whole host of myths and patented ideas about the war; an emblem capable of triggering a set of associations so familiar as not to require naming. As Hew Strachan remarked in 2013, expressing his fears about the upcoming centenary, "What we also 'remember' is the familiarity of Remembrance Sunday, of poppies and the Cenotaph, the symbols through which the First World War is still most commonly refracted today." If the centenary "simply reworks the familiar themes of remembrance, it will be repetitive, sterile and possibly even boring," he concludes. "If we do not emerge at the end of the process in 2018 with fresh perspectives, we shall have failed."[34] But failure threatens from multiple directions. Responding to the critique that barbed wire and bones would have made a more appropriate statement, Tom Piper, designer of The Poppies, countered, "For me, bones would have been a much triter, more obvious thing to do,"[35] underlining a central problem of postmemory memorials: how to avoid falling back on familiar images and tropes presumed to carry ready-made poignancy.

In a story incessantly replayed in media coverage of the exhibition, Paul Cummins, the artist who first conceived the project, described its inspiration: his stumbling across the words "blood swept lands and seas of red, where angels fear to tread" scrawled on the will of an unknown soldier who died in the conflict. "It read like a poem and it just seemed to fit," he explained.[36] One is left to wonder, however, whether one hundred years out from the event, the power and poignancy of the words derive from their familiarity rather than their haunting resonance. And one is left to wonder whether the immense popularity of the installation depends on the ease with which it fits popular perceptions of the war as horror, death, and futility—or, as Squadron Commander, the Lord Flashheart in *Blackadder Goes Forth* famously put it, "the blood, the noise, the endless poetry." The readiness with which the public responded,

12 **INTRODUCTION**

then, might also owe something to the way, as discussed in chapter 2, the British public has been trained to understand the war though its poets and poetry, with the "war poet" serving as a privileged site of memory. The words of the anonymous soldier, however, that did not make it into the exhibition's title—"where angels fear to tread"—point to another possibility: that the metaphors so movingly invoked in this fragment, the "blood swept lands and seas of red," might have been, even in the time of the conflict, already a cliché. This possibility appears all the stronger when one realizes that the lines chosen for the exhibition's title do not just read like a poem—they are in fact part of a poem considerably less forceful in its entirety than in the lines excerpted from it.[37] Lines of a similar nature, in fact, can be found throughout the archive of soldiers' writing. Santanu Das, for example, cites a letter from 1915 sent by an Indian doctor, Captain Kalyan Mukherji, to his mother: "Rivers of blood, red—everywhere." The evocative phrase raises the question of what the exhibition might have looked like if *this* soldier's words—a soldier who only a short time later laid the blame for the bloodshed on the "patriotism that the English have taught us"—were Cummins's launching point.[38] It is also perhaps worth questioning whether some might have heard in "Blood Swept Lands and Seas of Red" an echo of Enoch Powell's infamous "Rivers of Blood" anti-immigration speech of 1968.

The question, then, one might pose to centenary installations like The Poppies is whether, to borrow Hirsch's terms, the expressive forms and distant memorial structures that once marked the war's remembrance can be "reactivated" and "re-embodied" through present-day imaginative investments or whether they end up simply being recycled—a question whose answer has by no means been decided.[39] The afterlife of The Poppies, however, complicates the subject. For despite the creators' insistence that the installation would be temporary—that its meaning resided in its transience—a portion of the installation has been "saved for the nation," while the bulk has been dismantled.[40] Indeed, parts of the installation have been literally recycled—in the touring exhibition of its most dramatic structures, *Wave* and *Weeping Window* (figure I.6), and in the redistribution of the purchased poppies. Between July 2015 and November 2018, The Poppies traveled to seventeen locations across England, Scotland, Northern Ireland, and Wales, including castles, museums, parks, cathedrals, public meeting halls, a pottery, a mill, a barge pier, and the National Assembly of Wales, attracting four million visitors. A kind of "Poppies Lite," far short of the 888,246 poppies of the original, the installation was reimagined as a traveling site of memory, reinforcing its place in what Annette Becker has called "the new tourism of remembrance."[41] It was reimagined, moreover, as a way to give posthumous life to the exhibition—a chance to "revisit" the

THE AFTERLIFE OF COMMEMORATION

FIGURE I.6. St. Magnus Cathedral entrance with poppies. From The Poppies touring exhibition: *Weeping Window*, St. Magnus Cathedral, Kirkwall, April 22–June 12, 2016. Photo credit: Hans Henning, https://creativecommons.org/licenses/by-sa/4.0/deed.en

Tower of London installation for those who did not get to see it in its original manifestation. Indeed, the last stop on the regional tour before a final showing in London was the Middleport Pottery in Stoke-on-Trent where just under half of the poppies for the exhibition were created, reinforcing the tour's self-referential element. The "Where Are the Poppies Now" website provided another way for The Poppies to "live on" as a "virtual global installation," mapping the locations of the purchased poppies and providing a platform for their owners' stories; at the same time, it reveals how the individual poppies were refashioned by the people who purchased them—attached to lives beyond the World War I dead the exhibition commemorated.[42] At the end of the tour—and the end of the centennial season—*Wave* and *Weeping Window* were exhibited in the Imperial War Museum in London and Manchester, respectively, where both subsequently found permanent homes, thus institutionalizing the ephemeral and adding another layer to the commemoration of commemoration.[43]

The second centenary exhibition I turn to now operates from an opposite principle, testing the limits of the tropes and mechanisms of remembrance on which The Poppies depended—and which had been so central to a hundred

14   **INTRODUCTION**

years of the war's commemoration—by, in effect, dispensing with them. *Shot at Dawn*, a small photographic exhibition, unfolded largely below the radar, at least in comparison to The Poppies extravaganza; in medium, scale, aesthetic, and subject matter, it could not have been more different from the Tower of London poppies. The two, however, were both executed under the same national umbrella organization, 14-18 NOW: WW1 Centenary Art Commissions; both ran under the organization's banner, "Extraordinary arts experiences connecting people with the First World War"—the very formulation suggesting that connection can no longer be taken for granted but needs to be mediated. Both, moreover, could be understood as types of memorials, as were the other art commissions the organization sponsored, including those by Jeremy Deller and Rachel Whiteread, the artists badmouthed in The Poppies controversy.[44] *Shot at Dawn* was a photographic exhibition, commissioned by the Ruskin School of Art at the University of Oxford and executed by Chloe Dewe Mathews, an award-winning photographer. It consists of twenty-three photographs of sites where a thousand British, Irish, Belgian, French, French-African, and Commonwealth soldiers were executed for cowardice and desertion, or where they were held in the period leading up to their execution (figure I.7).[45] Like the late-stage iteration of The Poppies, it was a touring exhibition, running from November 2014 to July 2016, but its international itinerary—Edinburgh, London, Essen, Dresden, Dublin, Madrid—and its highbrow museum locations suggest a very different purpose from The Poppies' nationalist/populist agenda. In addition to the material installations, it appeared in multiple platforms: an art book, a web presence, and a University of Oxford podcast in "The First World War: New Perspectives" series.

If The Poppies surprised with its fanciful and abundant take on a familiar memorial icon, *Shot at Dawn* was an unusual choice for centennial representation for entirely different reasons. For decades after the war—indeed, until the late twentieth century—the stories of the 306 British soldiers shot at dawn for military offenses were largely suppressed in the United Kingdom and their names excised from public memory, as I will discuss in chapter 4; only in 2006, after a long and contentious campaign, did they receive retrospective pardons from the British government and some form of restitution in local war memorials. For many, however, their case remained controversial. For many, moreover, like Mathews herself, who did not know about the executions until she began the project, the story of these executed men has remained invisible. That they could now be showcased in leading educational and cultural institutions and appear under the banner of official sites of commemoration was a triumph of the once unthinkable. More than that, Mathews's exhibition was not the only shot-at-dawn event to be commissioned by 14-18 NOW,

FIGURE I.7. From Chloe Dewe Mathews, *Shot at Dawn* series. Private Joseph Byers, Private Andrew Evans, time unknown/06.02.1915; Private George E. Collins, 07:30/15.02.1915. Photo credit: © Chloe Dewe Mathews

although the other commission, *The 306*, a trilogy of plays, approached the subject from a very different angle.[46] Unlike The Poppies, Mathews's centenary commemoration did not focus exclusively on the British experience; Mathews, in fact, deliberately approached her subject from a transnational perspective. She had wanted to include German sites as well, but there were no available records, the silence and suppression surrounding such executions extending well beyond British borders. Mathews's photographs offer no clues to the national identity of the victims. Indeed, they offer no clue whatsoever to the soldiers' identities.

Mathews was not the first British artist to commemorate these soldiers. In 2001, Andy DeComyn's Shot at Dawn Memorial was unveiled at the National Arboretum in Staffordshire (figure I.8), but, as will be discussed in chapter 4, its aesthetic is strikingly different; unlike Mathews's exhibition, DeComyn's memorial was not a commission but rather, in the artist's words, "a gift to the families." And its design and location reflect what the family members of these soldiers had long been lobbying for and what the Shot at Dawn campaign had promoted: an affective relationship previously denied them—a relationship to

FIGURE I.8. Shot at Dawn Memorial, National Arboretum, Staffordshire. Photo credit: Harry Mitchell, https://creativecommons.org/licenses/by/4.0/deed.en

a family member, to the Great War, and to communal rites of commemoration. They were seeking, belatedly, to be part of the culture of memorialization—a culture whose rituals continue into the present. What the National Arboretum offered them was a ratification of their loss and a dedicated memorial location, even if it remained separate from established sites of remembrance and was funded by individual donations.[47] As the arboretum's director admitted at the time, not too many years earlier such a project would not have gotten off the drawing board. "I don't think there is a person alive today who would say these deserters should be shot," he proclaimed—a statement that, if undoubtedly an exaggeration, nonetheless expressed the new visibility of these soldiers' plight and a "sea change" in public opinion.[48]

By the time Chloe Mathews took up her commission, then, shot-at-dawn soldiers had commanded considerable popular attention, if not institutional legitimation in established war narratives. Conservative politicians and self-styled revisionist historians, with military historians at the forefront, continued to insist that the pardons, granted in 2006, constituted a rewriting of history—an imposition of anachronistic values—and that attention to these soldiers was disproportionate to their importance in the larger context of the war and an impediment to a more nuanced understanding of its operations.

THE AFTERLIFE OF COMMEMORATION　17

The cultural institutions that supported Mathews's exhibition are significant, therefore, as markers of the changing shape of World War I studies. Even more remarkable, though, than this official recognition was the way Mathews went about realizing the project. Refusing preemptive visualization, her work could not have been more different from DeComyn's memorial, with its oversize figure of a soon-to-be-executed soldier, and its heavy-handed symbolism, with the surrounding wooden stakes representing all of the victims. Nor did her work have much in common with the frequently reproduced photographic portraits of the soldiers that featured so prominently in the Shot at Dawn campaign any more than it did, as will be discussed in chapter 4, with the bios that accompanied them, fictionalizations and dramatizations of these unknown men's stories.

Working in an exact and methodical fashion to photograph the sites of executions at as close as possible to the precise time of day and time of year of the incidents—information she gleaned through meticulous research—Mathews spent two years studying and photographing these locations. What she recorded was a series of austere landscapes, sparsely filled places marked by absence—the absence of the person presumably at the center of the story, the individual who was executed, as well as the officers and men who made up the firing squad—figures DeComyn displays so prominently and symbolically (figure I.9). Generally shot at dawn (and occasionally sunset), the photographs cast an eerie light on their missing subject, creating the impression, as Geoff Dyer suggests, that "the thing that gives a particular spot its meaning—a dead body—has been painstakingly removed."[49] They provoke, then, by withholding. What it means to revisit these scenes one hundred years after the fact is at the heart of the project—one that demands an ethical engagement from the spectator, who must see what only becomes visible when one knows what has happened there. As Mathews explains, "Initially, I was wary of taking on a project about the first world war as I have no personal connection with it . . . but, from a documentary photography perspective, I was drawn to the idea of arriving somewhere 100 years afterwards."[50] Put another way, the project was born postmemory. In registering these present absences, Mathews insists on an alterity that resists conceptualization, while maintaining that the landscape bears traces of the trauma. "It's almost the opposite of war photography," she explained of her process. "So, instead of the photographer bearing witness, it is the landscape that has witnessed the event and I who am having to go into that landscape in the hope of finding anything tangibly connected to the event. It was almost like having to find a new language or way of seeing."[51] Tangibility, I should add, is here a manner of speaking; actual tangible items—a bullet embedded in soil, or scrawled words still visible on a wall where a condemned

18   INTRODUCTION

FIGURE I.9.   From Chloe Dewe Mathews, *Shot at Dawn* series. Soldat Ali Ben Ahmed Ben Frej Ben Khelil, Soldat Hassen Ben Ali Ben Guerra El Amolani, Soldat Ahmed Ben Mohammed El Yadjizy, Soldat Mohammed Ould Mohammed Ben Ahmed, 17:00/15/12/1914. Photo credit: © Chloe Dewe Mathews

man was held—are the exceptions in Mathews's photographic repertoire. If, as Winter repeatedly and crucially insists, "Remembrance is part of the landscape," Mathews gives this claim new meaning.[52]

The idea that the landscape bears the residue of the cataclysmic events performed upon it has also shaped centennial efforts along the old Western Front, efforts that have focused on site-specific commemorations. But these other European memorials come at the landscape from very different directions. As Annette Becker has documented, the dominant mode on the Western Front has been a kind of heritage-making, marked by the installation of museums, interpretive centers, signposts, and self-guided tour itineraries, shaping what visitors are invited to remember—often, she argues, at the expense of history. As the ultimate confirmation of this tendency, she notes, "A UNESCO committee is now classifying the traces of battlefields, under the heading of 'Landscapes and Sites of Memory of the Great War.'"[53] The locations Mathews chooses for her photographic testimonials, are, by contrast, not the stuff of UNESCO efforts; indeed, they exist in competition with that over-

THE AFTERLIFE OF COMMEMORATION   19

charged zone of memory—a realm so steeped in memory that, as Dyer argues, certain events like the ones that Mathews documents have inevitably been forgotten, gone missing, or been obliterated.[54] Mathews frames her shots to provoke remembrance, to reanimate and preserve these forgotten but emotionally loaded places, but she refuses signposts and interpretive guides, offering only the barest information to orient her viewer: name and rank of soldier and time, date, and place of execution. She refuses the personalizing stories, the pathos-filled anecdotes, that accompanied the Shot at Dawn pardons campaign, as I will discuss in chapter 4; even the names of the soldiers are barely legible in the exhibition's installation, given the small size of the print on the modest accompanying labels. Interestingly, reviews of her exhibition often supplied precisely this missing information and these missing narratives. Commenting on other Western Front commemorations, Becker speculates, "Perhaps the impossibility of projecting the self into a too-painful past underlies this intensive process of heritage-making."[55] Mathews, for her part, does not pretend to transcend the problem of projecting the self into a too-painful past but instead makes the problem her subject. "Rather than serving simply as memorials," Dyer suggests, "the photographs may be documentary depictions of remembering."[56] As such, they call into question the possibility that a posthumous existence can be materialized. By contrast, it could be argued, DeComyn's Shot at Dawn Memorial, by seeming to achieve this projection into a too-painful past, creates a space that, like The Poppies, ultimately divests us of the task of remembering. In this respect, Mathews's project is antiheritage and antispectacle. It is, rather, aligned with the idea of the countermonument, a subject I will touch on in chapter 3.

The same, of course, cannot be said for the Tower of London poppies installation, which stages the problematic of remembrance of a war not fought on one's own soil, not etched into the very landscape; indeed, the need to bring the war home might help explain its nationalistic focus and its reliance, in the poppies, on prosthetic devices to trigger remembrance. For the landscape must be transformed to perform an act of witnessing, a new heritage-making superimposed on a location already a world heritage site. Where Mathews vacates the space of execution, The Poppies overfills it, repurposing the Tower's bloody history into a new spectacle of remembrance.[57] Yet both have produced commemorations perceived as peculiarly poignant. They thus open up an issue that will concern me throughout the remainder of the book: the nature of the affective response that the war's remembrance solicits and the means by which affect can be mobilized. That these two very different commemorative acts have both appeared under the banner of 14-18 NOW is perhaps especially fitting, for they articulate the parameters for imagining the war *now*, one

20   **INTRODUCTION**

hundred years out from its inception. While one stunningly reimagines the already imagined war—and its obsessively practiced commemoration—the other unimagines it, disabling inherited memory to perform a new kind of remembrance.

The Importance of Being Posthumous

Posthumous Lives, as its title signals, is a book about afterlives—the afterlife of World War I, the afterlife of its remembrance, and the afterlife of individual soldiers. It is also, of course, a book about memory and memorialization. I have chosen to begin, then, with these two centennial performances of remembrance because they help to frame the question of how and why the memory of this war—and the memory of its commemoration—continues to exercise a compelling hold on the British imagination. They demonstrate, moreover, in striking fashion, the extent to which memorial-making functions as a self-(re)generating process, taking on a life and legacy of its own. These 2014 installations, the book argues, must be understood against the commemorative practices they reinvent and challenge, against the inherited, and now ritualized, tropes that have come to define the war's memory—practices I elaborate on in each of the following chapters. And they must be understood in relation to the formation of a postwar culture of memory—a culture obsessed with the need to remember, a culture that made "Lest We Forget" its watchword. But the book also argues that the process works the other way around. Practices of remembrance, as they have changed over time, and as my two examples demonstrate, open new ways to understand earlier commemorative rites and rituals, in part by reactivating the forgotten histories of their construction and reception but also by reactivating the impulse that drives them: the constant impulse to remember as itself a monument to the inevitable failure or inadequacy of memory.

Since the 1990s, commemorative practices, and the work of memory more generally, have emerged as an important locus for scholarship on World War I across a range of disciplines and geographic locations; the subject has also continued to grow as a matter of avid popular interest and populist engagement, as the Tower of London poppies illustrates. The extensive body of work produced by Jay Winter has been especially influential in constructing a lexicon and establishing a critical framework for the study of remembrance—in the context of the Great War and also more generally. His book *Sites of Memory, Sites of Mourning* (1995), in particular, helped to move the topics of memory and memorialization (and grief and bereavement) to the center of our understanding of postwar

European culture; my own decision to organize *Posthumous Lives* around four such sites, as well as the vocabulary of commemoration I draw on, owes a good deal to Winter. I have not, however, followed Winter in his call for a comparative approach as "the only way to break out of cultural history limited by national perspectives" because the national element, I believe, still offers an important avenue of investigation.[58] It is, in fact, precisely the peculiarities and particularities of the British perspective that I hope to illuminate, the qualities that have rendered British commemoration of the Great War a national obsession and that continue to shape the war's commemorative afterlife, as evidenced in both the design and the popularity of The Poppies exhibition. The sites I have chosen, then, as Alex King argues of "British commemorative practices" more generally, "[are], and were seen to be, distinctively British," despite overlaps with practices in other European countries.[59]

In thinking about this national component, I have benefited from the work of a cluster of scholars—including not only Alex King but also Adrian Gregory, Catherine Moriarty, and David W. Lloyd—who have produced granular histories of British war memorials and other commemorative practices of the interwar period.[60] Their work provides a historical template through and against which I read the memorial sites I have chosen, but ultimately my approach differs from that of Winter and these other historians of memory and commemoration in the nature and scope of the sites I explore and the kind and intensity of attention I pay to them. My sites, for example, all have at least some distinctly literary features—even if their aesthetic qualities are not my primary focus: memoirs of dead soldiers produced by friends and family as a species of life writing; the popular and academic afterlife of a war poet, as traced over the course of a century; Virginia Woolf's landmark book on women's writing, *A Room of One's Own*; the campaign to obtain pardons for the shot-at-dawn soldiers. The reading strategies I deploy, moreover, to illuminate their cultural operation grow directly out of my literary training, as does my broader understanding of memory practices and rites as imaginative constructions. Indeed, one of the distinguishing features of the book is to bring to the work of literary study a set of concerns about memorialization more often the purview of other disciplines and to bring to the study of commemoration a more literary perspective. Consequently, the objects I explore do not fall neatly into disciplinary categories. Rather, my analysis reveals the way commemorative objects also participate in cultural formations of a literary nature and the way literary objects—even highly canonical ones—can serve commemorative functions. It invites consideration of how these objects—and the practices that sustain them—might be read when we insert them into unaccustomed contextual histories. To this end, *Posthumous Lives* performs a series of symptomatic readings of the practices and processes that

22   INTRODUCTION

made memory of the war dead (and of the war) an ongoing British preoccupation, as these practices manifest over time in a representative set of cultural locations. And it makes the case for the type of intensive, close, and sustained attention such readings require—readings that both illuminate and test the rites of memory that constitute their focus. Putting literary and memorial practices into a new kind of dialogue, *Posthumous Lives* aims to advance our understanding of both by exposing their interdependence and their sometimes surprising convergences.

One of the principle takeaways from the now considerable body of scholarship on memory and commemoration is the recognition that remembrance is, and always has been, "an ongoing process of contestation," and that the work of memory is neither fixed nor static.[61] *Posthumous Lives* works to further unfix it and to expose its fault lines. It does so, in part, by introducing on occasion theoretical lenses like Hirsch's concept of "postmemory"—concepts derived from different historical traumas and contexts and from different memorial cultures and practices (e.g., the Holocaust, the Vietnam War, 9/11). Such a strategy, the book argues, opens up understandings of postwar practices that might not otherwise have been visible, illuminating not only the way such practices can become entrenched but also the way, despite appearances to the contrary, they sometimes function as sites of resistance. But more fundamentally, *Posthumous Lives* does this through its own somewhat idiosyncratic choice of objects and the dialogue it initiates between them, as it moves back and forth between the center of British memorial culture and its periphery; in addition, moving freely, as in this introduction, through past and present practices of remembrance, it performs remembrance both forward and backward, sometimes looping back to tell the same story from multiple directions.[62] In doing so, it exploits its own postmemory position both to retell a story of British memorial mania and to unsettle it.

More particularly, the book takes up this project by tracing the permutations of the trope of the posthumous life as it has shaped World War I memory practices and rituals. At first glance, this trope might seem unexceptional—something between an oxymoron and a tautology; as such, it has not garnered close critical attention. But it is important, I maintain, for a number of reasons—not least its omnipresence in postwar memorial culture. The historical centrality of the posthumous, I am arguing, makes it an ideal focus for elucidating the underlying structures that constitute the rites of memory developed in the midst of the war and in its immediate aftermath. Thus, it also provides a useful platform to revisit a set of questions and tropes that have preoccupied scholars of World War I commemoration—questions about remembering and forgetting; permanence and ephemerality; public and private; individual and collective; presence and absence; and the mobilization of affect. But it revisits these tropes in order to defamiliarize them. If the trope of the posthumous life is not itself a unique invention of its wartime and postwar context, the scale of loss and its reach across the entire population put singular pressure on it. It gave the desire to create posthumous lives—to give the dead a continued presence, to extend the interaction between the dead and the living—a new urgency as a mode of memorialization.[63] It even, one might argue, made it a requirement, allowing the practice to function as a cultural counterpart to the great innovation of postwar society: the commitment to naming individually each and every dead soldier. And for a grieving public, it became an indispensable corrective to the specter of dispensable lives that the war uncovered.

As *Posthumous Lives* demonstrates, one immediate legacy of the war was to unleash an unprecedented spate of posthumous publications as a form of commemoration: books of poems and letters by dead soldiers, most (but not all) justified more by the fact of the author's death than by the work's literary merit. In this they followed a logic quite different from posthumous publication's usual justifications: the opportunity to allow a beloved writer one last appearance before the public; the chance to champion a still unrecognized or underappreciated writer of genius. In these new instances, the fact of the author's death could be seen to create desire and value rather than fanning desire for an already-valued entity. As discussed in chapter 1, the war also unleashed a spate of amateur "biographies"—Lives, as it were, of the obscure dead—however inadequate as fleshed-out portraits. The effect of these publications was to put posthumous lives into circulation, to turn the posthumous into a familiar feature of public discourse. While theoretically the "posthumous life" was available to everyone, in practice it relied on the cultural and material resources of the more privileged classes for its fullest articulation, especially when it manifested itself in print publication. Where chapters 1 and 2, then, trace this circulation, chapters 3 and 4 register reactions against its exclusions.

During the war, moreover, and for some time after, posthumous births, both literal and figurative, were a demographic reality; these included not only the biological children of soldiers who died before their offspring were born but also the many children conceived in the immediate aftermath of the war who were named for soldiers who did not return, most often a dead relative or a surviving soldier's fallen comrade. In addition, many soldiers who survived the war—and some while they were still fighting it—describe experiencing their lives as posthumous, a notion that runs through much of the best-known World War I literature. Writing to Siegfried Sassoon in 1922, Robert Graves makes the point quite literally, projecting himself as the posthumous child of his own

24   **INTRODUCTION**

dead self: "You identify me in your mind with a certain Robert Graves now dead whose bones and detritus can be found in *Over the Brazier, Fairies and Fusiliers* and the land of memory. Don't. I am using his name, rank and initials and his old clothes but I am no more than his son and heir."[64] If Graves is more direct and more eloquent than some in expressing this sentiment, it was an experience shared nonetheless by many of his contemporaries, including traumatized civilians, and one he would amplify in his own war memoir, *Good-Bye to All That* (1929).[65]

The idea of the posthumous life, then, as the book will illustrate, was deeply embedded in postwar culture, making it a fallback option for commemoration; but the book argues for the idea's centrality not only for structuring the memory work of the time but also in determining the particular shape of the war's commemorative legacy, including the class assumptions that filtered into it. What are the consequences, the book asks, of investing in the posthumous life as the governing structure of memorialization? Close analysis of the trope's operations thus helps to explain how the rites of memory it initiated have been (and continue to be) locked into intractable contradictions—contradictions newly visible from our postmemory perspective. Indeed, if the posthumous life was appropriated in postwar commemorative discourse as something immediately available and accessible to the grieving—a source of comfort, stability, and meaning—the reality was more thorny and the relief not distributed evenly. What the long view allows us to see is that the need that the posthumous life was meant to fill was one that had to be filled over and over again; the posthumous life, in other words, was something that had to be repeatedly produced and reproduced rather than something to be definitively accomplished. The tensions between the particularities of a life that it attempted to capture and the recognition of the life as ultimately irrecuperable were not resolvable. As a trope, moreover, the posthumous life has been subject to other theoretical understandings considerably less comforting and less relentlessly humanistic. It has functioned as an emblem of the modern condition—a figure of belatedness and loss of continuity. As a specifically modern (or postmodern) construction, it has been associated with the postapocalyptic and the posthuman—what remains when humanity may no longer have a future.[66] As Jeremy Tambling observes in *Becoming Posthumous*, "the posthumous complicates," opening up a space that is inherently undecidable and unstable.[67] Its appeal for many writers and thinkers, he demonstrates, was precisely its power to disturb our certainties—even our sense of our very existence—which is the opposite of what many postwar mourners sought from it. Read this way, with attention to its contradictions, the trope of the posthumous life, this book will argue, becomes available for different ends than simply the replication of earlier practices of commemoration and for more multifaceted understandings of its historical operation, ones that open its history to its repressed narratives.

"Whose war? Whose memory? These are the crucial questions," Adrian Gregory affirms in his study of Armistice Day celebrations from 1919 to 1946, "for in Britain there were no undisputed guardians of the [war's] memory."[68] As for other scholars who have expanded our understanding of the war's actors and victims, these questions are also my starting point, although I come at them from a slightly different direction. Whose life qualifies for a posthumous existence? *How* is memory manufactured out of what is not there, and how is it transmitted? Whose needs are served in such an undertaking? What are the consequences of these practices for our current efforts to grapple with the war's legacy? If the first two chapters do not stray very far from familiar subjects of commemoration—the young men whose tragic deaths lie at the heart of established remembrance rituals—they shift focus away from the men themselves to the public and private hands that made possible an afterlife for them, and they remind us that the posthumous life is always a collaborative undertaking. The chapters serve as companion pieces and inverses of each other: one looking at the phenomenon at large, one zeroing in on a single soldier-poet; one focused on a set of now-forgotten figures and artifacts, the other on the overremembered and culturally canonized "war poet."

Chapter 1, "Material Boys: Lives of the Dead and the Objects of Biography," considers a body of material that has largely escaped critical attention— the eclectic, often privately published, memorial volumes compiled by family members of dead soldiers and published both during the war and in the years immediately afterward as posthumous tributes to a loved one. While often dismissed as ephemera, they turn out to be eloquent witnesses to the need to invent afterlives despite the lack of sufficient warrant or evidence. Patched together out of scraps and fragments, these commemorative volumes make up for lives that lacked recognizable fullness and dimension through a proliferation of materials. Stretching the limits of traditional life writing to accommodate their unconventional subjects, these volumes function simultaneously as texts and affective objects, repeatedly blurring the boundaries between public and private acts of remembrance. Reading these amateur efforts against the *Dictionary of National Biography*, on the one hand, and the emergence of the "new biography," on the other, "Material Boys" considers these once-ubiquitous biographical artifacts in relation to the challenge posed to traditional biography by the war's unprecedented death toll. It argues, moreover, that these works are more densely intertwined with other postwar cultural productions, including modernist inventions, than received literary history has previously recognized. As lives of the dead (quite literally, posthumous Lives), however,

26   **INTRODUCTION**

these hybrid, fragmented, and incomplete life stories demonstrate the limits to the invention of an afterlife that the living may cherish. They thus raise questions about the staying power of the posthumous.

Taking the poet Charles Hamilton Sorley, a soldier who died at age twenty, as its point of departure, chapter 2, "Sorley's Travels: The Afterlife of a World War I Poet," explores the surprising durability of his posthumous life and reputation. In contrast to the figures discussed in chapter 1, the war poets have suffered, if anything, from overfamiliarity; precisely for this reason, however, they are of interest to this book, attracting as they do such excessive emotional investment. By approaching the subject from an unfamiliar angle, the relatively unknown Sorley, the chapter opens to view what is often taken for granted: the underlying structures that facilitate this cathexis. Offering snapshots of memory-making at three different historical moments, it scrutinizes the work performed by individuals, coteries, and cultural institutions in sustaining the poet's afterlife, and it brings into focus the temporalities of the posthumous. The chapter considers the types of objects deployed to structure memory as well as their exposition venues (private networks, exhibition halls, museums, collected works, popular and critical biographies); most crucially, it considers the affective structures that drive these practices of remembrance, making it a pivotal chapter for the entire book. And it contrasts the efforts to maintain Sorley's posthumous life with Sorley's own poetic meditations on posthumousness.

Moving from the months immediately following Sorley's death in 1915 to the first decades of the twenty-first century, the chapter illuminates how the memory work countenanced and solicited by the commemorative practices that have grown up around him changes in its travels over time and location. How, for example, I ask in this chapter, does a "boy who wrote poems" (thirty-seven in all, and most written when still a schoolboy) become a "war poet," with a popular following and institutional afterlife extending into the twenty-first century? How does he sustain a posthumous life on such a slim portfolio? What happens when commemoration moves from private family parlors and closed circles of loved ones to public displays in formal publications and museum spaces? How does one explain the intensity of emotion "Sorley" continues to generate out of all proportion to personal knowledge or strictly measurable achievement? Using Sorley to illuminate the British fixation with the dead war poet as the locus of an affective response that makes continued remembrance possible, this chapter asks what it means "to fall in love with a dead man."

Where the first two chapters tracked the need of the living to invent posthumous lives as a form of consolation and a guarantee of continued connection to the war's affective nucleus, the last two chapters consider those shut out of this process, those excluded or sidelined from the performance of memory. Chapter 3, "Posthumous Was a Woman: War Memorials and Woolf's Dead Poets Society," argues that *A Room of One's Own* (1929), Virginia Woolf's foundational study of women's literary history, can be read as a monument to the unmemorialized: a commentary on and strategic intervention into the postwar culture of memorialization that the preceding chapters document—a culture that largely excluded women. Woolf's invention of Judith Shakespeare, a poet who never wrote a word and died without fulfilling her potential, stands, then, as a countermonument, if only an ephemeral one, to the memorials to the Glorious Dead popping up everywhere and to the fetishization of the soldier-poet as an emblem of the lost generation. By memorializing someone who never existed, Woolf underlines this exclusion, while demonstrating the drives and mechanisms that deliver the "posthumous" to living communities. Considering the way the legacy of the war haunts a text that would not seem to have the war as its ostensible subject, this reading of *A Room of One's Own* participates in a larger project inaugurated by feminist scholars, that of reconsidering what counts as "war literature." It participates, as well, in an ongoing debate about how modernism and the war speak to each other. The last part of the chapter flips the scenario, taking up the question of the hyperpresence of a single woman—Nurse Edith Cavell—in memorial literature and monument constructions. If "Shakespeare's sister" stands as the marker of the erasure of women in the postwar landscape of memorial culture, "Edith Cavell," this chapter argues, may well be her evil stepsister, the woman who was remembered seemingly everywhere. But the Edith Cavell produced through these processes of commemoration is as much an invention as Judith Shakespeare—an entirely posthumous construction. The subject of highly contested, even diametrically opposed, narratives and meanings, "Cavell" focalizes the question posed by Woolf of how and for what reasons women can be remembered in the postwar culture; in what her representation allows as well as what it represses, Cavell also provides an occasion to test the possibilities for commemorating pacifism.

The final chapter of the book, "Absent from Memory: Shot at Dawn and the Spectacle of Belated Remembrance," continues the consideration of those denied recognition in the official project of commemoration: the approximately 306 soldiers executed for cowardice, desertion, and other military offenses. Picking up on chapter 3's speculations about pacifism, it continues as well a consideration of those who said "no" to war—although for different reasons than those of pacifists and conscientious objectors. It reads the concerted acts of unremembering to which these shot-at-dawn soldiers were subjected at the time of their deaths and in the war's immediate aftermath

28   **INTRODUCTION**

against the contentious (and ultimately successful) turn-of-the millennium campaign to secure posthumous pardons and recognition for them. It argues that from the beginning, the contours of the debate surrounding these soldiers were shaped by the centrality of the posthumous life as the defining feature of remembrance, especially in the way the ideas of posthumous harm and posthumous restitution figured in governing formulations from both sides of the controversy. Drawing on Thomas Laqueur's work in particular, the chapter uses the case of these soldiers to revisit a postwar innovation in official practices of commemoration: the obsession with the naming of the dead in national and local memorials and books of remembrance. What does it mean in such a context, I ask, *not* to have one's name remembered—not to be afforded a posthumous existence? And what happens when remembrance comes only belatedly? If practices of remembrance are always a product of contestation—contestation driven not so much by actual lives and events as by the urgent motives of the living—this chapter makes such contestation its explicit subject. As a limit case for the project of remembrance, the shot-at-dawn soldiers, it argues, expose the fault lines of the larger memorial undertaking, opening to view the means and structures through which afterlives are created. In doing so, it exposes the blind spots and contradictions that continue to inform commemorative practices and rituals. In a coda to the chapter, I speculate on the consequences of the controversy's apparent closure, using the shot-at-dawn instance to reflect anew on practices the book as a whole has been illuminating and to question what is lost and gained in moves designed to redress earlier commemorative omissions by constructing new (if belated) posthumous lives to fill in for earlier missing ones.

As my chapter breakdowns indicate, the "culture of memory" of my subtitle might better be described as cultures of memory, given the diversities within the separate examples, all illustrating the ritualized operations by which the living create the afterlives they need or desire. If commemoration, then, was a national practice and pastime, it was not a monolithic one—even within relatively homogeneous communities. Still greater differences would emerge if this book were to consider more overtly diverse cultural locations—ones that, as Santanu Das reminds us, require attention to very different types of objects than "the letters, poems and memoirs that form the cornerstone of European war memory" and that cannot simply be subsumed under a presumptive national narrative.[69] But the "cornerstone" items, *Posthumous Lives* argues, can also benefit from the type of material and structural analysis that these other memory objects solicit, allowing us to see the way they, too, operate as objects and not simply as normative cultural landmarks. Memory, indeed, as I use the term here, alludes to something manufactured, and *Posthumous Lives*

THE AFTERLIFE OF COMMEMORATION 29

emphasizes the literal making of it—one reason I begin this book with homemade memorial volumes. Despite the considerable attention they have garnered, moreover, mainstream memory practices still house underexamined archives with valuable stories to tell us about the structures and processes that continue to shape our postmemory rites and rituals.

Memory, of course, as any student of the subject recognizes, remains a term with contested borders. Following Winter, it would be possible to make the semantic shift from memory to remembrance. Such a move would emphasize the act or process of remembering rather than the person or event remembered; it would open a space for the consideration of memory not solely based in personal experience. And it would help to underline the collective agency of particular constituencies in the memory-making process. All of these realignments illuminate a central piece of my argument: the way British memory practices are built on the commemoration of commemoration. But I preserve the more tricky term "memory," as I do the singular designation "culture," to highlight the tensions between competing understandings of these overcharged designations. My intent in this book, then, is not to resolve these tensions but to keep alive their different resonances. Indeed, preserving the term "memory" can reactivate one of its original meanings: remembrance of the dead.[70]

Adopting the singular "culture" also serves several purposes. In addition to signifying a group ethos—a set of shared attitudes, values, and practices—it invites attention to the cultural products memory generates and relies on: literary, artistic, and intellectual artifacts. Furthermore, it allows for a focus on how memory is cultivated and curated. I also use the singular because I want to argue that despite divergent interests and practices, something that could be called a "culture of memory" does function at times in a homogenizing manner, dictating appropriate affective responses to the war's devastating losses and enforcing an obligation to remember, even as these dictates continue to be contested. The culture of memory can thus be seen to perform as both product and agent of remembrance.

Finally, I preserve the formulation "culture of memory" to open this book out to larger considerations of modernism and modernity where memory has become something of a watchword. As Sarah Cole has argued, "In historicizing the practices of memory . . . we can locate particular moments when the notion of memory becomes especially burdened, when it plays a sharp and vital role in community or national consciousness, when its forms seem to tap into very basic and unsettled problems. The period after the First World War represents one such moment."[71] In this period, I am arguing, commemoration assumes the weight of memory's burden—and the commemoration of

30   **INTRODUCTION**

commemoration is one of its most lasting legacies. While considerable critical attention has been devoted to modernist engagements with memory in all its permutations, "modernism and commemoration" remains an underexplored subject; indeed, the two have been largely viewed as antithetical.[72] Approaches to the subject have generally been limited to considerations of modernist artworks as "anti-monuments"—conscious rejections of the principles and abstractions on which official commemoration depended—and to practices of resistant mourning.[73]

As a memory-suffused moment, however, the postwar period produced both an abundance of traditional forms and a profusion of experimental artistic creations; it generated a diverse set of responses to its memorial culture—many of which cannot be securely placed along some spectrum of resistance and conformity. In *The Great War and Modern Memory* (1975), Paul Fussell famously established a particular version of the war's shaping of memory, locating in the war the roots of a pervasive modern sensibility characterized by a new modern language and a determinedly ironic perspective.[74] His paradigm continues to haunt contemporary scholarship even as it has been critiqued from multiple directions, provoking new interpretations of the Great War's legacy in relation to both modernism and modernity. Fussell's book, as Leonard V. Smith argues, has itself become a *"lieu de mémoire* or 'site of memory' of the Great War";[75] indeed, as the continued echoes and riffs on its title indicate, it stands as a notable instance of creating an afterlife. While the book immediately resonated with academic and lay audiences, touched by its affective power as much as its provocative thesis, over time and through its increasing contestation, it has revealed itself as simply one more "afterlife" created according to the needs of a particular moment and particular constituencies. Its posthumous life thus shadows this book.

With the exception of *A Room of One's Own*, Woolf's genre-bending essay, the objects of my analysis do not include many items or practices that would conventionally be considered modernist—in some instances quite the contrary. The more literary artifacts are not for the most part characterized by aesthetic experimentation, impersonality, or irony—to name just a few modernist hallmarks—nor do they promote a particular "modernist" ideology. Indeed, the cultural praxes in which they participate often depend on a type of populist appeal to emotion and sentiment disdained by mainstream modernists. But one of the underlying arguments of this book is that analysis of these "nonmodernist" practices can open a space for reevaluating the more canonical objects of literary and cultural history and the genealogies that have shaped the meaning we give them. And they can open a space for expanding *what* we talk about when we talk about modernism.

THE AFTERLIFE OF COMMEMORATION   31

Posthumous Lives, then, takes as one of its central premises that the memorial practices it investigates have more significant and far-reaching connections to modernist undertakings than originally acknowledged, and that such practices cannot simply be dismissed as "nonconsequential expressions of private sentiment" or unquestioned acceptance of official doctrine.[76] They can help to illuminate less celebrated modernist preoccupations than the ones that have been institutionalized in the literary critical canon. As Jahan Ramazani argues in his afterword to *Modernism and Mourning*, the essays in that book "collectively establish mourning as an angle of approach to modernism no less generative than such interpretive templates as 'irony' and 'impersonality,' 'experiment' and 'gender wars.'"[77] A similar claim, I argue, can be made about other preoccupations of the postwar culture of remembrance, as my discussion of Woolf's engagement with war memorials demonstrates. But for the most part I approach this interface more elliptically, not through the modernist works and modernist practitioners themselves but through a set of works and practices outside the high modernist orbit. In doing so I hope to encourage a deeper understanding of modernism's relationship to the culture it grew out of and to excavate the ground for a future dialogue attentive to its parallels with as well as divergences from contemporaneous cultural formations. As Allyson Booth has argued, "We read modernism without fully realizing the extent to which it handles the bones of the war dead."[78] At the same time, I want to shift attention from some singular notion of Modernism as the only discourse that matters when thinking about this period and about the war's continued hold on the cultural imaginary.

I see this book, then, as contributing to a growing body of scholarship at the intersection of the New Modernist Studies and First World War studies—work that has been broadening the way we think about modernism in relation to the war and to the war's remembrance and that has been recovering underrepresented literary histories to highlight the existence of alternative modernisms and divergent modernities.[79] Like this work, my book is concerned with the long-term consequences of the institutionalization of singular practices and viewpoints to the exclusion of competing narratives. In the introduction to a special 2017 issue of *Modernist Cultures* titled "Modernism and the First World War," Andrew Frayn notes, "Much critical work has been done over the last twenty years to ensure that First World War Studies and Modernist Studies speak to each other," but as he also acknowledges, "reluctance remains to link the two."[80] This reluctance has been especially pronounced around the subject of postwar commemoration, given its association with official culture. *Posthumous Lives* provides a platform to revisit this vexed relationship. The fact that the New Modernist Studies emerged in the academy at the

32   **INTRODUCTION**

same moment that memory studies was gaining ascendance makes this an especially fertile space for further exploration. As modernist studies has expanded to accommodate not just a new global dimension but also middlebrow, sentimental, and vernacular modernisms, it is a fortuitous moment, I am suggesting, to test the claims of what might be called "memorial modernisms."

In "The Great War and Post-modern Memory," Michèle Barrett voices this possibility in terms of the power of modernist art to mediate bereavement: "The question is: can a modernist aesthetic, in which affect and emotion is rendered only obliquely in deference to a search for the inner truth in consciousness and perception, really address human grief in the measure required?"[81] Barrett reopens this question as a direct challenge to Jay Winter's certainty that the answer is a decided negative. "The cutting edge of 'modern memory,'" Winter writes in *Sites of Memory, Sites of Mourning*, "its multi-faceted sense of dislocation, paradox, and the ironic, could express anger and despair, and did so in enduring ways; it was melancholic, but it could not heal."[82] Barrett poses this question, however, from the vantage point of a present more than eighty years out from the signing of the armistice, and as part of a shift in emphasis from personal to cultural memory, where "healing" and "moving on" might no longer be the desired objective. Moreover, although war memorials are not her specific focus, she writes at a time when minimalism and abstraction have come to be seen as the "unofficial language" of contemporary commemoration, "the best available mirror for a modern world"—a near-complete reversal of the dominant arguments of the 1920s.[83] Barrett's question and the debates it resuscitates reprise the issues I touched on in my discussion of centennial exhibitions at the beginning of this introduction; the question of what memorializing can mean in an age of postmemory stands as a central topic that I return to throughout this book. But ultimately, *Posthumous Lives* approaches this subject from a direction opposite to Barrett's. As a study of the Great War and modern *remembrance*, it opens a space to reverse the terms of Barrett's question in order to ask, if somewhat speculatively, Can an aesthetic steeped in affect and emotion, of the type I consider in my chosen sites of memory, speak meaningfully to modernism? As my succeeding chapters will demonstrate, this is a question we have not yet settled.

CHAPTER 1

Material Boys

Lives of the Dead and the Objects of Biography

At the end of her 1919 memoir of her son, Edward Wyndham Tennant, killed on the Somme in October 1916 at the age of nineteen, Pamela Glenconner appends "A Fragment of Autobiography" (figure 1.1). Written only months before her son's death and found among his effects, the narrative is constructed in the third person, in the form of a biography of a fallen comrade, someone he calls "his dearest friend"—"a person," he coyly notes, "whose life and happiness were as much to me as my own."[1] In *The Missing of the Somme*, Geoff Dyer observes the eerie sense we sometimes get that the Great War "had been fought in order that it might be remembered, that it might live up to its memory"; its "fallen were being remembered," he repeatedly points out, "before they fell."[2] Samuel Hynes makes a similar point about some wartime combatant narratives: "It is as though they were already posthumous, even as they were being written."[3] As if to confirm this notion— indeed, to take it to its logical extreme—Tennant, in his autobiographical experiment, finds he can only tell his life by imagining his death and how he will be memorialized, by turning his life, as it were, into a memory object. In effect, for readers of his mother's volume, he renders his life doubly posthumous. Pondering what to include "to get the book to its 200th page," "to keep his ["friend's"] memory flowering in [his] heart" (*EWT*, 312), this resurrected voice replays a central problem of the memorial it follows: how to tell the story of those absent from themselves; how to reconstruct a life that may not have

CHAPTER 1

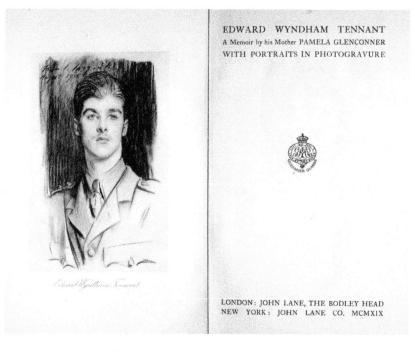

FIGURE 1.1. Frontispiece illustration, a charcoal portrait by John Singer Sargent, and title page from Pamela Glenconner, *Edward Wyndham Tennant: A Memoir by His Mother* (London: John Lane, 1919)

enough material to fill a volume. It thus encapsulates in miniature the paradoxical nature of the objects that form the subject of this chapter.

As a personal effect of the dead and one of the last remains of the living person, the autobiographical fragment would have had its own hallowed place in the material culture of remembrance, a culture that put a premium on "lastness"—last words, last letters home, last actions, last possessions to have been handled. Like other artifacts—war medals, pieces of soldiers' uniforms, certificates of service, postcards, photographs, trench souvenirs—it stands in for and provides access to the missing body. As a specifically autobiographical piece of writing, it is peculiarly situated to convey the personal experience embodied in the artifact. Over time, as the figure invoked by the material object drops out of living memory, the artifact itself—or the memory of it—replaces the memory of the commemorated person in much the way, as Susan Stewart has shown us, a souvenir operates.[4] As a textual object, however, the autobiographical fragment performs a kind of double action. While the manuscript itself accrues affective capital from its proximity to the departed, transmuted into print it is relieved of the taint of battle—relieved of "the smell of grave-yards and the Dead" that Vera Brittain so famously lamented adheres to ma-terial relics like the soldier's kit bag.[5] But appended to a memorial volume, the textual fragment acquires a new materiality; it constitutes a piece of the stuff out of which a "life" can be posthumously manufactured.

Scholars of the material culture of World War I have reconstructed the biography of Great War objects—the items found in dead soldiers' kits and returned to their families or brought home by survivors; the trench art manufactured by soldiers and civilians alike from a variety of war materials—to track the fugitive lives they reference.[6] I want to approach the subject here, however, from the opposite direction: to look not at the items made by or be-longing to the soldiers but at the items made about them; to track the fugi-tive Lives composed in their memory. This chapter, then, illuminates the objects of commemorative biography—the memorial volumes, collected, cu-rated, and often privately published, that became familiar relics in so many mourning households. It considers both the materials that went into these vol-umes, including the soldiers' own writings, and the volumes themselves as material objects. It therefore differs in its methodology from a strictly literary reading of the text but also from a strictly materialist one of the artifact. And it considers as well the object—or purpose—of these volumes. Patched to-gether out of scraps and fragments—letters and poems by the deceased; memoirs by family members; tributes from others; snippets of inspirational literature; photographs and drawings; diary fragments—these commemora-tive volumes deploy a proliferation of materials to make up for lives that lacked recognizable fullness and dimension. In doing so, I argue, these volumes cre-ated a new kind of biographical hybrid, occupying an ambiguous place be-tween text and object and an ambiguous place in a rapidly changing genre.

Genre Wars/War Genres

Like other wars, World War I unsettled established practices of life writing, "impos[ing] certain narratives" and "creat[ing] a demand for new life stories . . . not least through the impulse to memorialise."[7] Most of the critical attention to the subject, however, has focused on the pressures the war exerted on autobio-graphical forms and practices, already under stress, as they were adopted by an increasingly large and diverse cast of actors; but the war provoked a crisis, if anything even more profound, on biography as a genre.[8] On the one hand, the "new biography," inaugurated with the publication in May 1918 of Lytton

36   **CHAPTER 1**

Strachey's *Eminent Victorians*, called into question the possibility of traditional biography to fulfill what Sir Sidney Lee described as its primary commemorative object: "to transmit personality."[9] The timing of Strachey's manifesto, nearly four years into the war, was not accidental; as his friend David Garnett noted, "Lytton's essays were designed to undermine the foundations on which the age that brought war about had been built."[10] And they were designed to undermine the biographical practices that enshrined the exemplars of those discredited values. Although Strachey had begun his foray into Victorian biography before the war's inception, the war, Michael Holroyd argues, provided the catalyst that gave the book its theme and its coherence.[11] In effect, it transformed what started out as an amiable romp, the projected *Victorian Silhouettes*, into the more hard-hitting *Eminent Victorians*, fittingly introduced with the appropriated military metaphors that Strachey assigns to the "explorer of the past" who models the biographer of the future: "He will attack his subjects in unexpected places; he will fall upon the flank, or the rear; he will shoot a sudden, revealing searchlight into obscure recesses, hitherto undivined."[12] As Holroyd suggests, the text was Strachey's version of an antiwar "campaign," an alternative to the explicitly pacifist screeds of Bertram Russell and others, and a "counter-attack" to the religious posturing that informed so much wartime propaganda.[13]

Interestingly, in the decade following the war, as Laura Marcus documents, a new conception of biography, along the lines of Strachey's, appeared simultaneously in the literature of the major combatant nations—England, France, and Germany—as if, in the wake of the war, the very category of a "life" could no longer be taken for granted.[14] If biography depends on the assumption that a life follows a recognizable narrative, the "old biography," it was argued, had identified the wrong narrative and deployed the wrong narrative methodology. For biography, then, as for other literary genres, the war would seem to have sealed the notion that traditional narratives and traditional genre boundaries could no longer be relied on. The "new biography," by contrast, concentrated on the missing person, the person not captured by traditional biographical methods—the part of a life not translatable into action, what Lee dismissed as "a mere phantasm."[15]

At the same time, the possibility of biography was being challenged in even more fundamental ways by the presence of so many missing persons in the war's unprecedented death toll and the felt need to capture these lives for posterity—a need that neither the "old" nor the "new" biography could effectively answer. The challenge located itself at the intersection of private memory and national mourning. While the problem, then, was by no means unique to Britain, its solution took on a distinctly British aura through the appeal in the resulting texts to the national character. As early as May 1915, the *Times* was calling for a concerted effort to supplement "the little biographies that fill the columns of the newspaper," biographies reduced to the most skeletal data: "Their age, the name of their school and perhaps of their university, the date on which they gained their commission, and the date of their death make up the record of their short lives, with now and then a sentence or two from a letter telling how gloriously they ended them." To this, the *Times* urged as a kind of civic duty should be added "some frail memorial" in words; "If some one can collect their various memories and marshal them quite shortly and simply . . . he will be doing a real service. . . . Such a modest record is worth attempting if only for the sake of those who are now too young to remember and even of those still unborn." "If the attempt is to be made," the article went on, "it should be made soon, lest later it become almost impossible. . . . The whole machinery for making these unpretentious biographies will be out of gear."[16] Just two years later, the same arguments would be advanced for the formation of a national war museum, followed by public appeals for items related to servicemen who had been killed or had distinguished themselves in action—"photographs, biographical details and 'all kinds of mementos, even of trifling character'"—before such items were scattered in local and regional museums or private hands or were lost altogether.[17]

If the *Times* proposed through "such private records" a kind of dispersed national archive, postwar collections like E. B. Osborn's *The New Elizabethans* (1919) provided a more centralized home for what the *Sunday Times* reviewer called "sympathetically" rendered and "vivaciously" written "miniature biographies."[18] Organized as a kind of portrait gallery or collection of "types"— for example, "The True Amateur," "The Modern Actor," "The Absolute Poet," "The Student in Arms," "The Highland Soul," "An Irish-Torchbearer," "The Happy Athlete," "The Christian Soldier"—the book highlights twenty-five representative examples of fallen soldiers, some included in paired entries. As its title suggests, and like other contemporary works of its kind, it celebrates the "English" values that distinguished the nation's fighting men—"these golden lads," in Osborn's familiar if overblown rhetoric—linking them to their Elizabethan predecessors: "Their land was the Gloriana they glorified in their deeds."[19] Notwithstanding the fact that his exemplars include an Irishman, a New Zealander, a Canadian, a few Scotsmen, and several Americans, they fulfill their destiny as *English* "Renaissance men": "They were all scholars and sportsmen and poets"; "They had the Elizabethan exuberance"; they were "a race of conquerors" and "examples of antique heroism"; they were bound by "the instinct of brotherliness."[20] Advertised by its publisher as "a series of memoirs of

38   **CHAPTER 1**

men distinguished in all walks of life who have fallen in the war," *The New Elizabethans* was lauded in reviews for a design that represented "as worthy a conception as 'The Dictionary of National Biography.'"[21]

Like the *Dictionary of National Biography* (DNB), *The New Elizabethans*, of course, had certain inevitable biases; there is, for example, a decidedly aristocratic slant to its selections despite its stated aims of inclusiveness. More important, perhaps, it shared with its predecessor an unrealizable ambition. Like the *DNB*, whose 1912–1921 supplement needed to be scaled back lest the sheer volume of entries become overwhelming, *The New Elizabethans*, with its subtitle, *A First Selection of the Lives of Young Men Who Have Fallen in the Great War*, was a project that threatened to be endless; in almost its very first words, then, it referenced "the sequel," never in fact completed, "which the natural growth of the work has rendered necessary."[22] Similarly, *The Bond of Sacrifice: A Biographical Record of All British Officers Who Fell in the Great War*, a more comprehensive— and more formulaic—effort at national biography than Osborn's venture, had to be abandoned after its second volume, its coverage extending no further than the first six months of 1915.[23] But the reference to the *DNB*, I want to suggest, also signals, as with Strachey, the need in postwar Britain for new biographical possibilities and an alternate biographical repository. The war, in fact, precipitated a shift in focus for the nation's biographical manufactory; writing from the War Trade Intelligence Department in 1918, H. W. C. Davis reported a new consensus among the dictionary's editors: "that the tendency after the war will be towards the study of Movements and Developments rather than of pure biography."[24]

It is worth noting, moreover, that the vast majority of those who died in the war did not live lives that would have earned them entry in even the *DNB*'s original iteration. Put simply, they died too young and consequently did not achieve enough to merit inclusion, the measure of their life resting in their unrealized potential—in what could be memorialized only as an absence. In fact, not until the *DNB*'s 1993 edition of *Missing Persons*—recognizing 1,086 persons omitted from previous editions of the *DNB* from its inception until 1985—did even some of the best-known soldier-poets who died in the war find a place in this compendium. Writing a generation before the inception of the war, Sir Sidney Lee, the second editor to join the project, describes the hypothetical pool from which candidates for the *DNB* had been culled; if one includes all who have reached adulthood—and for Lee this means "omitting all who have died before reaching their twenty-fourth year"—then, he concludes, "I find that one in every 5,000 has in the last nine centuries gained the distinctive level."[25] Pressed to articulate the grounds for admission, Lee offers as a minimum, "No man's life should be admitted to a collection of national biography that does not

MATERIAL BOYS   39

present at least one action that is 'serious, complete, and of a certain magnitude.'" For the fallen World War I soldiers, however, often the only act to meet this criterion was their death—not an action that sufficiently distinguished them from others. "Actions which are accomplished, or are capable of accomplishment, by many thousands of persons," Lee observes, "are never of the magnitude which justifies the notice of the national biographer."[26]

These actions, however—these premature deaths—justified the notice of countless ordinary citizens, who felt moved to give their purely private recollections a kind of public framework and to produce a kind of biographical artifact, even if they did not name it as such. Indeed, as this chapter will argue, neither the traditional framework of biography nor new experimental models could provide a template for these biographical outpourings that began appearing during the war and peaked in the years immediately following it, though they had features in common with both. Like practitioners of other literary forms of the period, then, these would-be biographers experienced a genre problem, precipitated by the magnitude of loss they experienced and the ensuing sense of dislocation. As the structures of official mourning, moreover, became increasingly fixed—the impersonality of public monuments, the uniformity of official cemeteries, and their location on foreign soil—many felt the need for something more personal than mere names inscribed on tablets and for something more formal as a repository of memory than the homely family album, with which these volumes nonetheless had certain affinities. They felt the need, in other words, to record these lives in a *book-like* object and a *biography-like* genre. The fact, then, that these volumes were printed is an essential part of their story—and an essential reason for their class parameters. If not full-fledged exemplars of the biographical genre, these undertakings were nonetheless something more than the potted biographies in obituary notices, in regimental histories, and in school, workplace, and parish publications. As Jahan Ramazani argues of the modern elegy, these works could be seen as attempts to create a "person-filled counterforce" to what Gary L. Long has called the "'person empty cenotaphs of a rationalizing society.'"[27] Unlike the elegy, however, these memorial volumes also conveyed this personal dimension through their tactile elements, as I will discuss later in this chapter. While undoubtedly meant to be read, then, they also remained objects to be viewed and handled, household possessions infused with affective power and designed to trigger memory. For members of a certain class—and class was an important determinant for them—their presence was everywhere. Thus Michèle Barrett observes how, while staying at the home of some friends in the country while she was writing *Casualty Figures*, her own recent foray into World War I biography, she "predicted quite confidently that someone in

40   **CHAPTER 1**

that large family would have died in the 1914–1918 war, and that there would be a record of it." "It took all of four minutes," she notes, "to find it on the bookshelves: a volume of privately printed letters and papers, assembled by his sister, for his sons to know him by."[28]

So ubiquitous, in fact, were these collections that Samuel Hynes suggests they could be considered "a new genre of war writing," something that might be called "war memoirs of the dead": the "volumes of letters, diaries, and journals of men killed in action that were edited by friends or relatives, and were published primarily as memorials."[29] The implications of this claim, however, have not generally been pursued by World War I scholars, either literary or historical. Although the existence of such volumes has been noted, few have looked at them closely in the terms Hynes imagines.[30] In designating these volumes "war memoirs of the dead," Hynes was, of course, both linking them to and distinguishing them from a later but much more well-known genre: the now-canonical "war memoirs of the living," the so-called truth-telling volumes published by the war's survivors in the late 1920s and early 1930s and epitomized by the works of Robert Graves, Siegfried Sassoon, and Edmund Blunden. As Brian Bond intimates, however, in titling his study of such classic war memoirs *Survivors of a Kind*, survival was at best a relative term for those who experienced themselves as in some way already dead as a result of their war experience.[31] As I noted in the introduction, the soldiers themselves were the first to diagnose this condition, and the fact was not lost on their readers. When Edmund Blunden's *Undertones of War* (1928), for example, was first published, H. M. Tomlinson, echoing Blunden, wrote that it was a book "by a ghost for other ghosts," an assessment that would seem to collapse Hynes's distinction between memoirs of the dead and memoirs of the living.[32] If, however, one expands Hynes's rubric to include those works that supplement the posthumous papers they publish with personal reminiscences and testimonials— the commemorative volumes that more often than not simply bear the dead soldier's name as their title—the difference in the two types of memoirs becomes more evident. The more expansive memoirs of the dead of the sort considered here resolve the apparent oxymoron in Hynes's formulation, presenting themselves as memoirs not so much *by* the dead as *about* them; not so much about the war as about the person lost to it. They thus participate in a more explicitly *biographical* project than the later, much-celebrated autobiographical war memoirs. As Lives of the dead, these earlier volumes project a different kind of posthumous existence from the one that surviving soldiers claimed for themselves. Indeed, they would seem to operate from opposite motives: the one lamenting premature death and projecting the Life as consolation, the other displaying the spectacle of what Emily R. Wilson has dubbed "tragic overliving," an existence unnaturally prolonged in the face of intolerable loss and unassimilable experience.[33]

As posthumous Lives, however, these earlier memorial volumes have proved more difficult to categorize than their successors—the autobiographical narratives of the overlivers. Despite their superficial resemblance to biographies, they resist the structures of approved life writing—too incomplete to form a coherent narrative, too unknown and unknowable to be rendered legible, too ordinary to command public attention. They thus differ significantly—in their aesthetic as well as their immediate reception and ensuing oblivion—from the later, more literary memoirs that have come to define the war experience. With a few exceptions, they have remained largely below the radar of even most World War I scholars, of interest primarily to book collectors and Great War aficionados. Yet as a genre, I am arguing, these now-forgotten memoirs of the dead have a claim on the attention of the cultural historian and the literary scholar—as human documents and expressive objects that convey a distinctive sense of how the war meant, to both "the glorious dead" and those who strove to memorialize them. Appearing in large numbers and displaying certain features in common, they represent a distinct and consequential response to what Diana Fuss has called the problem of "dying modern," inventing a form, in the face of the anonymity of mass death, to render death more personal.[34] Unlike the belated memoirs of the former combatants, they carve out a space for the immediacy of personal grief and for the sentiments of home-front survivors—and they do so in a location that is not strictly private. At the same time, I will argue, they cannot simply be dismissed as expressions of conventional, sentimentalized mourning. Above all, as my analysis will illustrate, they reveal themselves to be hybrid objects, and their multifaceted hybridity facilitates a twofold argument. On the one hand, these volumes address devastating loss in a more complicated way than has generally been credited; on the other, they show themselves to be more densely intertwined with other postwar cultural productions, including modernist inventions, than received literary history has previously recognized. In both instances, they shed a critical light on the practices they at once contest and mirror.

Taken at face value, these commemorative volumes provide unusual access into how people negotiated loss and grief on a personal level, but from our own contemporary perspective they also illuminate how lines between public and private were repeatedly crossed and tangled in the process.[35] Occupying a liminal space as both texts and objects, they reveal themselves to be, like the modern elegy, a "compromise-formation" between the privatization of grief and its sanctioned public expression.[36] As domestic objects, for example, they generally occupied the more public spaces of the household, available at once for public display and private consumption, the two some-times bleeding into each other.[37] At the same time, as print publications, these memoirs blur these boundaries further, troubling the lines separating private recollection from public commemoration, conferring a public (or semipublic) status on personal memory and private sentiment and implying that lives too insignificant or too incomplete to merit biographical treatment nonetheless yield important biographical artifacts. Indeed, this latter claim might be seen as their defining feature. Thus, even when written by family members or com-missioned by them, as was generally the case, these memoirs almost invari-ably insist on the ordinariness of their subjects, even if only as a rhetorical gesture.[38] What the parents of Eric and Arnold Miall Smith wrote in *Two Brothers* (1918), their joint memorial to their slain sons, then, could be said of countless others: "They were just average, wholesome, healthy boys, full of joy of life, haters of war, good sports . . . and when war was declared, detest-ing war as they did, they simply had to go. Just as all the average, wholesome, right-minded boys had to go, and went."[39]

Other volumes, indeed, echo these sentiments. "There was little in the ac-tion of his days that was unusual," James Logan Mackie's biographer writes. "He had no particular intellectual gifts, no flair for things of an artistic, liter-ary or philosophical nature. He was not a youthful prodigy."[40] Contrary to the dominant myth of genius cut short that has come to define so much of World War I memory, many of these young men did not display in their early life any indicators of exceptional promise or achievement, and their families did not shy away from admitting as much. *The Book of Bentley* (1918), a memoir to John Bentley Freeman, for example, dutifully records two such assessments by former housemasters. "Three years ago I should not have picked him out as one who would make a fine soldier," his housemaster from his early years at Marlborough College wrote. "At School he was such a quiet boy, that his extraordinary power of rising to the great occasion would have seemed almost impossible," a later housemaster confirms.[41] The accounts, in fact, are often characterized by what would appear to be a disarming candor. Commenting in *Victor Alexander Ewart* (1921), for example, on her son's propensity for drawing—"almost always ships"—Evelyn Ewart notes, "He had no turn for drawing. . . . Also he was not musical. He learned scales and exercises on the piano, but nothing came of it." In fact, she seems at pains to underline her son's deficiencies. "Victor played games," she adds, "but showed no sensational form," and his school reports, duly noted, were consistently mediocre: "Term succeeded term, and Mr. Worsley always said Victor's conduct was good, but that he was indolent, and did not give his abilities a chance." Indeed, the most distinctive thing Evelyn Ewart finds to say—what she inscribes in almost the first words of her narrative—is, "From babyhood to the end of his twenty-five years and three and a half months of life, he enjoyed wonderful health."[42]

Of course, one cannot mistake a certain class accent here, the self-deprecation intimately tied to class privilege. Victor's father, as it turns out, was Crown equerry to Queen Victoria, and the queen was Victor's godmother, and many other such volumes pointedly celebrate aristocratic lineage. But class distinction notwithstanding, these memoirs testify to the problem of recording a life lacking in exceptionality—a problem magnified for those from classes where the ordinary lives of a household were less obsessively documented. Indeed, without these documents, and without the means to preserve them, those other families could rarely if ever produce comparable volumes. But while these memoirs undoubtedly function, at least in part, as "exclusionary consolatory fictions,"[43] in insisting on the ordinariness of their subjects and the attendant problems of representation, they also open a space, if only theoretically, for recognition of other human losses outside their class-bound existence. Implicitly or explicitly, they raise the question of what counts as noteworthy in a life that, as Evelyn Ewart indicates, must be counted in days and months as much as years—a condition not unique to the privileged. In doing so, they press the limits of their own enterprise, testing the possibility of biography for one without claim to singularity or preeminence. One can locate in these texts, then, a familiar refrain: "Anything in the way of a formal biography was not to be thought of," Charles Sorley's father writes of his son in *The Letters of Charles Sorley, with a Chapter of Biography* (1919).[44] "This little memoir, written by one who knew Logan Mackie for many years, does not presume to be a biography," Major A. Stodart-Walker affirms in his preface to *James Logan Mackie* (1919).[45] "For some, among the fallen, a crowning tribute will be laid hereafter upon the record of their years," Marc Noble's sister notes; "With these Marc Noble will not be recalled."[46]

As even this brief survey suggests, what these biographical memoirs lack is life, posing the problem of how to record a life that is missing because not sufficiently lived, that is unnarratable because its narrative trajectory has never taken off. What happens when life is, in effect, incomplete—not as Sir Sidney Lee worried because the subject is still alive but because of the life's extreme brevity?[47] As Marjorie Noble confesses, "Had life been added to the gifts of life, a memoir of Marc would have indeed done more than loosely indicate a general trend of character."[48] Writing about Rupert Brooke, Virginia Woolf identifies a similar problem: "Nothing, it is true, but his own life prolonged to the usual term, and the work that he would have done, could have expressed all that was latent in the crowded years of his youth."[49] Indeed, these memorial volumes are and are not nothing, for the sense of the war as a world-historical

44   CHAPTER 1

event of unsurpassed moment demands their memorialization of ordinariness, despite the evident obstacles it entails. The problem is in part one of narrative: how to shape a life with so little in it, how to render such a life in a persuasive manner. But it is also a question of the nature and sufficiency of the available material. As Woolf suggests, these men "leave so little behind them that can serve to recall them with any exactitude. A few letters, written from school and college, a fragment of a diary—that is all."[50] Some do not even leave that. And they lack the traditional milestones around which a Life can be organized. Indeed, mustering a "chronological biography" to preface the set of remembrances that make up *Horace A. Link: A Memoir* (1919), its compiler can barely fill a page with dates of importance even as he feels compelled to create such an artifact.[51] Reviewing Edward Marsh's memoir of Rupert Brooke for the *Times Literary Supplement* in August 1918, Woolf concedes "the enormous difficulties which beset the biographers of those who have died with undeveloped powers, tragically, and in the glory of public gratitude."[52] For those outside the privileged classes, the difficulties are even more insurmountable, rendering these memoirs a largely class-bound phenomenon.

As Woolf acknowledges elsewhere, however, similar problems confront the practitioners of the "new biography": "Many of the old chapter headings—life at college, marriage, career—are shown to be very arbitrary and artificial distinctions. The real current of the hero's existence took, very likely, a different course."[53] But if, for Woolf and other advocates of the "new biography," to reject these chapter heads is to choose an alternative aesthetic, for the young war dead, such chapters are not even possible, and the "real current" in their lives is inevitably fixed in childhood. Perhaps for this reason some memoirs dispense with descriptive chapter heads altogether, as John Buchan does in *Francis and Riversdale Grenfell: A Memoir* (1920), confining himself to a simple record of dates. If the new biography, as many have noted, inaugurated an unprecedented emphasis on childhood as a formative influence on the subject, these memoirs give us childhood with a vengeance—not necessarily out of inclination but because it is all that is available to them. Christopher Coombe Tennant, for example, in the "Autobiographical Fragment" included in Sir Oliver Lodge's memoir of him, *Christopher: A Study in Human Personality* (1918) (figure 1.2), projects the chapters his "life" might take although he insists his "is not an attempt at autobiography": "Like the lives of most other men, mine falls into periods: Before school—Private school—Public school—Sandhurst—the Army." Most men, however, do not take stock of their lives "at the age of 19 years 9 months" when, as Christopher acknowledges, the record "must necessarily be incomplete and lacking in detail" and the precarious circumstances of war render additional chapters uncertain.[54]

FIGURE 1.2. Frontispiece photograph and title page from Sir Oliver Lodge, *Christopher: A Study in Human Personality* (London: Cassell, 1918).

The configuration Christopher outlines, however, corresponds to the life span of many men of his generation and finds itself echoed in the formal subdivisions of the biographical record. Glenconner, for example, in *Edward Wyndham Tennant*, one of the most widely read and favorably reviewed publications of its type, elaborates this schema for the life she writes of her son who died just months after his nineteenth birthday—"Early Childhood," "Childhood," "Poems Written in Childhood," "Schooldays," "Later School Days (1911–1914)," "France," "On Leave"—after which she appends a set of assorted, nonchronological add-ons. Marie Leighton parses these divisions even more finely—and more sentimentally—in *Boy of My Heart* (1916), her semifictionalized tribute to her son, Roland Leighton, best known as Vera Brittain's fiancé: "The Extravagant Baby," "The First Steps of the Little Feet," "The Boy's Treasures and Other Things."[55] But even such chapters tend to be foreshortened, whether by the limitation of the life or the limitation of the biographer. "It would be a fascinating task to follow him through his life in a long and exhaustive chronicle with the four great Chapter-headings, Childhood, Growth, Manhood, Death," Guy Ridley writes in a memoir introducing *Poems by Ivar Campbell* (1917), "But such a chronicle would be the work of

46   **CHAPTER 1**

years and would require a master-pen to write it."[56] By contrast, the chronicles I consider here are amateur productions, written under the time pressure of occasional literature—to commemorate a death in a timely manner, or to mark the anniversary of the subject's birth or passing.

In many cases, moreover, even the simple narrative arc adumbrated by such chapter headings was disrupted by the miscellaneous material inserted within and between them: poems from childhood, letters from school, selections of verses, school magazine publications, impressions written by friends, letters from the front, doodles and drawings, diary fragments, funeral elegies, letters of condolence, or lists of hobbies and favorite pastimes. In *George Buchanan Smith, 1890–1915* (1916), one such insertion literally splits the official memoir in half, as the contents page indicates: "Memoir, Part I," "His Verses," "Memoir, Part II." These chapter divisions are followed by other assorted headings that self-consciously proclaim the book's hodgepodge construction: "Letters from His and Our Friends," "Published and Other Notices," and "Some Tramps and Climbs."[57] These random pieces, however, mirror the condition of their subjects. The editor of *In Memoriam: Harold Parry, Second Lieutenant, K.R.R.C* (1918), for example, in introducing a selection of Parry's poems, notes the happenstance nature of their composition and preservation: "They were to be found everywhere—backs of envelopes, untidy and half undecipherable scrapbooks, neat and orderly manuscript, prim typewritten portfolios."[58] Their significance, he seems to signal, lies not so much in the poems themselves as in their fragmentariness, their evidence of a life cut off before its literary output could be properly organized and collected.[59]

The works, indeed, are characterized by an excess of mismatched pieces, some only peripherally related to their ostensible subject. *Edward Wyndham Tennant*, for example, ends with Glenconner's poetic tribute to Edward's sister, the infant daughter who died on the day of her birth in 1916, presented as the volume's third appendix, "'Flower of the Field' or 'Hester.'" Lodge's *Christopher*, in its chapter-by-chapter unrolling, practically hemorrhages appended supplements: "A Message to the Bereaved" from those who have "passed over"; a memorial, composed by Christopher's mother, on the occasion of the death of her eighteen-month-old daughter; a complete list of boys who attended Christopher's preparatory school, West Downs, in 1909, with details of their military service; a Roll of Honour of the fallen from his public school house at Winchester; brief private notes and jottings by his mother, written within days of learning of his death. In some cases, the memoir proper, if such a term can be used, is merely a preface or appendage to some other publication: a collection of poems or a compilation of letters—or even an argument for afterlife survival. As ad hoc biographies these works put pressure on the genre

MATERIAL BOYS 47

by rendering themselves unreadable, their significance residing in their very miscellaneousness. In other words, it is the failure of the individual components to link up coherently that strongly conveys the evanescence of their subject to the reader. Yet, as discussed in the next section, these volumes create a new kind of afterlife as part of the material culture of remembrance, and their meaning exceeds their function as textual record.

Material Matters

Often printed in limited editions with sometimes lavish packaging, memorial volumes were designed to be dipped into, displayed, and privately circulated—and to be preserved as family heritage—as much as to be read in a linear fashion. Their life as objects thus complements their textual existence. Like other memorial artifacts such as the embellished photographs that Geoffrey Batchen analyzes in *Forget Me Not: Photography and Remembrance*, they depend on the physical intimacy of touch—the feel of the object itself and of its encasing framework—in order to trigger memory; and they depend on their hybrid and miscellaneous elements "to provide a compelling memorial experience" that would not otherwise be available to their makers and their recipients.[60] As objects, then, as much as texts, they stand as testimonials to the losses of the class, broadly defined, that can afford the cost of their publication or can command the attention and resources of established publishers.

The privately printed volumes, which prove especially susceptible to this object-focused analysis, range from modest efforts to elaborate art house productions employing special fonts, handmade paper, and sumptuous bindings. In some instances, at least, the expense must have been exorbitant, whether from the scale of the undertaking or the cost of materials and labor. Lady Desborough's memoir of her two sons, Julian and Billy Grenfell, *Pages from a Family Journal, 1888–1915* (1916), for example, runs to an encyclopedic 655 pages with twenty-five plates, significantly outpacing in this respect other similar productions and contributing to the appearance of conspicuous consumption—a notion reinforced by indications of a circulation considerably wider than the small circle designated as its intended audience: "For Julian and Billy's brother and sisters, and for their intimate friends."[61] Given its sheer bulk, it is hard to imagine anyone reading such a "book" cover to cover; the logic of accretion, moreover, that seems to inform its composition resists narrative containment despite the overarching chronological framework. Indeed, while ostensibly culled from a larger work, *Pages* gives the appearance of being just that: a barely edited collection of pieces. On an impossibly larger scale, then, the volume

48   CHAPTER 1

works through the same logic of miscellaneity that characterizes the more typ-ical memorial volumes, and it conveys, even in its outsize length, the same sense of evanescence.

In its parts as well as whole, moreover, it displays a conspicuous excess: in the sheer number of family letters it collates, most written to the boys' mother; in the family documents it preserves, no matter how trivial (e.g., "Bil-ly's History of the Family," dictated when he was five years old); in the copious testimonials it includes from schoolmasters, dons, family friends, and family servants (including detailed reports on the children composed in the parents' absence); in the numerous public notices it records of the brothers' deaths, as well as of their achievements at school, university, and the army; in the pages and pages of extracts from letters of condolence, a mere sampling of the hun-dreds of letters received by the family.[62] In its massiveness, then, it both magni-fies and brings into focus the materiality of its textual components, rendering them of a piece with the photographic supplements, themselves, in the scale of such things, similarly excessive. In the persistent markers of wealth—the staged portraits in fancy dress (figure 1.3), the leisure shots in country retreats—the photographs, in their repetitive iterations, provide further testimony to the privileged world the brothers inhabited, a world already in these images taking on the aura of the relic. While celebrating the life of Lady Desborough's sons, then, the book also mourns a posthumous lifestyle. But the relentless excess also serves another function: to signal a personal loss that remains incalculable. In doing so, it testifies to what, despite the volume's inordinate length, remains unspoken and unspeakable in a culture not given to the free expression of emo-tion: what it means to lose two much-loved sons, aged twenty-five and twenty-seven, within two months of each other. And it testifies to the impossibility of memorializing even the most well-documented of truncated lives.

After receiving a copy of *Pages from a Family Journal*, Evan Charteris, a close friend of the family and purportedly a former lover of the author, wrote to Lady Desborough, "You have done with your sons what no one has ever done before, and raised to them with your own hands a memorial of perpetual beauty."[63] Whether the achievement was as unique as Charteris claims—or as successful—remains open to question; but one way or another, this is what all such memorial volumes aim to accomplish, the volume itself a kind of substitute tombstone, a reaction in part to the prevailing condition of corpselessness, with bodies buried overseas or never recovered altogether. And private publication facilitates this am-bition. Like *Pages*, many such volumes stake the claim for their existence on their display value, as does *The Book of Bentley*, announcing on its back cover, "One hundred copies privately printed, for presentation only. / Issued on Bentley's 21st Birthday, January 20th, 1918." Inserting the book into a gift economy, the

MATERIAL BOYS 49

FIGURE 1.3. Julian and Billy Grenfell as pages to Lady Charles Cavendish-Bentinck at her wedding, 1897. From Ethel Anne Priscilla Grenfell, Lady Desborough, *Pages from a Family Journal, 1888–1915* (Eton: Eton College, privately printed, 1916), facing p. 34

cover statement at once decommercializes it and announces the highest admission price of all for it. Like *Pages*, moreover, many of these volumes honor a dead soldier by exhibiting the wealth and prestige of his household, even if they employ different exhibition strategies. *The Career of a Second Lieutenant in the Year 1914* (1915), for example, a volume of 120 pages with eight leaves of plates, includes on its title page the following dedication: "In Memory of Second Lieut. Bevil Tollemache / First Battalion Cold Stream Guards / Grandson of the First / Lord Tollemache of Helmingham."[64] In the British Library copy of this volume, printed on high-quality watermarked paper and bound in gold-tooled brown Niger Morocco leather with gilt-edged pages, the shield from the family's coat of arms, also gilded, is embossed on the cover. The luxuriousness of the materials calls attention to the volume as a precious object. A printed presentation note pasted into the volume suggests that this was not merely a single personal copy specially produced for the family and bound in this manner, which was a more common occurrence. A bookseller's description for a slightly less ornate surviving copy—this one bound in "the original white vellum"—suggests that even the

50   **CHAPTER 1**

more widely circulated version of the volume had an element of extravagance: "Without doubt the most lavishly produced memorial volume that I have had in my collection and possibly the rarest!"[65] The interior matter consists of the usual miscellaneous assortment: biographical information, personal impressions, letters from the front, descriptions of the battle where the twenty-five-year-old Bevil lost his life, and obituaries and letters of condolence. These materials, however, cannot be completely separated from the volume's lush exterior. Like *Pages*, the memorial betrays an implicit logic: the value of the deceased can be read in the value of the memorial object, even as the original readers recognized that it cannot be read in the miscellaneous scraps that constitute its contents; also like *Pages*—and like so many similar volumes—there is an added poignancy in the inverse proportion between the shortness of the life and the lavish expenditure on it. Viewed today, such objects testify to another failure—the failure in spite of copious resources to preserve a life from oblivion.

Such objects, however, continue to hold interest for the access they provide to the way memory is manufactured. In their immediate circumstances, these volumes derive much of their significance from being something "made"—in particular by the family (or by their surrogates), created by the resources the family commands if not by their manual labor. They are memorials, in other words, that the family itself has designed and executed out of materials precious in themselves or rendered so affectively. For subsequent generations, these memoirs acquire another valence because the biographical object replaces the memory of the biographical subject whom the text attempts to capture. Detached from any living memory of its title character, the object carries instead the traces of the hands that went into its production: in the soliciting, sorting, selecting, and ordering of the textual relics and physical materials out of which it is fashioned. John Buchan's *These for Remembrance: Memoirs of 6 Friends Killed in the Great War* (1919) provides an interesting illustration as a memorial made not *to* a family member, although Buchan lost a brother in the war, but *for* his own family, for his children, "to know something about [his] friends who fell in the Great War." Buchan's contemporaries were a half generation or so older than the young men whose memorialization I have thus far been tracking, but his memorial volume works through similar memory practices.[66] Affectively, Buchan installs his friends in the place of family—the most typical subject for such commemorative undertakings—and his personal copy, hand-bound by the foremost bookbinder of the day, bears the shield from the Buchan coat-of-arms. Indeed, *These for Remembrance*, of which only a few copies were ostensibly published, reproduces the material features of the most exclusive family productions, as a publisher's note to the 1987 reprint explains in some detail: "The book was privately printed in 1919 by monotype letterpress on hand-made paper, the illustrations being original photographs glued by hand on to the relevant pages, or drawings by Blackwood glued or bound in. The work was supervised by the Medici Society, and carried out at the Chiswick Press."[67] The emphasis here is on the handmade and the tactile and on the adherence to time-honored artisanal practices—qualities reinforced in Buchan's personal copy, with its opulent binding in red-brown Morocco leather and its gold blocking. The volume, it could be said, partakes quite literally of what James Young has described, in another memorial context, as "the texture of memory."

In these features, the book thus announces itself as something very different from Buchan's many commercial publications, and different even from the other memoir of the war dead that he wrote, *Francis and Riversdale Grenfell: A Memoir*—a book he was commissioned to write by the uncle of slain friends.[68] In his introduction to the modern reprint of *These for Remembrance*, Peter Vansittart has argued that while we may never know "the extent of grief for his friends," given Buchan's "inviolate personal reticence," Buchan "emerges more decidedly" in the pages of *These for Remembrance* than in his autobiography, *Memory Hold-the-Door*, written twenty-one years later.[69] I would argue, however, that the departure from his publishing norms in the original memorial volume and the extravagance of the publishing venture may tell us more about the extent of this grief than anything contained *inside* the volume. The material artifact, in other words, articulates the grief that cannot otherwise be chronicled. The fact, moreover, that Buchan recycles, nearly verbatim, two of the memoir's chapters when he comes to write his autobiography—the only such borrowings he acknowledges there, and then, in only a partial manner—provides further evidence of the book's anomalous status as an affective object.[70] His children, too, the intended audience for *These for Remembrance*, would undoubtedly have responded to the book's aura. For as Buchan explains, the book is written for them to read, "but not yet"—not, that is, at the time of its publication; consequently, it would have accrued added value as something that had to be held in reserve until they were old enough to understand it. Even before his children open it, then, the carefully preserved volume announces itself as a rare and precious object, conveying in this manner as much as in its words the depth of what their father's friends meant to him.

Few such volumes, of course, were anywhere near as lavish, but even the more modest undertakings invest in their status as affective objects—for their creators and for their presumed audience. As the editors of *The Prose Writings of Ivar Campbell* (1918) note, explaining their decision to publish privately what Campbell might not have wished to see published, such volumes aim to become "a cherished possession" in the hands of those who knew and loved the deceased (and even perhaps those without such claims of personal knowledge),

52   **CHAPTER 1**

the value of such objects residing not in the printed words themselves but in their association with the dead person.[71] Even then, when not reliant on expensive materials, these volumes present themselves as things to be preserved and treasured, and they project this aura even for contemporary readers encountering these objects a hundred years after their creation. In some instances, they amplify this effect through their very homeliness—evidence of their handmade and heartfelt construction, the qualities Batchen emphasizes in his study of what he calls "vernacular photographic practices."[72] Like Batchen's memorial artifacts, these memoirs trade on their vernacular quality, as in this homely address by Horace Link's parents to the readers of their volume: "We send this Memoir to our friends, and to those of our dear 'Hoddie,' as an expression of unceasing thankfulness for the twenty-five years of sunshine which his life brought us."[73] These unassuming volumes thus achieve the same end as their more lavish counterparts but from the opposite direction. In both instances, private publication allows the volume to function as a gift or offering for their producers (and their contributors) as well as their audience, something created out of love and decidedly not for profit. As reinforced by presentation cards, dedications, prefaces, and handwritten inscriptions, the significance of the gift lies in part in its ability to circulate within a self-selected circle. The affective pull, moreover, works in both directions. As the compilers of these volumes note, they are often produced, sometimes with considerable reluctance, at the persistent urging of others: the deceased's friends and other relatives or, in those cases where there have been prior publications, devoted readers and followers. These volumes then play a role in creating and sustaining a community of the bereaved linked by the creation and possession of the shared object. They participate in rituals of what Jay Winter has called "collective remembrance," made possible by ties of both real and fictive kinship.[74] And they participate in the promise, implied by such objects, of an afterlife for their subjects—a posthumous life explicitly announced in the many anniversary volumes that mark a birthday the subject did not otherwise live to celebrate.

These works, then, perform first and foremost as keepsakes and mementos, and their biographical aspirations are contained within their commemorative function—the very thing that has kept us from recognizing their place in the development of biography as a genre. Indeed, such a function aligns them with discredited biographical practices. Harold Nicholson, for example, singles out the "commemorative instinct," what he calls "the cenotaph-urge," as the single factor most responsible for the "impurity" of contemporary biography.[75] But if these works invoke commemoration, they do so without harnessing its monumental dimensions, thus shifting our understanding of the way the process operates. Instead, regardless of their actual size, they regularly insist on their diminutiveness. "This little book," "this little intimate volume," "this slight memoir"—these are the types of phrases that appear over and over again.[76] While few of these works are actual doorstoppers like *Pages from a Family Journal*, the variation in size is considerable, with many running well over a hundred pages. In some cases, of course, the volumes are quite literally "little books," as measured by their physical dimensions or their page tally. *The Book of Bentley*, for example, is a mere twenty pages; constructed out of stiff paper, with the pages loosely stitched together, it resembles more a booklet than a full-fledged volume, a book-like object rather than a book proper (figure 1.4). Its material features thus underline the instability of its location in a genre. Some volumes even announce their brevity in their titles, as in *George Roworth Parr, Prince Albert's Somerset Light Infantry: A Short Memoir* (1915), a publication fleshed out to eighty-seven pages by the addition of other material, as the volume's full title indicates: " . . . *Together with His Letters Written Whilst on Active Service during the Great War, and Some of His other Writings*."[77]

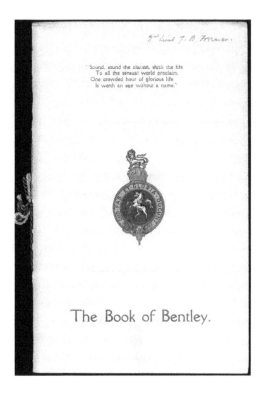

FIGURE 1.4. *The Book of Bentley* (Burton-on-Trent: W. B. Darley, the Caxton Press, privately printed, 1918). Photo Credit: © Imperial War Museum (LBY K. 87/542)

54   **CHAPTER 1**

Similar memorial volumes, however, stress the "little" even when their length is substantial, and they stress the offhand quality of the work even when, as occasionally happened, the author or contributor is a professional writer. Thus in the case of the Grenfell brothers, John Buchan dedicates "this little book"—a work of some 240 pages—to "the Twins' brothers and sisters," while the volume's sponsor, Field-Marshal Lord Grenfell, will not even go so far as to say the material at hand warrants a *book*, conceding only that his nephews' large cache of letters seemed worthy of "some form of publication."[78]

Hybrid Forms and Missing Persons

Despite their many disclaimers, these memorial volumes, I am arguing, offer an important commentary on both the practices of commemoration in which they participate and the practices of biography that they distinctly mimic. And they do so by virtue of their relentless hybridity, inserting themselves in the no-man's-land between the "old" and the "new" biography and between public and private memorialization. Recalling earlier associations of biography with commemoration, with the desire of a nation, in Lee's words, to accord "rational and efficient monuments" to its "distinguished sons and daughters," these volumes, in their determined understatement, question the commemoration they perform, collapsing public and private and rendering the idea of permanence suspect. In effect, they render themselves paradoxically posthumous—a living testimony to their own evanescence and the evanescence of the lives they commemorate. Speaking in 1896, Sir Sidney Lee cemented the association of national biography with the commemorative impulse. "If biography is to respond to a whole nation's commemorative aspirations," Lee asserted, "its bounds must be enlarged and defined, so as to admit, with unerring precision, everyone who has excited the nation's commemorative instincts, while the mode of treatment must be so contrived, so contracted, that the collected results may not overwhelm us by their bulk."[79] The makers of the commemorative volumes I have been considering, however, test the limits of this inclusiveness, stretching the bounds of biography by, in effect, provincializing it, turning its resources to their own intimate connections.

What Lee perhaps did not anticipate was the way the Great War would open a fissure in his formulation, producing a split between the large numbers of the recently dead exciting the nation's commemorative instincts and the small fraction who could be admitted to his repository of national biography.[80] Indeed, in an address to the English Association, published in September 1918, Lee admits the new challenge: "Biography will be called on—nay, is being called upon owing to the premature ending of so many lives of high promise on the battlefield of land, sea, and air—to perform its peculiar commemorative function on a vaster scale than ever before."[81] But this recognition of monumental sacrifice worthy of recognition does not prompt Lee to alter his earlier position on the magnitude required for a life to merit biographical treatment in the public arena or on the level of skill the biographer must demonstrate to perform this function, what he calls in an earlier publication "a commensurate sufficiency" of subject matter and style.[82] The task of memorializing what is not there—the truncated lives of unfulfilled promise—thus remains to be taken up by amateurs, by biographical outliers who render biography's "peculiar" practice even more peculiar. Lee's belief, moreover, in the superiority of biography to more ephemeral monuments, articulated in his address "National Biography" (1896), takes on a particular edge in the shadow of postwar mourning and the proliferation of names on public memorials, for it proleptically challenges the very premise of the nation's postwar memorialization project: "Monuments in stone or brass may preserve a man's name for two or three centuries, but little purpose is served by the preservation of a man's bare name. Even epitaphs, which supply something more than a bare name, are not lasting." By contrast, Lee affirms, "Biography is of its essence public and perspicuous; it is no less certainly permanent."[83]

But the kinds of biographical objects I have been looking at here occupy, as cultural forms, some uneasy place between a "bare name" and perspicuous and permanent memorialization, especially the many that were privately printed in small runs for circulation to friends and family. Even as they make claims to fulfill the need for some permanent record, they announce themselves in their intimate scope and in their amateurish construction as decidedly ephemeral, not likely to outlive those with firsthand knowledge of the departed; if they survive, they do so as mere relics. They thus remind us that for the kinds of posthumous people they enshrine, there is a time stamp on the posthumous. Insofar as they are biography, they project biography as ephemera, and they offer none of the traits Lee identifies as biography in its essence. For if they are neither fully public nor certainly permanent, they are also not perspicuous. They do not, then, fulfill the conditions of the "old biography" despite the centrality of their commemorative element. At the same time, they lack what Strachey articulated as the guiding principles for the "new biography"; they correspond neither to the biographical tomes, "those two fat volumes, with which it is our custom to commemorate the dead," that Strachey derided in his predecessors nor the "becoming brevity" Strachey advocates as an alternative.[84] Any resemblance to the "brief lives" Strachey popularized is a function of the brevity of the life they record rather than the

56   **CHAPTER 1**

biographer's judicious editing. When the biographies themselves are brief (which is certainly not always the case), they are not necessarily *becomingly* so. They lack clarity, precision, and a principle of selectiveness: they are, one might suggest, to return to Lee's language, neither rational nor efficient, and this critique extends to those volumes published for a general readership. As book-like objects and biographical approximates, they exert their power not by conveying meaning discursively (like Strachey or the *DNB*) but through affect.

The volumes, by and large, also share with each other the same eclectic aesthetic. Although none of these works exceeds a single volume, they often cannot escape feeling bloated, and they display all the faults Strachey rails against in their heftier precursors: "their ill-digested masses of material, their slipshod style, their tone of tedious panegyric, their lamentable lack of selection, of detachment, of design."[85] In the absence of enough material from which to cull a complete and coherent narrative of their subject—the absence, that is, of documentable experience—these volumes make a virtue of indiscriminateness, filling the gaps with whatever comes to hand. They include, it would seem, virtually everything; nothing appears too trivial or too inconsequential. Hence the impression these memoirs often give of being either too short or too long, if not both simultaneously. And hence the impression they convey of being alternatively, or at once, too private and too public.

Woolf, who reviewed several such volumes, diagnoses the two sides of the spectrum. In the case of Rupert Brooke, whom Woolf knew personally, the public profile projected in the memoir does not match her intimate, private knowledge. Reading Edward Marsh's 1918 memoir, a work largely derided today as unapologetic hagiography, and comparing it to her knowledge of the subject, Woolf admits that she has "seen enough to be made sceptical of the possibility of any biography of a man dying, as he died, at the age of twenty-eight." As Brooke's mother admits in her introduction, the volume is "of necessity incomplete," but not just for the reason she acknowledges: the inability to obtain reminiscences from his Cambridge contemporaries, most now themselves "scattered or dead."[86] The volume may be incomplete, Woolf suggests, because of what friends and associates are unwilling to say publicly in a volume intent on supplanting the living man—a complex and flawed individual—with a sanitized and sentimentalized posthumous invention. The problem, then, is not that the material for a life is nonexistent—Brooke even made it into the *DNB*'s 1912–1921 supplement—but that there is too much in the life that cannot be commemorated within the conventions of the genre. Indeed, the recent publication by the British Library of *The Second I Saw You* (2015), a never-before-published memoir of Brooke, written soon after his death by a former lover and hailed for exposing Brooke as a vicious sadist, tortured soul, and despiser of women, suggests just how much his contemporaries might have been withholding.[87]

In the case of Edward Wyndham Tennant, who died at nineteen, the situation is reversed, and a posthumous life even more elusive—the lack of a public dimension to the life exposed in the excessive display of what would ordinarily be kept private. In such circumstances, Woolf maintains, biography is not merely impossible but bordering on the indecent. If not quite the lurid spectacle Woolf bemoaned on "the night of the Cenotaph"—"A bright light in the Strand; women crying Remember the Glorious Dead, & holding out chrysanthemums"[88]—the excessive show of sentiment displayed in Lady Glenconner's memorial to her son (like the class privilege that bolsters it) was, Woolf suggests, similarly objectionable. Consequently, she calls out what she dubs "the aristocratic point of view"—the unthinking self-absorption, the unseemly demonstrativeness—betrayed in both the narrative and its central subject, "Bim," as he is regularly named there: "From his natural confidence spring all those demonstrative ways which are at once so charming and (to be honest) so strangely disconcerting when published in a book. For if, as is likely, one is neither related to Aunt Annie nor has ever heard of her existence, there is something indecent, though childish and disarming, in the amazing aristocratic irreticence which is displayed—the assumption that everybody must know you, and be interested in hearing all about you."[89]

The problem Woolf identifies is even more far-reaching than this one example, going to the heart of so many of these commemorative volumes, dependent as they are on making the "too private" public. If what they exhibit is more often dull than salacious, they nonetheless violate some implicit, and in some cases explicit, taboo about what can appropriately be revealed to the world: recollections of quaint childhood mannerisms and sayings; caches of letters home composed by a schoolboy; fledgling literary work not ready for wider circulation; excerpts from personal diaries meant for the eyes of the author only; transcripts of secret-society talks and other school proceedings; papers first discovered in the dead man's effects, sometimes in sealed envelopes or locked manuscript books. These items, as Constance Astley notes in the memoir she commissioned for her son, often refer "to trivial everyday matters of transitory and probably personal interest only."[90] However innocuous in themselves, "when published in a book," to borrow Woolf's words, they appear transgressive. As suggested by the memoir's title, *Richard Vincent Sutton: A Record of His Life Together with Excerpts from His Private Papers* (1922), they give the appearance of intrusion into confidential territory. For this reason, the prefaces to these works often take the form of an apology—for encroaching on private grief, exposing tender personal moments, disseminating immature work,

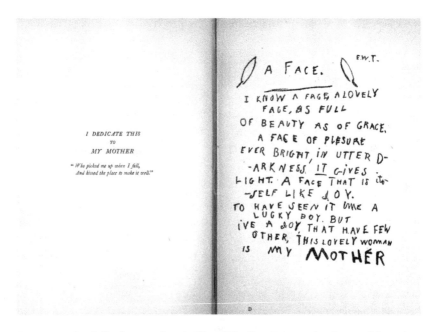

FIGURE 1.5. Facsimile of poem written by Edward Wyndham Tennant when he was eight or nine years old. From Pamela Glenconner, *Edward Wyndham Tennant: A Memoir by His Mother* (London: John Lane, 1919)

indulging sentimental effusions, violating the wishes of the deceased, or publishing altogether. It is hard to read these accounts, then, without feeling we—or the authors—are overstepping, that we are being forced to eavesdrop on what is too trivial or personal for us to witness. This sensation is particularly acute when, as Woolf seemed to recognize, what these volumes display results in the infantilizing of their subject:[91] the lingering on earliest impressions in the selection of remembrances, as in "'Hoddie'—In Babyhood and Boyhood: By His Sister" (*Horace A. Link: A Memoir*); the precious photographs of the subject as an infant or young child (see figure 1.3); the prattle of baby talk that echoes through these chronicles; the nursery names carried into adulthood (e.g., Bim, Hoddie, Little Yeogh Wough, Bez, Tadpole); the unabashed juvenilia that crams the pages, sometimes reproduced in facsimile format (figure 1.5); the seemingly endless excerpts from letters addressed to "My Darling Mum" or "Dearest Darling Mumsey."

Yet the very features of these works that made some contemporary readers squeamish—and that elicit cringes from present-day readers—also contribute to their peculiar poignancy: to the pathos they project in the types of materials they are forced to rely on. They thus offer unusual insight into the workings of grief and memory and the particular challenge posed by the elusive objects they commemorate. These same features, moreover, can also be read somewhat less sentimentally: to signal a resistance, if only an unconscious one, to the demands of the biographical genre in which these volumes so uneasily participate. In their fixation on the stuff of childhood, for example, they expose the standard biographical plot, with its emphasis on the accomplishments of manhood, to be a fictional construct. This is particularly true, as I have argued elsewhere, for the many memoirs written or compiled by women.[92] Refusing to prioritize acts of public interest and significance—indeed, exposing the impossibility of such a project for lives so abruptly and prematurely foreshortened—they insist instead on the importance of things traditional biography cannot accommodate. Indeed, implicitly at least, they make the case for the value of the banal and quotidian. Simultaneously, they contest the inscription of the life in a linear narrative, a narrative for which mature masculinity is the goal and death the necessary outcome. Yet they do not abandon the biographical project. Rather, they exploit the potential of biography to tell *personal* stories, to provide a platform where, as Marita Sturken has argued, "individual memories are shared, often with political intent, to act as counter-memories to history," even if, in this case, they do so without any defined political agenda.[93] Telling what might be called "*this* boy's life," in all its overspecificity, they resist having that life completely subsumed in the official narrative, the generic "soldier's story"; at the same time, they embrace those official conventions in the volume's memorial architecture (its title, dedication, and other paratextual materials).

Alongside the personal materials they amass, then, they collect more public documents: military testimonials (in the form of letters from both officers and men attesting to the soldier's distinguished service); obituary notices and letters of condolence, often replete with clichés of heroic sacrifice; death notices and war office correspondence; battlefield and burial site maps; funeral sermons. The awkward juxtaposition of these public and private components and their sometimes porous boundaries—the way, for example, public discourse infiltrates private correspondence—render these works unsettling hybrids in even more far-reaching ways than I have already documented. When Bevil Tollemache's mother, for example, addresses her dead son in a letter that opens the family's memorial volume, the public and private can be seen visibly vying with each other: "And now all is over, I know that nothing you could have done in this world is so glorious as the record of your great sacrifice for us all, which will live for ever written on the Golden Roll of England's Honour. I often think of you still as my little boy who often wanted my help."[94] Performing what Tanya Dalziell has called, in another context, "an extended and imaginative interaction between the dead and the living," she refuses in this epistolary

60   **CHAPTER 1**

exchange to cede her son to the public narrative that would otherwise decisively claim him, even as she affirms that narrative.[95] In a striking manner, these memorials demonstrate, as Thomas Laqueur reminds us, that "writing of the dead is never entirely either a private or a public function, especially in the writing of war dead."[96] These memoirs, in fact, can be defined by their mixed character, by the tension between their competing narratives and registers, by their different levels of both public and private discourse—both within and between their individual components.[97] Sturken has argued that this tension "converges in particular ways around those biographies that are important to the national image."[98] While individually these memorial volumes would not fit that category, collectively, they take on that status as illustrations of how, on a personal level, the nation absorbs (or fails to absorb) the exorbitant sacrifice demanded of it.

In the features, moreover, that render these memoirs aesthetically suspect—their patchwork and miscellaneous nature; their indiscriminate principles of inclusion; their refusal of distance, proportion, and decorum—they unravel the structures of memorialization in which they participate. Their very incoherence, I am suggesting, exposes the inadequacy of the cultural formations available to them. Few of these works overtly protest the war or question the larger purpose of the deaths they commemorate. Quite notably, they lack the gritty realism and the critical edge of the famous war memoirs that appeared around a decade after them. *The Diary of a Dead Officer: Being the Posthumous Papers of Arthur Graeme West* (1919)—one of the few publications of its kind to claim the attention of contemporary scholars—would be an obvious exception, but it suffered in its own day for voicing untimely political sentiments.[99] Significantly, moreover, this volume, which documents its subject's evolving pacifist convictions and his failed act of protest, was neither authorized nor approved by West's family, and Dominic Hibberd, in the introduction to a 1991 edition, has suggested that the family may even have tried to suppress it. Additionally, as this new edition documents, years later, West's sister is still concerned to rescue her brother's reputation from what she deems his original editor's mishandling of the papers.[100] More typically, the family-sponsored commemorative volumes tended to pay lip service at least, when not offering a full-throated endorsement, to orthodox views on the sanctity of death in heroic service and the justness and necessity of the war that claimed the lives of loved ones, sentiments that have not endeared them to modern readers. Indeed, for much the same reason that Ramazani has argued that Wilfred Owen rejected the traditional elegy, modern readers are likely to view these works, some even bearing telltale titles like *A Soldier of England* (figure 1.6), as "con-

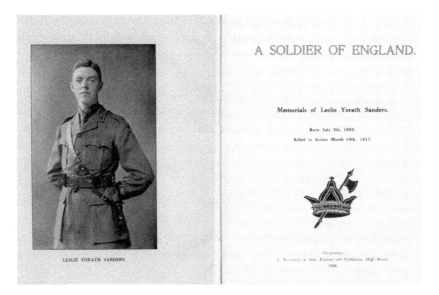

FIGURE 1.6. Title page and frontispiece photograph from Agnes J. Sanders, ed., *A Soldier of England: Memorials of Leslie Yorath Sanders* (Dumfries: J. Maxwell and Son, 1920)

taminated" by their "likeness to the compensatory discourse of patriotic propaganda."[101] If not immune from such charges, however, these works cannot be completely defined by them; nor should their investment in consolatory fictions of a more personal nature automatically disqualify them from engaging in ethical acts of mourning. As Diana Fuss pointedly asks, "Are inherited models for writing about sudden or enduring grief ipso facto unethical, and can modernist despair truly be said to be the only real ethical response?"[102]

These works, moreover, may be less straightforward than they appear in their consolatory apparatus. Their disparate parts frequently pull against each other and threaten the consoling and uplifting messages the volumes attempt to deliver. If, on the one hand, they write modern deaths in an acceptable manner, one that permits them to be absorbed into the national narrative, on the other—in their affective performance—they blow open the project, rendering the deaths an incomprehensible "affront to understanding."[103] These works, then, might have more in common with modernist resistant mourning than would be immediately obvious, or at least, they might be open to analysis in terms of "the complexity of affects associated with loss and consolation" that can, as Anita Helle has argued in the case of "ambivalent mourning," render expressions of loss difficult to pinpoint on a progressive/antiprogressive spectrum.[104] The dilemma, in the memorial volumes, is staged, quite literally,

62   **CHAPTER 1**

over the soldier's dead but absent body. In the testimonials included in *Richard Vincent Sutton*, for example, a family friend and ranking field officer writes to the family, "I feel Dick's death . . . as almost a national calamity," a sentiment that is common throughout this memorial literature.[105] But if such remarks elevate the death by exaggerating its public dimensions, they also risk tipping in the other direction, exposing a different sort of national calamity in the inevitable loss of the private individual. In her discussion of the "corpse poems" frequently found in the poetic output of the two world wars, Diana Fuss characterizes this phenomenon as "the loss of one's right to die as an 'I' and not a 'we,' the loss of one's personal, private, and singular death." Against what Fuss calls "the politically opportunistic overvaluation of the dead," with its attendant suppression of the individual in ennobling abstractions, these memoirs stubbornly insist on the intimate and particular, on "the sum and substance of being that has been painfully lost," even if they can do so only as an expression of their own needs.[106]

These memoirs, then, might be seen as an alternative or supplement to the decorum of the public structures of commemoration—structures Michael Heffernan argues were designed to ensure that "the dead were not allowed to pass unnoticed back into the private worlds of their families."[107] While their publication precedes in many cases the establishment of dedicated memorial locations, they maintained their popular hold in the face of the increasing bureaucratization of memory and mourning, insisting that the private claims of the families could not be simply eclipsed by collective commemoration. In one respect, they act as authorized addenda to official sites of memory, containing private grief by providing a channel for it; in another sense, however, they expose the deficiencies and limitations of the carefully carved out and properly regulated spaces of public memorialization. In a sense, then, they make the personal political. Troubling the boundaries between public and private, they occupy a space that is decidedly messy, if also generative: the fluid and amorphous space of the semipublic—a space of critical importance in making sense of Britain's commemorative culture. Even when not published privately, then, these memoirs of the dead are, as often as not, unapologetically and in all senses of the word memoirs written by persons too close to their subject. "It may sound harsh to say that biography has no place for the widow's tears or the orphans' cry," Sir Sidney Lee proclaims in *The Perspective of Biography*, but these works depend almost exclusively on precisely such a viewpoint.[108] They lack the detachment and disinterestedness necessary for proper biography, as defined by proponents of both the old and new varieties, and they lack the temporal distance to assess their subject fairly. Put another way, they lack perspective. They locate their own authority and agency, however, in the immediacy this lack affords them. Yet the closeness they proclaim does not necessarily produce as full a challenge to the impersonality of public commemoration as might be expected. For if these accounts sometimes feel too personal or intimate, they also fail for the opposite reason: they are not intimate enough. In the end, the abundance of sometimes overly personal elements remains insufficiently distinctive to individualize their subjects.

The obligatory letters from commanding officers and from men, for example, testifying to how well loved the young officer was and how inspiring his example, when read in bulk across a range of volumes sound disturbingly similar. The letters and tributes from friends and family members, though touchingly earnest, often fare only marginally better; indeed, the qualities they most often single out to distinguish the subject turn out to be precisely the things attributed to many others, and precisely the things hardest to document: a genius for friendship, a gift for living, an irrepressible vitality. Even the records in the subject's own voice—excerpts from letters, diaries, and autobiographical writings—do not always convey a compelling sense of personality. There are, however, some striking exceptions, such as Charles Sorley, whom I discuss in chapter 2. The documents that could most successfully convey individuality, Buchan implies, tend to be unpublishable for that very reason, as in the case of Raymond Asquith's letters. "He could not write a sentence without making it characteristic and imparting into it some ribald whimsicality," Buchan observes, explaining why he cannot reproduce even excerpts from these missives.[109] As Buchan reminds us, the documents that make it into these memorial volumes are the product of careful selection; even when privately published, the documents are regularly redacted—excerpted and abridged but also sometimes added to or "corrected." If these works betray a certain homogeneous quality, however, it is not simply the function of family scruples and wartime censorship; it is also a reflection of the similarities in the background and education of the men commemorated and the shared cultural conventions that shape their writing. Whether tantalizingly brief, therefore, or tediously overextended, these works remain haunted by what is missing from them.[110]

For all their quirky elements, I am suggesting, these volumes can risk becoming all too familiar, simply generic—a souvenir object or mere memento. Even the men these volumes celebrated seemed to anticipate this possibility. Thus Edward Wyndham Tennant, in the autobiographical fragment he composed in the summer of 1916—the item with which I opened this chapter—announces his cribbing from other sources in his very first sentence, establishing

64   **CHAPTER 1**

his "life" as self-consciously literary. At the same time, he explicitly invokes both the worn-out tropes of biography and the clichés of memorialization to introduce what he passes off as a memoir of a friend: his concern about what to omit; his faux apology for speaking ill of the dead; his acknowledgment of "a purely sentimental feeling about 'sacred memories'" (*EWT*, 312). The concerns he expresses would have been familiar to other young men of his generation, already aware of the generic quality of the volumes that would commemorate them—the types of volumes they were sometimes reading in the trenches. Indeed, in Tennant's case, by the time he began his "autobiography," his mother had already arranged for the private publication of a volume of his and his brother's letters, his brother then serving in the Dardanelles—a volume whose galley proofs he reviewed on his last leave home in March 1916. And he had arranged for Blackwell's to bring out a volume of his poems— what he referred to in his letters as the "litel boke" (*EWT*, 206)—poems that his mother would republish at the end of her memoir of him.[111]

Even the portraits of the men that regularly adorn these memorial volumes (generally photographs but sometimes paintings or drawings) appear unnervingly similar, especially the studio-produced photographs of the soldier in uniform, the most common type of frontispiece illustration (see figures 1.1, 1.2, 1.6, and 2.1). As the National Portrait Gallery's recent collection of biographies of World War I poets illustrates, in the postwar years the frontispiece had become a charged site of memory with its own requirements for conformity. "Had the National Portrait Gallery brought out a book of this kind in the years immediately after the First World War," the authors note, "it would not have shown Isaac Rosenberg on its frontispiece," the photographic image they chose for this privileged position. "For the generation that raised the Cenotaph in London and the Menin Gate at Ypres to the memory of its Glorious Dead there would have been something too disturbing in the poignant and unmilitary inadequacy of that face, yet now it is precisely those qualities that make this image, of all those included here, the one that seems to speak most vividly of the suffering and waste of war."[112] During the war, moreover, when most of these photographs were taken, the studio portrait was already recognized as a proleptic token of remembrance, assuming the pathos that would be posthumously projected onto it. In this context, we can understand how Sassoon could complain to Lady Ottoline Morrell that he found Glyn Warren Philpot's portrait of him, painted in 1917, "a little popular," while jokingly conceding, "No doubt it will help to sell my posthumous works."[113] Ironically, the portrait was actually used as the frontispiece for *Siegfried's Journey, 1916–1920*, the third volume of Sassoon's second major autobiographical undertaking, the first being the "Sherston" trilogy, in which Sassoon represented himself as a fictional character: *Memoirs of a Fox-Hunting Man* (1928), *Memoirs of an Infantry Officer* (1930), and *Sherston's Progress* (1936). Published in 1945 by a Sassoon still very much alive, at least in body, *Siegfried's Journey* would seem to offer a different type of testimony from his earlier memoirs—one both written in the first person *and* fully claimed by its author.[114] The portrait's presence in that volume, however, suggests the way, as I noted earlier in this chapter, even those who survived the war often experienced themselves as posthumous, rendering *Siegfried's Journey*, in effect, "Memoirs of a *Dead* Infantry Officer," and turning Sassoon's offhand comment to Lady Morrell into something strangely prophetic. Indeed, in working over the bones of his earlier memoirs, Sassoon confirms his own posthumous existence, his own "overliving"—a condition already implicit in the earlier volumes. Interleaving a new version of his life over an earlier record of it, he adds yet another layer to the retrospective filtering of the life he compulsively reiterates. But Sassoon's memorial project is ultimately at cross-purposes with the guardianship of the dead in the Lives that I have been considering, reserving the place of mourning, as Andrew J. Kunka has argued, for combatants only, and rendering the posthumous life their exclusive territory.[115]

Yet his project shares with the earlier memoirs an underlying recognition: the compulsion to give posthumous life to the dead cannot be realized with any certainty or finality. Rather, the posthumous life is something that must be repeatedly reinvented to meet the changing needs of its makers—a recognition that carries through to the present. Indeed, for many of the early memoirists, the Lives they compiled were not the only posthumous lives with which they dabbled. Lady Glenconner, for example, the author of *Edward Wyndham Tennant*, produced at least three different memorial volumes in a five-year period, the first, the privately published collection of her sons' letters, produced before the death of her eldest son, Edward, the last an account of afterlife communications with him. In this latter volume, *The Earthen Vessel* (1921), she both records communications received in a series of sittings with a professional medium in the months immediately following his death in September 1916 and describes a series of vivid dreams in which she senses her son's presence—dreams, she tells us, she "fully believe[s]" are "interviews." In one such dream, as he holds in his hands the proofs of her memoir of him, they discuss the volume; in a telling metaphor, she renders literal the posthumous life she gives him, while he vouches for the accuracy of the representation: "I told him how hard I found it, how I struggled to write, and how clumsy I felt, and helpless. Writing it was like bearing him over again, a moral parturition. Child-birth is painless, I said, compared to writing memoirs of one you love."[116] As if anticipating future erasure, Glenconner here claims seemingly

66   CHAPTER 1

unimpeachable authority for the posthumous life she generates: the authority of experience, of motherhood, and, most of all, of the imprimatur of the volume's own subject. Indeed, in other dreams, and in the transcripts of communications received through the medium, "Bim" reveals his knowledge of even the book's most minute details: its cover, dedication, and publishing venue. At the same time, Glenconner's spiritualist "companion volume" exposes the incompleteness and omissions of the previously published memoir, *Edward Wyndham Tennant* (1919)—a memoir that itself supplements the scattershot spirit communications, already received at that time, that ground the 1919 volume. Like Sassoon's unfinished recollections, then, and like those of his wartime contemporaries, memorial volumes like those composed by Glenconner stand as testimonials to irretrievable loss: to a life that cannot be made whole through the inscription of it. When the dead, then, speak in these volumes (as they do in the autobiographical fragment that concludes *Edward Wyndham Tennant* or in the transcripts of his spirit communications), and when their loved ones collect the scraps of their lives and repackage them for us, their utterances do not resolve the problem of loss but rather reproduce it in a new genre. If, at their worst, these memoirs of the dead devolve into pathos and sentiment and trade on consoling fictions both social and political, at their best they perform the work Ramazani claims for the modern elegy—work that justifies their continuing interest for us: "At its best, the modern elegy offers not a guide to 'successful' mourning but a spur to rethinking the vexed experience of grief in the modern world."[117]

As lives of the dead (quite literally, posthumous Lives), these hybrid, fragmented, and incomplete life stories expose the contradictions that inform them. Despite their best efforts, they belie the impulse that generates them: to commemorate a life and preserve it for posterity. They expose, in other words, the inherent paradox of making the posthumous life the privileged locus for mourning. For the project is one that depends on a necessary failure, if only to sustain the conviction that the person is more than what any formal structure can register. Indeed, this element of failure—the inadequacy of the object to its maker's desire—is the force that drives the genre. "Elegies, it would seem, inevitably come up short," Fuss writes, diagnosing a problem that these memoirs share with their sister genre; like elegies, "the literary genre of choice in times of personal and national crisis," these memorial volumes also rely on an "earnest attempt to buoy the living by holding on to the dead," by resuscitating and reclaiming them.[118] On the one hand, then, these memoirs stumble against the problem of the life, and on the other hand, against the problem of memory. As Horace Link's sister observes, words prove inadequate for the task before them: "We feel very strongly that no mere words can presume to paint a character which endeared itself to family and friends alike."[119] Like others exercising stewardship over the remains of a life, these memoirists cannot escape compromising their material.[120] Indeed, the authors of these volumes come up against what the modernists famously celebrated—the elusiveness of the subject. In the absence of the stuff that makes up a public record, they inevitably fall back on intangibles when not simply recording the quotidian. While it may not have been their intention, they expose the problems the modernists deliberately highlighted: the difficulty of transfixing a life; of pinning down a personality; of capturing, as Marjorie Noble suggests, "those subtle characteristics which never can be catalogued, since they are the very inward essence of the soul."[121] They do so, in part, by producing obsessive catalogs. But they also face a more particular challenge because of the nature of the lives they are attempting to memorialize—lives in which the personality has not yet been fully formed and the person has not yet achieved all that is in him. To record the essence of such a life, they must, where the modernist turned to fiction, resort to the counterfactual.

At the same time, these works trip up in the face of the capriciousness of memory. Many offer disclaimers similar to the one that prefaces *In Memoriam: Harold Parry*, "This little book will be some sort of memorial to him for his many friends, though neither print nor photograph can brighten the picture which will live in the memory of them all"; their very existence, however, suggests doubts about the intensity and longevity of memory and about the "sad permanence of print" that they adopt as their medium.[122] Memory, they suggest, requires props, if it is to be sustained and transmitted, even if those props inevitably fall short of the original. More troubling is the possibility that haunts these works: that even with the necessary prompts, those closest to us cannot be fixed in memory, let alone preserved for future generations. The works, indeed, appear dependent on living memory, even when dedicated to those without firsthand experience of the subject (e.g., children, nieces, nephews, the next generation). Intimating that the posthumous life—let alone a posthumous life of any duration—may be an impossibility, they question the capacity of their narratives to succeed as postmemory accounts; like Batchen's vernacular photographs, they raise "the specter of an impossible desire: the desire to remember, and be remembered."[123] It is precisely this questioning, however, that gives them a continuing claim on our interest.

At the end of *The Great War and Modern Memory*, Paul Fussell notes, as an indication of "the unique persistence of the war in England," a sign "above a large section of shelves in Hatchard's Bookshop, Piccadilly." "I have seen nothing like it in any other country," he adds. "It reads: 'Biography and War Memoirs,' in recognition of a distinct and very commonly requested English genre."[124] As

68   **CHAPTER 1**

Fran Brearton notes, however, "the sign in Hatchard's has long disappeared—no one there remembers it," and the world to which it belongs "is now itself the stuff of nostalgia."[125] While the entwining of "war memoirs" and "biography" into a compound genre would seem to capture perfectly the works I have been exploring in this chapter, the memoirs of the war dead I have been considering here dropped out of public consciousness long before the disappearance of such signs. Consequently, when Fussell came upon the sign, it would have referenced works of a very different order from the ones I have identified in this chapter. In their own era, the war memoirs of the dead were rapidly eclipsed by war memoirs of the living, by the flood of "war books" that appeared in the late 1920s and early 1930s, works which, unlike the memoirs of the dead, continue to be reissued and have been recognized to have had a shaping influence on the autobiographical genre as well as a defining hold on our memory of the war. Indeed, these later works displaced the entire earlier genre, promoting their alternative narrative as the only story that mattered. Over the years, moreover, the memoirs of the dead, produced when the biographical genre was in flux, were further displaced by popular variants on "war memoirs and biography"—works written by journalists, military historians, and professional biographers and more readily recognizable as biography. Yet even as relics, these forgotten books have been crucial to the making of modern memory.

In standard literary histories, these anomalous biographical artifacts have fared little better than in the public arena—absent from accounts of the biographical genre, as it has emerged in the early twentieth century, and absent from the established narratives we have told ourselves about literary modernism, where until recently neither biography nor "war books" have had much purchase. As Laura Marcus observes, "Few critics have attempted to situate early twentieth-century biography in the broader literary and cultural arena" despite "the extraordinary popularity and perceived significance of the genre in the period of 'high modernism'"; she links this popularity "to the new forms of, and experiments with, the genre," what we have come to call the "new biography."[126] Fewer still would attempt to situate the kinds of works I have been looking at here in this broader field of modernist cultural production; few would even situate them as exemplars of biography. I would suggest, however, that the heightened taste for biography in the period Marcus references, "the 1920s and 1930s, particularly," may have also been fed by the advent, from the mid-1910s to the mid-1920s, of a very different type of biographical artifact—one decidedly not experimental, except accidentally so, but one that also enjoyed considerable popularity. Indeed, in their most evident features, the works I have been considering in this chapter confirm Winter's argument about the appeal of traditional languages and motifs for the public and private expression of mourning and bereavement.[127] But as I have been arguing, these works also demonstrate more engagement with modernist concerns than might be immediately evident. Indeed, they perform a crucial modernist function in exposing the mixed nature of the biographical object and the impossibility of pure biography. In the ways they appropriate and resist the structure, logic, and conventions of biography, they illuminate central features—and central problematics—of the genre. In this they operate much like other modernist artistic practices. While no one would mistake these clumsily constructed artifacts for their high modernist counterparts in either fiction or biography, they excavate common ground in several respects, and they grapple, in their own way, with issues at the heart of the modernist project. Ramazani has argued that the great modernist icons T. S. Eliot and Ezra Pound were, in fact, authors of "closet elegies."[128] While I would not go quite so far as to label the elegiac lives of the dead that have formed the subject of this chapter the works of "closet modernists," there is territory to explore in their unlikely overlapping. At a critical moment, moreover, when the New Modernist Studies has opened the field to a recognition of a wide variety of modernisms, it might not be too much of a stretch to see these practices as constituting a strand of an alternative "memorial modernism."

In his monumental study *Self Impression: Life-Writing, Autobiografiction, and the Forms of Modern Literature*, Max Saunders has pressed Marcus's argument even further, claiming that "modern English literary history is shaped by its conflicting responses to life-writing—especially autobiography and biography. These have helped to define the literary field, the canon, modern and modernist literature, and modes of interpretation."[129] Focusing on the intersections between biography and autobiography and between auto/biography and fiction, Saunders moves well beyond the "new biography" in establishing his taxonomies. He uncovers and illuminates an extremely wide array of experimental biographical forms and aesthetic practices from the 1870s to the 1930s. These include the portrait gallery, composite portraiture, collage, posthumousness, hybridity—all having suggestive analogues to the forms and practices that I have been considering. While the works I look at are not part of Saunders's story, his exhaustive mapping of the field provides a significant context for recognizing these hybrid works as part of larger cultural movements and formations. If, moreover, as Saunders argues, "life-writing is central to modernism, in ways that have only recently begun to be appreciated," the distinct body of life writing produced in the wake of World War I contributes valuably to our ongoing reevaluation.[130]

70 CHAPTER 1

Whatever their limitations, in their time these works participated, implicitly if not explicitly, in the construction of a national archive of personal records, a virtual library, as it were, of lives rescued from oblivion. They stood as a bulwark against the temporal pull of forgetting. Like "the lives of the obscure" that Woolf envisioned, these lives "seem to merge into one another, their very boards and title-pages and frontispieces dissolving, and their innumerable pages melting" into each other.[131] They thus could be seen to form a kind of composite portrait or collective memorial. Indeed, a crucial part of their meaning—at least for us today—resides in their iterability, in the way they testify collectively to an untranscribable grief that exceeds their function as individual records. Like the public memorials that they anticipated and miniaturized, these memoirs of the dead contained their own built-in obsolescence, but on an accelerated timescale. At the time of their publication, the vogue for these works attracted considerable public notice. As Janet Watson points out, for example, when one of these books, *The Letters of Charles Sorley*, was published in 1919, the reviewer for the *Times Literary Supplement* anticipated public fatigue with the genre: "On reading the title of this book many people, we fear, will exclaim with dismay, 'Another long book about a young hero-poet!'"[132] Some of these collections, like this one of Sorley's, were, in fact, widely read, widely reviewed by influential figures like Woolf, and widely circulated, a few even running into multiple editions, but not many have had afterlives of any duration. Sorley was something of an exception, and the next chapter takes up the surprising story of his afterlife as a way to make sense of the British fixation on the war poets—a fixation that had its roots in the affective structures that these early memoirs of the dead modeled. Sorley's talents, of course, were not incidental to his reclamation, but they tell only part of the story of how he came to be distinguished from the mass of young men initially memorialized like him.

For the rest, they exist today largely in the archives of the national book depositories in the United Kingdom; in dedicated collections like those of the Imperial War Museum; in offsite annexes of university libraries; and in some instances, where the book circulated widely in the past, on internet archives or in on-demand reprint series like "Forgotten Books." For the twenty-first century, they constitute a virtual archive of the forgotten: forgotten biographies of forgotten people. Like so many of the memorials erected in the years immediately following the war, these biography-like productions are monuments to the missing—the missing subjects these Lives record, and the missing subject of biography itself. Yet they remain a valuable resource for our reevaluation of the postwar memorial practices that continue to shape the war's affective legacy. Paradoxically, our postmemory position might enable us to better appreciate them—not as personal documents but as a significant cultural formation. Detached from the subjects that provided their reason for being—detached, that is, from the constraints of memory—they articulate, collectively, the peculiar sense of magnitude and loss that those who lived through the war experienced and that we continue to grapple with.

CHAPTER 2

Sorley's Travels

The Afterlife of a World War I Poet

In February 1916, a month after *Marlborough and Other Poems* was posthumously published and only four months after its author's death, Robert Graves wrote to Edward Marsh, impresario of the Georgian poets, "I've just discovered a brilliant young poet called Sorley. . . . It seems ridiculous to fall in love with a dead man as I have found myself doing but he seems to have been one so entirely after my own heart in his loves and hates, besides having been just my own age and having spent just the same years at Marlboro' as I spent at Ch'house [Charterhouse]. He got a classical scholarship at University College, Oxford, the same year as I was up and I half-remember meeting him there."[1] In this and subsequent letters to Marsh, and to two other young soldier-poets, Siegfried Sassoon and Robert Nichols, Graves can barely contain his enthusiasm for the poems of Charles Hamilton Sorley. "Listen," "Don't you like this," "By the way, don't you love . . . ," he implores, as he cites, sometimes from memory, lines and stanzas from his spiritual twin and posthumous protégé.[2] With each retelling, moreover, the half-remembered meeting takes on additional solidity; less than a year after his initial discovery of "the brilliant young poet," Graves tells Nichols, "I met him at Oxford in 1913 . . . but didn't realize who he was—wasted opportunities, horrid to look back on."[3] Looking forward, Graves submits the dead Sorley to an orgy of attention, shepherding his career through his own private networks. As his letters document, Graves watches over Sorley's sales, follows each new edition of *Marlborough* (there were three separate editions within the first year of publication alone), and tracks every public notice of him.[4] He even uses his personal connections to "insist on a decent review of Sorley" in the *Spectator*.[5] And much as he and Sassoon were in the habit, at this time, of "patch[ing] up" each other's verses, Graves proposes "emendations" to Sorley's published writing—suggestions he submits to Sassoon for his confirmation.[6] In undertaking these interventions, Graves makes Sorley a poet in a way he never was in his lifetime: a poet fashioned in Graves's likeness.

That Graves was responding to the poetry itself—its language and sentiment—seems indisputable; indeed, these are precisely the features he cites in his enthusiastic reveries. His investment in Sorley's posthumous career, moreover, can be seen as a measure of his respect for Sorley as a poet, as can his investment in editing him. In this, Graves anticipates the grounds of much of Sorley's favorable reception. But his response, like that of so many of Sorley's early readers, was also overdetermined, as his exchanges with Sassoon demonstrate. For men who regularly exchange Sorley lines and Sorleyisms, share Sorley volumes, and trade tidbits of Sorley information, the likeness Graves constructs serves certain homosocial and homoerotic functions that the wartime context intensified.[7] "What did your Marlburian say about Sorley," Graves writes to Sassoon, "and was he 'so'? As his book contains no conventional love-lyrics and as he'd reached the age of 20, I conclude he was."[8] "Did you know Sorley before his death?" he asks Nichols in his first letter to him, after declaring himself "a very very ardent Sorleian."[9] Indeed, shared love of Sorley is what brings Graves and Nichols together, Nichols's own poetry merely an afterthought. "Bob Nichols of course is no Sorley," Graves tells Sassoon, "but he's next best, a devout admirer."[10]

In this chain of substitution, however, the dead poet can also stand in for his unnamed living counterpart. At the front, for example, thinking of Graves as he listens to the sounds of battle—"And Robert's somewhere in it, if he hasn't been shot already"—Sassoon turns to thoughts of his own death, as mediated by Sorley: "And I've still got my terrible way to tread before I'm free to sleep with Rupert Brooke and Sorley and all the nameless poets of the war."[11] As later diary entries make clear, if Sassoon does not quite sleep with Sorley, he sleeps with Sorley by him, reading his letters to cheer himself, rehearsing his poems in his mind, filtering even his visceral responses through Sorley's affinities. "It was raining to-night," he writes in one entry. "The rain (that Sorley loved) was dripping quietly down."[12] Like Graves, who, recuperating in the hospital from his near-death experience, counts Sorley his "chief standby," Sassoon carries his volume(s) of Sorley with him, carries Sorley on his person.[13] And like Graves, who once remarked of his own writing, "We aren't all

74   CHAPTER 2

Keats or Sorleys," Sassoon, faced with what Diana Fuss has called "the challenge of dying a linguistically meaningful death," fears he may have nothing to say in the face of death to match Sorley's grim eloquence.[14] In a diary entry for Christmas Day, 1916, for example, after quoting meditations on death by Donne and Webster, Sassoon quotes four lines from "When You See Millions of the Mouthless Dead" by "young Sorley"—the poem that today most secures Sorley's reputation—only to muse: "And when these professors have said their say, what shall I utter concerning the old ruffian? Nothing. I have jabbered at him too often. He'll glance his eye at me and tell me to wait my turn like a good lad."[15] At some point, moreover, the Sorley Sassoon sleeps with turns out to be Robert Graves's copy; for soon after Sassoon is admitted to Craiglockhart War Hospital, following the publication of his famous protest, "A Soldier's Declaration," Graves writes, "I'm longing to get my Sorley back. Hurry up with it."[16]

Falling in Love with a Dead Man

In this private network, falling in love with a dead man serves a number of functions through the displacements it facilitates. On the one hand, it offers a safe way to love a man, when such love is dangerous, subject to sudden loss in the war's grim death toll and to increasing surveillance and criminalization. At the time, indeed, Sassoon and Graves were both in love with other men with whom they had unconsummated relationships. More fundamentally, it offers a way to mourn one's own dead when the exigencies of war make death ungrievable because life is so precarious.[17] Thus Graves writes to Sorley's father, "I have 'Marlborough' by heart now, and feel your son's death more acutely than any of my many close friends whom the War (and especially the Loos fighting where I was nearly killed myself) has snatched away."[18] As his comments suggest, the war, as Sarah Cole has argued, "destroyed friendship" by, quite literally, destroying friends, creating an "urgent need to imagine new and untested types of male unity."[19] In "friending" Sorley, Graves can feel for a dead man what is otherwise blocked or not allowable—love for other live men, loss of other dead ones. Loving Sorley, then, allows him to grieve deaths that could not otherwise be apprehended, either because the scale is too large or the individuals too familiar—too well known to submit to idealization or too close to home to be contemplated comfortably, as Graves suggests in his parenthetical admission ("I was nearly killed myself"). It thus serves a function akin to that performed in the memorial volumes discussed in chapter 1, objects that also resist strict categorization. Graves's over-the-top formulations, however, as in the fantasy he shares with Sassoon about a dining club of Sorley admirers, succeed more fully in manufacturing content and value to justify what might otherwise seem an unwarranted excess of affect. Indeed, for a group of young poets whose own futures are uncertain, loving a dead man is a way to project their own continued existence through comparable feats of affection. For if, as Sally Minogue and Andrew Palmer argue, "When a poet wrote about the death of a fellow soldier, he was also imagining his own extinction," it might be reasonable to assume that when he celebrates a fellow poet's posthumous survival, as Graves does here, he was also imagining his own poetic afterlife:

> I think one of the tests for worthiness to enter our dining club premises must be an appreciation of Sorley: Masefield gets in easily as he said the other day that to him twice as severe a loss as the ravishing of Belgium and the sack of cities and cathedral burnings, and the loss of the cargo of the *Lusitania* and so on was the death of Sorley—or words to that effect. *The* great loss of [the] war.
>
> Eddie [Marsh] not quite so sound, because Sorley spoke evil of Brooke in one of his letters, but almost so.[20]

If love of Sorley functions here as a kind of secret handshake or admission price to an exclusive male company, that imagined coterie allows Sorley to circulate, preserving his memory by making new Sorleyites. Sassoon, for example, would appear to have introduced Wilfred Owen to Sorley in the time they spent together at Craiglockhart, where Owen was being treated for shellshock.[21] And in wartime benefits and postwar readings and lectures in the United Kingdom and the United States, Sassoon and Nichols, along with Masefield, continued to resurrect Sorley for contemporary audiences and future generations, as did Harold Monro, in the postwar readings he and his wife organized in their bookshop. Nichols, indeed, may be responsible for the survival in print of Masefield's encomium, a version of which he records in the preface to his *Anthology of War Poetry, 1914–1918* (1943): "The Poet Laureate once said to me that Sorley was potentially the greatest poet lost to us in that war, and that, had Sorley lived, he might have become our greatest dramatist since Shakespeare."[22] This hyperbolic judgment is one that few perhaps would find credible, although the quality of Sorley's poems certainly warrants recognition. But in the fresh wartime context of the 1940s, Nichols infuses this exorbitant praise with new life and urgency. Framed as a dialogue between Nichols and an aspiring poet, Julian Tennyson, about to embark on his own war service, the preface establishes "Sorley"—the subject of one of Nichols's lengthiest digressions—as a token of what an older poet passes on to a young

76   **CHAPTER 2**

disciple in times of national crisis, a function Sorley has continued to perform, as do the war poets more generally.

Graves, meanwhile, with more far-reaching consequences, famously enshrined Sorley in an offhand remark in *Good-Bye to All That* (1929) as "one of the three poets of importance killed during the War"—Sorley's death, he suggests, the only reason the Battle of Loos is worth remembering.[23] Undoubtedly, this comment has over the years directed countless new readers to Sorley, given the continuing popular appeal and canonical status of Graves's autobiography. The assessment, moreover, is one Graves never swerved from, offering variations on it in a number of postwar writings.[24] Graves also memorialized Sorley in his poem "Sorley's Weather," where he opts for the restiveness of Sorley and the pull of the "rain-blown hill" over the "the firelit study" of Keats and Shelley: "Yet rest there Shelley, on the sill, / For though the winds come frorely, / I'm away to the rain-blown hill / And the ghost of Sorley."[25] Indeed, to the end of his lifetime, Graves never stopped promoting Sorley, even long after he withdrew his own war poetry from his *Collected Poems* in 1927. In 1974, for example, Graves exchanged a series of letters with the writer Rex Taylor, a personal friend and literary protégé, who was considering bringing out a new edition of Sorley's poems, offering to help him find a publisher, to read over the manuscript, and to make introductory remarks for the volume, and reminding him that Sorley's eightieth birthday was approaching. He "was to my mind the best poet of my generation," he writes in the first of these letters; "One cannot over-estimate Sorley's poems," he writes in another; and, in the final letter, he concludes "HE WAS OUR BEST POET OF THIS CENTURY" (capitals in original).[26] Crediting Blunden with introducing him to Sorley (a version of the story that does not appear elsewhere), he cites Blunden and Sassoon, both recently dead, as Sorley's "keenest admirers."

I dwell on Graves and his circle, then, because their example, in its extremity, bares the logic of the memorial project that has sustained Sorley's afterlife—even into the twenty-first century—a logic that informs the veneration of the war poets more generally. Indeed, the enthusiasm of his better-known literary contemporaries has everything to do with Sorley's later reputation, as was also the case with Owen, who was initially shepherded into print by Sassoon and later Blunden; but Sorley, despite the power of his poetry, never achieved anything like Owen's independent standing, his afterlife remaining dependent on new bursts of enthusiasm or revivals of earlier ones.[27] But I also dwell on these episodes because they are symptomatic of the extravagant responses Sorley appears always to have generated from his dedicated followers, even when he largely drops out of public notice—responses disproportionate to any strictly measurable achievement. For Sorley's acolytes were not limited to

Graves and his followers; rather, they appear in a variety of venues and locations, and they do not confine their admiration to his poetry. In a 1920 review of *The Letters of Charles Sorley*, for example, a book in the mold of the memorial volumes discussed in the preceding chapter, John Middleton Murry waxes effusive, locating in the Sorley volume what the records of those other material boys fail to accomplish: "the authentic voice of those lost legions," the shimmering aura of the generation that perished. Rejecting the sentimental effusions that pass for adequate tribute in more typical publications, Murry concludes that Sorley "was not the stuff that 'our modern Elizabethans' are made of."[28]

Murry's Sorley, however, is no less invented. Like Graves, Murry represents himself as half in love with a mirror image of himself, albeit a more youthful one: "Sorley first appears before us radiant with the white-heat of a schoolboy enthusiasm for Masefield. Masefield is—how we remember the feeling!— the poet who has lived. . . . That was Sorley at seventeen."[29] He quotes with delight Sorley's passion for Hardy—a passion Murry shares—and a mode of engagement Murry's own essay mimics. "I am just discovering Thomas Hardy," Sorley writes. "There are two methods of discovery. One is when Columbus discovers America. The other is when some one begins to read a famous author who has already run into seventy editions, and refuses to speak about anything else, and considers every one else who reads the author's work his own special converts. Mine is the second method. I am more or less Hardy-drunk."[30] Like Graves and Sassoon, Murry is more or less "Sorley-drunk," even if Sorley's fame extends at this time only to four editions, unable to resist one more Sorley quote, one more instance of Sorley's wisdom of spirit, clarity of vision, and fearless detachment. Murry's wife, Katherine Mansfield, perhaps not surprisingly, was never one of his special converts. Indeed, a note she wrote to Murry in June 1920 suggests that Sorley was a source of particular contention between them. Apologizing for starting a fight, Mansfield concedes that she has overstated her position. "Of course, I am not as anti-Sorley as 'all that,'" she admits, but six months later, praising Murry's new book, she returns to her objections: "I still think your Sorley's a mistake, for example. You've made him up."[31]

The Sorley archives offer no shortage of equally besotted readers, dispersed over time and cultural location and largely unknown to any but other Sorley obsessives. These include Doris Dalglish, who, writing in the *Friends' Quarterly Examiner* in 1937, and citing Murry as an inspiration, expresses the "overwhelming grief" she and her contemporaries still experience at "the mere sight of [Sorley's] name," even more than twenty years after his passing.[32] J. B. Jones, a native of Marlborough, during World War II erects his own eccentric shrine

78   CHAPTER 2

to Sorley by persuading the Royal Air Force, then occupying the downs, to mark off a milestone, a favorite spot that Sorley references in his poems, as safe from demolition—even if that shrine consists of no more than a dozen red petrol tins forming a barricade around a stone marker inscribed with Sorley's initials.[33] Martin Stephen, a historian and high master of a boy's school, undertakes a different type of salvage effort, insisting that Sorley is "a great poet, for all that he wrote only a handful of poems of lasting merit" and dedicating his book *The Price of Pity: Poetry, History and Myth in the Great War* (1996) to "the memory of Charles Hamilton Sorley, 1895–1915."[34] Finally, Peter Parker, on repeated occasions in *The Old Lie: The Great War and the Public-School Ethos*, cannot restrain his outrage at the way some of the earliest wartime and postwar tributes to Sorley failed to properly appreciate him, arguing the case as if it were a still-live battle.[35] At their most excessive, these enthusiasts imagine Sorley as the potential savior of civilization. Jones, for example, concludes his article with the hyperbolic claim, "There were many soldier-poets killed in the First World War. Had they, especially Sorley, the greatest of them all, been spared, their influential voices would, perhaps, have averted the tragedy of the Second."[36] Even sober academics are not immune to hyperbole. Noting that "save in a few lines here and there, Sorley did not achieve uniquely memorable verbal expression," and admitting that much of his published poetry is "pleasant juvenilia," Bernard Bergonzi nonetheless concludes that Sorley's death was "a tragedy for English letters."[37]

If Sorley's admirers over the years have continually made him up, refitting him for their purposes, none better deserves this epithet perhaps than Thomas Burnett Swann, Sorley's first, though largely unacknowledged, biographer. An American writer best known for his fantasy fiction, Swann published *The Ungirt Runner: Charles Hamilton Sorley, Poet of World War I* in 1965, followed in 1971 by a novel, *The Goat without Horns*, in which a fictionalized Charles Sorley appears as a character. Swann derives the title for his biography from "The Song of the Ungirt Runners," Sorley's hymn to long-distance running, and his celebration of Sorley as this "ungirt" figure—"unencumbered by clothes or conventions, free from shackles"—informs his entire project. Admitting that he has "not attempted to write what scholars call a definitive biography, with every possible fact amassed and footnoted," he opts instead for something "which moves swiftly, as Charles himself moved, from birth to boyhood to the brief radiance of manhood," a biography that borders unapologetically on idolatry.[38] And his rapturous reveries read like those of a man who has fallen in love with his subject, as in this passage where he ponders a photograph of "Charlie" in uniform (figure 2.1)—a picture he suggests that "almost do[es] him justice":

FIGURE 2.1. Frontispiece photograph of Charles Sorley from *The Letters of Charles Sorley, with a Chapter of Biography* (Cambridge: Cambridge University Press, 1919)

His eyes are dark, luminous, and sad, with a faint and surprising hint of the Orient about them; they are like the eyes in the frescoes and terra cottas of those wandering Easterners misplaced in the West, the ancient Etruscans. They seem to say, like some of his poems, that new though he is to war he recognizes the old horror; the skull beneath the helmet. And yet, for all of his seriousness, he does not look more than his twenty years. The grave eyes, one suspects, may flicker into a smile, and Charlie, the ungirt runner, will exorcise the soldier and race the wind across the Marlborough downs. It was such a boy that his parents saw at Hythe.[39]

The fact that Sorley was long dead when Swann first encountered him underwrites the shape and intensity of his overheated adulation, as it did for other early admirers.[40]

Not surprisingly, perhaps, Swann's biography did not make much of a critical impression. The editors of *Choice* magazine for 1965, for example, note: "Although favorably received and republished five times through 1932, Sorley's 37 poems have since then received almost no attention. This book certainly

80 **CHAPTER 2**

will do nothing to revive an interest; in fact, it could have the reverse effect. A model of bad biography. . . . Definitely not recommended."[41] Jean Moorcroft Wilson, Sorley's most recent biographer, is more discreet in her dismissal, noting simply, "There is no English edition," in the notes to the *Charles Hamilton Sorley* exhibition that launched her 1985 biography of him.[42] In the biography itself, she does not even mention Swann. Swann's response is perhaps the most extreme among Sorley's admirers: his novel, for example, narrated by a dolphin, is a cross-species homoerotic love song to Sorley. But despite, or even because of, its extravagance, Swann's response remains symptomatic of a quality that Sorley appears always to have peculiarly generated among select readers. Sorley's posthumous life, I am suggesting, is a function of his capacity to make people fall in love with him—to generate an affective response in excess of his measurable achievements. In saying this, I do not mean to devalue the aesthetic qualities that have drawn readers to his poems, which, I believe, can stand on their merits, but I want to suggest that these qualities in themselves are not sufficient to explain the intensity and duration of his posthumous reputation. Indeed, Sorley interests me precisely because of the liminal ground he occupies as a poet generally considered a one-hit wonder, although that hit has shifted over time and with different constituencies.[43]

Even Wilson's decidedly more professional effort, *Charles Hamilton Sorley: A Biography* (1985), and the editions of Sorley's poems and letters that she has produced (discussed in the next section of this chapter) cannot fully escape the affective dynamic I have been tracking here. Calling her entire Sorley enterprise "a labour of love," Jon Stallworthy aligns the biography with Edward Marsh's much-maligned 1918 memoir of Rupert Brooke—the work that "launched the legend of the 'young Apollo, golden-haired.'"[44] At a certain level, however, "falling in love" with one's subject may be an occupational hazard for those engaged in the work of war poet recovery, given the difficulty of disengaging that subject from the pathos it generates and of disentangling the literary appeal of the poems from their extraliterary features. Swann, then, may claim for Sorley that "On the strength of his poems, the poet deserves a biography."[45] The question remains, though, whether thirty-seven poems (or thirty-eight, as they are numbered in the fourth and subsequent editions of *Marlborough*) can in fact justify such an undertaking, especially when many of those poems are admittedly juvenilia. And if one does take up such a project, is the cradle-to-grave format appropriate for a life with so little space between its bookends? Is it possible to imagine a different kind of biographical artifact—a life, as it were, of the posthumous Sorley?[46] For it could be argued that despite the resources and sophistication that a modern-day biographer brings to her project, traditional biography is no more adequate today to capture such foreshortened lives than it was for the family and friends who produced the idiosyncratic Lives discussed in chapter 1. Now, as then, "lovability" may be the quality best identified with those who do not live long enough to accrue a full roster of achievements, and labors of love what sustains their revival, as Wilson herself seems to acknowledge in her introduction to the *Collected Letters*: "Even those to less intimate friends, even the occasional duty letters, enable us to gain a clearer picture of the exceptional and loveable person Sorley was."[47] "Falling in love," then, I am arguing, and I use the term loosely, is a way to name the excess in Sorley's reception, and the reception of the war poets more generally. It constitutes a way to touch and be touched by these young poets, and it illuminates the way they function as objects of cathexis. Jahan Ramazani has argued, "'Pity' is Owen's term for emotional identification with the victims of war. But Owen's poetry suggests that 'pity' cannot erase the boundary that separates victim from onlooker."[48] I am making a similar argument about "love," my term for emotional identification with Sorley and with the power of his writing. In invoking this term, then, I do not mean to be patronizing or dismissive; rather, I want to open a space to think more expansively (and critically) about the deployment of affect in the reception of World War I poetry.

If such structures of feeling met an urgent need in the wartime and immediate postwar period, as I have been arguing in my discussion of Graves and his contemporaries, in our age of postmemory, the need has assumed new dimensions, requiring that such structures be reinvented. The poet Michael Longley puts it eloquently—and literally: "Charles Sorley produced a handful of great lines before being killed at the age of 20 ('When you see millions of the mouthless dead / Across your dreams in pale battalions go . . .'). Why am I compelled to track his name to the Loos Memorial to the Missing, and run my fingertips over the carved letters which are all that is physically left of him?"[49] As Longley makes clear in his own "war poems" and prose commentary, this obsession with the "war poets," and Sorley in particular, becomes a way to memorialize his father and gain access to the World War I experience his father never talked about. Longley, indeed, occupies a position analogous to that of "the generation after," as it figures so prominently in the scholarship on postmemory that has been articulated in the Holocaust context; but where the children of Holocaust survivors, as Marianne Hirsch documents, could be said to "inherit" their parents' traumatic memories, Longley for the most part seeks out the war poets to effect this transfer.[50] "My father's central, really, to my preoccupation with the First World War," he explains in the roundtable discussion that concludes *The Cambridge Companion to the Poetry of the First World War*. It is also for him a way to negotiate more immediate traumas, such as the Irish

82   CHAPTER 2

Troubles. As Longley illustrates, then, falling in love with a dead man—especially a dead poet—becomes a way to mediate private grief and public mourning through an appeal to affect. "I simply want to go on talking to my father," he concedes.[51] As Fran Brearton illustrates, however, Longley also explores this connection more directly—as the bequest from his father of a posthumous existence. Thus in his poem "In Memoriam," Longley "posits his origins, twenty years before his birth, in the landscape of the Great War," where he is "left for dead" in "No Man's Land" after his father suffers a shrapnel wound to his testicle.[52]

Even for those without direct personal connections to the war, the affective potential of poems like those written by Sorley performs a similar function. That Sorley's poems *as poems*—the "great lines" Longley references—can speak so powerfully to their audience makes Sorley all the more available for this dual project. Regularly eliciting responses, both emotional and aesthetic, in excess of reason, the dead poet both organizes and contains what might otherwise be unspeakable. In a context in which the sheer scale of death and the extreme foreshortening of life made the lives of the dead unapprehendable by ordinary means, falling in love with a dead man, I am arguing, was a means to make ungrievable lives grievable—first for a generation too close to the experience of the war to respond adequately, and later for a generation too distant from it. In this, then, Sorley illuminates how the war poets have functioned more generally to give face, voice, and body to unfinished mourning and how they continue to function to address a war whose magnitude of loss defies explanation and whose memory refuses to be settled.

Finally, as Sorley's reception illustrates, "falling in love" is a means to assert a response that is decidedly amateur—not academic and not institutionalized.[53] This, of course, was also the case for the makers of the homespun biographical artifacts discussed in the previous chapter, but for them love of the dead man was their starting point. For those, on the other hand, at some remove from the immediacy of loss, falling in love is a way to explain—and to share— an intensity of response that would not otherwise be explicable and to open a space for voices that might not otherwise be recognized or valued by the official culture of remembrance. In this context, falling in love is an act to be performed over and over again as a rite of communion, and Sorley is an especially powerful exemplar. Indeed, well into the twentieth century, Sorley continued to function as shared currency among like-minded individuals of a variety of leanings. Thus Frank Kermode, citing a letter from 1973, in his *London Review of Books* review of the Sylvia Townsend Warner/David Garnett correspondence, notes,

The correspondents are in some ways remarkably alike, distinguished inhabitants of the same distinguished literary parish. Whatever one quoted the other would already know; so Garnett could no doubt identify the source of the lines

> Earth, that grew with joyful ease
> Hemlock for Socrates—

which I can't.[54]

The quoted lines, as Bernard Bergonzi explains in a subsequent letter to the editor, are from Sorley's "All the Hills and Vales Along," although, as Bergonzi points out, Warner misquotes them.[55]

Remote from centers of literary and academic culture, moreover, Sorley has enjoyed a niche reception akin to fandom. Largely on the basis of a single, much-anthologized poem, "The Song of the Ungirt Runners," for example, he has acquired a cult status among runners.[56] And he finds some of his most ardent admirers among lovers of the Wiltshire countryside and devotees of Richard Jefferies, who, in a kind of cross-generational mutual admiration society, find in Sorley a kindred spirit—Jefferies the one youthful passion Sorley never repudiated. Indeed, Sorley carried Jefferies's *Life of the Field* with him to the battlefield.[57] Frances J. Gay, for example, in an article in the *Swindon Review*, published in 1948 on the occasion of the Jefferies Centenary, extolls Sorley in the voice of a passionate enthusiast. "Read his poem," she writes of "Barbury Camp," "or rather shout it aloud against the wind on the top of the hill. Listen for the answering shout from those men of two or more thousand years ago."[58] Lady Phyllis Treitell, in a talk delivered to the Richard Jefferies Society in 2006, "Charles Sorley (1895–Oct. 1915): Poet and Disciple of Jefferies," feels free to ignore all modern scholarship, opening her talk with the charmingly disarming admission that, as the society newsletter reports, "she had not read the recent book on Sorley by Jean Moorcroft Wilson, as her aim was to reveal Sorley's devotion to Jefferies' essays," evidence for which could be discovered from earlier publications—articles in journals of local history and culture, none of them scholarly.[59] In her address to "devotion," Lady Treitell's talk illustrates another feature of the afterlife of the war poets in which, as Dominic Hibberd has maintained, "public esteem" has long been "far ahead of academic knowledge," if not, I would add, frequently at odds with it.[60]

The dispersed and uneven ways Sorley has been remembered illuminate the competing efforts to anchor his life and create posthumous identities for and through him. One consequence of these heterogeneous rites of memory has been the relegation of Sorley to specialist preserves—a figure whose

84   CHAPTER 2

interest lies somewhere other than the main currents of literary history, even when that preserve is the capacious umbrella of "war poet" and "war poetry." Indeed, one might argue, Sorley's posthumous career reflects his movement from one niche to another, sometimes even within the same category, as with the adoption of Sorley as a *Scottish* war poet, amped up in the centenary season.[61] In 1916, Graves could celebrate the fact that "Sorely is still selling, and *The Times* has labelled him 'Enrolled among the English Poets' for which God bless that usually bloody paper."[62] But Sorley's long-term place in the canon of English literature turns out to be considerably less secure than Graves imagined; he enjoys a very different type of posthumous life from a poet like Keats, for example—the icon of the young poet who dies prematurely. As discussed more fully in the next section of this chapter, the conditions of Sorley's popular reception complicate efforts to secure him a more academic standing.

In the locations where Sorley has found his admirers, though, his case illuminates the way memory of the war has been mediated by print media, with all its dedicated enclaves. It depends on a robust market that in the United Kingdom at least would seem always to have room for one more war book—and especially one more book devoted to war poets and war poetry, one more contribution to the dead poets society. Whether in small specialist presses or large mainstream and prestige publishing ventures, the industry satisfies what Brearton has described as "the seemingly insatiable appetite for more work on the subject that the war still generates."[63] In this respect Cecil Woolf Publishers, a modern hub of Sorley studies, is a site worth scrutinizing, and one I will consider in more detail in the next section of this chapter. It is a small publishing house run by Cecil Woolf, the nephew of Leonard and Virginia Woolf, and his wife, Jean Moorcroft Wilson, whose biography of Sorley and editions of his poems and letters are all in-house productions. Cecil Woolf Publishers has often been seen as continuing the legacy of the Hogarth Press, with Woolf and Wilson following in the footsteps of their famous predecessors, even working together at the very table where the Hogarth press once stood. Wilson is today the general editor for the publishing house's War Poets Series and, as one critic recently put it, "the undisputed doyenne of War Poet biographers," a subject she first became interested in when assigned by her husband to research the life and works of Charles Sorley, a poet then unknown to her.[64] Cecil Woolf, the child of Leonard's brother Philip, was also the nephew of an unknown war poet, the Cecil Woolf whose posthumous poems the Woolfs published through the Hogarth Press, as discussed in the next chapter, and who was killed by the same bullet that injured his brother Philip, the younger Cecil's father. Like many of his generation who bear the name of a fallen soldier, then, Cecil Woolf himself can be seen as a kind of site of living memory, a custodian of a posthumous existence.

In November 2005, at a reception at the Imperial War Museum (IWM) in London, Cecil Woolf Publishers launched the first titles in its new series of monographs on war poets and war poetry. Along with its Bloomsbury Heritage Series, the War Poets Series identifies the press's main area of specialization, marking its location at the intersection of two of Britain's most flourishing heritage industries: World War I and Bloomsbury.[65] Since its inception, and with the IWM imprimatur at its inauguration, the War Poets Series has been issuing four titles a year, with publication timed for November, in anticipation of Remembrance Day commemorations. John Press's critical appreciation, *Charles Hamilton Sorley*, is number eight in the series (figure 2.2).[66] These publications have generally been pamphlets of about twenty pages, although some are book-length studies—all inexpensively priced, and available only by direct order from the publishers. They range from biographical studies, memoirs, and critical studies to selections of the subject's poems. As small booklets, these monographs have something of the feel of the works that proliferated in the wake of the war—the small volumes of posthumous poems, letters, and memorial tributes of the sort examined in chapter 1.

In their mode of production and dissemination, as well as their material format, they seem to occupy, like those earlier works, a space somewhere between souvenirs and collector's items. The Siegfried Sassoon Fellowship, for example, a society dedicated to honoring the life and work of the poet, featured the 2006 series (including the *Charles Hamilton Sorley* volume) on its website, with the note, "These little books make excellent Christmas presents for anyone with an interest in WWI literature." In the virtual networks, then, that reconstruct old alliances, Sassoon can once again be a portal to Sorley, ninety years after he and Graves first discovered him. Promoted and publicized by such groups as the War Poets Association, an organization devoted to advancing "interest in the work, life and historical context of poets whose subject is the experience of war," and by societies dedicated to the memory of individual war poets (in their meetings, conferences, newsletters, and journals, and especially their websites), the War Poets Series inevitably points us to today's guardians and gatekeepers of collective memory.[67] In the travels of its small volumes, including the one that bears Sorley's name, we can witness the dispersed locations and virtual sites through which World War I's dead poets continue to perform their part in the production, preservation, and dissemination of memory.

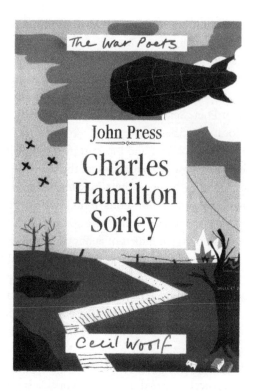

FIGURE 2.2. Book jacket, John Press, *Charles Hamilton Sorley*, War Poets Series (London: Cecil Woolf, 2006). Reproduced with permission of Cecil Woolf Publishers

Collecting Sorley

In October 1985, Cecil Woolf Publishers mounted the *Charles Hamilton Sorley* exhibition, the first retrospective to be organized solely in his name. Initially shown at Marlborough College, the exhibition enjoyed a one-week run at the Royal Festival Hall in London before its final showing in the Central Library in Cambridge in May 1986. As its organizers explained, the exhibition was timed to commemorate a number of events: "To mark the ninetieth anniversary of this First World War poet's birth; the seventieth anniversary of his death; the publication of the first full-length biography (*Charles Hamilton Sorley: A Biography* by Jean Moorcroft Wilson) and the first complete edition of his poems (*The Collected Poems of Charles Hamilton Sorley* edited by Jean Moorcroft Wilson)."[68] In its arrangement of artifacts, the exhibition tracks Sorley's travels—in months or at most handfuls of years—from birth and early childhood in Aberdeen, to Cambridge childhood and early schooling, through his five and a half years at Marlborough College, seven months of travel and study in Germany, nine months of military training in England, and four months of active service at the front. In another sense, the exhibition, as an event in its own right, tracks Sorley's travels from near obscurity—from the anonymity of being one of the thousands of nameless soldier-poets unleashed by the war or, as Sorley might have put it, one of "the millions of the mouthless dead"—to his arrival at one of the nation's premier venues for the arts and the revival of his life and works by a London publishing house precisely seventy years after his death. In doing so, it also testifies to the consolidation of his afterlife from one founded in the types of informal and personal networks described earlier in this chapter to one anchored in institutional praxis.

The Sorley exhibition and the publishing venture that underwrote it speak to the remarkable durability of World War I poets as cultural capital for the British public. They also speak to the extent to which rites of memory, as shaped by these poets, have remained remarkably static—"a timeless register," as Jay Winter has put it, "of terms and images through which later generations still frame their understanding of the 1914–18 war and its aftermath."[69] Despite persistent questions about the quality and enduring value of the poetry, and about the poets' representativeness, the passage of time has done little to loosen the hold of the soldier-poet as the war's iconic emblem, at least for the public at large. For scholars, the affective power of this figure and "the afterlives of such poetry and its place in cultural memory" have themselves become an important subject of critical inquiry.[70] Outside the academy, however, the privileged place of these poets goes largely unquestioned. Just weeks after the Royal Festival Hall showing of the Sorley exhibit, on November 11, 1985, the poet laureate Ted Hughes unveiled a memorial to the poets of World War I in the most hallowed of all locations: Poets' Corner in Westminster Abbey. The memorial, a slate footstone inscribed with the names of sixteen poets, confirms the extent to which the "war poets" by this time had collectively become a national institution.[71] Indeed, so deeply ingrained are the poets presumed to be in the national consciousness that the engraved words of their most famous exemplar, Wilfred Owen, go uncredited on the monument: "My subject is War, and the pity of War. The Poetry is in the pity."[72] At the same time, the collective nature of the memorial renders it anomalous in its location, as if to include these poets in the abbey requires an asterisk. For this reason, Dominic Hibberd excoriates the gesture as an absurdity: "Imagine a monument there to the Metaphysical Poets or the Restoration Dramatists or the Victorian Industrial Novelists."[73] Even as the memorial, then, enshrines this group of poets, it isolates them. Surrounded by memorial stones to such figures as D. H. Lawrence, Henry James, and T. S. Eliot, the poets of World War I remain quarantined, as they have been in traditional literary histories,

88   CHAPTER 2

occupying a space that is, quite literally, modernist-adjacent.[74] Among the sixteen poets mentioned by name on the memorial is Charles Sorley.

While by himself Sorley might seem too slight a figure for the level of attention lavished on him by the Cecil Woolf productions, his inclusion in the Poets' Corner memorial suggests his secure place in a readily identifiable, if loosely defined, collective identity: the "war poets." It suggests as well that his claim to continued recognition as an important literary figure may exist only within this category. In the world of "war poets," however, the Cecil Woolf exhibition is far from anomalous, requiring no special pleading and no exceptional justification. The decade preceding the publication of Wilson's two new Sorley volumes saw a spate of new biographies of World War I poets and a rush of new editions of their poems, many with similar claims to being the first of their kind. Ivor Gurney, Rupert Brooke, Robert Graves, Edward Thomas, and Isaac Rosenberg, for example, all were subjects of biographies—in Rosenberg's case, three separate ones, all published in 1975. New editions of Gurney's, Thomas's, Rosenberg's, and Owen's poems appeared, with novel claims to completeness—most notably, Jon Stallworthy's edition of Wilfred Owen, *The Complete Poems and Fragments*, a two-volume work that includes not only everything Owen wrote and drafted but also references to, if not reproductions of, every manuscript and textual variant.[75] Sorley, too, enjoyed a modest comeback in Hilda D. Spear's *The Poems and Selected Letters of Charles Hamilton Sorley*, published in Scotland in 1978 with support from the Scottish Arts Council, just a few years after Graves was involving himself in an edition of the poems that never materialized.[76]

By 1985, moreover, exhibitions commemorating war poets—whether singly, in pairs, or collective groups—were becoming well established, as was the linking of such exhibitions to anniversary dates.[77] As Geoff Dyer observes, "All of these dates are signposts pointing to one of the ways in which the memory of the Great War exerts itself more powerfully as it recedes in time."[78] Indeed, the timing of the exhibition and its attendant publications was no accident, riding a wave of renewed interest in the war poets that had begun in the 1960s and coming at the cusp of what Dan Todman has called "a second 'war books boom.'" With the fiftieth anniversary of the war as an impetus, this period had been a "key moment in the creation of the canon of war poetry which has come down to the present day," a canon institutionalized in the publication of anthologies of war poetry and the appearance of this poetry on the O and A level examination syllabus.[79] The moment also represented the onset of our postmemory era, just as all those who might have owned a living memory of the war were dying in increasing numbers. Whereas earlier the war had been an event with documented memories, by the mid-1980s it had become a "thing," a cultural event with its own dimensions. From this perspective the Sorley exhibition, however ingenious as a book launch, looked just like what one might have expected. Like other commemorative projects, it depends on a set of ritualized objects that render its subject at once individualized and generic. Composed of photographs, drawings, letters, personal items, copies of the Marlborough College literary magazine and other school documents, manuscripts of poems, and the various editions of Sorley's writings, as well as World War I memorabilia—a pair of German wire cutters; a British trench periscope; a piece of shrapnel; various trench signs; rifle grenades and steel helmets; a uniform of an officer of the Suffolk Regiment—the exhibition embodies what Pierre Nora has called "second-order" or "prosthesis memory," quite literally the "sifted and sorted historical traces" of a life no longer available to us.[80] Like the "photograph of a posthumous chalk drawing of C. H. S. by Cecil Jameson in 1917, based on a photograph of October 1914" (item no. 123 in the exhibition)—the original posthumous drawing, commissioned as a gift to Sorley's parents, now hangs in the National Portrait Gallery—Sorley can exist here only as a reconstructed object, as, in effect, the product of the collected "Sorleiana."[81] As with the multiple layers of remove displayed in the portrait, the impact of the exhibition is to render Sorley all the more posthumous.

Though distanced in time from the posthumous Lives discussed in the preceding chapter, this modest exhibition proceeds from a similar though updated logic of collecting. Like those miscellaneous volumes, it depends on a belief in the power of images and objects to convey meaning and affect, but this time "to embody and reconfigure personal and family memories" so as to make them available to outsiders when those with direct personal memory are no longer living, as was the case with donations to the In Flanders Field Museum.[82] It depends, in other words, on the assumption that "things, or their pictorial or literary representation should be assumed to lead to an imaginary space of forgotten memory," an idea that, as Susanne Küchler has noted, results from "an obsession with recollection that has beset the West since the death of Milton."[83] It is the same logic that has installed the war poets as Britain's memory keepers. This logic has been challenged by theorists of memory in a variety of memorial contexts, but even if we accept its terms, Sorley poses a particular challenge as a poet without the full panoply of writerly appurtenances.

Conspicuously lacking in the Sorley archive, with a handful of exceptions, are the types of items found among the effects of other World War I poets: manuscripts, drafts, typescripts, notebooks, early publications, correspondence with fellow poets or patrons. His entire poetic reputation rests, in fact, on one slim volume, *Marlborough and Other Poems* (four copies of which are displayed in the Cecil Woolf exhibition), for which only thirteen manuscripts survive. During his life, Sorley neither revised his poems nor attempted publication.

90   **CHAPTER 2**

His surviving papers offer little indication of his poetic method. And while he shared his poems with his parents and select friends, he was not part of any poetic networks, as were most of the best-known war poets. Nor is it clear that he thought of himself self-consciously as a poet or would have been recognized in those terms by his Marlborough contemporaries. As his housemaster at Marlborough maintained, "I don't think he would have given his life to literature if he had lived" (*L*, 62); "I don't suppose most boys in his house regarded him as a poet, distinctively so called" (*L*, 63). One cannot, then, imagine him writing home, as Owen did in December 1917, "I go out of this year a Poet, my dear Mother. . . . I am a poet's poet."[84] In this, he was unlike Graves and Sassoon, who produced major wartime publications. He was unlike Rosenberg, who published privately during the war to ensure his poems' preservation. And he was unlike Owen, who, though scarcely published in his lifetime, assiduously cultivated literary contacts who might advance his career, even advising his mother to type out portions of his letters for future publication. Sorley, by contrast, offers little evidence of having an eye to literary posterity. His life as a poet is, by and large, a posthumous reconstruction.

Yet, in part precisely for this reason, Sorley offers a useful vantage on the process of commemoration—on how "a boy who wrote poems" becomes a "First World War poet" susceptible to remembrance seventy years and more after his death. In the years since the Cecil Woolf *Charles Hamilton Sorley* exhibition, historians and literary critics have increasingly questioned the amount of attention given to a small group of elite male poets, to the exclusion of other voices and other experiences of the war less obsessively recorded and cataloged. In this light, the Sorley exhibition is illuminating, exposing the structures of privilege that underwrite his posthumous existence, just as they underwrite the poetry and the experience it records. Sorley himself had already begun to question this privilege while still a schoolboy. "The most awfully sad thing in history is, I think, that poetry up till now has been mainly by and for and about the Upper Classes" (*L*, 36), he told the Marlborough College Junior Literary Society in 1912; and before leaving Marlborough he informed his parents of his desire "to become an instructor in a Working Man's College or something of that sort" (*L*, 42)—a plan he is persuaded he can best achieve by first getting a degree, preferably at Oxford. His early escape from Marlborough, moreover, whose atmosphere he had come to find oppressive, was facilitated by his ability to spend what would have been his last two terms there studying and traveling in Germany. Sorley's turning away from his privilege thus still relies on it, and Sorley's afterlife is possible, the exhibition demonstrates, because his life has been preserved in the bits and pieces collected there. These include items maintained in the family through three generations—photograph albums, a scrapbook of letters and cuttings—and items, like the manuscripts of the poems, originally held by the family and subsequently sent to Marlborough College for preservation. And they include items housed in the college's archives: back issues of the *Marlburian*, where more than half of Sorley's poems saw their initial publication; proceedings of the Junior Literary Society, where Sorley delivered several papers; photographs of the college house to which Sorley belonged and the teams and clubs of which he was a member.

Sorley's life and work, then, can be recollected because he belonged to a family with the habits of preservation—and with the leisure and resources to collect family history—and because he went to a public school with the means to preserve his effects and a commitment to maintain and transmit Marlborough College heritage.[85] In addition to the usual school documents and records, Marlborough College houses the manuscripts of Sorley's poems, donated by the family in 1949. Its archives also include an assortment of items picked up by Sorley during his time in the army, including instructions in French for knitting, dutifully hand-bound by his sister in a memorial volume. However valueless in themselves, these miscellaneous objects survive because both the family and the institution could afford to collect and preserve them. His works, moreover, could be published because his family had the requisite resources and connections, including an association, through Professor Sorley, with Cambridge University Press, which published both his poems and his letters.[86] Of course, the quality of his writings is a necessary factor in this recognition, but as his circumstances make clear, the institutional infrastructure must also be in place for commemoration to happen. Sorley's case thus illustrates in miniature what the survival of other, more established, war poets demonstrates on a grander scale: the individuals and institutions that ensure the war poets' cultural prestige and robust afterlife. These include private collectors; surviving family members; estates and trusts; distinguished institutions of higher education; national, regional, and local history museums; major research centers; and national libraries.[87]

Because of its small scale, and because of Sorley's small output, the Sorley exhibition, along with the books that accompany it, offers an especially concentrated way to observe the acts of conservation that go into the making of a war poet. And it offers access to the acts of transmission through which "Sorley" travels, allowing us to trace the passage of objects and effects through private and familial channels. It thus supplements the discussion earlier in this chapter of the networks of exchange—the coteries and special interests—that have sustained a life for Sorley in the public imagination. And it allows us to trace the locations where memorials to Sorley have proliferated: Scotland

92   CHAPTER 2

(where a commemorative plaque was installed in 2018 in his childhood home in Aberdeen); Cambridge (where plaques bearing Sorley's name appear in two parishes); Marlborough College (in Memorial Hall, where Sorley's name is inscribed on a plaque next to one for William Morris; in the C-1 House Roll of Honour; in the street named after him in College Fields; and in the Sorley Signpost, discussed in the next section of this chapter, in the nearby countryside); and Oxford University (where Sorley is remembered in the Oxford University Roll of Service and the University College war memorial, even though he died before he could enroll in the university). These locations, moreover, have spawned anthologies in which Sorley is remembered, although not always self-evidently so. Sorley's status as a Scottish poet, for example, has been especially contentious. Over the years, his inclusion (as well as his exclusion) from Scottish anthologies (of war poets and of Scottish poets more generally) has been the subject of controversy, given the disparity between his Scottish birth and early childhood and his British upbringing.[88] While less contentious, his inclusion in *Cambridge Poets of the Great War: An Anthology* remains anomalous, as the only poet included not a member of a Cambridge college and as the author of one of the only poems not written and published either during or very soon after the war—a poem written when Sorley was about ten for his sister's school magazine. By contrast, Sorley's inclusion in *The Marlborough Anthology of Poets Educated at Marlborough College 1912–1969* and *Verses from Marlborough: Charles Hamilton Sorley*, both published by Marlborough College Press, perfectly fit Marlborough's embrace of him.

In taking the *Charles Hamilton Sorley* exhibition as my point of departure for this section, then, I aim to interrogate the work of memory performed by commemorative practices such as this one and the work of memory, changing over time, that circulates around the memorialization of a named individual—an individual for whom the "soldier-poet" has come to be seen as representative. I want, in other words, to consider what it means to think of a posthumous life as a "site of memory" and to think about the collecting practices that underwrite such an undertaking. As Samuel Hynes cautions, however, memory here is something of a misnomer; the memory on which the exhibition trades is what Hynes has called in another context "a collective, *vicarious* memory," and the work it performs is to transmit and refit received myths of the war and received myths of Sorley.[89] Indeed, by 1985, vicarious memory was close to becoming the only memory possible, and the Sorley replicated in exhibition, biography, and collected poems depends on recycled anecdotes and touched-up photographs, even as it introduces valuable new material.[90] In fact, at the time of the Sorely exhibition, few of Sorley's contemporaries would still have been living. Of the sixteen war poets commemorated on the contemporaneous

Westminster Abbey memorial, for example, only Robert Graves was alive at the time of its unveiling, and he died within a month of the installation. Both of Sorley's surviving siblings had been dead for nearly a decade when the Sorley exhibition opened, leaving the work of commemoration to be taken up by a niece and nephew on behalf of an uncle they never knew except through the stories passed down to them. At the time, moreover, Sorley would not have figured as among the most immediately recognizable of the war poets, who individually and collectively have exercised such a hold on the cultural imagination and collective memory of the British people. As the exhibition organizers explain, Sorley was "probably the last of the First World War poets not to have received full recognition."[91] From this perspective, then, the full-length biography and complete edition of Sorley's poems that occasioned this exhibition fill a space that the exhibition must first carve out as in need of filling. In other words, the exhibition must produce Sorley as a missed and missing person—in all his incompleteness—so that the "life" and "works" the new publications represent can flesh out the person enshrined and commemorated.[92]

As the somewhat contorted phrasing of the exhibition catalog indicates ("the last of the First World War poets not to have received full recognition"), Sorley's stature at this time—and into the twenty-first century—resists easy assessment. "If there had been a poll in late 1917 to identify the war's most distinguished soldier-poets," Dominic Hibberd and John Onions suggest in the introduction to *The Winter of the World: Poems of the Great War* (2007), "Brooke, Grenfell and Sorley would almost certainly have headed the list"—a position that has long since been usurped by other contenders.[93] In the years since Sorley was regularly in print (between 1916 and 1922, when five editions of *Marlborough* were published), however, he has continued to be anthologized and has continued to elicit respectful notice from scholars and devoted responses from general readers, even if he has never undergone a full-scale popular or academic resurgence.[94] There is ample evidence, then, that readers have found his poetry compelling. When W. B. Yeats notoriously excluded the war poets from *The Oxford Book of Modern Verse* in 1936, Sorley was one of the poets reviewers mentioned by name as a writer whose omission would be mourned by the public.[95] Four years earlier, *Marlborough* had been reissued in the Cambridge Miscellany Series, while in 1931 Ernest Benn Ltd. published a selection of his poems in its Augustan Books of Poetry series. And while Brian Gardner could lament in 1964 that Sorley was in danger of himself becoming a war relic, such claims had been voiced for more than twenty years (by John Press in 1943, for example, and Edmund Blunden in 1958), without any signs of his full-scale disappearance from modern consciousness.[96] Indeed, at least one critic saw in the publications of the mid-1960s evidence of an incipient "Sorley

94   **CHAPTER 2**

'revival.'"[97] If, moreover, Hibberd is right in his assessment that at the time of the Cecil Woolf exhibition "the average sixth-form audience" would be able to "name up to half-a-dozen" war poets, this hypothetical student most likely would have been able to name Sorley, even if such recognition did not necessarily carry over to the general public.[98] Sorley's visibility, then, is closely linked to the institutionalization of the war poets in the national consciousness and in the national curriculum in the years leading up to this event. In 1993, in perhaps the ultimate official act of recognition, Sorley was added to the *DNB* in its *Missing Persons* volume, along with 1,085 other people "unjustly omitted 'from the beginnings to 1985,'" the cutoff point for this reevaluation precisely the year of the Sorley exhibition.[99] Among the others also included for the first time were Wilfred Owen, Isaac Rosenberg, and Ivor Gurney. Moreover, in 2012, in anticipation of the upcoming Great War centenary, Cambridge University Press republished *Marlborough* for the first time in eighty years. In 2015 the Royal Mail honored Sorley with a commemorative stamp featuring his poem "All the Hills and Vales Along" (figure 2.3), and in 2018 he was featured in a major new oratorio commissioned to commemorate the end of the war—a piece I will return to at the end of this chapter. As with so much else surrounding Sorley, however, such signs of recognition coexisted with continued marginalization.

Sorley would seem to occupy, then, some ambiguous space between the remembered and the forgotten, the celebrated and the unduly neglected, and this ambiguity, I want to suggest, makes his case especially instructive. It locates the Cecil Woolf publishing ventures somewhere between necessary rescue work and the proverbial coals to Newcastle—simultaneously a bid for the cultural authority afforded the "war poets" and a deconstruction of it. And it sheds light on the competing demands placed on the war poet: to reflect both artistic value and compelling personal testimony, both literary finesse and emotional accessibility. It exposes, in other words, the problem Santanu Das diagnoses: "whether the accent should fall on war or on poetry, on cultural history or on aesthetic value."[100] For the figure of the dead soldier-poet had a special role to play, as Sorley's case illustrates, in negotiating between private recollection and collective remembrance. Indeed, from the start, with the earliest family publications, these poets performed a powerful function in channeling private grief into public ritual. As remembrance became more institutionalized, the poet's cultural capital accumulated in a manner and extent unseen outside Britain. Trotted out for the poignant anecdote or the apt poetic phrase and codified in the national curriculum and the ubiquitous war poetry anthology, the figure of the poet contributed in a peculiarly pervasive way to the public cult of the dead inscribed in official sites of memory—monuments, museums, cemeteries, and ceremonies, most notably those surrounding Armistice

FIGURE 2.3. Royal Mail commemorative stamp, "All the Hills and Vales Along, CH Sorley" (2015). Stamp design © Royal Mail Group Limited

Day. But if this figure was important for its symbolic and functional utility, it also served in its own right—and continues to serve—as a site of memory, a cultural locus where memories are crystallized and transmitted from one generation to the next, in often local and familial contexts.

In his contribution to *War and Remembrance in the Twentieth Century*, Jay Winter coins the term "sites of remembrance" to distinguish those locations where "individuals and groups, mostly obscure, come together to do the work of remembrance." Winter's semantic turn marks a strategic shift from both the

96   **CHAPTER 2**

overdetermination of Nora's "sites of memory" (for Nora, necessarily evacuated of authentic meaning) and the globalizing reach of categories like "collective memory." For Winter, the creation of these spaces, like the construction of the narratives to fill them, is "itself the process of remembrance"—a process unabashedly partial and particular. "Once completed in this initial phase," Winter insists, "these 'sites of remembrance' are never stable, never fixed"; rather, they are subject to dissolution, displacement, and reappropriation.[101] In this, *Charles Hamilton Sorley*, as a site, is no exception, but the displacements to which Sorley's memory has been subjected uniquely illustrate how British culture has negotiated the challenges facing postmemory generations. The rites of remembrance organized in his name were, as was generally the case in responses to the war, performed first at the familial level. And, as was the case with so many other bereaved families, one of the first acts the Sorleys performed was to collect and preserve their son's words in print, publishing *Marlborough and Other Poems* in January 1916, followed closely by *Letters from Germany and from the Army* (1916)—privately printed in an edition of sixty copies "for members of the writer's family and for some other friends who cherish his memory"—and finally, *The Letters of Charles Sorley, with a Chapter of Biography* (1919).[102]

Marlborough, published by Cambridge University Press, enjoyed a wide and continuous readership during and immediately after the war, running to five editions between 1916 and 1922. It was republished as number two in the Cambridge Miscellany series in 1932, a sign of its continuing stature. Despite publication by a prestige press, however, and despite its multiple reprintings, *Marlborough* had much in common with the hundreds of similar slim volumes of posthumously published poems that inundated the wartime and postwar market, many published privately and intended for only the most limited circulation, and most of which disappeared in short order, as did the more fully fledged memoirs described in chapter 1. Like these other volumes, Sorley's poems appeared just months after his death, and like so many others they were unrevised and unfinished. Shortly before his death, Sorley himself had insisted that the poems were not yet ready for publication, and that publication while the war was underway was somehow unseemly. "Had the author lived," Sorley's father explains in his preface, "his poems, if published at all, would not have appeared without revision; but no editorial liberties have been taken with the present text. Readers who find something in the book that appeals to them will pardon the occasional lack of finish as well as the inclusion of some verses which may seem of personal interest only."[103] As these comments make clear, if publication constitutes a duty to the dead and an obligation to memory, the poems depend for their efficaciousness as agents of remembrance on this very lack of finish and on a certain unsuitability for public consumption. Indeed, as the *OED* intimates, unfinishedness is practically a definition of the posthumous when paired with publication.[104] These volumes function, then, as a kind of inverse ruin, exposing in their fragmentary and unpolished state the loss they commemorate—not, as with conventional ruins, the loss of what once was whole and complete but rather what never had the chance to come to fruition.[105]

In important respects, moreover, it was the act of bringing the poems to publication—performed by the survivors in the collecting, sorting, dating, ordering, and arranging of them—as much as the actual publication that fulfilled the memorial function. As mentioned in the previous chapter, this was also the case with the more miscellaneous volumes of letters, memoirs, and tributes that families regularly assembled. Publication, indeed, unmoored these sites from their familial location, allowing memory to travel in unanticipated directions. As W. R. Sorley illustrates in the preface to *The Letters of Charles Sorley*, it opened the way for others to lay claim to the memory of his son and to make demands on that basis. Thus he recounts a response he received from an "unknown correspondent" a few weeks after the publication of *Marlborough and Other Poems*: "'I have had it a week,' [the correspondent] wrote, 'and it has haunted my thoughts. I have been affected with a sense of personal loss, as if he had been not a stranger but my dearest friend. But indeed his personality—the "vivida vis animi"—shines so strongly out of every line, that I feel I have known him as one knows very few living people.' . . . 'I venture to beg you,' the writer went on to say, 'before it is too late, to give the world some fuller account of his brief life'" (*L*, v). The words, in fact, sound uncannily like those Graves wrote to Sorley's father and like the sentiments he shared with his poet friends in his first rush of Sorley enthusiasm; in this light, Graves's hyperbolic response to the lively force of Sorley's soul begins to sound less eccentric—a fact Professor Sorley seems here to acknowledge. Noting that many other readers made the same request or urged the general publication of the privately printed *Letters from Germany and from the Army*, W. R. Sorley explains the family's initial resistance to making their son's life public: "It seemed to us that enough had been done by publishing the poems and that, for the rest, so dear a memory need not be shared with the world" (*L*, [v]).[106] Each successive edition of *Marlborough*, however, entailed the doling out of additional biographical features, from the sentence or two the second edition added to the first's terse statement, to the "prose illustrations" in the third (excerpts from Sorley's letters, cross-referenced with the poems), to the supplementary notes appended to the fourth. These new features, moreover, were consistently presented as a wrenching out of reluctantly proffered information.

The result of these negotiations over the public and private claims of memory is a new act of sifting, sorting, selecting, and editing, resulting in, on the one hand, the fourth edition of *Marlborough and Other Poems* (1919), extensively annotated

98　　**CHAPTER 2**

and "rearranged and reset" in "a form which is intended to be definitive," and, on the other, the expanded volume of letters, produced in collaboration with his wife, that W. R. Sorley's comments preface.[107] "Anything in the way of a formal biography was not to be thought of" (*L*, vi), Sorley explains in the preface, but like the volumes discussed in chapter 1, this volume is more than a mere collection of their son's correspondence. Part biographical fragment, part photographic portrait, part series of letters (familiar and familial), part testimonials from masters and tutors at Marlborough, part papers written for the Marlborough literary society (locked away under seal of secrecy and now recovered and brought to light), this hybrid and patchwork book reflects what stands in for a life when life has been cruelly foreshortened and when biography is unthinkable because there has not been enough of a life to warrant one. As a memorial volume, moreover, *The Letters* reveals how much such volumes share with later commemorative exhibitions, like the Cecil Woolf book launch, for example, that attempt to piece together a life out of shards, fragments, and exhumed relics.[108] At the same time, it reminds us of the private life that such public displays—publications as well as exhibitions—cannot breach, as Professor Sorley acknowledges. "Of the author personally, and of what he was to his family and friends, I do not speak," he insists in the "definitive" 1919 edition of *Marlborough* (*M*, vi).

The Cecil Woolf exhibition demonstrates that the passage of time has rendered thinkable what the family could not imagine—a formal biography, as well as a "collected" poems, and, in 1990, a "collected" letters, the final piece of Wilson's Sorley project. Together, these undertakings reflect Wilson's bid to establish herself as the editor of record for the Sorley corpus, a role formerly assumed by the family. In their divergence from the family-sponsored productions, however, her volumes raise the question of who controls Sorley's afterlife, a question similarly raised by Sorley's idiosyncratic followers. Indeed, the family's decision to destroy the originals of Sorley's letters after the 1919 publication of *Letters* could be read as an attempt to forestall any future "full-length" biography as well as any comprehensive edition of his correspondence.[109] Like other modern editions, then, Wilson's new volumes overwrite a certain historical withholding, and they standardize the material included in them, dispensing with the items that rendered the earlier volumes hybrids. In effect, they edit out the memorial architecture, such as the frontispiece photograph and the chapter of biography, and, with it, the shaping hand of the family.

These new editions, then, participate in an act of disarticulation. Collecting the poems, they suggest, entails an uncollecting of the person (and the personal), a severing of the poems from the biographical ephemera that surround them. Wilson, however, does not completely dispense with these elements, for the exhibition that launches her volumes collects precisely what the editions eliminate.

The editions, moreover, as collections, attempt to make Sorley's life conform to an internal logic uncovered by the editor. Professor Sorley, pursuing a different logic, grouped the poems in four broad thematic categories—"Of the Downs," "Of School," "Of Life and Thought," and "Of War and Death"—seeking to illuminate the spirit of the author; Wilson's restored chronology attempts an alternative narrative—one of poetic growth and aesthetic development, a narrative insistently reinforced, if not strained, in her companion biography.[110] To make this argument in the biography, for example, Wilson has Sorley "beginning his literary career in earnest" at the age of seven when the family moves to Cambridge, and a poem written when he is ten provides evidence that "Charles's poetic career had begun."[111] The "stages" of his mature career, moreover, that Wilson attempts to articulate, following his "apprentice work" at Marlborough, could not have lasted more than a couple of months each. Yet if these are the terms that justify Sorley's present-day survival, *The Collected Poems* exposes a certain tension in the project, leading Wilson to retreat from strict adherence to her own chronological schema when, in her opinion, the poems in question do not provide "a good introduction to Sorley."[112] These tensions can be seen as symptomatic of the contradictions in our modern-day memory project—between the aesthetic and the cultural, the amateur and the professional, the miscellaneous and the methodical. And they raise the question of whether the Sorley experience is improved by these practices of regularization.

Wilson's edition, moreover, raises the question of what "collected" means for a poet whose output consists of a single posthumous volume. Indeed, Wilson adds only 7 poems to those previously published in *Marlborough and Other Poems*, all of them relegated to the book's back matter in a section labeled "Juvenilia and Occasional Poems." And her edition offers little of the infrastructure one might expect from a collected volume.[113] While the edition may be, as Cecil Woolf Publishers advertised it, "the first complete edition of his poems," it offers no substantial change to the Sorley canon—a corpus already complete, for all essential purposes, in 1919. By contrast, some of the major World War I poets have seen an exponential extension of their posthumous canon, no one more so than Wilfred Owen. Where the first edition of Owen's poems, published in 1920, included 23 poems, by 1983 Stallworthy had gathered 177 poems and 172 fragments.[114] With one of its two volumes devoted to describing and in some cases transcribing the manuscripts in type facsimile, Stallworthy's edition appears, in Bernard Bergonzi's words, "as much a shrine or a memorial as a book." But if Owen here reflects one extreme in the possibilities for recuperation and canonization—a "reverential editorial presentation" rarely accorded "older and longer-lived English poets"—Sorley represents another: a limit case of the stand-alone "war poet" and the scholarly apparatus that supports such a designation.[115]

100   **CHAPTER 2**

The *Collected Letters* reflects a similar tension, sitting somewhat uneasily between scholarly edition and popular compilation, a reflection, perhaps, of the ambiguity of the position of the war poets in the broader culture. Unlike the letters of Keats, for example, Sorley's letters yield no great insights into his poetic process and no major articulation of a governing aesthetic; inevitably, the war trumps the poet in what the letters can illuminate. Nor do his letters, like those of Keats, offer any startling revelations of a personal nature. While Wilson insists that the letters "stand in their own right as remarkable literary achievements" (*CL*, 29)—some would even argue of more literary interest than the poems[116]—their publication remains dependent, as it was in their original context, on their wartime associations; as the list of illustrations, all dated between 1912 and 1915, indicates, it is access to the experience of this wartime world and its prewar formations that the volume promises. And while the edition expands the body of Sorley material widely available to the public— collating letters previously printed only in the rare 1916 *Letters from Germany* with those contained in the long-out-of-print 1919 *Letters*, along with some unspecified number of letters published for the first time—it by no means supplies all of Sorley's letters.[117] In the absence of manuscripts, it cannot fill in the family's omissions from the previously published letters (letters, Professor Sorley acknowledges, generally "not given in full" [*L*, viii]); nor can it include letters the family chose not to publish in either of these volumes—letters Professor Sorley describes in *Letters from Germany* as "too intimate for the cold light of print," or ones they never succeeded in collecting. Missing, for example, as Wilson acknowledges, are Sorley's letters to his closest friend at Marlborough, another war casualty, and letters, if they were ever written and delivered, to his host family in Germany. Like the biography of Sorely, the *Collected Letters* must make do with the limited archive of a life that is anything but full-length.[118] As a collection, it remains the collected fragments of a half-lived existence.

Unlike the earliest editions of the poems and letters, which, like other volumes of their kind, were often distributed as gifts and memento mori and preserved as treasured possessions, modern editions like Wilson's are not in themselves, *as books*, affective objects. As texts, however, they derive much of their power, as did their earlier counterparts, from their ability to trigger affective responses in their audience, to invoke, for example, as the *Times* review of Wilson's biography advertises, "the marvellous boy cut off in his prime" (January 2, 1986). They operate, to borrow from Marianne Hirsch, as postmemorial objects, demonstrating how "certain images and certain narratives have been able to circulate in the culture of the postgeneration," although not necessarily in the way Hirsch advocates.[119] Produced by individuals a generation removed from direct experience of the war and its traumatic losses, editions like Wilson's demonstrate how "postmemory" can be generated and transmitted over time through textual circulation—literally, through the republication of the texts that first generated these narratives and the framing of them within well-established parameters. In doing so, they reveal a danger that Hirsch identifies in the postmemory enterprise: the risk "of falling back on familiar and often unexamined cultural images" rather than shifting the paradigms and broadening and enlarging the archive.[120] Indeed, like the collected items that prop the publications in the Cecil Woolf book launch exhibition, Wilson's new editions work to recover an affective connection to the past for which the war poets have long been privileged representatives and Sorley a particularly powerful exemplar.[121] But in replacing familial memory with an affiliative postmemory connection, they do little to dislodge the underlying structures of representation and do little to shift interpretive frameworks. In exhuming Sorley from out-of-print oblivion, these publications aim for a certain freshness of perspective; like other postmemorial work, they attempt "to re-embody and re-individualize" a distant historical subject,[122] offering insight "into an unusual young man" (*CL*, 28), as Wilson notes of the *Collected Letters*. At the same time, however, Sorley remains a mere variant of the established individuals and institutions that have traditionally provided access to popular memory of the war, and his collected works appeal, as Wilson implicitly acknowledges, to a nostalgic invocation of the past promoted in the war's customary reception. As Wilson notes of the letters, they can be read for "the picture they give of a vanished world" (*CL*, 29), whether of prewar public school life or of World War I France. As a site of memory, then, the Sorley embodied in these publications stands at once as emblem of an irrecoverable past and the instrument of its transmission in a process defined by ritualized recollection. Above all, these publications reflect a particular moment in the war's remembrance and in the institutionalization of the war poets. At the same time, they raise the question of the future of the collection as the privileged vehicle for moving memory of the war into the twenty-first century.

Sorley's Signpost

> Sorley is the Gaelic for wanderer. I have had a conventional education: Oxford would have corked it. But this has freed the spirit, glory be. Give me *The Odyssey* and I return the New Testament to store. Physically as well as spiritually, give me the road.
>
> —Charles Hamilton Sorley to Arthur Watts, June 16, 1915

When the Imperial War Museum of London launched its largest ever exhibition on the Great War poets, *Anthem for Doomed Youth: Twelve Soldier Poets of*

102   **CHAPTER 2**

the First World War, in October 2002, it chose as the centerpiece of the Charles Sorley section a battered signpost that once stood on the Marlborough downs, not far from where Sorley attended school. As a repository of sentiment and affect, this was a somewhat unusual choice. Unlike many of the exhibition's most conventionally stirring objects—the pocket watch that stopped when Edward Thomas died; the trench boots belonging to Siegfried Sassoon, pulled open across the instep as if to admit a foot; the locks of Rupert Brooke's hair; Wilfred Owen's copy of Keats's *Endymion*, with annotations in his hand; the map of Belgium, returned with Julian Grenfell's effects, still soaked through with his blood—the signpost does not bear the imprint of Sorley's body. It is not something he owned, touched, made, or held in his hand. Indeed, although the exhibition caption labels the item "Sorley's Signpost," it is not Sorley's in the ordinary sense of the word. Rather, as the caption explains, it is "the original signpost which Sorley passed on his many walks on the Marlborough downs"—although solitary runs might be a better description of Sorley's habitual activities. What the caption does not mention is that in 1976, well before the IWM exhibition, Marlborough College had already established Sorley's Signpost as a commemorative site, installing a new signpost dedicated to his memory on the spot where the original one had stood (figure 2.4); hence the inscribed sarsen stone, borrowed from the Marlborough memorial site, lying at the signpost's base in the exhibition. How and why the original signpost would have been preserved remains an open question.[123] But whether or not the signpost displayed in the IWM is the original one, its presence in the exhibition speaks to a dilemma that the passage of time has only intensified: how to make these poets (and their poems) live as the war recedes into ever more distant history, poets at once under- and overremembered in twenty-first-century culture.

Anthem for Doomed Youth, which ran for six months to an enthusiastic reception, drew on the IWM's rich archives and storehouses for its display of World War I artifacts and personal documents; it boasted many items exhibited for the first time, including some still in private hands and others gathered from remote locations. It exploited multimedia platforms and artifacts: interactive displays; film footage and video; timeworn photographs and newly minted photographic enlargements; music piped into exhibition spaces; a headphone area for voice recordings; and musical scores, paintings, and drawings to supplement the manuscripts and printed poetic materials. It was thus an exhibit on an entirely different order from the homely displays of earlier decades. But if the extravagant objects and technological innovations of the IWM retrospective demonstrated advances in the practices of collection and curation, the subject of the exhibition—the perennial soldier-poets—and the

FIGURE 2.4. Sorley's Signpost dedication, October 3, 1976. Photo credit: Kumud Dhital, "Sorley's Signpost," in the *Marlburian*, Michaelmas Term 1976, © Marlborough College 1976

specific figures it chose to highlight exposed the extent to which the memory of the war was still being constituted through the same individuals and the same social institutions as in the mid-1980s. Indeed, the IWM exhibit contains only one poet, Francis Ledwidge, not included in the Poets' Corner memorial. The exhibit exposed, moreover, the extent to which the war's memory was still being constituted through the mechanism of collection. In the dawning years of a new millennium, however, the museum had to reach for ever more spectacular artifacts and an ever more immersive experience to trigger affective engagement. As the choice of the signpost demonstrates, this was perhaps a bigger problem for Sorley than for some of the others; for despite earlier recovery efforts like Wilson's, accounts of museumgoers to the IWM exhibition suggest that Sorley still occupied the place of the "not so familiar" in the cohort in which he found himself there.

The IWM exhibition was, of course, entirely grander in size, scope, and public footprint than the modest Cecil Woolf exhibition-cum-book-launch discussed earlier in this chapter. Sorley, moreover, was only a small piece of the

104   **CHAPTER 2**

IWM extravaganza. But even in the "Sorley objects" collected for the respective showings, certain continuities are evident as well as certain stark differences. Where the Cecil Woolf exhibition, for example, showcases a photograph of the Cecil Jameson chalk drawing of Sorley, along with the photograph on which it was based, the IMW displays the original drawing, on loan from the National Portrait Gallery. And where the IWM installs the actual signpost, with the memorial stone beside it, the earlier Sorley exhibition proffers a case of derivative signpost artifacts: a 1922 etching of the signpost by a former Marlborough art master, Christopher Hughes; an undated drawing by Hughes; a photograph, taken in 1931 by the Reverend R. H. Lane, showing the actual position of the original signpost; a watercolor painted by Sorley's nephew Julian Bickersteth, while he was a student at Marlborough in 1938; and a sketch of the design for the memorial stone's inscription, created by an Old Marlburian, Simon Verity. Where the IWM, then, can trump the earlier exhibition in nearly every instance, it constructs its Sorley out of largely the same materials.

Seen in this light, the signpost, far from being an idiosyncratic choice for a memory object, turns out to be a well-established signifier for Sorley—and one already performing the work of transferring affect across generations. What makes its presence in the IWM so surprising, though, is the decision to install the physical article itself—a decision that complicates the memory work the signpost performs by crisscrossing the messages it delivers. On the Marlborough / Poulton downs, where the original signpost stood, the signpost is indexical. As a directional signal, it performs a function independent of Sorley, naming the locations to which it points on a spot where four grass tracks converge. When Sorley's name is attached to it, however, as in the Marlborough College memorial, the signpost becomes referential, fixing Sorley's memory in a particular location. In effect, it proclaims, "Sorley passed this place"; "Sorley wandered here." Installed in the IWM, however, the signpost does not point anywhere—at least not to any of the geographic locales it indexes. There is, in other words, no "here" to designate as the site of Sorley's wanderings. Even as its presence attempts to tether "Sorley" to the lived experience of a flesh-and-blood individual in the particular time and place that the captions identify, then, the signpost resists its referential function. Dislodged from its topographic location, it memorializes Sorley's memorialization, the signposting of his memory.

That memory has been intimately tied to place, although the place so designated has not remained stable. Like the signpost itself, Sorley's memory turns out to be multidirectional. In the first instance, it locates Sorley's memory at the site where he has found some of his most devoted admirers: the town of Marlborough and the surrounding Wiltshire countryside. In effect, the exhibition deploys Sorley's own commemorative marker, referenced in three of his poems, to fix his memory in an affectively charged location; it thus repeats the gesture Sorley's father performed when he chose "Marlborough" as the title poem for the volume he published in 1916 to commemorate his son. If his father secured Sorley's identification with a place he loved, however, he also, perhaps inadvertently, secured it with the more narrow confines of the school, Marlborough College—a place toward which Sorley's feelings were more deeply ambivalent.[124] And Marlborough College has not hesitated to claim Sorley for itself, stamping its claim on him on and through the signpost—not only on the downs but in college histories, publications, and rituals.

In the IWM, however, the signpost issues contradictory directives. On the one hand, the exhibition literalizes the item, insisting that this is the very signpost Sorley passed; on the other, at least in potential, it opens up the signpost's symbolic dimensions by liberating it from the ground it once occupied and unleashing it from habitual associations. For the young Anglo-Scotsman who somewhat fancifully attributed his free roaming spirit to his Gaelic roots when he wrote to his friend Arthur Watts from his billets in France—"Sorley is the Gaelic for wanderer"—there is perhaps a certain poetic justice in this act of displacement. Indeed, for the Sorley who, in that same letter, projecting his life a year into the future, imagined himself virtually anywhere—"I am sometimes in Mexico, selling cloth: or in Russia, doing Lord knows what: in Serbia or the Balkans: in England, never. England remains the dream, the background: at once the memory and the ideal" (L, 275)—the uprooted signpost might be an even more fitting insignia than its grounded prototype.[125] Poised in possibility, its "arms askew" (as Sorley affectionately described it in a poem), the signpost could stand as a tribute to wandering itself, the material embodiment of Sorley's self-proclaimed mantra: "Physically as well as spiritually, give me the road." As such, the signpost marks not only Sorley's life, with its unanticipated perambulations, but also his unpredictable travels in the years since his death, as evidenced in the disparate locations where efforts to claim his memory have materialized. These include, as I have already suggested, virtually every place Sorley lived, or anticipated living; *Marlborough*, its place-name notwithstanding, was even republished in 2014 as part of a "Scottish Lost Treasures Collection."

Sorley's penchant for wandering, in fact, could be read as a hallmark of his brief life, prompting him, when he was just sixteen, to walk from Marlborough to his home in Cambridge, a journey of about a hundred miles, and then, a year and a half later, to perform the solitary journey in reverse, lovingly recording the walk in his letters and poems. It found an outlet while he was at school in his lengthy rambles, especially his long runs in the rain that became the stuff of college lore.[126] His wanderlust, moreover, skewed the path of what

106   **CHAPTER 2**

might otherwise have been a typical schoolboy trajectory, leading him, in what would have been his final two terms at Marlborough, to reject the power and privileges of the public school for an opportunity to live and study in Germany, where he discovered strong affinities, and where he briefly found himself an enemy alien when war was declared in August 1914. Even in the army, where he sought a commission immediately upon his return to England, he resisted entrenchment—in both action and thought. At the front, he found "a freedom and a spur" (*L*, 305) in no-man's-land, where, as a brother officer records, he sometimes went crawling "just for the fun of the thing" (*L*, 294). In his letters, he allowed himself equal latitude to roam from the expected path: "England—I am sick of the sound of the word. . . . I think that after the war all brave men will renounce their country and confess that they are strangers and pilgrims on the earth" (*L*, 240).

As a wanderer's totem, then, the signpost captures something of Sorley's spirit, as I have tried to suggest in my protracted meditation on it. But ultimately the signpost owes its inclusion in the IWM exhibit, as it did in the earlier Sorley exhibition, to its presence in Sorley's poems, where it has functioned as a kind of "homing" device: at once a marker of home and the mechanism for getting there. It owes its inclusion, as well, to the posthumous life Sorley's poems have conferred on him, where the signpost has assumed the stature of a signature or trademark, appearing on the inside and outside covers of modern editions of his work. The signpost, for example, forms the cover design of Hilda D. Spear's edition of *Poems and Selected Letters* (1978) (figure 2.5), the first edition of his works to be published since the Cambridge Miscellany edition of *Marlborough* of 1932. It appears, superimposed on Sorley's image, as a feature of the cover art for Wilson's editions of *Collected Poems* (1985) (figure 2.6) and *Collected Letters* (1991). Wilson also incorporates the signpost into the endpaper design for all her Sorley publications. In effect, the signpost has become an authorized Sorley portal. In the poems, however, all written while Sorley was in the army, it initiates a different type of memory work—one triggered by the war's radical and traumatic dislocations. Rehearsing divergent forms of a posthumous existence, the poems both complement and contest the memory work of Sorley's public memorialization in material monuments, commemorative exhibits, and print publications.

If the first of these poems, "Lost," registers the visceral shock of exile and estrangement—"Across my past imaginings / Has dropped a blindness silent and slow" (*M*, 29, ll. 1–2)—the last and slightest, "I Have Not Brought My Odyssey," indulges the fantasy of a joyful return to the place of recovered memory, the speaker blithely indifferent to whether the journey be achieved before or after his death, "with the body or without it." The last of the familiar markers

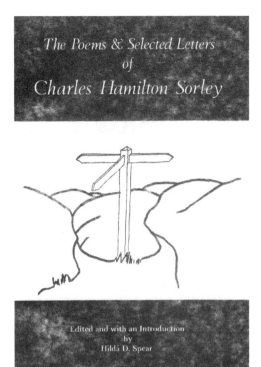

FIGURE 2.5. Book jacket, *The Poems and Selected Letters of Charles Hamilton Sorley*, ed. Hilda D. Spear (Dundee: Blackness Press, 1978). Cover drawing: David Millar

pointing the wanderer home, the signpost, in the "Odyssey" poem, takes on the cumulative force of unchecked nostalgia:

> And that old signpost (well I knew
> That crazy signpost, arms askew,
> Old mother of the four grass ways).
> (*M*, 83–84, ll. 79–81)

A verse epistle addressed to a former master and composed in "jingling" couplets, "I Have Not Brought My Odyssey" performs as licensed regression—a retreat from the "battered trenches" through a return to the position of schoolboy (*M*, 84. ll. 87–88).[127] In the memory work the poem performs, the signpost functions as an instrument of magical thinking.

By contrast, "Lost," a poem Sorley wrote before being deployed overseas, operates under the sign of prohibition, and the signpost serves as a kind of "Do Not Enter" sign, marking the place from which the speaker is shut out—his mind now forced to bend to other things.

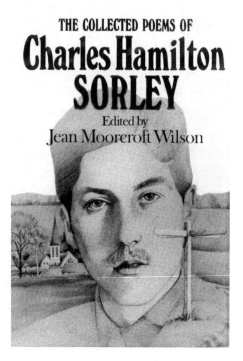

FIGURE 2.6. Book jacket, *The Collected Poems of Charles Hamilton Sorley*, ed. Jean Moorcroft Wilson (London: Cecil Woolf, 1985). Jacket design: Bill Botten. Reproduced with permission of Cecil Woolf Publishers

> I may not think on those dear lands
>   (O far away and long ago!)
> Where the old battered signpost stands
>   And silently the four roads go
>
> East, west, south and north,
>   And the cold winter winds do blow.
>   (M, 29, ll. 5–10)

If the signpost bars the speaker's access to a place of cherished memory, however, it also fills it; as it accumulates details, it spans, in the space of the poem, even the stanza break, leaving the speaker hovering between a bereft present and an unknowable future.

Sending the poem to a Marlborough friend, A. E. Hutchinson, in December 1914, Sorley underlines the importance of the memory work it performs, as it were, under erasure. The poem, he suggests, might be his most successful effort to date "to express in words the impression that the land north of

Marlborough must leave" on those whose minds have not been deadened and diverted by "the artificial machinations that go on within the College Gates": "Simplicity, paucity of words, monotony almost, and mystery are necessary. I think I have got it at last here" (*L*, 250). But if Sorley "gets it" *here*, it is in part because he is no longer *there*, and his absence lends the poem a memorial cast. Four months later, sending the poem to his parents, he calls it "the last of my Marlborough poems" (*M*, 129). If "Lost" is a valedictory poem, however, the Marlborough it leaves behind is radically distilled, the landscape bared of specifics.[128] And the signpost that oversees this land points nowhere in particular—only "East, west, south and north."

Sorley's poem, then, entails a reorienting of "his" signpost to accommodate the new imaginative terrain that the war has forced on him—even while he still occupies English ground. In his most fleshed-out signpost poem, a sonnet written six months later while his battalion was stationed near the front line in Ploegsteert, Belgium, the signpost undergoes its most radical metamorphosis. The poem is one of "Two Sonnets" addressed to Death, and as the speaker acknowledges halfway through its opening sequence, Death has usurped the place of the known and familiar, imposing its signpost everywhere:

> You, so familiar, once were strange: we tried
> To live as of your presence unaware.
> But now in every road in every side
> We see your straight and steadfast signpost there.
>
> ("Two Sonnets: I," *M*, 76, ll. 5–8)

These new circumstances invert the memory work the poem must perform. Unlike "Lost," which tracks a process of estrangement, the signpost sonnet performs an act of refamiliarization, making the familiarity of death even more familiar. It achieves this end by, as it were, transforming death's pointer into *Sorley's* signpost—by transforming the "your . . . signpost" of the poem's opening into the "my" signpost ("that signpost in my land") of the poem's second half:

> I think it like that signpost in my land,
> Hoary and tall, which pointed me to go
> Upward, into the hills, on the right hand,
> Where the mists swim and the winds shriek and blow,
> A homeless land and friendless, but a land
> I did not know and that I wished to know.
>
> ("Two Sonnets: I," *M*, 76, ll. 9–14)

110   **CHAPTER 2**

The signpost, in fact, is a shifting signifier—the hinge on which the poem turns—and the transition from octave to sestet, "I think it like that signpost in my land," begins the work of remaking the new signpost in the image of the old, of transposing the old onto it. This transformation, however, requires an act of strenuous imaginative effort, for the likeness between the two is anything but self-evident. One effect of this transaction is to give the shadowy signpost material shape, to clothe the deathly signifier in homeliness, turning it into something the speaker can embrace. In effect, it works to habituate the speaker to his own posthumousness. But the process also works the other way around, tingeing the original signpost with unearthliness and revealing the beloved downs to be, as "Death—and the Downs," Sorley's working title for the poem, intimates, a landscape that has always harbored death.[129] In the sestet, then, in a term Sorley invokes in his most famous sonnet, "When You See Millions of the Mouthless Dead," the poem "spooks" remembrance to produce an awareness of a forgotten presence, a reminder of the strange that haunts the familiar.[130]

In "Lost," in the absence of the signpost, the speaker finds himself directionless. In the sonnet, he finds his direction through the uncanny affinity by which the past signpost illuminates the present one, uncovering a path on the threshold between the known and unknown—a place of peril, promise, and possibility over which the speaker pauses in suspended animation. Writing of Keats, Brendan Corcoran identifies such states of suspension with a "posthumous positionality"; in their own way, all three of Sorley's signpost poems occupy this liminal territory, gesturing toward what Corcoran describes as a "posthumous poetics."[131] Blurring the lines between life and death, they can be read, like the "last-word" poems Diana Fuss discusses, as "literary exercises in premature dying"—the signpost sonnet most especially.[132] Voiced from the very verge of death, however, the poem offers no words of consolation, prophecy, or protest, only an expression of dispassionate curiosity. Indeed, the sonnet is addressed to Death, not to the speaker's prospective mourners. Even as the poems, then, perform a posthumous identity, they refuse its conventional expression.

In the IWM exhibit, the manuscript of "Two Sonnets" was displayed in a glass showcase opposite the signpost. It is dated June 12, 1915—just four months before Sorley himself was killed in action. A caption notes, "The signpost referred to in the poem is one he passed on his walks in the countryside around Marlborough," and directs the viewer to the displayed object, turning the material signpost, at least momentarily, into an oversize gloss to the sonnet and the sonnet into a proleptic epitaph. It is perhaps, then, not surprising that in the IWM the signpost also stands beside a panoramic photograph of the battlefield of Loos, showing the spot where Sorley died, for in the logic of the exhibition, the sonnet, with its invocation of Death, is also a gloss to the signpost. To some extent, then, the exhibition constrains the signpost's free flow of associations, reducing its meaning to its most transparent function: a prop for the familiar narrative of "doomed youth" that the exhibition trades on.

In the exhibit space the signpost thus becomes simultaneously the emblem of Sorley's life and the marker of his death, exposing a doubleness at the heart of the memorial project that has grown up around him. On the Marlborough downs, where the new signpost, erected in 1976, commemorates his memory, Sorley's Signpost performs a similar dual function (figure 2.7). On the downs, however, the signpost does not stand out as a displaced object. Only the sarsen stone, with its lettered inscription, names the signpost a memorial site, distinguishing it from its merely functional counterparts. The presence of the stone, though, with its dedication, "C H S—1895–1915," could be seen to convert the crossroads marker into a cross, lending the solitary signpost the aura of a grave site, reminiscent of the provisional ones that once dotted the battlefields of Belgium and France. For Sorley, whose name appears on the Loos Memorial to the Missing, it is perhaps the closest thing to a known grave that he has. It is a burial place, moreover, that Sorley might have liked. But, of course, there is no body buried there. Perched on its lonely spot, however, Sorley's Signpost performs its memorial work for those with the knowledge to seek it out, even as the passage of time renders its inscription increasingly illegible.[133] As a memorial, however, the signpost has its additional ironies, not the least of which being that it is not, in fact, Sorley's signpost. Instead, it bears witness to what is no longer there: Sorley's signpost as well as Sorley himself.

The modern signpost, moreover, does not perform the same function as the signpost that Sorley wrote about. In its new designation, the signpost names the man identified with it, and by extension it names as "Sorley country" the land to which it points. Sorley had decided opinions on such memorial impulses; he could not bear even the idea of a photograph of himself circulating his image to friends and family. There is something incongruous, then, in the nature of this memorial work—this effort to imprint Sorley's name (literally, his initials) on a spot of the earth in order to record his brief transit there, as if to say, "That there's some corner of the Marlborough downs / That is forever Sorley." Sorley balked at Rupert Brooke's famous sonnets, calling them "overpraised," and accusing Brooke of taking "the sentimental attitude."[134] He balked as well, despite his unwavering admiration for the Wiltshire naturalist, at the "passion for labeling everything" that had led overzealous critics to "refer to the country between Swindon and Marlborough," the same country

112 CHAPTER 2

Figure 2.7. Sorley's Signpost in winter. Photo credit: © Vieve Forward, "Signpost and Charles Sorley Memorial Stone, Poulton Downs," https://creativecommons.org/licenses/by-sa/2.0/

Sorley adored, "as the Richard-Jefferies land" (L, 55). He rejected, in other words, the type of posthumous life implicit in such acts of "heritaging," just as he rejected it in his poems.

In "All the Hills and Vales Along," one of his most frequently anthologized poems, Sorley revels in the earth's indifference to human passing:

Earth that never doubts nor fears,
Earth that knows of death, not tears,
Earth that bore with joyful ease
Hemlock for Socrates,
Earth that blossomed and was glad
'Neath the cross that Christ had,
Shall rejoice and blossom too
When the bullet reaches you.
    Wherefore, men marching
    On the road to death, sing!

SORLEY'S TRAVELS   113

Pour your gladness on earth's head,
So be merry, so be dead.

(M, 72, ll. 19–30)

Simultaneously buoying and chilling, the poem has baffled critical efforts to place its tone and attitude. As Elizabeth Vandiver observes, "This disturbing poem has inspired radically different interpretations. Some critics read it as a straightforward expression of joy in nature and in death, enhanced by the jaunty metre; others, 'as an oblique subversion of jocular stoicism.'"[135] Whether or not one reads the poem as ironic, however, the reabsorption of the dead into earth's elements—the return of the human to the humus[136]—remains the only posthumous life the poem acknowledges.

Sorley's last poem, the one for which he is most remembered today, pushes the excavation of this terrain even further, rejecting out of hand all memorial sentiments. Found in his kit after his death and frequently read as a further response to Brooke, the poem is unrelenting in its assertion of the irreducibility of death:

When you see millions of the mouthless dead
Across your dreams in pale battalions go,
Say not soft things as other men have said,
That you'll remember. For you need not so.
Give them not praise. For, deaf, how should they know
It is not curses heaped on each gashed head?
Nor tears. Their blind eyes see not your tears flow.
Nor honour. It is easy to be dead.
Say only this, "They are dead." Then add thereto,
"Yet many a better one has died before."
Then, scanning all the o'ercrowded mass, should you
Perceive one face that you loved heretofore,
It is a spook. None wears the face you knew.
Great death has made all his for evermore.

(M, "A Sonnet," 78)

"No sonnet or anti-sonnet," Edna Longley has argued, "has ever had more effect."[137] Generally known today by its haunting first line with its invocation of "the mouthless dead," the poem, in its voice of dispassionate assessment, meticulously deconstructs every consoling fiction that the war's death toll prompted, dispensing with any idea of a sentient afterlife and any rationale for our mourning rituals. The poem, I want to argue, constitutes Sorley's most

114   **CHAPTER 2**

extended meditation on the idea of a posthumous existence. While the speaker is never explicitly identified as a voice-from-beyond-the-grave—indeed, the "you" and "I" of the poem remain stubbornly indeterminate—the poem achieves much of its disconcerting power from the sense it conveys of being spoken posthumously, a sensation reinforced, if not in fact created, by the "poignant circumstances of the poem's posthumous discovery."[138]

If the speaker can speak for the mouthless dead—can be their mouthpiece—it is, the poem implies, because he is in effect already one of them. This sense is further reinforced by the poem's pivotal pronouncement, "Say only this, 'They are dead'"—immediately qualified by a postscript, "Then add thereto, / 'Yet many a better one has died before,'" an allusion, though unmarked, to Achilles's words in *The Iliad* on the death of Patroclus.[139] Emily R. Wilson maintains that "when Achilles lives on after the death of Patroclus, it is as if he is himself already dead."[140] When Sorley's speaker takes on Achilles's words as his own, I am suggesting, he assumes his posthumous position. But as with the corpse poems Fuss discusses, where the dead rebuke the living for their senseless mourning, Sorley's poem operates through a paradoxical logic; it assumes a posthumous voice to reject the idea of any kind of posthumous communication.[141]

In its final movement, then, the poem refuses the last remnant of conventionalized solace. Entertaining the illusion that we can make contact with our own personal dead—that we can identify the particular face of a loved one in the "o'ercrowded mass"—Sorley pulls the reader up short to effectively efface such a comforting fiction: "It is a spook. None wears the face you knew." Robert Graves has suggested that Sorley's father changed the word "spook" to "ghost" in the second edition of *Marlborough*—perhaps to provide a more comforting message, perhaps to correct a perceived solecism—a correction Graves rejected. For his part, in his correspondence with Sassoon, Graves proposes "lie" as a preferable postmortem emendation.[142] But the unsettling "spook" has the advantage of more effectively jolting the reader, revealing, as Vandiver argues, that "anything the 'you' of the poem may see or imagine is only that, imaginary, not even worthy to be dignified by the term 'ghost.'"[143] If in its opening lines, the poem invokes the "pale battalions" of the dead, it does so only to reject, in its closing lines, any idea of an afterlife of the ghostly legions and any idea of survival through living memory. Sorley's objection to the notion of a continued personal existence thus appears at once principled and pragmatic; even if a posthumous life for the individual was once possible to conceive, he seems to suggest, it becomes unthinkable under modern conditions when deaths are numbered in the millions.

The memory work performed by Sorley's poems, this last one most particularly, thus stands at odds with the memorialization of him, the affectless, unsentimental voice of the poem in stark contrast with the way Sorley himself has come to function as an affective trigger for the war's tragic losses. This discrepancy is perhaps nowhere more striking than in the commemorative plaque installed on Sorley's childhood home in Aberdeen in 2018 (figure 2.8). Inscribed with the poem's antimemorial injunction, "Say not soft things as other men have said, that you'll remember for you need not so," the plaque prompts precisely such remembering, exposing the gap between the power of Sorley's words as poetry and the memory work of public memorialization. As the city councilor remarked at its dedication, it is meant to ensure "that the community and particularly young people, will see it and be inspired to take up the torch of Remembrance for the next 100 years."[144] Sorley's signpost, I have been suggesting, as it moves from his poems to its memorial locations, performs a similar function of contradictory inscription, encrypting the kind of posthumous life that Sorley himself rejected and that his family resisted authorizing. It thus points to the way that commemorative objects and objectives can be reshaped and repurposed over time.

As a material site, moreover, the signpost holds particular interest because of the protracted memorial history behind it. In 1916, for example, Sorley's family rejected the suggestion, made by a fellow officer in Sorley's regiment, that a white stone bearing Sorley's name be placed on the Marlborough downs on the very spot where the new Sorley's Signpost now stands; in doing so, they cited Sorley's own reluctance to have a volume of his poems published, on the

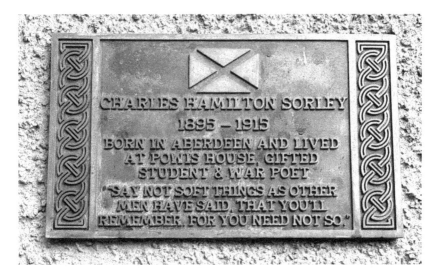

FIGURE 2.8. Plaque commemorating Charles Hamilton Sorley, Powis House, Aberdeen, Scotland. Photo credit: Watty62, https://creativecommons.org/licenses/by-sa/4.0/deed.en

116   **CHAPTER 2**

grounds that war was no time for such self-aggrandizing gestures.[145] In 1940, when an old Marlborough schoolfellow wrote to the *Times* with a similar suggestion for a memorial, Mrs. Sorley reaffirmed the earlier decision and its rationale.[146] The presence of the current Sorley memorial on that very site, then, celebrated in the 1976 dedication ceremony attended by some sixty people, and complete with a reenactment of one of Sorley's famous runs (see figure 2.4), reflects the passing of Sorley's memory to other hands—to those less intimately tied to the subject than the principal mourners of his death.[147] And it illustrates the way memory is repeatedly remade to serve the changing needs of the living.

Similarly, in the IWM, the signpost anchors an effort to reanimate Sorley for viewers for whom he is no longer a known entity, much as the exhibition as a whole seeks to "revitalize and repersonalize the social memory of the war" for an audience without direct access to the war's living memory.[148] As Andrew Motion explains, "A large part of their purpose in putting on the show [was] to introduce these poets to a new generation of readers, and to do so in a way which makes remote history seem recognisable and familiar."[149] The project, then, has certain affinities with the kind of postmemorial work Marianne Hirsch advocates—work that "strives to *reactivate* and *re-embody* more distant political and cultural memorial structures by reinvesting them with resonant individual and familial forms of mediation and aesthetic expression," allowing them to persist "even after all participants and even their familial descendants are gone."[150] But if the IWM exhibit succeeds in refreshing its models, it often does so to generate the same affective responses that previously defined the war's memory, deploying the poets to render the war "recognisable and familiar."

As a familiar object in an unfamiliar context—an object that quite literally stands out from those that surround it—the Sorley signpost performs this operation in superlative fashion, inviting museumgoers to attach a resonant story to it. As an object, moreover, that does not belong to the cultural storehouse of the war's iconography, it opens the possibility for alternative narratives and pathways. At the same time, as I have already suggested, its choice is overdetermined—by the prior reception of Sorley and by the fetishization of the war poets. Seen in this light, the signpost underscores the limits of the memorial project and its necessary incompleteness, pointing away from the showcases' ineffectual efforts to preserve a life under glass. In the IWM, then, as on the downs, the signpost becomes a testimonial to transience, at once a fixed marker of memory and an ephemeral monument.

If, as I have been arguing, Sorley's signpost can provide an entry to Sorley, its efficacy depends on the afterlife it makes possible, on its capacity to put Sor-

SORLEY'S TRAVELS   117

ley back into circulation beyond the exhibition's confines. Within the museum, moreover, it operates unevenly for different audiences. The narrative, for example, that I have been teasing out from the signpost would most likely be available only to dedicated Sorleyites, to those already deeply familiar with Sorley's writings and with a range of writings about him. For the casual museumgoer, the "Sorley experience" would be considerably foreshortened. If, within the architecture of the exhibition, the signpost marks a space to pause over a relatively unknown poet's brief life, it also points the way out to the more open, spacious, and familiar ground of the iconic war poets—the Owen and Sassoon rooms on the other side. Even as it invites a fresh take on a familiar subject, then, the exhibit, "aptly but unimaginatively called Anthem for Doomed Youth" (in Andrew Motion's words), locks into place the space Sorley occupies in the established topography of the "war poets," the passageway and connecting link between the idealism of Rupert Brooke (the entry point for the exhibit) and the searing disillusionment of Owen, Sassoon, and Rosenberg, as if no other narrative were imaginable. In its persistent appeal to pathos, moreover, the exhibit reinforces the linking of the war poets to their precarious lives, rendering them inaccessible except through the lens of loss. It thus locks them into the timeworn category of "doomed youth," leaving unanswered the question of whether the war poets might be susceptible to other configurations and alternative forms of remembrance.

In an effort to move the work of postmemory out of its entrenched positions, Marianne Hirsch calls attention to the ubiquitous figure of the lost child in Holocaust art and narratives, aligning her project with those who would both scrutinize the figure and refuse its sentimentality. In the World War I context, the war poet, as an emblem of lost youth, has operated in a similarly privileged fashion to mediate the memory of the war's trauma. Given the weight of Britain's memorial culture, it has been difficult for new commemorative efforts that invoke this figure, however innovative, to escape being absorbed into inherited paradigms—to escape the appeal of falling in love with a dead man. When Neil McPherson's *It Is Easy to Be Dead*, a play "based on the brief life, letters and poetry of Charles Hamilton Sorley," was performed in London in 2016, the press responded in predictable fashion; the *Guardian*, for example, headed its review, "Requiem for a Forgotten War Poet" (June 21, 2016), exposing both the staying power of this ruling trope and the extent to which Sorley was once more in need of revival.[151] Indeed, the play, which materializes Sorley through the staging of his parents' struggles to memorialize him, replays, in a literal fashion, the recurrent dynamic by which Sorley must be rendered freshly dead in order for some new proponent to revive him. For theatergoers, the fact

118   **CHAPTER 2**

that Sorley was relatively unknown rendered him newly ripe for mourning; the play's careful curation of his words could then work to foster the emotional attachment necessary for catharsis when, at the play's end, the resurrected Sorley was required to die again. Calling the play "at once requiem and reclamation," the *New York Times* review (July 2, 2016) captured this paradox—one that has characterized Sorley's entire afterlife.[152]

Similarly, when James MacMillan produced his oratorio based on five Sorley poems, *All the Hills and Vales Along*, commissioned by the London Symphony Orchestra and the 14-18 NOW arts program to commemorate the one hundredth anniversary of the war's end, Sorley, "the obvious choice" according to MacMillan, required reintroducing to audiences in both Scotland and England. MacMillan himself had been introduced to Sorley many years earlier, after being given a copy of *Never Such Innocence: A New Anthology of Great War Verse*, edited by Martin Stephen, a great admirer of Sorley, and the poems were ones to which he returned years later. Not surprisingly, perhaps, for its London performances, the Barbican incorporated the oratorio into a commemorative series titled "For the Fallen"—the title, like the IWM's *Anthem for Doomed Youth*, at once appropriate and overburdened by cultural baggage.[153] Critics were quick, moreover, to seize on the poignancy of McPherson's inclusion of the National Youth Brass Band of Britain among the featured performers, its members little younger than Sorley at the time of his death. By contrast, when the play premiered at the Cumnock Tryst festival in Ayrshire, Scotland, the composer's birthplace, it featured a string quintet and solo winds instead of a full orchestra, and the brass band that played was an amateur ensemble, the very one in which the composer's coal miner grandfather once played euphonium. The performance thus tapped the local and familial and, like McPherson's play, claimed Sorley for Scotland.[154]

As one of the youngest fallen poets to attract continuing attention—and, according to many, one of the most promising—Sorley has epitomized one of the war's iconic narratives: the Keats-like tragedy of "a greatly talented boy-poet greatly cut off."[155] Sorley, however, never achieved Keats's posthumous reputation, or even the reputation of more prolific and better-established war poets similarly romanticized; indeed, as a poet seemingly doomed to be repeatedly revived and repeatedly forgotten, Sorley amplifies the war poet's lostness. Might it be possible, then, to do with his figure what Hirsch enjoins her readers to do with the lost child, "to queer that figure and to engage in alternative patterns of affiliation beyond the familial, forming alternate attachments across lines of difference"?[156] If Graves and his circle offer one model of such "queering," it is by no means the only possible one. As I have tried to document, other networks have radiated out from Sorley, promising different, still underexplored paths of connection. Indeed, we might now, a hundred years and more after the fact, return to Graves's coded question about Sorley's sexuality, "Was he *so*?," and read its encrypted message somewhat differently: *Must* he be *so*—what the weight of British cultural memory has made of the war poets? As I have argued, Sorley himself has been a signpost for various coteries with special affinities and, like the other war poets, has functioned as a signifying marker in the construction of the war's cultural memory; but like his signpost, "he" need not point in only one direction. The patterns of affiliation that I have been documenting, with their intricate interconnections and crossovers, begin to map a new kind of cultural work to which Sorley might lend himself; these attachments, however, remain ones largely formed along lines of sameness, although that sameness has diverse referents. If one were to take up Hirsch's challenge more fully, what would attachments look like formed around more radical lines of difference? What other posthumous lives would they facilitate? In such a project, might the posthumous life, and the affective power that underwrites it, be a further opportunity in opening the war to a more multidirectional memory?

CHAPTER 3

Posthumous Was a Woman
War Memorials and Woolf's Dead Poets Society

> Now my belief is that this poet who never wrote a
> word and was buried at the crossroads still lives. . . .
> For great poets do not die; they are continuing
> presences; they need only the opportunity to walk
> among us in the flesh.
>
> —Virginia Woolf, *A Room of One's Own*

When Virginia Woolf wrote these words, she was not, of course, referring to the dead soldier-poets of World War I: the men like Charles Sorley (see chapter 2) who also "died young," their gifts still unrealized, and who were buried near where they fell in the battlefields of Belgium and France, if not more far-flung places. Yet Woolf's invocation of Shakespeare's sister, coming as it did ten years after the peace was declared, followed a period of national obsession, as the preceding chapters have demonstrated, with the fate, in spirit if not name, of Shakespeare's brothers.[1] These young men "of brilliance, promise and innocence, who were snuffed out in the carnage of the First World War," were even being explicitly promoted by some contemporaries as the "new Elizabethans."[2] And these war dead—these dead poets, as they were most commonly figured—were still very much alive in the public consciousness when, in *A Room of One's Own*, Woolf took up the woman writer's cause. The years immediately succeeding the war, in fact, saw an unprecedented display of public and private acts of commemoration, most notably, as mentioned in the introduction, the erection of the Cenotaph, or "the empty tomb," in Whitehall in July 1919 and the burial of the Unknown Warrior in Westminster Abbey on Armistice Day 1920, timed to coincide with the unveiling of a new Cenotaph, now made permanent by popular demand (see figures I.2 and I.3). The response to these memorials was not one that could be easily forgotten: "By the end of the week, it was estimated that one million people had visited the Cenotaph and the graveside, and that no less than 100,000 wreaths had been laid either in the Abbey or in Whitehall."[3]

And the process did not stop there; what, as discussed in the introduction, Woolf called the "lurid scene" of the "night of the Cenotaph"—a scene "like one in Hell"—was followed, as Karen L. Levenback reminds us, by "approximately forty thousand memorials throughout England," reaching their height in the early 1920s, when memorial tributes and unveilings could be observed on a daily basis.[4] This memorial mania, to borrow Erika Doss's term, could in many ways be traced to the government's decision, first declared in 1915 and reaffirmed in 1920, not to repatriate any of the bodies of the soldiers who died overseas or to allow private memorials in the military cemeteries.[5] Consequently, local memorials situated on home ground came to serve as surrogate gravesites. In central London, memorials cropped up in churches, workplaces, government centers, transport hubs, tourist sites, parks, and other public spaces; among the most arresting were the London and North Western Railway Company Memorial in Euston Square (1921), the Great Western Railway War Memorial in Paddington Station (1922), and the Royal Artillery Memorial at Hyde Park Corner (1925). Farther off London's tourist map, memorializing efforts were no less vigorous. In East London alone, Mark Connelly has identified "the unveiling and dedication of some twenty-six memorials in East and West Ham between January 1919 and Armistice Day 1921, forty-one in the City, twenty-two in Tower Hamlets, ten in Ilford and three in Romford."[6] And throughout the 1920s, Sir Edwin Lutyens, the designer of the Cenotaph and one of the key architects for the Imperial War Graves Commission, continued to leave his mark on London memorial architecture, including the Royal Naval Division memorial at Horse Guards Parade (1925), where a statue to Kitchener was erected a year later, and the Mercantile Marine memorial at Tower Hill (1928), not far from the Tower of London.[7] The London Woolf so avidly longed to inhabit again with the return of peace—a longing she recorded in her letters and diaries—could be seen, then, as an urban landscape that was being transformed into a testimonial tract. Indeed, as Geoff Dyer has argued, in the postwar years, Britain entered a "phase of protracted mourning" only "formally completed with the inauguration of the Memorial to the Missing of the Somme at Thiepval in 1932."[8]

Missing Memorials

This chapter proposes to read *A Room of One's Own* through and against this postwar context. The culture of remembrance, it suggests, provides an important

122   **CHAPTER 3**

but not generally noted frame of reference for understanding Woolf's own meditation in *Room* on the absent and the missing, just as it did for other modernist literary artists. But in invoking—and inhabiting—the tropes of remembrance, Woolf also displaces them. One might even argue that she "queers" them—and this at a time when reverence for the war dead was still a powerful cultural imperative. In staging a commemoration for someone who never existed, Woolf opens to view and thus makes transparent the process by which communities shape a past for themselves through the production of afterlives—a past in the case of the actual war dead no less dependent on the needs and experiences of the living than Woolf's admittedly partial ritual. And she exposes the fiction of inclusiveness promoted in the nation's official structures of memorialization. For while the overseas military cemeteries were, as Thomas W. Laqueur reminds us, explicitly designed to avoid a landscape of inequality and to cultivate a democratic "community of the dead," their domestic surrogates, Woolf insinuates, could not help but re-perform the exclusion of women from this newly sacrosanct community.[9]

Like the ubiquitous war memorials, the cult of the soldier-poet, as it surfaced in the public arena, was a commemorative site where the exclusion of women was cemented and enforced through an appeal to affect. As the previous chapter illustrated, the "immense investment in war poetry as 'marketable sentiment' in newspapers and anthologies," and in stand-alone volumes, already evident by the middle of the war, continued unabated in the immediate postwar years, with the figure of the dead young poet acquiring a luminous presence.[10] Woolf's densely allusive text attends to the way this affective investment functioned as an alternative structure of remembrance and to the gendered interdiction that underwrites its operation. For poetry by women could not attract the same attention or elicit the same emotional expenditure—something Woolf feels compelled to remark precisely because it goes without saying; she does so, however, by addressing the absence of women poets not in this specific postwar moment but in history more generally.

If the first phase of this enthusiasm found its apotheosis in the canonization of Rupert Brooke, eulogized as the personification of self-sacrifice and the exemplar of British manhood at its noble best, this act of enshrinement, Robert Wohl suggests, effectively transformed Brooke himself into "a patriotic monument of marble."[11] Lesser-known figures like Sorley, however, as discussed in chapter 2, also attracted considerable public attention and outsize emotional investments in this period, even if their deaths were not commemorated with comparable fanfare. Woolf herself, in fact, while decrying Brooke's grotesque transformation, made her own small contribution to the burnishing of Sorley's reputation and the narrative that supported it, proclaiming that "he was destined, whether in prose or in verse, to be a writer of considerable power," while lamenting the tragic circumstances of his death that left these powers unrealized.[12] Woolf, however, would have recoiled at the excesses of his admirers, as discussed in the preceding chapter, even if she was willing to deem him, unlike Brooke, a "genuine writer."

The counterstory of war to the patriotic narrative Brooke epitomized—one focused on the horrors of war and the fate of a generation callously delivered to meaningless slaughter—was already finding voice in the posthumous collections of Wilfred Owen (1920) and Isaac Rosenberg (1922), although these poets were yet to find their large audiences; their new perspective, however, did not so much displace the central icon of the doomed youth of unfulfilled promise as resituate it, preparing it for a different kind of romanticization at the hands of later generations. By the decade's end, moreover, "a rash of books about the generation of 1914 and their war experiences, many of which became runaway best-sellers,"[13] was promoting this alternate war story and giving a new turn to the figure of the "poet" done in by the war: the sensitive young man who survived the war, only to experience himself as a "ghost." These memoirs, autobiographies, and autobiographical novels—the most famous, in the British context, all authored by poets (Siegfried Sassoon, Robert Graves, Edmund Blunden, and Richard Aldington)—performed, Jay Winter has suggested, as "a kind of war memorial, a ritual entombment of and separation from those who had fallen by those who had survived."[14] But I would argue it was their former selves as much as their fallen comrades that these authors were ritually entombing and their present selves that they were enrolling as members of a lost generation. In this "war book" publication bonanza, 1929, the year *A Room of One's Own* was published, was recognized as the "big year for war books in England," with 1928, the year Woolf delivered the lectures on which she based her text, a close second.[15] Woolf's bid for a forgotten poet she calls Judith Shakespeare, then, comes at a time when the poet killed in the war, literally or figuratively, was still exercising an enormous influence on popular memory.

S. P. Rosenbaum's publication of the manuscript versions of *A Room of One's Own* makes clear that "the fiction of Shakespeare's sister was not part of Woolf's original Cambridge talk."[16] Nor was the trope of "the blank spaces on the shelves," of "looking about the shelves for books that were not there" (*AROO*, 54, 47). In introducing these elements, Woolf was doing, with a vengeance, what Sarah Cole claims Eliot did in 1925, when he added the words "mort aux Dardanelles" to his original dedication of *Prufrock*, "To Jean Verdenal, 1889–1915" when he republished it in *Poems 1909–1925*. Woolf was, to tweak Cole's words, putting *her* "own stamp on the familiar signifier of the

124   CHAPTER 3

tragically dead young man."[17] The evolution of these motifs in the year between the talk that gave rise to *Room* and the published volume locates these developments at precisely the moment a new orthodoxy of disillusionment with the war was being consolidated in the belated war memoirs discussed above and the moment, Wohl suggests, the idea of a "lost" generation, initially associated with disorientation and discontinuity, "was increasingly being equated with [a] 'missing' generation," and "the suggestion of physical absence."[18] When, in *A Room of One's Own*, then, Woolf writes, "When the guns fired in August 1914, did the faces of men and women show so plain in each other's eyes that romance was killed?" (15), she echoes what surely must have seemed, at that moment, a familiar antiwar refrain: the death of romance. Indeed, in focusing on the ugly truths the war brought to light, Woolf aligns her work with the gritty realism and new truth-telling that defined those works, even as she elsewhere expresses resistance to their overexplicitness. The romance, however, so systematically dismantled in the "war books" of the late 1920s—the romance of war—was romance of a different kind from the one Woolf spotlights. For those works had as an implicit target the idealistic rhetoric of adventure, heroism, patriotism, glory, and self-sacrifice that the experience of trench warfare quickly shattered. And when Woolf prefaces this passage, her most extended and explicit reference to the war in this text, with the question "Shall we lay the blame on the war?" (15)—indeed, when she inserts the question in this seemingly unlikely place (a discussion of dead vs. living poets)—she does so at a moment when "blaming it on the war" had become something of a fashionable pastime, a point her holograph insertions to the Fitzwilliam manuscript of *Women & Fiction* underline.[19] In fact, in what is sometimes referred to as the War Book Controversy, vocal detractors of these new "truth-telling" volumes made precisely this objection, accusing the books of trafficking in lies and antiwar propaganda. Woolf's intervention in this debate thus both aligns her with and counters the popular war books that Janet Watson has argued were increasingly sidelining women.[20]

This passage, culminating in the only half-rhetorical question, "But why say 'blame'? Why, if it was an illusion, not praise the catastrophe, whatever it was, that destroyed illusion and put truth in its place?" (*AROO*, 15), is cited frequently in Woolf scholarship. What is less frequently noted is the way the passage specifically invokes the postwar literature of disillusionment from which it takes off—both literally and figuratively. In the very next sentence, relaying her trek from the men's to the women's college, Woolf identifies "truth" as the place where men's and women's paths depart: "For truth . . . those dots mark the spot where, in search of truth, I missed the turning up to Fernham" (*AROO*, 15).[21] As this line suggests, truth, for Woolf, is always at least half in quotation marks. As in her refocusing of the question of romance earlier in the passage, Woolf's mimicry allows her to both participate in and distance herself from the newly articulated postwar project. Truth-telling, indeed, was the sine qua non on which the "war books" staked their claim for significance, even if, as with Graves, sometimes in a tongue-in-cheek manner. From the start, *A Room of One's Own* fancifully claims this same territory as a modernist birthright; for in a dazzling array of rhetorical flourishes, "truth" becomes the ideological battleground for Woolf's modernist/feminist assault on facticity, marking the spot that Woolf uncovers in the preceding passage (the denoted ellipsis, ". . .") as a site where "war writing and Modernist writing [have] interpenetrated each other."[22] Swerving from the main path, as she does throughout the essay, Woolf at once engages the war and decenters it, turning the War Book Controversy into a literary dispute being fought on very different terrain.[23]

Woolf's recognition of the importance of the war in opening careers for women, a point her narrator makes in distinguishing "the chief occupations that were open to women before 1918" (*AROO*, 37) with those now before her audience, has also been noted as a crucial context for *A Room of One's Own*. It lays the ground for her closing appeal to her audience to do the work that would give "the dead poet who was Shakespeare's sister" the "opportunity to walk among us in the flesh" ([118], 117). Indeed, in insisting, apropos of Shakespeare's sister, that with the proper commitment from women, "she will be born" ([118]), Woolf gifts her a posthumous birth, encroaching on the territory of one of the war's most poignant legacies—the many children fathered by soldiers who died before they were born and whose births, at least among the upper classes, were often advertised in public notices in the press.[24] In doing so, Woolf shifts the limelight from the sacrifice of the traditionally privileged to the opportunities of the newly enfranchised. In fact, not only were the professions opening to women, but the Equal Franchise Act of 1928 extended to women, for the first time, the same voting rights as men. Yet despite the acknowledged importance of these moments, and despite a growing consensus that Woolf, throughout her career, was deeply engaged with issues of war, *A Room of One's Own* has not generally been read as one of Woolf's "war books."[25] Nor does the text, for the most part, call attention to what Teresa Winterhalter has called its "lexicon of war," and what I would like to call its "lexicon of war memorialization," as often as not representing it through a rhetoric of indirection and displacement.[26]

What would it mean, then, this chapter asks, to read Woolf's influential contribution to a history and theory of women's authorship against this largely unspoken backdrop, to uncover the memorial culture that underwrites the

126   **CHAPTER 3**

work in which Woolf both does and does not take part? And what can such an undertaking tell us about the tangled roots of modernism in the culture of remembrance? For a start, Woolf's homage to the Unknown Poet she calls Judith Shakespeare, the commemorative gesture that forms the centerpiece of her work, could be seen as precisely that: a commemorative act. Pointing to Vanessa Bell's jacket design for the original Hogarth Press edition of the text, Jane Marcus says as much: "She has managed to articulate absence, to suggest infinite possibility, to design a monument for Judith Shakespeare, to picture the tomb of the 'Unknown' woman artist. It is both a memorial and a stage set for a resurrection."[27] Woolf's spectacular fiction of this unknown poet's life, I would add, might be heard to echo—indeed, to answer and improve—"the fanciful essays in which the life of the Unknown Warrior was re-created" in the newspapers of the time of the 1920 Armistice Day rites.[28] As an appropriation of a sacred icon, moreover, it performs a feat potentially more daring than the appearance of the Unknown Warrior on the stage in 1928, an event David Lloyd notes was beset by controversy.[29]

Indeed, Woolf's extended meditation on "Women and Fiction," even as it shifts the discourse away from men and war, draws on precisely the tropes Jay Winter has identified in his landmark work, *Sites of Memory, Sites of Mourning*, as constituting the distinctive logic of the memorialization project that followed the Great War: the return or rising of the dead; the obligation of the living to make good their sacrifice; the dialogue with the dead through the conferral of a posthumous voice.[30] Woolf, however, draws on these tropes in order to turn them inside out; in mimicking them, she refuses to play it straight, treating her culture's rituals of hushed reverence and pious sentiment with casual abandon and mock solemnity. When Woolf enjoins her audience to "let flowers fall upon the tomb of Aphra Behn" (69)—in Westminster Abbey, no less—and dedicate themselves to bringing Shakespeare's sister (back) to life, she is evoking, I want to suggest, the well-established rituals of collective mourning which she then displaces with her own idiosyncratic rites. And when she confers on Shakespeare's sister the promise of belated authorship and a posthumous life, she is self-consciously occupying forbidden ground, carving out a space for the emergence of a novel form of women's authorship in a territory newly excavated by the war.

For World War I posed in particular and pressing ways the problem of posthumous authorship, if for no other reason than that it "produced a phenomenal number of poets who wrote a vast quantity of verse," and it produced an extremely large number of deaths among this poetry-writing class.[31] In *A Room of One's Own*, the absence of women writers in the Elizabethan age—a time "when every other man, it seemed, was capable of song or sonnet"

(*AROO*, 43)—prompts Woolf to speculate about a female Shakespeare. The Great War seemed another such time of creative outpouring and another time when the absence of women's voices was pronounced. In a rubric that appears to have had some purchase for his contemporaries, E. B. Osborn dubbed the war's fallen heroes "The New Elizabethans": "They were all scholars and sportsmen and poets—even if they did not write poetry, they had a conviction that life ought to be lived poetically. They had the Elizabethan exuberance."[32] As a publisher, a reviewer, and an avid reader of newspapers and journals in which such works were regularly noted, Woolf would have been well aware of this flood of war poetry appearing in monographs, books, anthologies, and newspapers, as well as postcards, pamphlets, broadsides, and other ephemera. In her published essays, and even more in her letters and diaries, Woolf expressed a certain ambivalence about the work of the surviving war poets—Sassoon, Graves, Blunden—some of whose volumes the Hogarth Press published over the course of the 1920s.[33] But as her *Times Literary Supplement* and *Athenaeum* essays suggest, she was even more keenly aware of the peculiar delicacy of judging posthumous works, of which there were so many, given, as she put it in one review, the "large number of . . . young men who left behind them enough verse to fill a little book before they were killed." Consequently, she often appears at pains to mitigate the harshness of her criticisms when reviewing such poets.[34]

These little books, of radically uneven quality, appeared literally as well as figuratively as voices from the dead. This was no less true of what we have come to see as the major and defining war poetry of the period as it was of its more minor and private manifestations. Wilfred Owen, for example, who published only five poems before his death in battle one week before the end of the war, could be said to be defined by his posthumousness, his public literary career emerging, Geoff Dyer suggests, not so much as protest to the nation's official rites of remembrance but rather as one of the coordinates: "the Unknown Soldier and the poet everyone knows."[35] When Edith Sitwell brought out the first edition of Owen's poems in 1920, Siegfried Sassoon, in his now famous introduction, insisted that Owen's poems (poems Owen himself had called "elegies") could "speak for him" and turned the poems, in effect, into Owen's elegies for himself: "All that was strongest in Wilfred Owen survives in his poems," Sassoon wrote; "these poems survive him as his true and splendid testament."[36]

Yet if Owen's words bear witness from the other side of death, they require, as in any form of posthumous authorship, the efforts of the living to reach an audience. More common than the case of Owen, however, were the volumes of posthumous poems by authors of admittedly lesser genius—volumes published

128   **CHAPTER 3**

in small runs as acts of private or semiprivate commemoration, as discussed in chapter 1. Virginia and Leonard Woolf, for example, along with Leonard's brother Philip, published in 1918, as the second publication of the Hogarth Press, a posthumous edition of Cecil Woolf's poems for private distribution among family and friends. As Philip's dedication intimates, these were poems that were perhaps not yet ready for publication, poems that were, like their author, prematurely released: "Had he lived longer, some of these poems, revised and re-polished, might have appeared one day in a volume under both our names. Now that he is gone, I dedicate them, as they were left, to the memory of the dearest and bravest brother that a man was ever loved by."[37]

Even more common, however, as chapter 1 indicated, were the tributes, in the form of memorial volumes, to the young men who died before making their name, the "dead poets" who, like Woolf's Judith Shakespeare, "never wrote a word" (or at least did not write enough of them to fill a volume), and whose Lives, reconstructed by family and friends, stood in the place of their posthumous poems. So common had these books become that in 1924 Woolf could introduce a book review thus: "The war has made us familiar with the type of book of which Mr Graham's is a good example. A young man impresses his friends with his powers, writes one novel of great promise, and is killed at the age of thirty. The friends then attempt to record what he was to them, and to adumbrate what he might have been to the world. Those who did not know him follow with sympathy, but necessarily with some bewilderment."[38] In saying this, Woolf seems to put her finger on the overdetermination factor: the remains are not enough to constitute literary achievement, so the audience has to contribute its own goodwill, its own desire (which she calls sympathy) in order to warrant readability.

The need for such a leap of faith on the part of the audience—and for a corporeal intermediary to shepherd the dead man's words to a living readership—finds its logical fulfillment in the most bewildering instance of such volumes: the spiritualist tracts that doubled as memorials. The most famous of these was undoubtedly *Raymond; or Life and Death*, published in 1916, by Sir Oliver J. Lodge, a distinguished physicist. Part memorial to his youngest son who died at Ypres at the age of twenty-six, part collation of evidence for the "survival" of his son, including transcripts of séances in which "Raymond" communicated from the other side, part theoretical explication of the spiritualist hypothesis, *Raymond* "went through a dozen printings between 1916 and 1919 and was republished in abridged form as *Raymond Revisited* in 1922."[39] Successors to *Raymond*—in published volumes and in private records of sessions with mediums—were part of the daily fare of the postwar reading public; Lodge himself followed Raymond with another memorial volume two years later, *Christopher: A Study in Human Personality* (1918), mentioned in chapter 1. Few of these later efforts commanded the public attention Lodge's original volume generated. In their sheer persistence, however, these acts of remembrance remind us that the revival of spiritualism, especially among the educated classes, was one of the striking effects of the war; it was also, as Woolf would have recognized, an occasion for new forms of posthumous authorship and posthumous publication, even if she did not actually read these spiritualist publications. Such works, I am arguing, formed part of the culture out of which Woolf conceived her own quirky take on a posthumous existence.

As testimonials like Lodge's suggest, moreover, in their hybrid commemorative/spiritualist structure, the argument for "life" after death is the ultimate extension of the memorial impulse: they materialize the assertion that the dead survive, as Woolf would say, as "continuing presences" (*AROO*, 117), even if they do not follow Woolf in suggesting that they "walk among us in the flesh."[40] As such, these works make explicit what is already inherent in memorial tracts produced without what Lodge calls "supernormal" assistance: the dead survive, quite literally, in pieces and fragments. In the case of the volumes with a spiritualist cast, the kinds of pieces gathered as evidence of "survival" require even more decoding to be rendered legible as "authorial" pronouncements than their testamentary counterparts—the array of miscellaneous documents the young men leave behind. But even the more ordinary manifestations of a posthumous life present considerable hurdles. In the case of the "material boys" discussed in chapter 1, their families compensated for the central lack at the heart of their memorials by amassing an excess of bits and pieces connected to the commemorated person. For Woolf, creating a "material girl" proved infinitely more formidable because of the utter paucity of available materials.[41] Indeed, *Room* would seem to suggest that the problem of commemorating those who die too young pales against the problem of remembering those who have never lived at all. The task Woolf sets herself thus appears even more daunting than the spiritualist attempt at afterlife communication, requiring Woolf's own mediation, her own sleight of hand—backed by the collective will of women everywhere—to "prove" that "life" continues for one not yet even born.

For those who die prematurely in a cause of recognized national importance, by contrast, the language of remembrance lies ready to hand. Thus Lodge locates *Christopher* (see figure 1.2), his memorial to Christopher Coombe Tennant, the son of a distinguished medium and close friend of the family, within this larger commemorative discourse. Announcing his work as a tribute to "latent capacity" and "nascent genius," the "altar" he feels compelled to raise to the memory of doomed youth, he declares, "It is mainly of these unfledged songsters, these undeveloped athletes, these youths of blighted

130   **CHAPTER 3**

promise, that I write."[42] Asking in "Youth and the War," the introduction to the volume, the fundamental question, "Why pick out for special remembrance one rather than another of the glorious company of those who have sacrificed themselves in this high cause?," Lodge rationalizes his choices for their typicality: "Each has done his duty, each is one of a type" (*C*, 6). Woolf, on the other hand, when she takes up a parallel project, must conjure a type from the silences of history that have doomed Shakespeare's sister to be one of a kind. Offering *Christopher* as, in effect, a sequel to *Raymond*, Lodge explains that, having already dealt with "the engineering practical type" in that earlier volume, his tribute to his son, he is now attempting to limn "the scholarly, the more artistic type, the undeveloped man of letters . . . the youth of intelligent and cultivated emotion" (*C*, 6). Writing of the Cenotaph, Winter observes, "It is a form on which anyone could inscribe his or her own thoughts, reveries, sadnesses."[43] Though not yet erected at the time Lodge penned this volume, the Cenotaph, in its universalist aspirations, models what Lodge attempts here. Like the Cenotaph, with its blank marble surface and empty center, Lodge's "incomplete" memorialized "lives" remain to be completed by what his readers project onto them: "Each may stand for a multitude, and I trust that many parents will realise, in one or other of those commemorated, a sufficient picture of what their own son was like, and will feel that in endeavouring to commemorate a few we are really commemorating a large and increasing number" (*C*, 6).[44] More than a decade later, Woolf would remind her readers of what Lodge leaves out, inventing in Shakespeare's sister her own surrogate figure for such uncompleted lives—"the undeveloped *woman* of letters," a blank slate for women to reflect collectively upon.

Part personal memoir, part exposition, *Christopher* is, like *A Room of One's Own*, a meditation on genius, as Lodge's opening words suggest: "In this great massacre of youth, in which we are all, to the best of our ability, heavily engaged, . . . what slaughter of heaven-sent genius must there inevitably be!" (*C*, 1). Like Woolf, moreover, Lodge recognizes that genius rarely flourishes where the necessary conditions have not prevailed (birth, education, wealth, a congenial family environment): "One undoubtedly who possessed such advantages is the subject of this memoir" (*C*, 7).[45] Like so many others in that time, however, Christopher's genius is not allowed the opportunity to bear fruit: he is nearly stifled first by the uncongenial atmosphere of the public school, then by the demands of the war that shut him out from "his cherished ambition to go to Cambridge" and force him to abandon "the anticipated enjoyment of rooms in the Great Court of Trinity, wherein, when he tried for his scholarship, he had passed a glorious week" (*C*, 17). In the place of such rooms of his own, Christopher experiences the oppressive discipline of Sandhurst and the grim realities of the trenches, where he is quickly struck down three days after his arrival at the front. Perhaps more interesting than this familiar recital of promise, however, is the digression Lodge allows himself in order to lament the daily slaughter of genius among those of the lower social ranks, simply by virtue of their class: "Of the wastage we hear less, but it must be appalling. Slaughter in war is but another and more obvious form of slaughter; it attracts more attention, but, save in quantity, it need hardly be more repined than the less obtrusive moral and intellectual slaughter always going on in time of peace" (C, 9).[46]

Returning to *Room* with these works as a backdrop, one sees that the war appears at once nowhere and everywhere. As if in response to Lodge, Woolf draws attention to her own reworking of an undertold tale of tragic waste. "That, more or less, is how the story would run, I think, if a woman in Shakespeare's day had had Shakespeare's genius," she proclaims, relegating her heroine to a choice of grim fates: she "would certainly have gone crazed, shot herself, or ended her days in some lonely cottage outside a village, half witch, half wizard, feared and mocked at" (*AROO*, 50, 51). The more familiar story, however—the one the war impressed on the national consciousness through repeated iteration—informs, at almost every level, the counternarrative Woolf spins, constituting a sustained reference point for her address to female authorship. The accounts of latent genius snuffed out by the war, for example, of those "mute and inglorious Miltons" who never got to express themselves in song, would have been only too familiar to Woolf when she imagined "some mute and inglorious Jane Austen" (*AROO*, 51) as *A Room of One's Own* took shape in her mind. And the would-be poets trapped in soldiers' bodies and forced to bring their mangled work out before its time—poets of whom Woolf wrote on more than one occasion—may well have cast their shadow as she pondered "the heat and violence of the poet's heart when caught and tangled in a woman's body."[47] This led her to speculate, in what has become one of her most cited pronouncements, "Indeed, I would venture to guess that Anon, who wrote so many poems without signing them, was often a woman" (*AROO*, 50, 51). But in putting material conditions front and center in her analysis, Woolf also aligns herself with the exposé of the forms of wastage that the war's all-too-conspicuous carnage obscures. As it did for Lodge, I am arguing, the much-celebrated slaughter of war provided Woolf with the occasion to repine—and thus to make "obtrusive"—"moral and intellectual slaughter" of another kind, although for Woolf that other kind had more to do with gender than class. The war is thus crucial to Woolf's articulation of female authorship even though—perhaps even because—it is not Woolf's explicit subject; the war becomes that which must be forgotten for other stories to come to

132   **CHAPTER 3**

light, helping to explain why the young men of the "lost generation" so volubly lamented in public and private memorialization rites hover as silent ghosts behind the "dead poets" Woolf would bring to life.

Woolf, of course, does not note such presences directly. Rather, her argument proceeds through what Melba Cuddy-Keane has called, in a different context, a "trope of substitution."[48] Most fully materialized in the insertion of Shakespeare's sister in the dead soldier-poet's place, such substitutions run through the entire work, shadowing even its most foundational claims: "A woman must have money and a room of her own if she is to write fiction" (*AROO*, 4). For a room of one's own—"let alone a quiet room or a sound-proof room" (*AROO*, 54)—is precisely what soldiers fighting in the trenches did not have.[49] Five hundred pounds a year, moreover, the symbolic figure Woolf selects as a necessary competency to achieve independence—the figure, incidentally, T. S. Eliot set as the minimum annuity that would allow him to quit his job at the bank and devote himself entirely to writing poetry—is a shorthand she first introduces in her diary in 1915 in reference to Leonard's brothers, enlisted in the war effort. Speculating on what they will do after the war is over, Woolf notes, "Cecil would like to stay in the Army, which however, one can't do, unless one has money, & neither of them has a penny. Five hundred a year is considerably more valuable than beauty or rank."[50] With the cessation of war, Woolf returns to this theme, writing on November 15, 1918: "The first effect of peace on our circle is to set Desmond loose, & to bring Gerald Shove up to London saying that he must find a way of making £500 a year. Before long the crowd of out of work intellectuals looking for places will be considerable."[51] When Woolf urges her readers to earn five hundred pounds a year, then, she inserts them in the place of the crowd of out-of-work intellectuals who preceded them: the returning soldiers, civilian volunteers, and conscientious objectors (COs), displaced by the war.

Woolf herself was not immune to the myth of a lost generation. "Our generation is daily scourged by the bloody war," she wrote in her diary in June 1920. "Even I scribble reviews instead of novels because of the thick skulls at Westminster & Berlin."[52] And a few months later she returned to the theme of the war's generational cost, noting that it is "life itself, I think sometimes, for us in our generation so tragic—no newspaper placard without its shriek of agony from some one."[53] In opening *A Room of One's Own* with a fictive visit to Oxbridge, however, Woolf situates her work where a particular version of the myth was at that moment being solidified: the myth of the loss of an entire generation of brilliant young men who served as junior officers in the war. In this context, Woolf's meditation on the cost of privilege—her critique of Oxbridge for the toll it extracts from those who are locked in as well

POSTHUMOUS WAS A WOMAN 133

as those who are locked out—takes on an added significance, given the very different way that cost was being construed in contemporary public discourse. For at the heart of this new myth was the idea that it was the elite who bore the heaviest burden of the war and that the loss of so many cultivated intelligences had left the world sadly and irreparably depleted. Woolf was well aware of the class bias that went into dominant versions of this myth. In her diary, for example, she repeats Arnold Toynbee's catty attack on the Oxford war heroes, apparently enjoying the opportunity to cut them down to size: "He knew the aristocratic heroes who are now all killed & celebrated— Grenfells, Lister, Shaw Steuart, Asquith, & loathed them. . . . He described their rows & their insolence & their quick snapping brains, always winning scholarships, & bullying & bringing bath chairs full of rats into Chapel. . . . It reads much like a Mrs Ward novel."[54] This myth, however, as Wohl suggests, was not entirely without foundation: "The younger the junior officer and the more privileged his education, the more likely he was to be killed."[55] The more likely, it could be added, he would have been a soldier-poet, given the intellectual emphases of the most privileged public schools and universities.[56] Indeed, "the propensity of Oxford and Cambridge men to join up early," and thus "to receive a commission from an early date," can be explained in part by the fact that they had the leisure as much as the character to do so; they were also, Winter explains, more likely "to serve in the infantry rather than in specialist units, where some scientifically trained undergraduates and graduates of other universities were directed," resulting in a disproportionate number of deaths. As Winter concludes, "The privileges enjoyed by Oxford and Cambridge men in 1914 were paid for by higher than average losses in the First World War."[57]

These losses did not go unnoticed by the guardians of these institutions. The imagined rooms in Oxbridge, for example, that Woolf describes in *A Room of One's Own* with such a mixture of envy and ambivalence were, in reality, at this time, well-established memorial sites. In Merton College, Oxford, for example, there was a tradition of putting up wooden plaques in rooms bearing the names of former inhabitants who died in the war.[58] And by the mid-1920s, virtually every college in Oxford and Cambridge had its own war memorial, where the names of "sons of the college" were inscribed in stone on a wall of the college or engraved in brass plaques. Even without these marks on the wall, however, the rooms were haunted by the young men whose university careers had been aborted or interrupted—often permanently. As Harold Macmillan recalled in old age, "I did not go back to Oxford after the war. . . . I just could not face it. To me it was a city of ghosts."[59] The "famous library" that bars Woolf's narrator from its premises, then, also has other ghosts to answer for,

134   **CHAPTER 3**

as Woolf herself recognized. In "These Are the Plans," for example, she laments the young poet "ordered from a Cambridge library to the front with the likelihood of death."[60] But the rooms were haunted as well by the motley crew of outsiders who became the temporary and unlikely occupants of these seats of privilege, when the colleges in Cambridge and Oxford were nearly emptied out: Belgian and Serbian refugees; soldiers in training; officers, who were sometimes billeted in college rooms and invited to eat at high table; injured and disabled soldiers; and even women, like Vera Brittain and her Oxford women cohort, displaced into vacated men's rooms in Oriel College, when Somerville College became a war hospital. The grounds as well, where Woolf's narrator is not allowed to walk, have their own history of prior usurpation, with the Trinity backs having been transformed into a temporary hospital and the King's and Clare cricket grounds a place where a permanent hospital was installed.[61]

Karen L. Levenback has argued that Woolf "studiously avoided ritualistic and stylized commemoration of the dead."[62] Not surprisingly, then, Woolf's accounts of her trips to Cambridge make no mention of the university's many memorial sites. Nor does she mention the statue of the returning soldier, "The Homecoming," which stands as one of Cambridgeshire's two major tributes to native sons who fought in the war. Although K. S. Inglis notes, "When you arrive in Cambridge by train, the first monument you pass on the way into town is a war memorial," Woolf never acknowledges taking in this sight.[63] Indeed, she appears to go out of her way *not* to notice it. Thus while she recounts, in February 1923, eight months after the unveiling of this memorial, her walk from the train station to the bottom of Station Road, she does not mention the monument that stands at precisely this location, the intersection of Station Road and Hills Road. And she does not mention it in any of her subsequent journeys to Cambridge, by train or car, including her October 1928 visits. The omission would appear to be pointed, given Woolf's sense of the unhomeliness of Cambridge for those not natural inheritors to the uninterrupted flow of gold and silver that endowed fellowships, chairs, and lectureships and furnished libraries and laboratories. For similar reasons, perhaps, "The Glorious Dead"—the soldier-poets and aristocratic heroes so obsessively celebrated in postwar commemorations—appear in *A Room of One's Own*, even on their home ground, only through their absence, through the figures Woolf installs in their place. Even when Woolf expressly raises a ghost or phantom, as in the possible twilight appearance of Jane Harrison—"could it be the famous scholar, could it be J—H—herself?" (*AROO*, 17)—the figure of the woman scholar appears where other ghosts might have been expected: the missing young university men who went to war and never returned.[64] In fact, when Woolf's narrator forbears even attempting to enter the chapel in Woolf's fictionalization of her Cambridge visit, she avoids the opportunity to witness its recently installed war memorial, for, as Angela Ingram notes, "At the time when Virginia Woolf spoke at Girton and Newnham the most recent addition had been—what else?—the King's College Chapel War Memorial to the fallen of the First World War."[65]

During the 1920s, as I have been demonstrating, Woolf clearly shared the British preoccupation with the war dead and the rites of commemoration, but not for the officially sanctioned reasons; instead, she turns this fixation on its head, recasting the "millions of the mouthless dead" as the silenced women writers of England or, as she puts it in "Thoughts on Peace in an Air Raid" (1940), an essay written in the midst of World War II, the "millions of bodies yet to be born."[66] In doing so, she anticipates, in some ways, the arguments that would inform revisionist histories of World War I at the end of the century. Gail Braybon, for example, summarizes this later development: "From the 1990s onwards, there has been an increasing interest in the complexity of the war's impact on different societies and social groups, and a growing recognition that there was no one 'war experience.'"[67] This awareness has led to a re-evaluation of the way our understanding of the war has been shaped by the experience and posthumous reputation of a relatively few privileged men, the members of the junior officer class, and more particularly the canonized war poets. Stacy Gillis, for example, has argued, "While the reasons for the resonance of these myths surrounding the literary output of the war have been the subject of much work, what has received less attention is the way in which the myths surrounding these literary figures have resulted in the exclusion of other accounts of the war, accounts which spoke to other kinds of experiences and traumas."[68]

A rich and considerable body of feminist scholarship has responded to this oversight by attempting to recover women's experience of the war by recovering the extensive body of women's "war poetry." As Claire Buck observes, "Poetry was the preeminent genre for women writing between 1914 and 1918," accounting for a quarter of the two thousand poems about the war published during this period.[69] In putting the woman artist, or would-be artist, in the dead soldier-poet's place, however, Woolf was not particularly interested in reclaiming women war poets, even where their poems might be seen to explore concerns aligned with hers. Woolf's letters and diaries, in fact, are filled with dismissive comments on contemporary "poetesses," some of them writing what has now come to be seen as war poetry. Rather, her text works through a complex series of displacements whereby the woman artist (in Woolf's formulation, a person who never existed) can, in effect, rescue "poetry"—what

136   **CHAPTER 3**

comes from the mind of the artist "whole and entire" and "unimpeded" (*AROO*, 58, 59)—from "war poetry," the poetry that is not poetry, that has taken its place.

Woolf's critiques of the war poets are in fact far-reaching. In her reviews of lesser-known poets, and in her private comments, Woolf repeatedly notes the failings of their poetry—poetry that most likely would never have been written and certainly would not have been published if it had not been for the war. Of Cecil Woolf's poems, for example, she admits, even as she begins setting them in type, "They're not good."[70] Of Geoffrey Dearmer, one of the soldier-poets she reviews alongside Sassoon, she acknowledges, his "imagination is neither strong enough nor trained enough to do the work he asks of it"—a criticism she tempers with the concession that "the war, perhaps, has brought these pieces forth before their time."[71] When it comes to the better-known poets, her objections are even more pointed. She expresses amazement, for example, that a trusted friend and fellow artist "thinks Rupert's poetry was poetry," admitting that she had come to think Brooke's poems "mere barrel organ music."[72] In the case of Sassoon, despite declaring him "able-bodied in his poetic capacity" and insisting he "requires no excuses to be made for him," she concedes that "it is difficult to judge him dispassionately as a poet, because it is impossible to overlook the fact that he writes as a soldier." She then goes on to say, "Mr Sassoon's poems are too much in the key of the gramophone at present, too fiercely suspicious of any comfort or compromise, to be read as poetry."[73] And of Sorley, an aspiring writer she admires because he "was experimental" and "always making an effort to shed the conventional style," she admits that he can ultimately do no more than indicate his promise, the direction his work would take not yet discernible.[74] Woolf, in fact, might have appreciated Vincent Sherry's wry formulation, "This dearth of 'combat modernist verse' might be taken as one more grim statistic of war dead—how many proto-modernist poets perished in the trenches?" It is not clear that Woolf could have identified any such protomodernists from her own reading and reviewing of these figures. She would, however, undoubtedly have appreciated Sherry's redirection of our gaze to "the other major modernist poets who lived out the war in London, specifically Pound and Eliot and Yeats."[75] For ultimately Woolf invokes her own dead poet to make space for "living" poetry. Thus she defends Eliot—"a true poet, I think; what they will call in a hundred years a man of genius"—from those too staid to appreciate him: "I say poetry is defunct; & Tom &c anyhow try to animate it."[76]

In *A Room of One's Own*, however, Woolf's chain of substitutions is effected through the agency of Shakespeare—Woolf's shorthand for poetry that is timeless, impersonal, and vital. For if Shakespeare's sister stands for great poetry, she does so, quite literally, by standing in for Shakespeare. In 1916, the year of the three hundredth anniversary of Shakespeare's death, a commemorative volume, *A Book of Homage to Shakespeare*, was published by Israel Gollancz, containing entries by 166 contributors from around the world. The volume, as John Lee explains, marked a radically scaled-down realization of the prewar project envisioned by Gollancz, "a memorial that would 'symbolize the intellectual fraternity of mankind in the universal homage' accorded to the genius of Shakespeare, the greatest Englishman"—a project to be implemented through the building of a new theater. The war rudely shattered Gollancz's dreams and, as Lee argues, also shifted the focus of the commemoration, the collection itself becoming "one of the very earliest anthologies of war poetry, and perhaps the first such international anthology. For, as is suggested by the title given within the book—*1916 / A Book of Homage to / Shakespeare*—many of the contributions, and most of the poetry in English, were more concerned with Shakespeare's relationship to the events of the Great War than with the arrival of the tercentenary itself."[77] Woolf, however, had other ideas about the uses to which Shakespeare should be put, and her own alternative memorial in *A Room of One's Own* could be seen to make good Gollancz's original intention; for Shakespeare's sister, with the promise she holds for intellectual sorority, provides a way to recuperate this "universal homage" by making the name of Shakespeare more truly universal.

Toward the end of *A Room of One's Own*, when the narrative has turned to the present, Woolf's narrator observes "a sudden splitting off of consciousness" if one is a woman, "say in walking down Whitehall," when "from being the natural inheritor of that civilisation, she becomes, on the contrary, outside it, alien and critical" (*AROO*, 101). Woolf's choice of Whitehall, of course, is not as arbitrary as she suggests—"say in walking down Whitehall." Indeed, Christine Froula has demonstrated that this "sentence cost its author some pains, particularly in respect to the pronouns," and the extended discussion it inaugurates is one of the most worked-over in Woolf's manuscripts.[78] The seat of government and power, Whitehall was also, as no contemporary would miss, the site of the Cenotaph and the annual Armistice Day ceremony.[79] In *Mrs. Dalloway*, it is "a pavement of monuments and wreaths" down which Peter Walsh walks, as he follows a group of young boys in uniform bearing a wreath to the empty tomb—a scene David Bradshaw has painstakingly illuminated.[80] Over the course of the 1920s, Whitehall continued to function as a ready designation for this site of remembrance and its requisite rituals. In May 1925, for example, Woolf records a bus trip—"crossed Westminster Bridge; admired the Houses of Parliament & their fretted lacy look; passed the Cenotaph, which L. compromised by sitting with his hat off all the way

138   **CHAPTER 3**

up Whitehall"—and a year later she notes, "Silver & crimson guard at White-hall; the cenotaph, & men bare heading themselves."[81] David Lloyd in fact notes, "In 1928 the Cenotaph was still referred to as 'the only monument in London which passersby naturally and of their own accord salute.'"[82] A focal point of collective mourning, the Cenotaph, it was proudly proclaimed at its unveiling, made England "one soul," "one body," "one society"—an assertion reiterated, and even fortified, following the first-ever radio broadcast of the Cenotaph ceremony and the two minutes of silence on November 11, 1928. As Adrian Gregory explains, "The crucial feature of the radio Silence was less the actual broadcast than the knowledge that the listener was one of millions doing exactly the same thing."[83] But if this society was not one (or not one to which women could naturally belong), Woolf, in appropriating the rhetoric of memorialization that surrounded the Cenotaph, constructs in her "fantas-tic" conclusion to *A Room of One's Own*, a society of a different sort: a dead poets society, whose members are linked by the "survival" of Shakespeare's sister in her living counterparts ("She lives in you and in me" [*AROO*, 117]).[84]

In thus configuring "Shakespeare's sister," Woolf turns her text into a kind of countermonument—one that calls attention to its own creation and its own essential constructedness. Indeed, from the outset, Woolf makes up "Judith Shakespeare"—and unmakes her—before our very eyes. In invoking the idea of the countermonument, I am drawing freely on James E. Young's formula-tion, which despite its very different context (Holocaust memorials in East-ern Europe) remains suggestive for thinking about how Woolf's figure operates. "By defining itself in opposition to the traditional memorial's task," Young argues, "the countermonument illustrates concisely the possibilities and limitations of all memorials everywhere. In this way, it functions as a valuable 'counterindex' to the ways time, memory, and current history intersect at any memorial site."[85] In contriving her own counterindex, Woolf calls attention to the public dimension of her art, for her monument does not exist apart from its public life. Its meaning *is* its performance, and what its audience makes of it, as Woolf's final flourish makes clear. Woolf's text thus functions as a mem-ory site—a testament to an absent monument, the unmarked grave where the remains of the missing Judith Shakespeare lie; and it remembers this absence by reproducing it, by allowing "the negative space of the absent monument" to "constitute its phantom shape."[86] In doing so, it demonstrates the empti-ness at the heart of the official culture's memorialization project. In this it per-forms an aesthetic feat Allyson Booth has identified as a particularly modernist response to the war: "inventing architectural shapes to stand in the place of those absent bodies." "Architecture," Booth writes, "supplied many modern-ists with a vocabulary for articulating loss." Modernist fiction, moreover, like war memorials, could point "toward corpses buried elsewhere, providing proxies for those bodies that were simultaneously absent and present, physically gone but stunningly felt in psychological and emotional terms."[87]

Read in this light, the choice of Elephant and Castle for the burial site—a late addition in the evolution of the text—underlines the countermemorial impulse, for it is a location that is markedly not sacrosanct, a locus of urban congestion if not yet urban blight, precisely the kind of location often favored for conceptual art. More specifically, it functions as a kind of negative space, a location defined by the fact that it is decidedly *not*-Whitehall and *not*-Westminster Abbey. Once dubbed the "Piccadilly of South London," by the late 1920s Elephant and Castle would already have seemed something of a distant outpost, "'desperately remote and inconvenient' and 'psychologically . . . miles away' from Whitehall."[88] As such it resists the museumification or rigidification of monuments like the Cenotaph, and it stands as a counterpoint to the official structures of ceremonial mourning—the structures that I suggested at the beginning of this chapter were turning London into a memorial tract. But if Woolf refuses the consolatory mourning offered by traditional memorial sites—and refuses the patriotic jingoism attached to them—she does so not simply by rejecting their structures but by inhabiting them, and thus opening them to the stories they have left out.[89] For this reason I see Woolf more aligned with Young than with Hynes, who offers a more straightforwardly oppositional notion of the modernist "anti-monument."[90] In occupying the space that the war carved out—the empty shelves where the books of the lost generation were *not*; the grave of the Unknown Warrior; the empty tomb of the Cenotaph—Woolf, I am suggesting, establishes the woman author in no-man's-land. And in taking up the mantle of authorship by raising a voice and body from the dead, Woolf offers yet another twist to the literary history she rewrites, proclaiming, as it were, "Posthumous was a woman."

A Room of One's Own, as has often been noted, is structured around a "series of turns and counter-turns."[91] I want to close this section with one of my own. Shakespeare's sister, it could be argued, represents in my final formulation a kind of special pleading for women; in another more utopian strain, *A Room of One's Own* gestures toward a time when gender as we know it will cease to be relevant. If Shakespeare's sister, then, functions as a kind of monument, like other countermonuments, it is an ephemeral one—a monument that encodes its own dissolution.[92] For when, at some unknown time in the future, Shakespeare's sister comes to life, "she" will cease to be a site of remembrance. Having been born, she will no longer require a monument to mark her failed existence. At the end of chapter 2, Woolf's narrator speculates, in the future

140   **CHAPTER 3**

perfect voice, on a time, "in a hundred years," when "women will have ceased to be the protected sex" (*AROO*, 40). There are no limits, she suggests, to what is imaginable should such a time come to pass: "Anything may happen when womanhood has ceased to be a protected occupation." "Remove that protection," she writes, in a disconcerting illustration, "expose them to the same exertions and activities, make them soldiers and sailors and engine-drivers and dock-labourers, and will not women die off so much younger, so much quicker, than men that one will say, 'I saw a woman today,' as one used to say, 'I saw an aeroplane'" (*AROO*, 40–41). In a passage laden with Great War references (the airplane not the least of them), women, Woolf suggests could become the new lost generation.[93] "But what bearing has all this upon the subject of my paper, Women and Fiction?" (*AROO*, 41), Woolf asks at the end of this section. If "Shakespeare's sister," as I have been suggesting, offers one way to make the connection by reminding us that "Posthumous was often a woman," Woolf's essay contains the possibility of a potentially even more radical suggestion. For if we recognize gender as socially constructed and historically contingent, we can, Woolf conjectures, envision a more perfect future whose refrain might be, "'Woman' is posthumous."[94]

The Monuments Woman

In the "Present Day" section of *The Years* (1937), Peggy and Eleanor Pargiter, riding in a taxi in central London, find themselves "stopped dead" under an imposing statue. "'Always reminds me of an advertisement of sanitary towels,' said Peggy, glancing at the figure of a woman in nurse's uniform holding out her hand."[95] The figure, though never named in the novel, is Edith Cavell, the British nurse, matron of a Red Cross hospital in Occupied Brussels, who was executed by the Germans in October 1915 for aiding Allied troops to cross the border, a death that earned her instant fame as a martyr.[96] Her statue, opposite the National Portrait Gallery in St. Martin's Place, London (figure 3.1), was one of hundreds of memorial sites erected in her name in the interwar years—sculptures, plaques, hospitals, nurses' rest homes, schools, street names, even a flower varietal designation—not to mention a run of biographies, plays, novels, and films, many bordering on hagiography. As Katie Pickles has documented, these homages to Cavell were a transnational phenomenon, extending well beyond the United Kingdom and even beyond the British Empire.[97] The rapidity with which they emerged, moreover, is striking; the earliest biographies appeared within weeks of her death while the first film, *Nurse and Martyr*, appeared less than two months after her execution. Even the name

Figure 3.1. Edith Cavell Memorial, St. Martin's Place, London (2018). Photo credit: Matthew Skwiat

"Edith" enjoyed a revival in the years following Cavell's death, Edith Piaf being the most famous beneficiary, creating a kind of collective living memorial to her. The passage in *The Years* has attracted considerable critical attention, but Woolf was not the first to comment on Cavell's commodification in these memorial structures. As Sue Malvern documents, at the time the London

142   CHAPTER 3

statue was unveiled in 1920, the *New Statesman* noted that "she looks like an advertisement for a complete nurse's outfit."[98] In Peggy's offhand comment, however, Woolf went further than most in exposing the gender politics that sustained the token inclusion of Cavell in the pantheon of war heroes. If, as I have been arguing throughout this chapter, "Shakespeare's sister" stands as the marker of the erasure of women in the postwar landscape of memorial culture, "Edith Cavell," I want to suggest here, may well be her evil stepsister, the woman who is remembered seemingly everywhere.

Only weeks after her death, when the Germans refused to surrender her body, a memorial service for Cavell was held in St. Paul's Cathedral, attended by the prime minister, various cabinet members, and other dignitaries, as well as hundreds of nurses and wounded soldiers. Reportedly, within fifteen minutes of opening its doors, the cathedral was filled to capacity. The service followed a day of national tribute—an event that some even argued should be made an annual observance.[99] The *Daily Telegraph* announced a public subscription to raise funds for a monument, and the city of Westminster offered the site, with the artist Sir George Frampton volunteering his labor. In May 1919, Cavell's exhumed body was transported to England, where a funeral service was held in Westminster Abbey (figure 3.2), followed by burial in the precincts of Norwich Cathedral near Cavell's birthplace in Swardeston. Anticipating, and in some respects rivaling, the reception of the Unknown Warrior, who was buried in Westminster Abbey a year and a half later, the event was marked by considerable fanfare: a special gun carriage, drawn by horses, was commissioned to carry the flag-draped casket (the same that would later transport the Unknown Warrior); an escort of soldiers accompanied the body; a procession of nurses preceded the coffin, along with a guard of women from the armed forces; military bands played while tens of thousands of people thronged the streets to pay respects to a national heroine; Queen Alexandra and Princess Victoria attended the ceremony. "No triumphant warrior and no potentate," the *New York Times* reported, "could have received a more impressive tribute than was paid today to the mortal remains of Miss Edith Cavell as they were borne through London on their way to their last resting place at Norwich" (May 16, 1919).

The Edith Cavell Memorial in London completed the ritual, the unveiling ceremony in March 1920 another occasion for marked public tribute. The memorial was unveiled by Queen Alexandra, with the queen of Belgium participating, and the flags of both countries draped the statue. The King's Guards formed a Guard of Honour, and "Last Post" and "Reveille" were performed.[100] The edifice itself is at once austere and massive, so much so that contemporary audiences were unsure whether its central feature, a large stone block mounting

FIGURE 3.2. Nurse Edith Cavell, funeral service in Westminster Abbey, London, as reported on the front page of the *Daily Mirror* (May 16, 1919). Photo credit: © John Frost Newspapers/Mary Evans Picture Library/agefotostock

into a cross, was sculpture or architecture.[101] Indeed, the monument is heftier—in height and weight—than the Cenotaph at Whitehall. Perched on a pedestal and rising to half the height of its immediate backdrop, an oversize figure of Cavell, sculpted in white Italian marble, stands poised against a huge mass of gray Cornish granite. Squarely above her head, the word "Humanity" appears, while a scroll proclaims, "For King and Country." Topping off the structure, and extending its height to forty feet, a stone cross rises, along with the half figure of a woman carrying a child. At the rear of the block, a relief of a lion crushing a serpent (the lion a traditional symbol of Britain) confirms the installation as a national monument.[102]

In fact, the Cavell memorial was one of the first public war memorials to be erected in central London and one of the few in England to highlight women's contributions to the war effort, the notable exceptions being the IWM's Women's War Shrine at Whitechapel Art Gallery, exhibited in October 1918 before the war was even over, and the restored stained glass window in York Minster, dedicated in 1925 to "the memory of the women of the Empire who gave

144   CHAPTER 3

their lives in the European War of 1914–1918"—a memorial the *British Legion Journal* dubbed "a women's cenotaph."[103] The Cavell memorial is one of the few war memorials, moreover, to a named individual and the only such to a woman.[104] In the more ubiquitous memorials, where individual names appear as but one among a list of others, women's names are scarcely present—absent entirely or dwarfed by the litany of male casualties. As Janet Watson points out, women who died in service overseas were buried with full military honors in military cemeteries alongside soldiers.[105] Back home, however, they were inconsistently and unevenly remembered on local war memorials and in local remembrance ceremonies, and they received few of the official tokens of recognition granted families of fallen soldiers.[106] Even when memorialized, they were subject to diminishing visibility. The immensely popular Women's War Shrine, for example, with its Roll of Honour of 500 women war casualties, was part of the *Women's War Work* exhibition that ran for only six weeks in its initial installation; it was revived in 1920, with another 300 names added, when the IWM moved to its "permanent" home in the Crystal Palace, but the shrine did not make it into the exhibition space in either Kew Gardens, where the IWM relocated in 1924, or Lambeth Place, where the IWM has been located since 1936.[107] Even in York Minster, as Vivien Newman has noted, the wooden doors bearing the names of 1,465 women are tucked away in a side chapel, rendering the women's deaths a kind of footnote, sidelined even at the site of their fullest commemoration.[108]

By contrast, both the timely completion and the prominent public position of the Cavell monument, as Pickles has argued, signal "Cavell's important place in the commemoration of the Great War"—and in national remembrance more generally.[109] Its close proximity to Trafalgar Square aligned it with Nelson's Column, marking it as a stop on what Sue Malvern has described as "a processional axis of commemoration"; the subsequent installation of the permanent Cenotaph in nearby Whitehall and the tomb of the Unknown Warrior in Westminster Abbey cemented Cavell's position as a cornerstone of "the national war shrine."[110] Cavell, however, remained the lone woman occupying this position—her situation, in almost every respect, anomalous, starting with the fact of her body being repatriated. As Hughes notes, "She was remarkable because she was the exception, the only woman to have become one of the famous war dead who could rival in renown the Unknown Warrior."[111] If the near-universal reverence Cavell was accorded suggests a kind of parity between men's and women's sacrifices in the war effort, this parity proved short-lived; as Watson has documented, the postwar years saw the increasing erasure of women from the public war narrative—a process nearly complete by the time *A Room of One's Own* was published. Cavell's posthumous celebration, then, marked her as the exceptional woman rather than the representative one, and in this nothing could be more different from what Woolf imagined for Judith Shakespeare, absent from history and buried in an unmarked grave in an out-of-the-way location. Indeed, as Pickles notes, Cavell was decidedly "not an afterthought, or a forgotten figure later recovered."[112] In fact, Cavell's grave in Norwich, like that of the Unknown Warrior, became a popular postwar pilgrimage destination, as did the cell in Brussels where Cavell spent her last hours.[113]

Yet Cavell, one might argue, was every bit as "made up" as Woolf's fictional creation, her "life" an entirely posthumous construction.[114] From the moment of her death, Cavell's story was appropriated for its propaganda value and accordingly sensationalized. She was, in effect, transformed into a poster child for recruitment, a tool so powerful the bishop of London once suggested that further recruiting campaigns would be superfluous (figure 3.3). Her image, plastered on posters, broadsides, calendars, and postcards, cast Cavell as the embodiment of imperiled British womanhood and her death as the ultimate emblem of German brutality. Indeed, despite the fact that Cavell was a forty-nine-year-old professional woman, early representations projected her as young and defenseless. Although the London statue presents a mature, even sternly formidable, figure, traces remain of this ideological baggage. The banner "For King and Country," mirrored on the reverse side of the monument by the words "Faithful unto Death," locates Cavell's significance, like that of her male compatriots, in her patriotic sacrifice. The other words that flank the four sides of the central block of the monument—"Humanity," "Devotion," "Fortitude," "Sacrifice"—reinforce this message, lifting her out of the realm of the merely human into one of universalizing abstractions.

Beneath her feet, the particulars of her death appear in an inscription: "Edith Cavell, Dawn, Brussels, October 12th 1915." With these words, the monument announces itself as arguably the war's first "Shot at Dawn" memorial. Inviting viewers to visualize her execution, the words fix Cavell as "The Woman the Germans Shot," as the title of a 1918 silent film dubbed her, a woman celebrated because of the way she died. Indeed, the widespread outrage generated by her death was fueled by the perception that to carry out such a sentence on a woman—a woman, moreover, who had devoted her life to the selfless care of others—transgressed all bounds of civilized behavior. Left unquestioned in this outburst of righteous indignation was the morality of the "legitimate" executions carried out by the British and the Allied forces—on foreign nationals and on their own citizens.[115] By the time of Cavell's death, seven "enemy civilians," all of them foreign nationals and all of them men, had been shot at dawn as German spies in the Tower of London, only the first of these

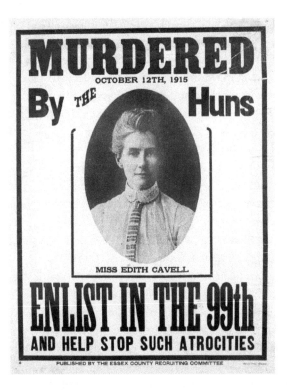

FIGURE 3.3. Edith Cavell enlistment poster. Produced by Essex County Recruiting Committee © Imperial War Museum (Art.IWM PST 12217)

cases widely covered in the press.[116] Even less visible to the public, more than fifty British soldiers had been shot at dawn for cowardice, desertion, and other military offenses—a number that would rise to more than three hundred by the end of the war. Not until 2001, as I will discuss in chapter 4, would these other shot-at-dawn casualties, "the men the British shot," be commemorated in an official memorial—a monument, like the one to Cavell, that also foregrounds an oversize figure ostensibly facing a firing squad (see figure I.8)—and not until 2006 would they be officially pardoned.

At the base of the statue, in letters considerably smaller than the overtly patriotic exhortations, a legend reads, "Patriotism is not enough. I must have no hatred or bitterness for anyone"—allegedly Cavell's last words, spoken on the eve of her execution. "The only fine thing that was said in the war," Woolf has Eleanor proclaim in *The Years*, as she reads aloud the words on the pedestal, although Peggy immediately deflates the sentiment by pointing to the words' ineffectuality: "'It didn't come to much,' said Peggy sharply."[117] Significantly, however, Peggy's disclaimer notwithstanding, more than twenty years after Cavell's death, Woolf assumes an audience that will recognize the words even though she never actually quotes them—indeed, even though she never identifies Cavell by name. In *Three Guineas*, Woolf would take Cavell's stance one step further, suggesting that for women, as outsiders, patriotism was irrelevant—"as a woman, I have no country"[118]—but however insufficient the words may have been in themselves, they remained for Woolf a significant touchstone. About a year after the publication of *A Room of One's Own*, for example, Woolf cites Cavell's words, although misremembered, in a letter to Ethel Smyth: "And enthusiasm (as Nurse Cavell said), is not enough. No, nor discrimination either."[119] The actual words, "Patriotism is not enough," also resonated for the greater British public—so much so that when the Cavell statue was originally unveiled in 1920 without the words being included on it, there were immediate protests. Four years later, after a campaign spearheaded by the National Council of Women of Great Britain and Ireland, the Labour government added the words, though not without some vocal opposition.

What precisely the words meant, however, was by no means self-evident, nor was it certain that these were the exact words Cavell spoke on the occasion or that they were in fact her last ones.[120] Contemporary responses to the sentiment expressed thus fell along a wide spectrum. At one extreme were those like Sylvia Pankhurst, who registered the words—words that "made one's heart thrill"—as a clear rebuke to the warmongers. A 1915 cartoon by Herbert Cole, for example, in Pankhurst's *Dreadnought*, derides the government's distortion of Cavell's message, upended within months of its utterance, into a rationale for the escalation of militaristic aggression.[121] In his preface to *Saint Joan* (1924), George Bernard Shaw followed suit, representing Cavell as an "arch heretic" for resisting the partisanship patriotism dictates—for declaring in the middle of war that "patriotism is not enough" and assisting Allied and enemy soldiers alike, without making distinctions between them. And he excoriated the British for their moral cowardice in erecting a statue to Cavell and omitting her words from it.[122] Others, significantly more numerous, however, saw in her words no more than the perfect expression of her Christian convictions—a set of beliefs that did not necessarily challenge the established order of things. The same bishop of London who in eulogizing Cavell represented her death as the solution to Britain's recruitment crisis did not hesitate to repeat the words when blessing the statue at the monument's unveiling. While some at the time undoubtedly heard in the words an expression of radical pacifism, as have some later commentators, many who responded to the uplifting humanitarian message saw outright rejection neither of patriotism nor of participation in the war

148   **CHAPTER 3**

effort. As Adrian Gregory suggests, "'Pacifist' attitudes could also be complex. A disdain for the traditional elements of patriotism did not prevent the possibility of approval for certain varieties of military action."[123]

Woolf, who once remarked, "We were all C.O.'s in the Great war," may well have discerned in Cavell's words a vindication of the antiwar stance of her Bloomsbury cohort.[124] Lytton Strachey, for example, purportedly proclaimed that his "one ardent desire" was to see Lloyd George, as one of the prime instigators of the war, "publicly castrated at the foot of Nurse Cavell's statue."[125] Like Strachey, Woolf was surely outraged by the way Cavell's image was manipulated first to ramp up the war effort and later, after the war's cessation, to uphold the "big words" that continued to provide its retrospective justification. She may well have sympathized with Cavell's family, who purportedly declared they wanted no monuments to her, if not necessarily for all the same reasons.[126] Whether Cavell would have identified with Woolf's particular brand of pacifism remains a more open question. As Michèle Barrett has argued, Woolf's "we" ("We were all C.O.'s") was actually "a tiny number of cases" out of the relatively small group of COs during the war, the majority of whom resisted war for religious reasons—reasons perhaps closer to Cavell's sentiments, if she were indeed a pacifist, than Bloomsbury's high-sounding rhetoric.[127] Cavell's other "last words," moreover, spoken immediately before her execution—"My conscience is quiet. I die for God and my country"—are decidedly less at odds with the patriotic sentiments inscribed on her monument than the "last words" later appended to it. According to Pickles, it was "these last words that were widely reported around the world," as opposed to the more famous "Patriotism is not enough" statement.[128] Further complicating the matter, the question of the extent to which Cavell may have been involved in providing intelligence to the British remains unsettled, with new evidence of espionage surfacing as late as 2015, raising the question of whether the pacifist Cavell is any less a posthumous construction than the patriotic exemplar.[129]

Today, the Cavell monument is listed as a "peace memorial" on the Peace Pledge Union (PPU) website, and the London branch of the Women in Black, a worldwide network of women committed to "peace with justice," holds monthly antiwar vigils at its location; it was a stop on the 2014 Peace Walk through London, an event staged to coincide with the hundredth anniversary of the assassination of Archduke Ferdinand. In the 1920s, however, such a coherent antiwar message would have been less clearly legible. As the history of her commemoration demonstrates, Cavell could be many things to many people—martyr, saint, patriot, exemplar of British womanhood, even honorary soldier—but full-fledged pacifist was at best only one of them, and one that could not be readily sustained in the official sites of remembrance. Hence the competing rhetoric that adorns the London monument. In fact, during the war, and for some time after it, actual card-carrying pacifists—the men who refused to fight and the men and women who supported them; the COs and the antiwar activists; the leaders of the No-Conscription League and the Women's International League for Peace and Freedom—were more likely to be deemed treasonous than to have statues erected to them.

Cavell, by contrast, inspired statues in abundance. "During the interwar years," Pickles has argued, "there were arguably more statues, busts and plaques made to commemorate Edith Cavell than any other woman of her generation." Indeed, images of Cavell literally reduplicated themselves, with replicas of a bust sculpted by Frampton distributed to a variety of institutions around the world and throughout the British Empire. Even Cavell's dog was embalmed as a sacred relic, eventually finding a home in the Imperial War Museum.[130] At stake in the inordinate attention accorded this single woman was the question of how, at this historical moment, women could be remembered and represented—a question clearly on Woolf's mind when she invented Shakespeare's sister. Indeed, with the afterlives of men taking on ritualized patterns and assuming the force of a national obsession, there was little space left for alternative forms (and subjects) of remembrance; women, given their very different experience—both in the war and out of it—could not easily be accommodated into existing memorial paradigms except, as in the case of Cavell, as evident exceptions. For postwar memorial culture, then, remembrance of women was not, as in the case of men who died, a recognized obligation but rather a problem to be tackled—a problem that has persisted into the twenty-first century, as the controversy surrounding the Memorial to the Women of World War II, unveiled in Whitehall in 2005, demonstrates.[131]

Cavell's deification suggests the degree to which public recognition in her time depended on conformity to traditional feminine values, to the fact that, as Nicoletta Gullace puts it, "As a nurse ministering to the sick and wounded, Cavell glowed with the idealized aura of nurturing femininity."[132] Indeed, one of the early objections to the London monument was that Cavell did not appear feminine enough. This could be repaired, however, at the symbolic level. The inclusion at the top of the monument of the figure of a mother and child—a figure, some have argued, so superfluous to the main design that it cannot even be seen properly—demonstrates that even an unmarried and childless woman cannot be honored outside the maternal context. As Jane Marcus has forcefully argued, it is precisely these fetishized roles—nurse and mother—that Woolf was challenging in her late works, and in her invocation of the Cavell monument in particular.[133]

150   **CHAPTER 3**

The commemoration of Cavell, replete with military pomp, posthumous honors, medals, plaques, and pageantry, was nothing if not excessive.[134] With the London monument as its flagship, it could be seen as a ready-made argument for why, as Woolf would insist in *Three Guineas*, women should reject all such acts of ceremonial recognition and all such marks of personal distinction. Cavell, indeed, as embodied in the memorial structures representing her, reads like a cautionary figure for what Woolf described there as the pitfalls awaiting the *living* professional woman: "You will have to wear certain uniforms and profess certain loyalties. If you succeed in those professions the words 'For God and the Empire' will very likely be written, like the address on a dog-collar, round your neck" (*TG*, 85). But Cavell's commemoration reads, I would suggest, as an even more powerful warning of the pitfalls awaiting the *dead* (professional) woman, exposing what happens when the body is given over to the state and its official structures of commemoration. It thus offers a clue as to what Woolf may have had in mind when, in *A Room of One's Own*, she contrived her undecorated antiheroine, and it helps to explain why Woolf chose not to raise a tomb to Judith Shakespeare, not even a small one. For, as Woolf recognized, Cavell's posthumous glorification is only an extreme example of the way afterlives are always constructed to serve the needs of the living, with consequences, Woolf insists, that need to be registered.

Crucially, Cavell's outsize presence crowds out the space for alternative configurations of women—in the war effort or, as important, out of it. Dick Sheppard, for example, the vicar of St. Martin-in-the-Fields, worried in 1920 that Cavell would be remembered at the expense of other women, writing in the *St Martin's Review* "that this memorial should have been dedicated to all women at war, with Edith Cavell taking a leading position."[135] Sheppard, who would found the Peace Pledge Union in 1934 and become one of the movement's most powerful and charismatic advocates, may have later come to think of the memorial differently, but his comments point to a significant issue: the very visibility of Cavell's name and image renders anonymous all the other women who contributed to the war effort.[136] The monument privileges, moreover, one kind of war work—work conceived as woman's "natural" occupation—over other forms of women's labor more generally performed by working-class women: munitions work, service in the auxiliary armed forces, land work, motor transport work, and so forth.[137] Prominently sculpted in nurse's uniform, Cavell thus visibly encodes dominant gender and class assumptions.

As one of only a handful of monuments honoring women, moreover, the Cavell memorial raises the question of whether war work (and wartime sacrifice) is what women should be celebrated for, their only achievement worth mentioning. Indeed, in co-opting Cavell for the war dead and making her a celebrity, official culture could be said to have effectively masculinized her according to its own needs and processes, even as it continued to accentuate her feminine attributes. In doing so, it foreclosed other ways of thinking about women's contributions to culture and society. For this reason, perhaps, in *A Room of One's Own*, it is Shakespeare's sister, not Tommy's sister, who commands Woolf's attention, allowing her to short-circuit the conventional process by which afterlives are created.[138] In *Three Guineas*, Woolf argues that far from a spontaneous outpouring of women's genuine patriotism, the rush with which they threw themselves into the war effort was a demonstration of the desperation middle-class women felt with the stultifying conditions of their existence: "How else can we explain that amazing outburst in August 1914, when the daughters of educated men who had been educated thus rushed into hospitals, some still attended by their maids, drove lorries, worked in fields and munition factories, and used all their immense stores of charm, of sympathy, to persuade young men that to fight was heroic, and that the wounded in battle deserved all her care and all her praise?" (*TG*, 49). In the Outsiders' Society that Woolf envisions in *Three Guineas*, entry into her club requires disavowing precisely these activities; women, she argues, must "refuse in the event of war to make munitions or nurse the wounded," and they must pledge themselves "not to incite their brothers to fight, or to dissuade them, but to maintain an attitude of complete indifference" (*TG*, 126–127). As she acknowledges, however, with the exception of inciting men to fight, most of these activities were "mainly discharged by the daughters of working men," and thus not overly burdensome for middle-class women to repudiate.[139] In urging her audience to disavow these things, Woolf is, in effect, engaging in a process of preemptive de-memorialization, dismantling the grounds on which conventional commemoration rested.

In demanding this refusal, moreover, Woolf was invoking a suppressed history of women's wartime activities by reviving arguments made during the war by antiwar suffrage advocates—women who resisted the jingoistic call of the Women's Social and Political Union, led by Emmeline and Christabel Pankurst, to suspend political activism and throw themselves into supporting the war effort or who broke with the National Union of Women's Suffrage Societies over its more measured endorsement of the war's necessity. Many suffragists and suffragettes refused to engage in war-related work, confining their efforts to relief of noncombatants, and many refused to assist the government to recruit men to fight or women to work in munitions. Others actively opposed the war through participation in the peace movement's various branches.[140] These women, however, have suffered a double erasure. In the commemoration of women's war work—a crucial feature of the IWM's

152   **CHAPTER 3**

earliest instantiations between 1918 and 1924—there was no space (and no will) to acknowledge the war resisters, especially the most militant ones.[141] Women's acts of resistance to the war, moreover, have remained largely invisible in the dominant narrative of the suffrage movement that solidified in the 1920s and 1930s—one that promoted the notion of women's war work and women's demonstration of patriotism as the decisive factors in the awarding of the vote to them in 1918.[142] As many scholars have noted, however, the initial restriction of suffrage to women over thirty who met a property qualification, not expanded to include all women until 1928, meant most women munitions workers, the largest group of women war workers, would have been excluded from the vote; this did not, however, deter the promotion of a version of history that made their enfranchisement its rhetorical centerpiece.[143] In this "official" narrative, Cavell was frequently invoked as an exemplary instance of women's worthiness for full citizenship. Herbert Asquith, for example, "attributed his 'conversion' to women's suffrage to the heroic actions of women like Edith Cavell, who had 'taught the bravest man amongst us a supreme lesson of courage,'" while Lord Haldane "battled a last-ditch effort to derail women's suffrage in the House of Lords" by pointing out the tremendous sacrifices made by women, noting, "There have been women, like Edith Cavell, whose names will not be forgotten, women who have died under shell fire, died under bombardment, died by bullet wounds just the same as men have died."[144] This argument, whatever its legitimacy, had sufficient currency at the time for Woolf to rail against it. In *Three Guineas*, she goes so far as to question whether women who opposed the war should refuse the vote granted under such false pretenses.[145] Gullace suggests that the situation might be even more complicated and the vote even more compromised, for if the Representation of the People Act of 1918 was primarily intended to enfranchise soldiers, as many historians have argued, the corollary of this was the disenfranchisement of pacifists and COs—men who failed to fulfill their patriotic duty. In extending the vote to a subset of women, Gullace argues, the government found a means to lend this disenfranchisement legitimacy. "Rarely, if ever," she argues, "has so much parliamentary capital been spent to disenfranchise so few men."[146]

Seen in this light, Woolf's choice of Shakespeare's sister as an object of remembrance begins to feel prescient, the advance guard of the Outsiders' Society that Woolf would invent in *Three Guineas*. If the fictional poet does not share the commitment to end war that Woolf would later exact from the members of her imagined organization, she, significantly, does nothing to enable or promote it. Woolf endows her with no opinions on the subject. Rather, as a poet (and pointedly *not* a war poet), she stands as a salient reminder that there is something other than "women at war" worthy of celebration at this historical juncture. As such, she appears as Cavell's antithesis: not saintly, not passive, not pure, and most important, given the very different circumstances of her life, not in the service of the war machine, even if only, as in Cavell's case, perhaps unwittingly. Whether or not the comparison was intentional, in creating Shakespeare's sister, Woolf registers an implicit protest to Cavell's hyperpresence as the acceptable face of women's sacrifice and of women's noteworthy achievements. Shakespeare's sister, by contrast, like Aphra Behn, is decidedly not respectable. Nor is she selfless. She demands nothing less than a fundamental shift in the grounds of remembrance. For unlike Cavell, she stands as a presence to be remembered not for how she died—the underlying logic of established memorial structures—but for the new lives that will make her actuality possible. In doing so, she figures a new kind of posthumous existence—one that repudiates the kind of posthumous lives the postwar memorial culture popularized and Cavell epitomized in favor of one that affirms what has yet to be thought into existence.

Such a reading would locate *A Room of One's Own* as more of a transitional work—between the aesthetic phase of Woolf's career, culminating in *The Waves*, and the more overtly social and political one, culminating in *Three Guineas* and *The Years*—than has generally been recognized.[147] It would underline the way *Three Guineas* functions as a sequel and companion piece to *Room*, as Woolf alleged when she first imagined it, and it would allow us, retrospectively, to read *Room* as a "pre-meditation" on the feminist and pacifist concerns of her later writings. It might even allow us to see Woolf's deflections from the war as a form of engagement with it—a means, as Melba Cuddy-Keane suggests of an earlier essay, for Woolf to "confront the war by invoking an alternative discourse—one, in her view, more in accord with the interests of democracy and peace."[148] For the collective work Woolf urges her audience to undertake in the name of Shakespeare's sister—work performed in the service of freeing (women's) thought and cultivating (women's) creativity—is precisely what Woolf offers in "Thoughts on Peace in an Air Raid" as the work that women ("not this one body in this one bed but millions of bodies yet to be born") must do to "think peace into existence."[149]

In 1928, when Woolf was preparing the lectures that would eventuate in *A Room of One's Own*, Cavell was once more in the public spotlight with the appearance of Herbert Wilcox's silent film *Dawn*—an account of Cavell's life as a nurse and of her trial and execution; the subject matter was perceived as so politically sensitive that a major censorship controversy grew up around it.[150] Even before its release—indeed, even before the film was completed—there were efforts to suppress it on the grounds that it might reignite wartime animosities. At

154   **CHAPTER 3**

the instigation of the German embassy, Sir Austen Chamberlain, secretary of state for foreign affairs, urged its suppression, questioning whether its release would be politic, given current efforts at international cooperation and understanding. At the same time, Lord Birkenhead, secretary of state for India, decried in the *Daily Telegraph* the exploitation for profit of "the agony and the sacrifice of the noblest woman whom the war produced"—a sentiment apparently shared by Chamberlain.[151] These cries of outrage ironically point up the way the government itself had sensationalized Cavell's death for its own purposes during and after the war, but they were nonetheless effective. So persistent were the allegations of exploitation that Wilcox "promised to devote a portion of the profits to the Edith Cavell Rest Homes for Nurses."[152] Both Wilcox, the film's director, and Reginald Berkeley, its scriptwriter, insisted that the film was meant as an antiwar statement—an indictment, in Berkeley's words, "not of the German people nor even of the German Army, but of the whole damnable system that produced the War of 1914 and of the hideous obligations which the rules of war throw upon unwilling people" (*Times*, February 20, 1928); nonetheless, the British Board of Film Censors refused to issue it a certificate on the grounds that it was "inexpedient in present circumstances" to revive such an inflammatory subject, the implication being that it would stoke anti-German feelings that would make a new war more likely.[153] The London County Council, however, followed by other local authorities, overruled this decision, allowing the film to be shown in numerous locations. For about a month, beginning in February, well before the film's scheduled release, the controversy occupied the London newspapers, with impassioned letters and editorials appearing on a nearly daily basis; the limited release of the film in April 1928 revived the public attention that had earlier greeted its announcement. What the discourse surrounding the film made explicit was that no telling of Cavell's story, however careful, could avoid misperception if not misrepresentation, and that Cavell could not be separated from the ways she had been instantiated in modern memory. Even Cavell's "own" words on the publicity poster, "I Must Have No Hatred or Bitterness towards Anyone," were not enough to quell the controversy. Rather, the episode exposed the limits of deploying Cavell as a potential spokesperson for an antiwar message—an object lesson in the way memory is constructed, revised, and regulated.

In *A Room of One's Own*, Woolf imagines a different kind of heroine and a different kind of memorial structure—a monument that does not exist in material form for a person who never existed. As a subject not bound by the usual rites of memorialization and their motives and constituencies, Shakespeare's sister can present herself as fully available for Woolf's fictionalization. And Woolf can be transparent about her agenda and her fabrications. Ironically, this fictional construction may now enjoy a more robust afterlife than the woman the world vowed never to forget. When London Remembers, a website that publishes its mission as "aiming to capture all memorials in London," was launched in 2004, it announced the Edith Cavell Memorial as "the obvious memorial to choose" for its first featured entry.[154] But to a large extent, by this time Cavell herself had already faded from memory, with people regularly passing the memorial without even noticing it, let alone understanding its significance; Cavell's name, moreover, no longer provoked immediate and universal recognition. As Pickles has argued, "For all the cries that Cavell would be remembered forever, by the end of the twentieth century her memory has largely disappeared in both the metropolitan and colonial areas that had belonged at the time of her death to either the Allied world, the British world, or both."[155] The Royal Mint's creation in 2015 of a five-pound commemorative coin to honor her memory on the centenary of her execution may, paradoxically, be further evidence of the extent to which she has become a mere relic—a figurehead on a coin that does not circulate as currency.

In 1923, far from the shadow cast by the Cavell monument in the center of London, a Canadian artist, Dorothy Stevens, carved a memorial plaque to conscientious objectors, recording the names of seventy-three British COs then known to have died as the result of their wartime ill-treatment—harsh prison conditions, grueling hard labor, force-feeding, near starvation.[156] At the peak of the war memorial frenzy, this obscure antiwar plaque was an anomaly, a tribute to the unsung casualties of a war its dedicatees had unflaggingly protested. Created at the suggestion of a German woman, the secretary of the German section of War Resisters International, the plaque was initially installed at the headquarters of the League of War Resisters in Berlin, although after several relocations, it eventually found its way to London thirty-five years later.[157] The German location was, of course, symbolic, a testament to the fact that resistance to war transcends nationalism and national identity. Interestingly, the erection of the plaque in 1923 coincided with the push to have Cavell's famous "dying words," "Patriotism is not enough. I must have no hatred or bitterness for anyone," added to her memorial in London—a gesture, as its proponents explained, toward international understanding. Given the resistance to even this modest gesture, it is hard to imagine a conscientious objectors' memorial finding a welcome home in England in the 1920s.[158] That posthumous might be a pacifist, as the scroll of names testifies, was simply not part of the national narrative at that historical moment.

In the intervening years, the situation has shifted considerably. Today, in Bloomsbury, amid Virginia Woolf's old haunts, a dedicated memorial redresses this oversight. Unveiled in 1994, the Conscientious Objectors' Commemorative

156   **CHAPTER 3**

Stone stands on the north side of Tavistock Square (figure 3.4); across the square, near where Woolf's house once stood, Woolf herself is commemorated by a small bronze statue, installed in 2004—a copy of the bust sculpted by Stephen Tomlin in 1931, not long after the publication of *A Room of One's Own*.[159] Both memorials are fittingly understated. Almost blending into the background, the memorial to the COs—essentially a rough slab of slate—is one Woolf might have appreciated, despite her disdain for monuments. It is the type of peace memorial Edith Cavell could only ever imperfectly figure. Indeed, it is the opposite of the massive statue erected to Cavell and of the conventional war memorials that the Cavell monument mimics. Where the Cavell memorial occupies a space in central London near important national landmarks and cultural institutions, the Conscientious Objectors' Commemorative Stone occupies a countercultural stronghold: Tavistock Square is home to a number of other peace monuments, including the Hiroshima tree (planted in August 1967) and the Gandhi statue (unveiled in 1968). The conditions under which the Conscientious Objectors' Commemorative Stone emerged are also markedly different from those surrounding the Cavell monument. No royalty presided over the unveiling of the Conscientious Objectors' Commemorative Stone, and no assemblage of powerful interests comparable to the Cavell Memorial Committee underwrote its installation. Instead, it was installed and created under the auspices of the PPU, which sponsors an annual Conscientious Objectors Day celebration at its location.

Unlike the Cavell monument, no sculptures adorn the memorial, and no high-sounding words are etched into the face of the stone. In fact, no individual names are recorded for posterity. Rather, like the figure of Shakespeare's sister, it is a blank slate, in this instance literally so, for viewers to project upon. An inset plaque reads, "To all those who have established and are maintaining the right to refuse to kill / Their foresight and courage give us hope." Around the four sides of the plaque, creating a frame, the inscription reads: "To commemorate men & women / conscientious objectors to military service / all over the world & in every age," while the base of the plaque proclaims, "This stone was dedicated on International Conscientious Objectors Day." Where Woolf imagined that the future accomplishments of women could breathe retrospective life into her fictional figure, the Conscientious Objectors' Commemorative Stone invokes past exemplars to inspire future resisters. Foremost among these predecessors are the British COs of World War I, as the PPU website makes explicit. This was the group, moreover, singled out for a high-profile event staged at the memorial site in the run-up to the Great War's centenary. Sponsored by First World War Peace, a consortium of peace societies, the 2014 Conscientious Objectors Day celebration honored the "First

FIGURE 3.4. Conscientious Objectors' Commemorative Stone, Tavistock Square, London. Photo credit: Thomas Hahn

World War COs and women peace workers who said No to the war" by showcasing descendants and archiving the stories of COs and peace workers. As with war memorial ceremonies, the ritual included the reading of names and laying of flowers, as well as the production of brochures with thumbnail portraits and minibiographies. As Woolf so famously did with her creation of Shakespeare's sister, the promoters of the event were engaging in a project to recover those "absent from history" (*AROO*, 45).[160] Like Woolf, moreover, they invoked a kind of magical thinking by which the work they do today might change the past's trajectory—might transform, as the consortium's title suggests, war into peace. The proximity to Woolf of this belated memorial invites reflection: it reminds us of the space she carved out to "say No to war," in *A Room of One's Own* and in her later, more explicitly pacifist writings. As I have tried to suggest in this chapter, Woolf did this by occupying the space of remembrance, refiguring it for new ends and still-to-be-imagined futures.

CHAPTER 4

Absent from Memory

Shot at Dawn and the Spectacle of Belated Remembrance

In Bailleulmont Communal Cemetery in Pas-de-Calais, France, in the small plot devoted to graves for British soldiers from World War I, a singular text appears on the headstone of Grave B 12, Private A. Ingham: "SHOT AT DAWN / ONE OF THE FIRST TO ENLIST / A WORTHY SON / OF HIS FATHER" (figure 4.1). The cryptic words allude to a fact that was generally kept secret in the three hundred and more comparable instances: that the soldier was killed by his own comrades, the subject of a judicial execution. Allowed the regulation sixty-six characters for a personal inscription, George Ingham, the father of Private Albert Ingham of the Manchester Regiment, chose these defiant words to adorn his son's gravestone. Such a dedication was not what the architects of the Imperial War Graves Commission (IWGC) envisioned when, in the early 1920s, they invited the next of kin to personalize the uniform headstones erected for the Great War's fallen soldiers. Rather, they hoped for something "of the nature of a text or prayer," something tasteful and comforting, as Sir Frederick Kenyon suggested in his 1918 report to the commission on the design of the cemeteries.[1] Surprisingly, perhaps, given the kinds of sentiments that the commission sometimes rejected, the inscription was not censored.[2] Certainly, the words chosen by Ingham stand out from the more anodyne sentiments—the biblical quotations, the formulaic expressions of grief and assurances of remembrance—scattered among the hundreds of thousands of tombstones in the IWGC's military cemeteries. The bald declaration, "shot at

158

ABSENT FROM MEMORY 159

FIGURE 4.1. Grave of Private Albert Ingham, Bailleulmont Communal Cemetery in Pas-de-Calais, France. Photo credit: Simon Godly

dawn," moreover, flies in the face of the commission's 1922 internal directive not to allude to the cause of death or differentiate in any way the graves of the soldiers executed by order of Field General Courts-Martial—a decision designed as much to appease the families of the other soldiers buried in their vicinity as to protect the families of the executed soldiers from the embarrassment of public disclosure. The compromise solution suggests that the question of

160   **CHAPTER 4**

containing posthumous harm was part of the calculus behind the IWGC's thinking from the beginning—whether its concern was the (further) harm to the executed soldiers and their families or the harm to the "honorable dead" who might be contaminated by their presence.

If Ingham's choice of inscription breached the IWGC's notions of discretion, his fighting words also violated, on a more personal level, the expected response to news of such a tragedy: to succumb to shame and retreat into silence. Indeed, at the time George Ingham demanded this inscription, the last thing one would have expected was for a family to parade the circumstances of a loved one's execution. As it turns out, three other shot-at-dawn soldiers are also buried in Bailleulmont Communal Cemetery, including Ingham's "pal," Alfred Longshaw, with whom he signed up, with whom he went absent, and with whom he was executed. None of the others bear any personal inscription on their headstones.[3] In contrast to what we now know about how other families handled the situation—some disowned the offenders, hushed over their deaths, or consigned their stories to the realm of dark family secret—Ingham's testimonial stands as a remarkable assertion of pride in his son's sacrifice and in his filial relation. Pointedly, the inscription does not mention the crime for which his son was purportedly executed: desertion. Instead, it points a finger at the government and military institutions that initiated and then covered up these dark proceedings. Indeed, part of the anger that prompted this tombstone inscription arose from the fact that Ingham only learned the true cause of his son's death some years after the official notification.[4] Composing a text that should be unreadable—its individual lines bucking against each other—Ingham turns the shame of his son's death on a country that would do this to its own and then hide behind official euphemisms. At the same time, his inscription stakes an implicit challenge to the hometown communities that wrote off soldiers like his son as if they never existed, excluding them from local war memorials and books of remembrance.

What was barely speakable for George Ingham's contemporaries would find a new voice—and an appreciative reception—at the turn of the millennium when, as discussed later in this chapter, under the auspices of the Shot at Dawn (SAD) movement, relatives of executed soldiers began speaking out about their families' trauma and demanding due recognition for the men's service and sacrifice—a campaign that culminated in the 2006 awarding of posthumous pardons to all of these soldiers except those convicted of murder or treason. When these relatives and descendants did speak, they told nearly identical stories of how their families had previously dealt with this tragedy: no one ever talked about it, or if they did, it was only under conditions of strictest confidence, making George Ingham's gesture all the more striking. Inspired by the stories of others in a similar condition, and equipped with new tools to interpret a relative's purported infractions, including more up-to-date knowledge about battle fatigue and PTSD, the relatives of these men proved quite voluble, some even becoming minor media stars. Under pressure of the new light that the campaign shed on the subject—indeed, often on the discovery of an unknown local connection to this history—many communities began to reexamine their commemorative practices, restoring names to memorials where they had long been missing and, in the process, belatedly refiguring the nation's commemorative landscape. And in a twist George Ingham surely could not have anticipated, the graves of Albert Ingham and other shot-at-dawn soldiers became sites of pilgrimage, if not always for precisely the same reasons George Ingham articulated. In the wake of the successful pardons campaign, moreover, George Ingham himself, and his remarkable decision, would become the subject of yet another piece of commemorative shot-at-dawn literature, Mark Hayhurst's play *First Light*, which premiered at the Chichester Festival in June 2016.[5]

I begin, then, with this idiosyncratic instance of commemoration because George Ingham's solitary gesture anticipates many of the terms that some seventy to eighty years later would inform the nation's collective reckoning with this troubling piece of the Great War's legacy. As a modern military practice, the executions are very much a World War I phenomenon. As Gerard Oram notes, "Between 1870 and 1914 the British Army executed just three of its own soldiers," and by 1930 the policy had been abolished for all military offenses except mutiny and treason.[6] The pardons campaign, with the widespread media engagement it generated, however, speaks to a different historical moment: one in which the nation had lost virtually all of those possessing a living memory of World War I. In this context, the shot-at-dawn soldier could become one of the war's distinguishing features—a counterpart and foil to the ubiquitous soldier-poet. Like the much-commemorated war poets (discussed in chapter 2), the executed soldiers have attracted a level of attention—and exercised an emotional power—that many believe to be disproportionate to their historical significance. Unlike the soldier-poets, however, the shot-at-dawn soldiers have not generated the same level of academic attention—the subject largely confined to military history. Yet their place in public and private memory raises issues of scholarly as well as popular interest. Indeed, coming at a time when the motives and conduct of the war had been repeatedly called into question, the turn-of-the-millennium debate over these executed soldiers reflects in particularly striking fashion the challenges of commemoration in the age of postmemory.

I also begin this way because the episode highlights the problem that, from the start, soldiers shot at dawn posed for the nation—how would these men

162   **CHAPTER 4**

be remembered?—the problem writ large in remembrance more generally. More fundamentally, they raised the question of whether they could or should be remembered. These soldiers, then, like the forgotten women discussed in chapter 3, stand as a limit case for questions of inclusion in a commemorative practice that fetishized a comprehensive and democratic naming. Unlike the women, however, these men were in fact soldiers killed in the war, making their treatment seem even more exceptional. Included and excluded simultaneously, they were not so much overlooked as actively passed over. As such, they test the powers of accommodation in the great innovation of postwar commemoration—the naming of the dead—and open this practice to reexamination. And they shed light on a corollary formation: the creation of posthumous lives as a signature of commemoration. Obliterated in the war and its immediate aftermath, the deaths of these soldiers became a site over which the dictates of memory would repeatedly be contested; they emerged as a barometer for changing attitudes to the administration of the war and to the understanding of the exorbitant sacrifice it exacted. And they stand as a textbook illustration of how the lives and deaths of those once occupying the margins—indeed, those whom the official culture tried to expunge—can move to the mainstream in the practices of remembrance.

Names of the Dead

When in February 2007 Private Harry Farr, executed for cowardice in October 1916, became the first of the newly pardoned shot-at-dawn soldiers to be officially recognized in a ceremony of remembrance, his ninety-three-year old daughter, Gertrude ("Gertie") Harris, remarked, "I cannot believe that his name is now going to be remembered for future years, proving that he wasn't a coward but a very brave soldier" (*Northern Echo*, February 19, 2007). At the ceremony in Wealdstone honoring Farr, a temporary plaque was unveiled, bearing Farr's name and that of James Swaine, another executed soldier. The plaque had been added to the town's war memorial in anticipation of the permanent entering of the names later that year when weather conditions would make inscription feasible. This adding of names was one of many such ceremonies that would follow the British government's announcement in August 2006 of its intention to posthumously pardon 306 British and Commonwealth soldiers executed during World War I for desertion, cowardice, and other military offenses, but it was by no means the first such act of belated remembrance. Over the preceding decade, in the wake of intensive lobbying by advocates for pardons, many local communities struggled with the question of how they would remember their own forgotten war dead, and many local memorials were similarly "corrected."

Harris's remarks point to the almost talismanic power accorded to the act of naming: to be named is to be remembered, and to be remembered is to have the stigma of execution lifted, to have the taint of cowardice rewritten as bravery. Her comments, moreover, underline the gap between private memory—where presumably the name has never been forgotten, even if in this instance private memory had also been severely compromised by the family's own silence—and public remembrance. Hence the importance of not merely naming the dead but inscribing the names in the public record and having these acts of inclusion publicly witnessed. But her comments also suggest that the presence of the name is itself an act of witnessing; remembrance will be achieved, the name implies, even when no one is left who can remember the individual, even perhaps if no one reads it. It was not unusual, in fact, for inscribed names to be buried at memorial sites, or placed in otherwise inaccessible locations, behind walls, or in sealed caskets. At issue is the question of posterity. As Daniel J. Sherman has argued, "The inscription of a name attests to an individual's place in that society, without which a place in history would be literally unthinkable."[7] What does it mean, then, I want to ask in this chapter, *not* to have one's name remembered, as was the case with the executed soldiers? And how are we to understand the belated acts of remembrance that have erupted since the late 1980s, much of their fervor fueled by popular sentiment? The discourse of posthumous harm and posthumous redemption offers one potential explanation, but both concepts prove more variable in their meaning and their objects than might immediately seem apparent.[8]

The absence of names on memorials and books of remembrance, I want to argue, was not merely an omission but an active act of erasure, an act as it were of unremembrance. It produced an enforced anonymity in an era Thomas Laqueur has characterized as one of "commemorative hyper-nominalism"—a time when "the state poured enormous human, financial, administrative, artistic, and diplomatic resources into preserving and remembering the names of individual common soldiers."[9] This anonymity, moreover, carried through to the late twentieth century. As Anthony Babington, the first author to be granted access to the sealed court-martial records, noted in his book *For the Sake of Example* (1983), "They are the unremembered"—a position he both confirms and corrects in his own decision, out of deference to the soldiers' families, not to name them, even as he recounts their histories. "They are the central figures in this grim story," he writes, "but throughout the following pages they must remain anonymous."[10] On the home front, this anonymity had surrounded the soldiers from the time of their trials, and it was enforced

164   CHAPTER 4

by the government's decision in 1919 to seal the court-martial records for a hundred years—scaled back to seventy-five after the leaking of the names in Julian Putkowski and Julian Sykes's *Shot at Dawn* (1989) rendered further secrecy superfluous.[11]

During World War I, questions in Parliament about the executions were met with evasive answers to the effect that fuller disclosure was "not in the public interest," and this position was enforced in other government records; it continued in the postwar commissions that took up the subject in 1919 and 1922, and as late as 1972, Don Concannon, MP for Mansfield, asked if the surviving records could be destroyed, "to prevent the names ever being released" and becoming public.[12] Much earlier, in the 1920s, Ernest Thurtle, MP for Shoreditch, championed these soldiers as part of his campaign to abolish the death penalty for wartime military offenses; he nonetheless deliberately suppressed "the names of the unfortunate victims," along with other identifying details, in order "to avoid the possibility of giving unnecessary pain to relatives or friends," when he published his exposé, *Shootings at Dawn*, in 1924.[13]

In the immediate postwar context, the anonymity of the executed soldiers takes on particular significance because, as Laqueur notes, the war ushered in "a new era of remembrance"; no other age put so much importance on the individual naming of each and every dead soldier. "World War I, in short," Laqueur has argued, "witnessed the most dramatic explosion of names on a landscape in world history."[14] In the official structures of mourning, moreover, names took on an almost sacred aura—so much so that when, for example, a church in Hull came to be demolished, the memorial plaques bearing the names of individual World War I soldiers were buried in consecrated ground when no family member could be found to claim them.[15] "Their Name Liveth for Evermore," Kipling's choice of inscription for the Stone of Remembrance, a memorial fixture found in all of the larger military cemeteries, became a grieving nation's mantra; the afterlife of the name, as it proliferated on local monuments, served as a testimony to and consolation for the life sacrificed. The name, indeed, in this formulation, *constituted* the posthumous life its inscription promised. For the soldiers shot at dawn, however, the only place their name would appear to live was in the overseas military cemeteries, where they were afforded the same burial rites as other soldiers. But most of their families would have had little or no access to these overseas sites of commemoration.

Back at home, far from living for evermore, the names of these fallen soldiers were systematically wiped out, as if they never existed. They were not, for the most part, included on local war memorials or in books of remembrance in villages, townships, parish churches, schools, and workplaces if the cause of their death was known to the public. In a few instances, however, such exclusions were contested, as in the village of Fulstow, Lincolnshire. In 1918, when officials refused to include the name of Private Charles Kirman, who was shot at dawn for desertion, the village simply abandoned its plans for a memorial—only erecting one in 2005 when the names of all the World War I dead could be recognized.[16] More often, however, the exclusion of these soldiers was a matter of policy. They were not included in national monuments such as the Canadian Book of Remembrance in the Peace Tower on Ottawa's Parliament Hill, or the Scottish National War Memorial at Castle Rock, Edinburgh. Although their families were informed of their deaths at the time of their occurrence (though not always with the actual cause of death specified), their names were excluded from official casualty lists, and their deaths, in most instances, went unrecorded in regimental histories. After the war, when the army compiled its comprehensive list of men who died in active service, *Soldiers Died in the Great War, 1914–1919*, published between 1920 and 1921 in eighty parts and organized by regiment, corps, or unit, the names of the executed soldiers, with a few exceptions, did not appear there.[17] These men were casualties of war, then, but not named as such.

The consequences of this namelessness were far-reaching. The soldiers' deaths were not commemorated in the local press, nor were in memoriam notices published. Indeed, if a death was publicly noted, it was almost always a sign that the circumstances of the death had not been disclosed. Arguing late in the war against a proposal to spare the families knowledge of their relative's execution, Lord Derby, secretary of state for war, went so far as to suggest "that such deception in the past had resulted in the production of memorial cards, and other such methods of marking the honourable passing of a loved one"—practices he clearly deemed inappropriate in these cases.[18] Death plaques and memorial certificates were not offered to the families of executed soldiers, and medals they had earned were forfeited, although this was not the case for the more than three thousand soldiers convicted of identical crimes whose death sentences were subsequently commuted.[19] Indeed, only about 10 percent of the soldiers sentenced to death actually had their sentences carried out. On a private level, then, families were left without tokens and keepsakes to display as testimony to their loss and evidence of a loved one's service; they also were left without a place to go—a name to visit on a local monument—where their loss could be acknowledged publicly. They were left, in other words, without what Catherine Moriarty has called "sites to which memory could attach itself."[20] These lives were thus rendered, in Judith Butler's terms, "ungrievable"—both literally and figuratively. This state of oblivion also had more material consequences: the monthly service allowance a soldier's family received was suspended, and widows of executed soldiers were routinely

166   **CHAPTER 4**

denied pensions and child support benefits.[21] Given that all but three of the executed soldiers were privates or noncommissioned officers, the financial impact was dramatic, a pension often being all that kept a family from abject poverty.

These soldiers, then, could be seen as the ultimate version of "the missing," but unlike those remembered on the Menin Gate Memorial to the Missing in Ypres, these were soldiers to whom "the fortune of war" denied not "the known and honoured burial given to their comrades in death," as the Menin Gate inscription reads, but the known and honored *remembrance*. What they were denied was, in effect, the posthumous life promised as the reward for their sacrifice. Their treatment thus opened a rift where one had not previously been visible. Pushed to its logical extreme, the cultural equation of death and remembrance— if you died in the war, you would always be remembered—might mean that if you are not remembered, as was the case with the executed soldiers, you are not really dead; at the least, such soldiers did not belong to the ranks of war casualties, as the *Daily Mail* intimated when it announced Harry Farr's reinstatement with the headline "Soldiers Shot at Dawn Finally Join the Ranks of the Fallen" (February 18, 2007).[22] If in the years leading up to the pardons the case of the shot-at-dawn soldiers proved difficult to put to rest—repeatedly reemerging despite governmental efforts at suppression or partial appeasement—it may well be because the dead still occupied some limbo; they occupied "unquiet graves," as a guidebook to the execution sites in Flanders puts it.[23] Indeed, the official records for these deaths are rife with inconsistencies, with different causes of death frequently listed on different documents for the same individual: death certificates, casualty lists, routine orders, service records, next-of-kin notifications, gravestones, cemetery registers. These notations ranged from the bluntly factual "sentenced by court martial to be shot by firing squad" or "Shot by sentence of FGMC for 'Desertion,'" to the charitably deceptive "Died in action," to the more waffling "Died of wounds" or "Died at service," to, finally, the starkly uncompromising "Died." The ambiguities surrounding the executed soldiers' deaths have rendered the deaths themselves ambiguous and the dead soldiers ghostly, accounting in part for the way their stories have haunted both the British imagination and the families of the victims, unable to resolve their loss and grief. As Andrew Mackinlay, MP for Thurrock, noted in urging the case for pardons to the House of Commons in October 1993, "The demand for this remedy is like a cry from the grave."[24]

In an uncanny way, such cries became especially audible—and the sense of haunting rampant—at the moment the entire memory of the war seemed susceptible to disappearing; at that point, it became imperative to recover those who were deliberately expunged from the record and to invent new rites of memory for them. The failure of official channels to respond to this cry had already, at the time of Mackinlay's pronouncement, inspired a grassroots effort. The Shot at Dawn pardons campaign, officially launched in 1990, represented its mission as an act of restitution—a belated undoing of posthumous acts of exclusion and erasure. As such, it set out to repair the posthumous harm that had been done to the dead in declaring them unfit for recognition and the second-order posthumous harm done to their families by short-circuiting their ability to properly grieve a loved one.[25] By refusing to consider individual cases, the earlier government investigations of the executions—the Darling Committee on Courts-Martial (1919) and the Southborough Committee on Shell-Shock (1922)—had perpetuated the soldiers' anonymity and ensured that the dead could never be exonerated (and hence never be commemorated). By contrast, the pardons campaign recognized that to name the dead is at once to perform remembrance and make remembrance possible; in the case of *Unquiet Graves*, the guidebook to the graves in Flanders, it did so quite literally by identifying the graves so that they could be visited.

It is probably no accident, then, that Putkowski and Sykes's *Shot at Dawn*, the first work to name all the executed soldiers, reaches back in its design conventions to the format of rolls of honor or books of remembrance produced in the wake of World War I: it records the name of each man, offset in bold typeface, the regiment and unit in which he served, accompanied by line drawings of the regimental insignia, the date of his enlistment, the date (and even hour) of his death, the place of his death, and often his age at dying. It thus restores to the men the particulars their enforced anonymity had denied them. Even the capsule biographies that accompany these entries are not entirely unlike the annotations that sometimes accompanied a parish roll of honor. Where the official *Soldiers Died in the Great War* excluded these men from the casualty lists of their regiments, *Shot at Dawn* reinserted them in this very place that their ignominious deaths had denied them representation. In doing so, it laid the ground for the site-specific acts of local monument inscription in English villages and townships that would become one of the centerpieces of the Shot at Dawn movement.

At the level of the state, the pardons campaign began to gain real traction in 1997, when Tony Blair's administration agreed to take up the pardons question. Even though it declared a year later that the granting of pardons was unfeasible, effectively shutting down the question for the future, it publicly acknowledged that "in a sense, those who were executed were as much victims of the war as the soldiers and airmen who were killed in action." Although the decision was far from satisfactory to pardons advocates, it was nonetheless a rhetorical victory, confirming the soldiers' status as victims, on a par with

168   **CHAPTER 4**

others (or almost so), and worthy of recognition as such—by members of Parliament and by the general public. In lieu of pardons, then, in 1998 the minister for armed forces, John Reid, urged the adding of these soldiers' names to war memorials and rolls of honor. Significantly, this concession occurred at the moment when the last World War I veterans were dying. As Reid noted, "There remain only a very few of our fellow countrymen who have any real understanding or memory of life and death in the trenches and on the battlefields of the first world war."[26] There were few, in other words, in a position to understand or judge what these soldiers went through. Whether those few would approve or disapprove recognition for the executed soldiers—and over the years, whenever the subject emerged, the presumed (and actual) responses of the World War I veterans were passionately invoked by both sides of the controversy—remembrance, it would appear, could be achieved only in the absence of living memory. Only then could the idea of these men as victims, as much so as other soldiers, become intelligible, for only then could the discourse of "victims of war" be applied to all soldiers and their service and sacrifice. Indeed, not only were World War I veterans dying off, but so were the wives and children (and nieces and nephews) of the executed men, lending a certain urgency to the inscription ceremonies.

In the media coverage of the Shot at Dawn movement, these living relatives figured prominently. When Putkowski and Sykes first published *Shot at Dawn* in 1989, the decision to name names was attended by a certain amount of controversy, as the book stood to be the first intimation some family members would receive of a relative's execution. In the event, the book—and the formal Shot at Dawn campaign, founded by John Hipkin in 1990, that followed close upon it—prompted many relatives of executed soldiers to go public with their stories, breaking a silence in which their own families had often collaborated. The disclosure of names, in fact, unleashed not only a flood of stories about forgotten soldiers but also an outpouring of testimonials from the executed men's relatives and descendants, attesting to lives derailed by shame and outrage, and exposing what Michèle Barrett has called "the personal and human consequences of war."[27] And the public proved as hungry for these stories of continuing family trauma as for the soldiers' stories of battle fatigue and fatal lapses. The youthful faces of long-forgotten soldiers, then, captured in faded photographs reproduced in the media's shot-at-dawn stories were regularly accompanied by videos and color photographs of the aging faces and bodies of the executed soldiers' present-day advocates. Through a sequence of widely reproduced images, Gertrude Harris became the "poster senior" for the campaign: eighty-seven and wheelchair-bound, participating for the first time in a wreath-laying ceremony at the Cenotaph in November 2000; ninety-one and accompanied by her daughter, standing outside the High Court where a request to seek a conditional pardon for her father, Harry Farr, had been filed; ninety-three and flanked by children, grandchildren, and great-grandchildren at the ceremony honoring her father in Wealdstone in February 2007.[28] For the general public, these images stood as a visible reminder of the years that had elapsed since the teens and the twenties when such gestures of recognition for soldiers like Harris's father would have been timely. By the 1990s and 2000s, few remained who could claim such close descent to an executed soldier as Harris; those most active in the campaign more frequently belonged to the next generation or the generation after, typically nieces and nephews, and increasingly great-nieces and great-nephews, of childless soldiers or more distant cousins. Their presence at memorial ceremonies spoke to the years this solace was denied them, and it invoked the mourners *not* there beside them—the executed men's widows, sweethearts, siblings, friends, and children. It spoke to their need in the present to invent rites of memory that could, as it were, provide retroactive consolation. At the same time, it made visible the shift in understanding of how posthumous harm could be calculated.

For the rest of the nation, there would have been a long history of communal remembrance, much of it centered in the village or township where the family resided. In *At the Going Down of the Sun*, his study of British World War I memorials, Derek Boorman recounts the experience of a woman who, like Gertrude Harris, lost a father to the war when she was a young child; the story is instructive for its contrast to Harris's experience and that of other relatives of shot-at-dawn soldiers: "Mrs. Hilda Jones (née Coombes), now approaching 80, can remember her father's name being engraved on the war memorial at Shipton-under-Wychwood in Oxfordshire. She sat by the stonemason's side, proud of the engraved name but barely realising the full implication of what was happening. . . . Hilda and another little girl whose father had died in the war, [*sic*] unveiled the memorial when the ceremony was held in 1921."[29] For Gertrude Harris, in her eighties and into her nineties, there was no such memory to claim. And the little girl, Gertie, who was three years old when her father was shot—a father she had not seen since she was a four-month-old baby—was a woman of eighty-seven when she was invited to unveil the Shot at Dawn Memorial at the National Arboretum in June 2001 (see figure I.8). The statue she uncovered, however, was not one of her father; rather, it was a figure modeled on another executed soldier, Herbert Burden, meant to stand as a placeholder for all the shot-at-dawn victims.[30] The existence of such a memorial in such an official location—a site sponsored by the Royal British Legion, the Ministry of Defence, and the Heritage Lottery Fund, among other charities and institutions—was, in itself, a remarkable indication

170   CHAPTER 4

of a decisive shift in public opinion. But it would be another five and half years before Harris would finally see her own father's name engraved on a memorial plaque on a local war memorial, following the government's formal conferral of pardons. As with other shot-at-dawn families, then, the loss of a father, son, husband, or brother was compounded by the loss of the memory of his memorialization. If, as Moriarty has argued, these memorial services functioned to sanctify personal loss, transforming private sorrow into civic pride, this transformation could not be accomplished for mourners like Harris.[31] Indeed, like Harris, who first learned how her father died when she was forty (a secret she kept for another forty years), many of the aggrieved did not learn of the circumstances of their relative's death until well into adulthood, when all living connection to the events of the war was disappearing; private grief, like public remembrance, could thus be fully experienced only belatedly. Marina Brewis, for example, was fifty-nine when she stumbled on the truth about her uncle Peter Goggins after seeing the family name on a BBC documentary in the 1990s. Sam Watts was seventy-three when his sister revealed to him how his uncle had died. Tom Stones was fifty-five in 1996 when he first learned not only the circumstances of his great-uncle's death but of his very existence— all mention of Joseph "Willie" Stones having been systematically expunged from his family's records. As he explained in November 2000, when families of executed soldiers were first allowed to join the annual Cenotaph march-past ceremony, "This is the first time any of these families have been able to honor their relatives with the rest of the nation" (*Northern Echo*, November 11, 2000).[32]

Stones did not live to see his great-uncle pardoned, and Gertrude Harris was too ill in November 2006 to attend the first Cenotaph ceremony following the institution of pardons; as Harris's daughter explained, however, "The engraving ceremony is what she is really looking forward to so hopefully it will spur her on to get better" (*Yorkshire Post*, December 27, 2006).[33] In this respect, Hilda Jones's story is also instructive for the emphasis it puts on the materiality of inscription: what it means to actually see the name of a loved one being etched by the stonemason. Maya Lin, who credits World War I memorials as an inspiration for her Vietnam Veterans Memorial, makes a similar observation about the other monument that inspired her: "Any undergraduate who was at Yale when I started there in 1977–78 saw one or two men always etching out the names of the alumni from Yale or of the Yale students who had been killed in Vietnam. As you walked through the hall to and from classes, you'd register that there were these two men etching in the names. And you'd unconsciously register the time it was taking to etch in each name, and the time somebody had lost. It was always *there*. It was ever-present." As

Lin elaborates, this inscribing of names has a tactile element: "Also, you couldn't *not* touch the names."[34] These comments help to explain why the adding of names to memorial sites has acquired so much symbolic force in the SAD campaign, and why for so many the pardons, when they did finally come, would not be complete without an act of inscription to follow.

The need Lin points to, moreover, would have been felt even more powerfully in the shot-at-dawn cases because of the time elapsed and the distance from the actors and events celebrated; the inscription ceremonies were, quite literally, a way to make these losses legible after years of erasure. In the months and years following the government's historic decision, then, the question of how and where to name these dead continued to be fought out in local venues. Commenting on the profusion of local monuments that emerged in the postwar years, Laqueur noted, "This most bureaucratic and global of wars produced the most intense local writing of the names of the dead ever seen."[35] The pardons campaign replayed this localization with its own second-wave memorial mania, demanding space on these sites for the names yet to be written there. Even before it achieved its end in the halls of government, its claims were dividing villages and townships. In Shoreham, for example, where a contentious struggle in 1999–2000 ended with Thomas Highgate, the first British soldier to be shot at dawn, being denied a place on the town memorial, the situation remains unresolved at the time of this writing, despite the continuing and vociferous efforts of his great-nephew, Terence Highgate. When the original memorial plaque was replaced in 2000, however, a space was left for Highgate's name, "should people want it to be added at a later date" (*BBC News*, August 16, 2006). This unusual accommodation was perhaps a concession to the fact that the community had actually voted overwhelmingly to add his name—a decision overruled by the parish council on the advice of the British Legion. As the empty space on the memorial plaque reminds us, it is not just the presence of the name that signifies, but also the act of adding it to an existing monument—an act that can only be understood in relation to the history that preceded it.

For this reason, perhaps, in the many instances where memorials have been successfully updated, the unveiling ceremonies have had a good deal of theater about them, and the meaning of the victory that the new names announce can be read in the labor their inscription requires. To add names to war memorials at the start of the new millennium required the overcoming of certain technical difficulties, and it required the skilled labor of masonry workers, metal engravers, and calligraphers, undoubtedly in shorter supply than they were in the 1920s when memorial making was the order of the day. The labor and difficulty of these belated inscriptions, I am arguing, were an integral part

172   **CHAPTER 4**

of their expression of meaning, just as they were when the memorials were originally erected—something we tend to forget, as Laqueur observes, now that these memorials are fixed in the landscape.[36] When the books of remembrance for the Melbourne Shrine of Remembrance were being compiled in the 1930s, for example, the *Melbourne Argus* reported, "It will be nearly a year before the [89,100] names . . . are satisfactorily copied on to cream-tinted parchment with quill pens in lasting Indian ink." Unlike the majority of British monuments, the Australian memorial lists all who enlisted for service and not just those who died; as a deliberate part of its effort, moreover, it selected ex-servicemen for several of its calligraphers. As Moriarty explains, "Here, then, was another instance of the 'added value' achieved by the amalgamation of the activity of making, by those with direct association with the dead, and the use of 'meaningful' materials: long lasting, expensive, symbolic in origin."[37]

In the case of additions made to books of remembrance and war memorials at the turn of the twenty-first century, the "value added" attached in no small measure to the individual. The labor required to add a single name could be seen as an assertion that the life (and death) of that individual had meaning and value, something actively challenged in the not infrequent representation of these soldiers as "worthless men" in court-martial records.[38] To name these men was, in effect, nothing short of a conferral of personhood, making possible the construction of posthumous lives for them. In much the same way, the reading of "the tragic story" of a single individual, Private James Smith of Bolton, into the parliamentary record in March 2009 was a means for Brian Iddon, the MP for the constituency in which Smith lived, to affirm the value of his life and sacrifice in advance of the vote by the Bolton Town Council to add Smith's name to its book of remembrance; at the same time, it was a way to call attention to the fact that Smith was just one of many otherwise anonymous soldiers still unmemorialized more than ninety years after their deaths.

In the immediate aftermath of the war, the unimaginable scale and volume of death confronted memorial architects, as Laqueur has argued, with a series of challenges: "How do we actually *imagine* a million dead people?" If the answer was "by showing them as specifically as possible" by naming them individually, the architects were then left with "tremendous design problems"— problems at once aesthetic and technical—"in how to list names in an era when nobody had actually built memorials listing numbers of such magnitude."[39] Local memorials, of course, dealt in much more manageable proportions, but there, too, the logistical problem of how to list names and how to account for every individual remained paramount. Underlying this dilemma was the question of who should be memorialized in the wake of the war—a question whose answer was by no means self-evident despite an ostensible commitment to all-inclusiveness. Each local community had to invent its own guidelines. Should a memorial be a record of all those who served or a record of deaths, and if the latter, how long after the war ended could one die and still be included on the monument? What counted as a war-related death for an ex-serviceman? Death from wounds? Illness (the influenza epidemic, for example)? Alcoholism? Suicide? Should civilian casualties be considered? A further question was posed in how the names should be organized: alphabetically, by rank, by unit, chronologically, or by theater of war.[40]

The problem is one that continues to beset the inheritors of these memorial traditions, as the controversy surrounding Lin's Vietnam Veterans Memorial makes evident. With its stark minimalism—the black granite walls, the V-shaped design, and the complete absence of figural ornamentation—the memorial provoked polarized responses. Some, especially veterans, attacked it early on for these unconventional features (including the decision to represent the names of the dead in chronological order), while others extolled the memorial for the uniquely moving experience the mirrored walls of names generated. As Marita Sturken documents, the memorial sparked a national debate about "precisely how wars should be remembered, and precisely who should be remembered in a war."[41] The struggles over World War I memorials were no less animated, even if more decentralized, with much of the debate centered within local constituencies. Moreover, the solutions reached on both the large- and small-scale order, reflected a similar negotiation between the specificity of the name, with its insistence on the fact of an individual behind it, and the antirepresentational nature of its inscription, the fact that the name tells us virtually nothing about the person. As Sturken observes, writing of other memorial contexts, "The name evokes both everything and nothing as a marker of the absent one."[42] Because of the particular form World War I memorials took, the Shot at Dawn controversy shone unanticipated light on these contradictions. It thus helps to explain why these memorials could plausibly produce polar opposite responses. What Siegfried Sassoon excoriated in 1921 in "On Passing the New Menin Gate," as the spectacle of "these intolerably nameless names," Maya Lin found extremely moving—albeit more than fifty years later: "What I found most influential was the expression of great loss and tragedy surrounding these works; they focused on the people who gave their lives rather than on a country's or leader's politicized statement of victory. You begin to see emerging the acknowledgment of the individual."[43]

As Bob Bushaway notes, the desire for such acknowledgment drove much postwar practice: "Part of the function of the obsession with lists and rolls was the concern of the bereaved to see proper recognition accorded to the individuality of their loss."[44] This concern has also been central to the Shot at

174   **CHAPTER 4**

Dawn movement, even as its practice also pulls in the opposite direction—toward the absorbing of the "nameless names" into the consciousness of the public. As the movement's organizers recognized, public sentiment could be mobilized for pardons once the executed soldiers became individualized—once they had names and faces attached to them, even if these identities were post-memory surrogates. In this way, the harm done to these soldiers and their families could—ostensibly—be rendered legible for a public without personal stakes in the subject. In addition, then, to providing talking points and history tutorials for those grappling with the pardons question, one of the campaign's central strategies was to saturate the public with human interest stories, highlighting the plight of individual soldiers. If a key element of the posthumous harm that the executions generated was the "second death" of its victims in the erasure of their life stories, the campaign filled this gap by creating biographies for them.[45] At the same time, it created new rites of memory that would allow a distant public to feel they could inhabit the past thus recovered.

The Shot at Dawn website kept the work of the campaign in the spotlight, giving *Shot at Dawn*, the book, a second life in a new format; it provided a cache of ready-made stories that the press could draw on and a set of narrative templates that proved remarkably durable. The local press, however, was also inventive in uncovering stories of the "local boy done bad" variety and rallying local sympathies through them. In the national press, special attention, not surprisingly, was given to the cases that appeared most egregious: where there was clear evidence of shell shock, as in the case of Harry Farr; where the soldiers were very young, sometimes underage, and often undefended as in the case of Herbert Burden, the soldier on whom the central figure in the Shot at Dawn Memorial was purportedly modeled; or where the trials were shockingly brief and most questionable in their proceedings, as in the case of Willie Stones, a case even Hughes-Wilson, one of the campaign's most voluble critics, concedes might be seen as a clear miscarriage of justice.[46]

The media flurry was helped by the fact that the subject so readily lent itself to tabloid drama: the boy soldiers, summarily tried, hardly knowing what was happening to them; the pronouncement of sentence on the eve of execution, sometimes only hours before its enactment; the shootings at first light by a firing squad of the soldiers' own compatriots; the prisoners, blindfolded, manacled, and tied to posts, with white patches pinned to their breasts to provide a target for the shooters; the young officer commanding the squad, often forced to shoot the soldier in the head when death was not instantaneous. The elements were in fact much the same as those that had caused a minor media sensation when, in February 1918, the popular periodical *John Bull* took up the case of Sub-lieutenant Dyett, one of the three officers to have been executed during the war, with blazing headlines, "Shot at Dawn: A Trench Tragedy," "The Tragedy of a Boy Officer." In the Shot at Dawn campaign, however, the cases grabbing headlines were not those of the officers but of the ordinary soldiers—a trench tragedy for the groundlings. Unlike Dyett's case, where his family had the resources to rally public interest, the cases of the ordinary soldiers only began to gain traction at the turn of the millennium.[47]

Ironically, however, the more these shot-at-dawn stories circulated, the further removed they became from real individuals. Those with the closest ties to the executed soldiers were now two or three generations removed, while the even larger audience for these stories was a general citizenry without personal connections to the men in question. The stories themselves, moreover, in their repetitive iteration, sounded increasingly formulaic. The removal in chronological time thus virtually ensured that the rites of memory organized in the soldiers' name were not about the actual experiences of the dead but about how the dead can be made to matter to the living. The actual dead, indeed, were not available for this project any more than they were for the "material boys" discussed in chapter 1. The problem, in part, was the scarcity of information to work from. Neither the extant court-martial files—which contained summaries of the trials rather than full transcripts, sometimes amounting to no more than a couple of pages—nor family "archives" supplied enough material to flesh out the person or fully explain the circumstances that resulted in his execution. Many of the records held in the War Office in London, moreover, were destroyed in the London Blitz in 1940. Even family members were forced to fill in gaps with what they could only imagine in order to produce a coherent narrative from the scraps and fragments available to them.

The compressed life stories produced in this manner stand in striking contrast to the memoirs of the dead discussed in chapter 1, and they push considerably further the question of what might count as biography. While those earlier posthumous lives are no less fabricated—and no less constrained by the representational challenges posed by a truncated life that proves unfathomable—the families who produced them could spin their Lives out of actual material, textual and otherwise; this material, as I argued, was not always noteworthy, but there was generally lots of it, making these lives appear not so much fictionalized as overdocumented. And the default story line of heroic sacrifice was ready to hand, whether or not there were significant accomplishments to warrant it. The memory work these "material boys" generated thus entailed making something out of "nothing." By contrast, for the shot-at-dawn soldier, few documents survive, and the families of these soldiers would likely have had neither the habit nor the resources for preserving textual artifacts; given the circumstances of the men's death, moreover, they would probably have

176 **CHAPTER 4**

been less inclined to hold on to reminders of the person. In the aborted memory work their situation prompted, the substance of their lives, like their service to their country, was effectively nullified. The passage of time, then, only widened the gulf between the "life" and the person. The disappearance of memory traces, moreover, was a harm not repairable by the efforts of the SAD campaign or its resolution in the conferral of posthumous pardons. The irreducibility of this loss thus points to the limits of the posthumous harm/posthumous restitution model.

The leavings of these lives—often no more than a single photograph of the soldier in uniform, a few statements from his trial, some lines from his last letter home—were all the more poignant for being all that survived to testify to the man's existence. In some cases, moreover, not even that much remained. Nora High, for example, the great-niece of an executed soldier, Billy Nelson, noted, "We have a prayer book and a button from his coat and that is all we have left of him but we will make sure he is never forgotten" (*Daily Mirror*, June 22, 2006). Inevitably, these scraps of information were repeated, with minor variations, each time a soldier's story was publicized, thus becoming the defining stuff of the person. If, as Gertrude Harris suggests, for example, her fourteen-year effort to gain a pardon for "Harry" made her father, Harry Farr, "more real, more of a person for [her]," the father thus recovered was one who had never existed as such—one constructed through the years of reciting his story. As she told a reporter, "When I was a little girl I would say to my friends 'My dad died in the war' but it didn't mean anything to me because I never knew him. All this has given me a father. I didn't have one before, did I?"[48]

In a similar way, members of the public seemed to respond to the "reality effect" produced by the shot-at-dawn narratives with which they were inundated, often talking about the long-dead soldiers as if they knew them. Such responses reflect the success of the campaign in creating memories the public felt they could own and inhabit. Some were even tempted to produce their own fictionalizations of the life and death of local heroes, as in Les Smith's *Early One Morning* (1998), a play about Bolton soldier Private James Smith; Peter Drake's *The Prisoner's Friend* (2004), a drama focused on the events leading up to the execution of Durham soldier Lance Sergeant Joseph William Stones; and Bob Ashmore's *Rough Justice*, a play based on the last letter home written by Coventry native Private Albert Troughton, performed at the opening of the Shot at Dawn Memorial in June 2001. Martin Lynch's *Holding Hands at Paschendale* (2006), a play based on the author's grandfather, an arresting officer who was handcuffed to a young soldier for four days before the soldier's execution, though first performed after the pardons were announced, also fits this pattern. These plays were frequently performed in site-specific locations:

in Bolton, in the case of Les Smith, and later in Ypres, to coincide with the Unquiet Graves conference; the Drake play in a series of locations in and around Durham; the Lynch play in Dublin. In several instances, families of the deceased were invited to special performances with open discussions following.

Subjected to repeated retellings in popular culture and the media, however, the stories of executed soldiers crystallized into a set of fixed tropes and predictable anecdotes, never really moving beyond the same reductive choices: victim or rogue, hero or coward. If the shot-at-dawn soldiers posed the problem of commemorating those who were not heroes, the campaign resolved the issue by conferring heroic stature on them. What passed for posthumous lives, then, emerged as a set of formulaic fictions. Indeed, as these subheadings from two 2006 *Daily Mirror* articles suggest, the stories coalesced into a set of interchangeable sound bites or taglines, with only the parenthetical name of the executed soldier individualizing them: "Family Crisis Led to a Firing Squad" (William Nelson); "A 'Nervous' Boy Who Ran Away" (Charles Nicholson); "Executed to Deter Deserters" (Peter Goggins); "Pluck in the Trenches" (William Stones); "Confusion in the Smoke" (Harry Ashton); "Stowaway Missed Sick Wife" (Albert Ingham and Alfred Longshaw); "No Mercy for Ill and Injured Dad" (Harry MacDonald).[49] Unabashedly "sob stuff," the stories were nonetheless effective in soliciting public interest, and thus in helping to create a collective memory in the face of a no longer rememberable event.[50]

Many individuals were undoubtedly moved by the particulars of specific shot-at-dawn stories, but they were moved as well by the sheer volume of such narratives. Perhaps for this reason, the public seemed largely uninterested in discriminating between the cases, content to read them all through the lens of a small sampling that had acquired life for them—much to the dismay of the pardons opponents. When the Shot at Dawn Memorial, for example, appealed to the public for funding—a twenty-pound donation paying for a pinewood stake bearing a metal plaque with the name, regiment, age, and date of death of one of the 306 British and Commonwealth soldiers executed for desertion, cowardice, and other military offenses (figure 4.2)—the public was quick to "adopt a soldier." While some made commitments to particular soldiers based on local, regional, and national affiliations, for a majority of those who responded to the appeal, all the soldiers seemed equally worthy. When the *Daily Telegraph*, for example, announced in January 2001 that sixty-eight stakes still needed sponsoring, within a day of publishing this information its readers had contributed more than enough money to sponsor all 306 soldiers. As David Childs, director of the National Memorial Arboretum, noted, "Each deserter is likely to be sponsored by two or three people" (*Telegraph*, January 6, 2001). The

FIGURE 4.2. Pinewood stake and metal plaque bearing the name of Herbert Francis Burden, Shot at Dawn Memorial, National Arboretum, Staffordshire. Photo credit: Alan Samuel, https://creativecommons.org/licenses/by/2.0/deed.en

moral outrage at the treatment of the executed soldiers that the shot-at-dawn cases generated, prompting donations from people with no previous connection to or interest in them, then, was both specific and general—attached to the particular circumstances of particular named individuals and attached to a composite shot-at-dawn figure. And the prevailing sense that these cases signified a flagrant miscarriage of justice reflected both the public's conviction of particular soldiers' innocence, as extrapolated from the court-martial records and the anecdotes told about the soldiers, and the conviction that whatever the soldiers had done, nothing could justify their punishment.

What is striking in this turn of events was the readiness of such a large segment of the public to seize on these long-dead, unrecoverable soldiers and claim them as objects for collective commemoration in the present. By making distant suffering feel immediately real to so many people—the suffering of the soldiers but also of their families—the campaign provided a way for the public to experience (or believe they were experiencing) a live connection to the war at a moment when living memory was dead or dying. It thus tapped into a powerful need on the part of the postmemory population—a need these soldiers were all the more available to fill because the common soldier, by this time, had come to be seen as the war's callously sacrificed victim. In the end, when in 2006 the Labour government acceded to public sentiment and issued a blanket pardon, dramatically reversing its 1998 decision, it was the continuing trauma of the soldiers' living relatives, it claimed, that tipped the balance. As Secretary of Defence Des Browne explained, "Although this is a historical matter, I am conscious of how the families of these men feel today. They have had to endure a stigma for decades. That makes this a moral issue too" (*Guardian*, August 17, 2006). The issue, of course, was also a political one, and the government's show of empathy was meant to reach an audience much larger than the long-suffering families—the considerable segment of the public that required having its newfound feelings for the soldiers validated. The soldiers themselves, however, given the passage of time and the circumstances of their deaths, remained accessible only through fictional reconstructions. Even the television documentaries that proved so influential in awakening the public's interest in the wartime executions—Carlton TV's BAFTA-nominated *Shot at Dawn* (1998) and BBC1 Everyman's *Conviction* (1999), for example—were inevitably dependent on dramatic reenactments of a speculative reality. The entire campaign, in fact, depended on a popularization of history, demonstrating what Sturken has described as "tangled memories": the entwinement, in the public sphere, of history and cultural memory, as transmitted "through popular culture, the media, public images, and public memorials."[51]

What made the campaign so successful, I have been suggesting, was its ability to turn those without direct links to the soldiers into interested parties, initiating a process that could produce a kind of surrogate public memory, going beyond individual recollection and personal motives. Imaginative treatments proved yet another force in the overdetermined process that elevated the executed soldiers into memorial icons. In the absence of actual lives to draw on—in the absence, that is, of lives that were well documented—fictionalized lives assumed lopsided importance in the Shot at Dawn movement; they were able to do so, however, because actual fictions had laid the ground for receptivity to these soldiers long before the campaign took off. The public's ability to seize on these soldiers was made possible, then, not only because of the campaign's effective propaganda onslaught but also because literary works had provided a template for making the otherwise incomprehensible acts of these men both comprehensible and sympathetic.

While before the 1970s imaginative works treating the subject of the executions appeared only sporadically, advocacy for the soldiers through humanizing literary representations long preceded the SAD movement. As early as 1919, A. P. Herbert had published his novel *The Secret Battle* to publicize a case of what he believed to be judicial injustice—a book Winston Churchill claimed "should be read in each generation, so that men and women may rest under no illusion about what war means."[52] Like other early treatments of the subject, the book, which was reissued repeatedly from the time of its publication

180   **CHAPTER 4**

into the twenty-first century, achieved a new popularity when the Shot at Dawn campaign started engaging the public's attention.[53] In the following years, C. E. Montague's *Rough Justice* (1926) took up the subject, and shot-at-dawn figures made appearances in the memoirs published by Graves, Sassoon, and Blunden during the war book boom of the late 1920s. At midcentury J. L. Hodson's *Return to the Wood* (1955), focused in part on an inarticulate soldier accused of desertion and the officer assigned to defend him, provided the source text for John Wilson's play *Hamp*; the play, first performed in 1964, along with Hodson's novel, was adapted in Joseph Losey's film *For King and Country* (1964) and in a 1988 BBC radio play.[54] The extended life of the work through these adaptations provides testimony to the capacity of these shot-at-dawn stories to be repeatedly resurrected and reframed to meet the needs of audiences in different cultural moments.

Since the 1970s, when interest in the executions began to be revived in a more sustained manner with the publication of popular histories on the subject,[55] the pace of these literary publications accelerated sharply, helping to create and maintain a kind of shot-at-dawn literacy that could be tapped by the SAD campaign when it took off in earnest. Jennifer Johnston's *How Many Miles to Babylon* (1974) had a particularly rich afterlife. Adapted by the BBC in 1982 as a television drama starring Daniel Day-Lewis, it was later, after being adopted in the Irish secondary school curriculum, adapted for the stage by Alan Stanford for the Second Age Theatre Company in Dublin (2005)—these latter developments following the formation of the Irish Shot at Dawn movement in 2002. In England, Reginald Hill's *The Wood Beyond* (1997), part of his popular Dalziel and Pasco detective series, was adapted in 1998 for season 3 of the BBC television series. Across the Atlantic, Laurie King took up the subject in one of her Mary Russell / Sherlock Holmes books, *Justice Hall* (2002), while the mother-son team, writing as Charles Todd, made this the premise of its Inspector Rutledge series, begun in 1996, whose shell-shocked detective is haunted by the voice of a soldier in his regiment whom he was forced to execute. Implicitly or explicitly, most of these works presented themselves as part of the advocacy campaign on behalf of the soldiers, as evidenced in epigraphs, afterwords, author interviews, and publicity materials. As such, they worked in concert with other political and cultural forces that were propelling the cause of these soldiers into public consciousness, and they were instrumental in helping the SAD movement to gain traction by reaching large national and international audiences.

Elsewhere, shot-at-dawn characters figured prominently in genre fiction and young adult literature but also, at least episodically, in a sizable portion of all the imaginative work produced about World War I, so much so that when Cathryn Corns and John Hughes-Wilson published *Blindfold and Alone* in 2001, they could lament, "Every modern author or screenplay about the Great War appears to feel the need to include an obligatory execution scene in the interests of dramatic licence."[56] British television was no exception; *The Monocled Mutineer* (1986) and *Blackadder Goes Forth* (1989), with its "Corporal Punishment" episode, were especially influential in both popularizing and mocking the executions at the very moment the not-yet-formalized SAD movement was gaining momentum. *Downton Abbey*, which began airing four years after the pardons were settled, joined a long line of popular cultural representations, a highly visible but belated example of this phenomenon. Introduced in season 2 (2011), with the story of Mrs. Patmore's nephew, the shot-at-dawn motif returned in a season 5 follow-up, with the (somewhat anachronistic) war memorial inscription controversy that aired just as centenary commemorations were getting underway in November 2014.

No single work, however, reached as far into British culture in redefining the subject as Michael Morpurgo's *Private Peaceful*. Constructed as a monologue produced over a long night's vigil, the novel tells the story of a young soldier on the eve of what is eventually revealed to be his brother's execution, his prior life revealed in a set of vivid flashbacks. The 2003 novel, marketed for children ten years and older, was the first work Morpurgo published after being named children's laureate, although it was not his first attempt to celebrate the war's unsung victims; Morpurgo published *War Horse* in 1982, but it did not reach the stage until 2007, after *Private Peaceful* paved the way for its reinvigorated reception. *Private Peaceful*, indeed, quickly became something of a sensation, garnering enthusiastic reviews and coveted prizes and enjoying a parallel life as a hugely successful stage drama. In the stage adaptation, the narrator himself turns out to be the soldier about to be executed—a decision undoubtedly made for greater dramatic effect but also one that reflects the popular desire to give voice to the executed soldiers that the SAD campaign had awakened. *Private Peaceful* proved successful as a crossover commodity, appealing to adults and children, and its afterlife corresponded to the final amping up of the SAD movement. First performed in August 2004 at the Bristol Old Vic, the play enjoyed sellouts at the Edinburgh Festival Fringe and London's West End, with a UK tour in 2005 and a second London stint in 2006. It had also been performed, in collaboration with the a cappella group Coope, Boyes and Simpson, as *Private Peaceful: The Concert*, and in June 2006, less than two months before the announcement of pardons, it was released as a CD. By the time the government reached its decision about pardons, then, *Private Peaceful* had become a familiar icon for the shot-at-dawn soldier—highly sympathetic and thoroughly respectable. Indeed, *Private Peaceful* was already becoming entrenched in the English school curriculum, required reading in many classrooms.[57]

182   **CHAPTER 4**

Morpurgo, who was driven to write the novel after a journey to Ypres in which he visited execution sites and viewed the cells in Poperinghe, where the condemned prisoners spent their last hours, happened upon the grave of a soldier named Private Peaceful in a military cemetery and knew he had found the name for his title character. The character he created, however, was entirely imaginary. Morpurgo himself described the real Private Peaceful, who was *not* shot at dawn, as a true unknown soldier and in adopting the name for his creation transformed *his* Private Peaceful into a kind of World War I Everyman, the ultimate figure of sacrifice.[58] Presenting Private Peaceful in a manner calculated to evoke empathetic identification, Morpurgo lifted the figure of the shot-at-dawn soldier out of the messiness of history, making it safe for consumption by audiences of all ages. The success of *Private Peaceful*, in all its manifestations, might be seen as symptomatic of a broader shift in public perception. Fueled by a barrage of media representations over several decades, the dominant view of the war in the public arena had become one of a war of futility—an unmitigated tragedy whose victims were, above all, the common soldiers senselessly slaughtered by inept and unfeeling generals. These perceptions were heightened by a surge in battlefield tourism, where the sheer scale of loss was visibly imprinted on the visitor and where execution sites and graves of shot-at-dawn soldiers had become regular features of the itinerary, as in the Unquiet Graves Tour. In this climate, the shot-at-dawn soldier could become the ultimate figure for the horrors of the war—the stand-in for all the war's victims.

When in June 2006, then, one of the relatives of an executed soldier told a reporter, "There should be a statue in London of the soldiers who were shot at dawn rather than the one of General Haig," the comment was not entirely fanciful.[59] Eight years earlier, as the eightieth anniversary of the armistice was approaching in 1998, the *Express* ran a cover story, "Why Do We Let This Man Cast a Shadow over Our War Dead?," calling for the statue of Field Marshal Haig in London to be dismantled and replaced by a memorial to "one of the ordinary soldiers whose lives were lost in that great conflict . . . not of the general who, often needlessly, dispatched them to their deaths."[60] However farfetched the suggestion, it reflects in a striking manner how memorialization changes according to the needs of the living and how the ideas of posthumous harm and posthumous honor are subject to mutation; at the same time, the proposal proceeds through the logic of substitution, replacing one monument with another rather than, as with Woolf, for example, challenging the whole monument-making effort.

In a follow-up to the 1998 story questioning Haig's continued prominence in memorial culture, the *Express* noted the chorus of voices joining the protest, including Julian Putkowski, who commented, "I would like to see the statue melted down and the metal used to mint medals for the families of those executed as deserters and mutineers, even though they were shell-shocked and burnt out." Both stories circulated on the Shot at Dawn website. If in 2006 the moment was ripe for the government to take action, it was in part because the rhetoric of the pardons campaign had so successfully infiltrated public consciousness as to make such a reversal thinkable. But it was also because the campaign was symptomatic of a larger cultural transformation to which many forces contributed. This process was significantly aided by website links and social media. As early as 1993, Andrew Mackinlay, the MP for Thurrock who spearheaded the pardons campaign in Parliament, was announcing "overwhelming public support for it." "We now know," he proclaimed, "that, in a sense, the soldiers have already been pardoned by the highest court in the land—British public opinion."[61] It was a statement he would repeat over the years with increasing evidence to back him.

Over that time a variety of sites within the culture, drawing on different media and different social interests, came together to bolster the perception of a unanimous take on the subject. By the end of the campaign, so effectively had a single narrative come to dominate the public discourse on these soldiers that when Haig's son rose to defend his father's role in authorizing the executions, offering his demurral from the general enthusiasm for the impending pardons—"many were rogues, persistent deserters and criminals, or they were guilty of cowardice. They had to be made an example of" (*Northern Echo*, November 5, 2006)—his rhetoric sounded distinctly outdated, even churlish. Much the same could be said for the academic—mostly military—historians who continued to question the advisability of pardons, even after the government committed itself, as these dueling headlines from the *Telegraph* demonstrate: "Tears for the Families Who Lived with Shame"; "Historians Express Unease over Pardons" (August 17, 2006).

These interventions point to another twist in the posthumous harm narrative, turning attention from the soldiers as the injured parties to those who oversaw the military policy. In doing so, they transposed the locus of harm from the executions themselves and their toll on memory to the purported remedy supplied by the pardons and the new rites of commemoration that they generated.[62] For these detractors, the executed soldiers remained irredeemable. For the public at large, by contrast, the shot-at-dawn soldier had been effectively evacuated of controversy. The once-scandalous figure of the coward or deserter—a person no one talked about—had become a household name, had become in fact Private Peaceful. If it was in this context that the executed soldiers could be pardoned, it was also on these terms that they could

184   **CHAPTER 4**

now be named—named because they had become effectively nameless, increasingly detached from actual historical actors.

If the belated naming of the dead on war memorials marked a certain end to the legacy of shame and silence, the resolution was not without its ironies. For one thing, when new names were added to memorials and books of remembrance, their addition was far from seamless: the names appear out of order, often with obvious discrepancies in the size or style of the lettering, differences in materials, and an absence of weathering. They thus testify to the fact that their presence is an afterthought, reminding us that they were once missing and that an exclusion of so many years cannot simply be repaired by the stroke of a chisel. There is, in addition, a certain irony to the winning of this specific form of recognition at a time when, in many instances, the names on public monuments were becoming no more than that: names without faces or stories attached to them.[63] Many local memorials were suffering from neglect and disrepair, the brass in need of polishing or the stone so weathered as to render the inscriptions nearly illegible. Village memorials, moreover, were no longer the hub of community life or the site of collective mourning as they might have been in the 1920s when the unveiling of war memorials was a nearly daily occurrence. The spectacle of towns adding names to monuments, with their accompanying unveiling ceremonies, thus appears distinctly anachronistic.

In recalling these earlier times, however, the shot-at-dawn cases, with their long, contentious history, recall the forgotten histories of the monuments they modify, reminding us that the existing monuments were themselves the product of often fierce debate, persistent negotiation, and hard-won compromise over competing understandings of remembrance.[64] The absences their names repair, then, speak to other absences—some accidental omissions corrected in the past, others the results of deliberate decisions. They thus invite interrogation into the other war dead excluded, or unevenly represented, on existing monuments—nurses, Voluntary Aid Detachments (VADs), munitions workers, colonial soldiers and laborers, conscientious objectors—and other casualties such as those Michèle Barrett highlights, "survivors" of the war who struggled with postwar adjustment and disappeared into another kind of oblivion. "Had these men died," Barrett explains, "they would have been commemorated, as individuals, by name, on one of the memorials on the western front or at Gallipoli."[65] As it is, they have no formal recognition.

In *The Missing of the Somme*, Geoff Dyer observes, "By the mid-thirties the public construction of memory was complete. Since then only a few memorials have been built: addenda to the text of memory."[66] As self-conscious addenda to this text, the shot-at-dawn inscriptions, and the campaign that preceded them, call into question the project's completeness. As belated acts of remembrance, moreover, they expose the informing paradoxes they share with the larger memorial project in which they participate. Against the enforced anonymity of official erasure, to insist on a shot-at-dawn soldier being named, as their advocates demanded, is to insist on the fact that the life in question had meaning. At the same time, to do so is to choose for that soldier an alternative anonymity: to become merely one of the "millions of the mouthless dead" that Sorley so famously summoned; it was, in other words, to become just like all the others. In a context where naming became the new norm, it is the absence of a name, as the Shot at Dawn controversies remind us, that requires a narrative. To be included, to have one's name recorded, is no longer to be a name with a story attached to it. The plight of the executed soldiers has been marked by prohibitions on naming, remembering, and honoring, by the prohibition on telling men's shot-at-dawn stories. To a large extent, in the immediate postwar context, these soldiers were remembered only when their stories were not known or deliberately repressed, as on the gravestones in the military cemeteries.

The Shot at Dawn pardons campaign, launched in 1990, worked to put these names in the public consciousness, with its almost compulsive retelling of the men's stories; retelling their "offenses," it refused the shame attached to them, insisting that these men be known not in spite of the circumstances of their deaths but because of them. Indeed, the Shot at Dawn Memorial, with its oversize sculpture of a young soldier's body—blindfolded, hands tied behind his back, and on the verge of execution, surrounded by stakes representing all 306 victims—makes the manner of the soldier's death unmissable (figure 4.3). Marzena Sokolowska-Paryz has argued that the memorial's central figure is "the anti-thesis of the statues of the common soldier that had become immensely popular in the aftermath of the Great War." For unlike the more typical monuments, where heroic figures are found on raised platforms in central public locations and command the viewer's admiration, here "the statue of the condemned soldier is situated directly on the ground. There is no plinth to erect it to a position towering over the passer-by. The tied hands and the blindfold render the soldier defenceless against the fate awaiting him; he is a lonely and vulnerable figure, commanding pity."[67] Erected in 2001, a time when these men were publicly accorded little other recognition, the memorial celebrates the soldiers as victims. But the monument was also designed to disturb spectators by its overbearing presence, leaving open the question of the kind of memorial work it will perform in a postpardons context and how many people will continue to visit it. In these new circumstances, the memorial might become an even more emphatic act of witnessing, a testimony to the shame that persists despite the controversy's apparent resolution. With its chorus of dead and

Figure 4.3. Shot at Dawn Memorial, National Arboretum, Staffordshire. Photo credit: Alan Samuel, https://creativecommons.org/licenses/by/2.0/deed.en

living witnesses (the 306 stakes that surround the central figure, representing all of the dead soldiers, and the live spectators who visit the memorial), the memorial enshrines an episode in British history that provokes revulsion, whether or not one believes the government's actions were justified.

So successful was the publicity effort for this memorial and for the pardons campaign more generally that for a brief period the names at the center of the campaign became among the best known of the war's casualties: Harry Farr, for example, celebrated for being "Shell Shocked and Shot," was the subject of folk ballads, the inspiration for amateur poetics, and the onetime "owner" of a MySpace page.[68] Redacted in the tabloid press, circulated on the Internet, and broadcast on radio and television documentaries, the stories of shot-at-dawn soldiers passed into common parlance. There is perhaps a final irony: if the granting of pardons and the restoration of names to memorials and books of remembrance do indeed bring closure to this contentious subject, it may well be that what remembrance has earned these soldiers is the right to be forgotten, to, in effect, have their name inscribed without "Shot at Dawn" beside it.

Coda: Beyond Naming

Today, the naming of the dead has become such an established feature of the fabric of remembrance that scholars of commemoration have begun to put new questions to it. Jenny Edkins, for example, has argued that, given the "fundamental ambiguity and uncertainty" that surrounds all deaths (the fact that "in death as in life, a person is ultimately unnameable and unknowable, even to themselves"), "memorials that carry the names of the dead and missing— ubiquitous these days—need to be reexamined." This is particularly the case, she suggests, "when people are missing after wars or terrorist attacks, or after disappearances," when even the basic facts of time, place, and cause of death are open to contestation. It is also the case when the persons in question are migrants and the ambiguities of their status are accentuated, "bodies displaced from their established location, without documentation or recognition by governments, and often, of necessity, unacknowledged by their families."[69] The soldiers shot at dawn, of course, were not literally missing persons in this sense, although in some instances, as with other soldiers, their bodies were not found when the military cemeteries were being established; the belatedness in adding their names to memorials, moreover, was not connected to the problems of locating or identifying their bodies, as in the case of the 9/11 casualties, "the disappeared" in Argentina, or migrants missing at sea, some of the examples

188   **CHAPTER 4**

Edkins considers. In the strict sense of the terms as Edkins uses them, then, the shot-at-dawn cases represent neither of her paradigms: "bodies without names" or "names without bodies." In another sense, however, because of the British government's decision not to repatriate the bodies of any World War I soldiers, and the official suppression of names of the executed soldiers, they function in fact as both of these things. As I have tried to argue in this chapter, these men, after their deaths, were made to vanish; they became a version of the missing, even, in a sense, "the disappeared," unacknowledged and unevenly documented in both official and unofficial sites of remembrance, including family memory. The types of monuments that Edkins questions, moreover, are the inheritors of the Great War's memorial lexicon. Edkins's critique, then, might suggest some interesting avenues for further interrogation of World War I commemorative practices.

Edkins notes that although "it may seem obvious that bodies should be identified and relatives informed of a death, and that memorials should bear the names of those commemorated . . . it is important to think through what naming a body does politically."[70] The inherent paradox in Edkins's position (the tension between the obvious and the counterintuitive), I want to argue, is suggestive for thinking through the continuing legacy of the Shot at Dawn controversy and the closure promised by its naming ceremonies. Such a reexamination may be all the more pressing because in this instance so much energy has gone into thinking through the consequences of un-naming. In the case of these soldiers, as I have demonstrated in this chapter, the "obvious" was not initially self-evident. The issue of what relatives would be allowed to know about these deaths—would it be kinder, for example, to withhold the circumstances from them?; if they were informed, should they have access to the court-martial files?—and the question of whether these men should be publicly commemorated alongside other soldiers were both hotly contested, with anything like a consensus only emerging nearly a century later. Precisely because of this delay, seeing the men named openly on official memorials— and having the government publicly acknowledge what was done to them— emerged all the more emphatically as an imperative, the logical resolution to their systematic exclusion from practices of commemoration. For the relatives and advocates of these men, to name the dead was to confer on them a legitimacy that had long been denied them and to find for themselves some closure for their never-completed mourning. For the larger public, those with no direct connection to the dead, these acts validated a collective memory of the war they might not otherwise have been able to access. The "political" work that naming does, then, would seem in this case to be unambiguous.

Edkins's questioning of the obvious, however, invites speculation into other political agendas, into other interests served by memorialization as a form of closure: the transformation, to extend her argument, of the shot-at-dawn soldier into a "body that no longer disturbs," a body that can be reincorporated into "the body of the nation-state" and co-opted "into narratives of heroism, sacrifice, or national pride"—narratives, it should be added, that the soldiers' advocates actively embraced.[71] It invites, in other words, speculation into the narratives that were closed down or marginalized by the particular form the Shot at Dawn campaign assumed with its emphasis on posthumous restitution—on recognition, rehabilitation, and reincorporation within established frameworks—and, paradoxically enough, by the success of its efforts. One of the reasons the shot-at-dawn figure provoked so much uneasiness was the threat it posed to the British nation's image of itself—whether for those who were horrified that British soldiers could act the way they did in flouting their duty or those who were shocked that the British government could treat its own so inhumanely. It thus brought to the fore what postwar commemoration deliberately excluded: "the disturbing emotions of horror, shame and guilt that often embroil the survivors of carnage." In exposing "the abject realities of trench warfare," it threatened to expose the field of battle as itself "ignominious."[72] In this respect, the *inability* of these soldiers to be subsumed into traditional structures of commemoration may signal their most forceful political statement: their capacity to call into question the very pieties through which war is rationalized.

Writing about the Vietnam Veterans Memorial, Sturken critiques the rush to closure provoked by the belatedness of this recognition, roughly ten years after the cessation of a war in which American involvement had been both lengthy and contentious: "When, for instance, *Newsweek* printed a story entitled 'Honoring Vietnam Veterans—At Last' in 1982, the desire not only to rectify but to *forget* the mistreatment of veterans was obvious. To forget this episode in American history is not only to negate the ongoing struggles of veterans . . . but also to cease to examine the reasons why these men and women had been scapegoated."[73] In the case of the shot-at-dawn soldiers, the "rupture in public commemoration" was of considerably longer duration, and the pressure, after practically ninety years, "to draw a line" under this unhappy episode, as was frequently suggested, even more urgent.[74] The awarding of pardons, then, and the naming ceremonies that for a period of time accompanied them were met with a resounding chorus of "at last's" in media headlines and public proclamations. Sturken's critique, however, invites us to consider whether a similar desire to forget also informs these reparative gestures: Do these acts of

190   **CHAPTER 4**

remembrance allow the nation to forget an episode people would prefer to put behind them, to forget, in fact, precisely the treatment of the soldiers that made them a cause célèbre? And do they foreclose further examination of why these men were scapegoated in the first place—first by the military and then by the larger public?

In this context, the language and scope of the pardon are worth noting. As the official document appended to the courts-martial dossiers attests, "This pardon stands as recognition that [the named soldier] was one of the many victims of the First World War and that execution was not the fate he deserved." Significantly, the pardon does not vacate the soldier's prior conviction; it falls short, moreover, of any admission of wrongdoing on the part of the government and scrupulously avoids assigning blame for the executions. As Des Browne explains, "The pardon should not be seen as casting doubt on either the procedures and processes of the time or the judgment of those who took these very difficult decisions."[75] The blanket pardon, in addition, spares the government the thankless task of re-adjudicating the cases and becoming responsible for equally difficult present-day decisions. However humane the gesture, then, and however sincere its motivation, the desire to forget and move on is also unmistakable. In effect, one might argue, it is the nation that the pardon ultimately exonerates. At the least, it delimits the ways the executions are meant to be understood for the future, foreclosing the moral doubt their presence insinuated into the collective memory of the war and its rites of memorialization.

Sidelined in this resolution are uncomfortable questions about inequities within what was already a contentious military practice—questions provoked by differential applications of military law and differences among the men who were its victims. In the years and months preceding the British pardons decision, for example, the Irish had been extremely vocal in alleging disproportionately harsh treatment of their soldiers and demanding separate pardons for them; they may have been on the verge of winning this concession when their claims were subsumed in the blanket pardon.[76] Indian soldiers, who constituted a considerably larger portion of the British armed forces than the Irish, did not provoke similar advocacy, in part because no records of courts-martial in the Indian army have survived and consequently individual soldiers could not be pardoned. Nonetheless, Gerard Oram concludes that "the overall impression is that the Indians were treated particularly badly by the courts martial and it appears likely, from the surviving fragments of evidence, that most death sentences were carried out."[77] As Santanu Das suggests, moreover, in opening *Race, Empire, and First World War Writing* with the story of an Indian deserter, desertion itself might be understood and remembered very differently in a colonial context; it could, among other things, be considered an act worthy of being remembered, helping to explain how a deserting soldier's diary becomes "a rare, if not the only surviving, example of a trench notebook by an Indian soldier of the First World War."[78]

Colonial and other nonwhite laborers, who were executed mostly for murder, lie outside the purview of the pardons campaign, and they were not included in official government records of military executions. The exact number of such cases is unknown, but Oram speculates that it would have been considerable.[79] Julian Putkowski and Mark Dunning have recently advanced the case that pardons for soldiers executed for murder deserve reconsideration.[80] Within a larger context where all of the executed soldiers could be considered to have been scapegoated or killed "for the sake of example," the possibility that particular groups were subject to further scapegoating—the mentally deficient, the physically weak or undersized (as in the Bantam units), the psychologically damaged, colonial soldiers and laborers—raises disturbing questions that we might not want to prematurely silence. Although it was undoubtedly the case that a good number of the soldiers whose death sentences were carried out were, as apologists for the executions maintain, the most egregious offenders, there is also evidence to suggest that, as Oram has argued, in some instances at least, sentencing decisions were influenced by ideas about race, degeneracy, and eugenics, as they intersected with issues of discipline.[81] The disturbing specter of the shot-at-dawn soldier can thus shed light on the larger question of what it meant, in this war, with its massive death toll, to think of men as expendable. And it reminds us of why the unquiet graves of these soldiers should continue to call to us.

I am not, I want to make clear, arguing against the pardoning of the executed soldiers or against the recognition of these men on national and local memorials and monuments. I do want to suggest, however, that closure, if it is being achieved, may be premature, and that naming these dead is not necessarily the end of the story. Rather than simply neutralizing this figure as a victim like millions of others, we may also want to continue to critically examine the work it accomplishes through its power to disturb, particularly as we reevaluate the war and its legacy in the twenty-first century. However much proponents on both sides of the controversy have tried to draw clear lines under the subject, part of what has given the shot-at-dawn soldier such a hold on collective memory is precisely its ambiguity. His is a figure hard to classify, both collectively and individually—one that does not fit easily into available categories like "hero" or "coward." Nor does it fit into categories like conscientious objector or antiwar activist. When the designation of graves in the military cemeteries was being debated in Parliament in 1919, Colonel Lambert

192   CHAPTER 4

Ward appealed to his fellow MPs to treat the graves of the executed soldiers the same as all the others, arguing, "They were not cowards in the accepted meaning of the word."[82] What makes the figure of the shot-at-dawn soldier so troubling, I want to suggest, is also what makes it productive for further thinking—it challenges the accepted meaning of words, unraveling terms like "hero," "patriotism," "coward," and "sacrifice," rendering them ambiguous not just for its own special case but for soldiers more generally. As a figure of contagion, moreover, it threatens to unravel other narratives it touches on; it thus stands as a visible reminder of what the culture of memory may not want to remember.

I want to end this chapter where I began, at the grave of Private Ingham. In *The Missing of the Somme*, Geoff Dyer meditates on his culture's obsession with the Great War's memory through the vehicle of a road trip to the battlefield cemeteries in this sector—a trip that culminates at the great monument to names, the Memorial to the Missing of the Somme at Thiepval. Along the way, Dyer makes a significant detour, calling attention to the effort he expends to find the village of Bailleulmont and the grave that Ingham's father marked so idiosyncratically. "The deserter's grave has become a hero's grave," Dyer intones at the grave site; "pride has come to reside not in the carrying out of duty but in its humane dereliction."[83] Prefacing his visit with the observation, "Perhaps the real heroes of 1914–18, then, are those who refused to obey and to fight, who actively rejected the passivity forced on them by the war, who reasserted their right not to suffer, not to have things done to them," Dyer explicitly links the shot-at-dawn soldiers to antiwar resisters. He cements this point with a footnote to the newly dedicated Conscientious Objectors' Commemorative Stone in Tavistock Square—a memorial, as discussed in chapter 3, "To all those who have established and are maintaining the right to refuse to kill."[84] In doing so, he opens the way for the shot-at-dawn soldier to serve other uses, much the way German deserters in World War II were subsequently honored as agents of resistance; long before the Shot at Dawn movement achieved its signal victories, he claims for these British soldiers a different type of heroism from the state-sponsored variety upheld on traditional monuments, and he claims for them a form of active agency that lifts them out of victimhood.

Dyer's move returns us to Edkins's questioning of the traditional memorial project but also to a potential reservation she voices about her own practice: "Does contesting naming prevent one sort of co-option but entail another: the co-option into alternative, oppositional narratives?"[85] Dyer's narrative, unrecognizable perhaps to either Ingham or his father, might be a prime example of such co-optation, although this fact does not necessarily completely invalidate it. After all, the question remains whether the story of these soldiers has ever been anything but co-opted, their identity subsumed in the shot-at-dawn rubric. From the moment of their arrest, their narrative was circumscribed by the legal constraints and administrative protocols of military justice, and their executions packaged for their deterrent value. By and large, the men themselves were not absent and missing in any sense other than the fact and conditions of their execution. For their advocates as much as for their detractors, their story became what others could make out of it. They thus stand as the ultimate example of a process I have been tracing throughout this book. Beginning in 2001, each year at the annual Remembrance Day ceremony at the Cenotaph, the National Union of Journalists would lay a wreath in memory of these SAD soldiers. One such wreath bore the inscription "May those who could not stand the tumult of battle rest in eternal silence. We will speak for them."[86] Unable to speak in their own defense at their trials, and unable to speak in the long afterlife their notoriety earned them, these men were persistently spoken for.

More so than other war dead, the shot-at-dawn soldiers were defined by the condition of posthumousness—by their ability to live on after death as the ingloriously executed. Officially expunged and forgotten, they returned to haunt the national memory. It remains open to question what kind of afterlife they would have enjoyed had they died some other way. In 1998, John Reid, then minister for the armed forces, called on his fellow citizens to recognize "those who were executed for what they were—the victims, with millions of others, of a cataclysmic and ghastly war."[87] What these soldiers *were*, however, is precisely what cannot be answered—what cannot be easily distinguished from what they *did* and, even more, what was *done to them*, and what cannot be readily reconstructed in the absence of intimate personal histories or even detailed biographical information. Reid's inclusive gesture thus glosses over the defining paradox of their troubled existence: their posthumous lives, ironically enough, have been much better documented than any life they lived before their executions. This of course is true to some extent for all the figures this book has been considering: the material boys, embalmed in memorial volumes that at once expose and contest the missing life they record; the boy poet Sorley, repeatedly refitted to meet the affective needs of succeeding generations and disparate constituencies; the missing female Shakespeare Woolf would conjure into existence; or Edith Cavell, lost in the obsessive commemoration she generated. In the case of the shot-at-dawn soldiers, however, the contradictions in their survival are even more telling. Their prolonged existence in the public imagination, indeed, has everything to do with the fact

194   **CHAPTER 4**

that they were victims *unlike* millions of others. The story of their lives, then, is the story of their deaths in a way that separates even as it joins them to the others.

In 1993, in explaining his government's refusal to consider the question of pardons, Prime Minister John Major famously remarked, "I have reflected long and hard but I have reached the conclusion that we cannot re-write history by substituting our latter-day judgement for that of contemporaries, whatever we might think" (*Independent*, February 20, 1993). In replacing the military tribunal with the court of public opinion, the Shot at Dawn campaign opened the question of remembering the past to a variety of interlocutors. At the heart of the subject's contentiousness was the possibility it posed of wresting the war story from a class of military and academic professionals and of appropriating the discourse of remembrance for those who had been purposefully forgotten. If the case of the shot-at-dawn soldiers stages these concerns in an especially dramatic fashion, it also returns us to fundamentals: Whose war? Whose memory?[88] In doing so, it illuminates concerns that have run through this entire book. Whose memories survive, and whose are obliterated? How is memory manufactured? How is remembrance legislated and contested? Is there a space for resistance? What kind of affective responses do particular commemorative practices countenance and solicit, and how do such practices change over time? If "Lest We Forget" constituted a postwar watchword, the phrase is curiously unspecific in its object, leaving space for competing understandings of our obligation to remember. As I have been arguing throughout this book, and as other scholars of commemoration have argued before me, neither history nor remembrance is something static. In *The Work of the Dead*, Thomas Laqueur observes, "Names of the dead, like exhumed bodies, can remake history for the present."[89] In the case of the shot-at-dawn soldiers, the names of the dead, as I have tried to show in this chapter—in their presence and in their absence—do this by injecting ambiguity into established narratives about the nature of the war and its practices of remembrance. Like the other figures this book considers, they thus contribute to our understanding of the way the afterlives of the war have been enlarged and enriched by being reimagined and rewritten from a multiplicity of directions.

Notes

Preface

1. Gail Braybon, introduction to *Evidence, History and the Great War: Historians and the Impact of 1914–18*, ed. Gail Braybon (New York: Berghahn Books, 2003), 8.

2. See Dan Todman, "The Ninetieth Anniversary of the Battle of the Somme," in *War Memory and Popular Culture: Essays on Modes of Remembrance and Commemoration*, ed. Michael Keren and Holger H. Herwig (Jefferson, NC: McFarland, 2009), 27.

3. Geoff Dyer, *The Missing of the Somme* (New York: Vintage, 2011), 2. Dyer's book was originally published in 1994. Todman has argued that, in fact, "not everyone could easily claim a familial link," but he acknowledges, "by 2006, after repeated appearances in novels, documentaries and news reporting, the rhetoric of family history as a means of participation in the commemoration of World War I had become so strong that those who could not draw a link would either seek one out or be left jealous and bereft." See Todman, "Ninetieth Anniversary," 31–32.

Introduction

1. "Tower Poppies' Debt to the Potteries / Letters: Tristram Hunt MP," *Guardian*, December 29, 2014, https://www.theguardian.com/world/2014/dec/29/tower -poppies-debt-to-the-potteries; Mark Brown, "Blood-Swept Lands: The Story behind the Tower of London Poppies Tribute," *Guardian*, December 28, 2014, https://www .theguardian.com/world/2014/dec/28/blood-swept-lands-story-behind-tower-of -london-poppies-first-world-war-memorial. The *Financial Times* went even further, calling the exhibit "largely the most effective expression of commemoration in British history." Quoted in Paul Hardin Kapp and Cele C. Otnes, "The Poppies Exhibit: Producing and Consuming Commemoration of World War I in Britain," in *Heritage of Death: Landscapes of Emotion, Memory and Practice*, ed. Mattias Frihammar and Helaine Silverman (New York: Routledge, 2018), 112.

2. Alex King, "Remembering and Forgetting in the Public Memorials of the Great War," in *The Art of Forgetting*, eds. Adrian Forty and Susanne Küchler (Oxford: Berg, 1999), 147.

3. PRO: War Cabinet and Cabinet Minutes 23/11, July 4, 1919, War Cabinet 588, Minute 1; quoted in Jenny Edkins, *Trauma and the Memory of Politics* (Cambridge: Cambridge University Press, 2003), 60.

4. Quoted in David W. Lloyd, *Battlefield Tourism: Pilgrimage and the Commemoration of the Great War in Britain, Australia and Canada, 1919–1939* (Oxford: Berg, 1998), 88.

NOTES TO PAGES 4–9

5. Marianne Hirsch, *The Generation of Postmemory: Writing and Visual Culture after the Holocaust* (New York: Columbia University Press, 2012), 5.

6. Tom Piper, "A Note from the Designer," in Imperial War Museum [hereafter IWM], *Poppies: Blood Swept Lands and Seas of Red* (London: IWM, 2018), 12.

7. Quoted in Brown, "Blood-Swept Lands." For responses to the Unknown Warrior, see Thomas W. Laqueur, *The Work of the Dead: A Cultural History of Mortal Remains* (Princeton, NJ: Princeton University Press, 2015), 481.

8. Jonathan Jones, "The Tower of London Poppies Are Fake, Trite and Inward-Looking, a Ukip-Style Memorial," *Guardian*, October 28, 2014, https://www.theguardian.com/artanddesign/jonathanjonesblog/2014/oct/28/tower-of-london-poppies-ukip-remembrance-day. The comment about the Unknown Warrior is from the *Bradford Pioneer* for November 12, 1920; quoted in Laqueur, *Work of the Dead*, 482.

9. Quoted in Ben Riley-Smith, "David Cameron Defends 'Stunning' Tower of London Poppy Memorial amid Criticism from Guardian Writer," *Telegraph*, October 29, 2014, https://www.telegraph.co.uk/news/politics/david-cameron/11195377/David-Cameron-defends-stunning-Tower-of-London-poppy-memorial-amid-criticism-from-Guardian-writer.html.

10. See Brown, "Blood-Swept Lands."

11. Kapp and Otnes make a similar argument, calling the installation a "remarkable instance of the simultaneous commemoration and commercialization of death heritage." See Kapp and Otnes, "Poppies Exhibit," 107. The same convergence can be seen in the sites chosen for the 2015–2018 touring exhibition of two sculptures from The Poppies: *Wave* and *Weeping Window*. Concerns about these problematic intersections were heightened when it was revealed that only approximately one-third of the money raised by the sale of the individual poppies was actually going to the designated charities. See, for example, Sam Greenhill, "Just a Third of Tower Poppy Cash Is Going to Help Our Heroes: So Who WILL Be Pocketing the Rest?," *Daily Mail*, September 12, 2014, http://www.dailymail.co.uk/news/article-2754319/Just-Tower-poppy-cash-going-help-heroes-So-WILL-pocketing-rest.html.

12. See James F. English, *The Economy of Prestige: Prizes, Awards, and the Circulation of Cultural Value* (Cambridge, MA: Harvard University Press, 2008), 34.

13. See "Rachel Whiteread Nissen Hut: Part of the Shy Sculpture Series," 14-18 NOW, October 10, 2018, https://www.1418now.org.uk/commissions/nissen-hut-part-of-the-shy-scultpure-series/.

14. Kate Connolly, "Closed Books and Stilled Lives," *Guardian*, October 25, 2000, https://www.theguardian.com/world/2000/oct/26/kateconnolly.

15. Brown, "Blood-Swept Lands"; "Tower of London Poppies Honor 'Lives They Would Have Led,'" *NBC News*, November 10, 2014, https://www.nbcnews.com/nightly-news/tower-london-poppies-honor-lives-they-would-have-led-n245621.

16. Jay Winter, *Sites of Memory, Sites of Mourning: The Great War in European Cultural History* (Cambridge: Cambridge University Press, 1995), 54. See also Michèle Barrett, "The Great War and Post-modern Memory," *New Formations* 41 (Autumn 2000): 138–157.

17. Edkins, *Trauma and the Memory of Politics*, 72.

18. Quoted in "14-18 NOW to Take Poppies Art Installation around the UK," 14-18 NOW, November 8, 2014, https://www.1418now.org.uk/news/14-18-now-take

NOTES TO PAGES 9–11   197

-poppies-around-uk/. For a discussion of the nationalist component in Cameron's vision of the centenary, see Ben Wellings, Shanti Sumartojo, and Matthew Graves, "Commemorating Race and Empire in the First World War Centenary," in *Commemorating Race and Empire in the First World War Centenary*, ed. Ben Wellings and Shanti Sumartojo (Liverpool: Liverpool University Press, 2018), 8.

19. Winter, *Sites of Memory*, 80.

20. Virginia Woolf, *The Diary of Virginia Woolf*, vol. 2, *1920–1924*, ed. Anne Olivier Bell (New York: Harcourt, 1978), 80, 81.

21. See Marlene A. Briggs, "D. H. Lawrence, Collective Mourning, and Cultural Reconstruction after World War I," in *Modernism and Mourning*, ed. Patricia Rae (Lewisburg, PA: Bucknell University Press, 2007), 204.

22. See Lloyd, *Battlefield Tourism*, 90–91; Adrian Gregory, *The Silence of Memory: Armistice Day 1919–1946* (Oxford: Berg, 1994), 59.

23. Paul Cummins, "A Note from the Artist," in IWM, *Poppies*, 8. Although Cummins did sometimes mention this fact in interviews at the time of the exhibition, he did not do so consistently, and it received very little attention in the media feeding frenzy that surrounded The Poppies.

24. Santanu Das, "The First World War and the Colour of Memory," *Guardian*, July 22, 2014, https://www.theguardian.com/commentisfree/2014/jul/22/first-world-war-whitewashed-eurocentric.

25. Claire Buck, *Conceiving Strangeness in British First World War Writing* (London: Palgrave Macmillan, 2015), 2.

26. See Jenny Kidd and Joanne Sayner, "Unthinking Remembrance? Blood Swept Lands and Seas of Red and the Significance of Centenaries," *Cultural Trends* 27, no. 2 (2018): 68–82, https://doi.org/10.1080/09548963.2018.1453448.

27. Laqueur, for example, refers to the "spurious precision in any narrative collection of names." See Laqueur, *Work of the Dead*, 659n20. A 2018 memorial, the "Poppy of Honour," advertising itself as "the first national memorial holding the collective names of every person killed or missing in action in WWI," puts the death toll at 1,115,471. For colonial burial practices, see Michèle Barrett, "Afterword: Death and the Afterlife," in *Race, Empire, and First World War Writing*, ed. Santanu Das (Cambridge: Cambridge University Press, 2011), 301–320; and Barrett, "'White Graves' and Natives: The Imperial War Graves Commission in East and West Africa, 1918–1939," in *Bodies in Conflict: Corporeality, Materiality and Transformation*, ed. Paul Cornish and Nicholas J. Saunders (London: Routledge, 2014), 80–90.

28. Judith Butler, *Frames of War: When Is Life Grievable?* (London: Verso, 2009).

29. Nicholas J. Saunders, *The Poppy: A Cultural History from Ancient Egypt to Flanders Fields to Afghanistan* (London: Oneworld, 2013), 106–111. The practice of hiring war veterans was echoed in Cummins's decision "to employ only artisans whose family had experienced a direct, personal loss in the war" for the creation of the poppies for the 2014 Tower of London exhibition. See Kapp and Otnes, "Poppies Exhibit," 113.

30. Quoted in Gregory, *Silence of Memory*, 111, 155.

31. "Five Reasons People Don't Wear Poppies," *BBC News*, 9 November 9, 2015, http://www.bbc.com/news/magazine-34720464.

32. Gregory, *Silence of Memory*, 153. In yet another controversy, Sri Lankans established their own alternative flower-selling movement in the interwar years, the Suriya-Mal

198   NOTES TO PAGES 11–14

Movement, when "the British decided that money raised by the sale of poppies was exclusively for the benefit of *British* ex-servicemen; money would not be given to support Sri Lankan veterans." See Saunders, *Poppy*, 155–156.

33. See IWM, *Poppies*, 158.

34. Hew Strachan, "First World War Anniversary: We Must Do More Than Remember," *Daily Telegraph*, January 17, 2013. Kidd and Sayner's survey of 1,488 visitor responses to The Poppies concludes that the exhibition did little more than reactivate the familiar. See Kidd and Sayner, "Unthinking Remembrance?," 75–78.

35. Quoted in Alastair Sooke, "Tower of London Poppies Creator Tom Piper on Being Snubbed by the Art World," *Telegraph*, May 26, 2016, https://www.telegraph.co.uk/theatre/what-to-see/tower-of-london-poppies-creator-tom-piper-on-being-snubbed-by-th/.

36. Steph Cockroft and Corey Charlton, "From the First Ceramic Poppy to the Last: How the Tower's Moat of Flowers Grew over Four Months to Create Unforgettable Memorial," *Mail Online*, November 11, 2014, https://www.dailymail.co.uk/news/article-2829776/How-poppy-memorial-nearly-never-Artist-installation-called-reinforcements-realising-never-able-produce-flowers-time-Armistice-Day.html.

37. The full poem appears in IWM, *Poppies*, 15.

38. Quoted in Santanu Das, "Indians at Home, Mesopotamia and France, 1914–1918: Towards an Intimate History," in Das, *Race, Empire, and First World War Writing*, 78, 79.

39. See Hirsch, *Generation of Postmemory*: "Postmemorial work, I want to suggest—and this is the central point of my argument in this book—strives to *reactivate* and *re-embody* more distant political and cultural memorial structures by reinvesting them with resonant individual and familial forms of mediation and aesthetic expression" (33).

40. As David Cameron explained, "By displaying parts of the installation around the country and then permanently in the Imperial War Museum, we have ensured that this poignant memorial will be saved for the nation." "Tower of London Poppies: Thousands to Go on Tour," *BBC News*, November 9, 2014, http://www.bbc.com/news/uk-29965477.

41. Annette Becker, "Museums, Architects and Artists on the Western Front: New Commemoration for a New History?," in *Remembering the First World War*, ed. Bart Ziino (Abingdon, Oxon: Routledge, 2015), 97.

42. See IWM, *Poppies*, 12. According to the website, forty thousand poppies have been "planted" online: https://www.wherearethepoppiesnow.org.uk (accessed October 1, 2019).

43. Such practices had historical precedents. Battlefield tourism was a central feature of postwar commemoration, and both the Cenotaph and the Tomb of the Unknown Warrior drew tourists from across England. After being dismantled, the temporary Cenotaph found a home in the Imperial War Museum at Crystal Palace.

44. Jeremy Deller's *We're Here Because We're Here* was a UK-wide performance art event in which fourteen hundred volunteers dressed in World War I military uniforms started popping up in locations all over the United Kingdom on July 1, 2016, each representing a soldier who had died on that day; see 14-18 NOW, "We're Here Because We're Here," YouTube, November 10, 2016, https://www.youtube.com/watch?v=1pd1XYx27_U.

NOTES TO PAGES 14–22   199

45. The complete set of photographs can be viewed at Chloe Dewe Mathews's website, http://www.chloedewemathews.com/shot-at-dawn/.

46. *The 306*, a series of plays written by Oliver Emanuel and composer Gareth Williams, and directed by Laura Sansom for the National Theatre of Scotland, focuses on the lives of three executed soldiers. The first part was performed in 2016, with parts 2 and 3 following in 2017 and 2018. In filling in and giving dramatic shape to the missing lives of these soldiers, the plays take an opposite approach to the subject from Mathews.

47. One of the conditions for the erection of the memorial in the National Arboretum was that no public funds would be used for it.

48. Bess Twiston-Davies, "Public Pays Its Respects to the First World War Deserters," *Telegraph*, January 5, 2001, https://www.telegraph.co.uk/news/uknews/1313221/Public-pays-its-respects-to-the-First-World-War-deserters.html; Jonathan Black, "'Thanks for the Memory': War Memorials, Spectatorship and the Trajectories of Commemoration 1919–2001," in *Matters of Conflict: Material Culture, Memory and the First World War*, ed. Nicholas J. Saunders (Abingdon, Oxfordshire: Routledge, 2004), 146.

49. Geoff Dyer, "Dead Time," in *Shot at Dawn*, by Chloe Dewe Mathews et al. (Madrid: Ivory Press, 2014), n.p.

50. Sean O'Hagan, "Chloe Dewe Mathews's Shot at Dawn: A Moving Photographic Memorial," *Observer*, June 29, 2014, https://www.theguardian.com/artanddesign/2014/jun/29/chloe-dewe-mathews-shot-at-dawn-moving-photographic-memorial-first-world-war.

51. O'Hagan.

52. Winter, *Sites of Memory*, 1.

53. Becker, "Museums, Architects and Artists," 91.

54. Dyer, "Dead Time," n.p.

55. Becker, "Museums, Architects and Artists," 90.

56. Dyer, "Dead Time," n.p.

57. As I discuss in chapter 3, during the war, the Tower was the site of executions of German spies who were shot at dawn. Its "bloody history" is thus even more complex than might immediately be apparent.

58. Winter, *Sites of Memory*, 10.

59. Alex King, *Memorials of the Great War in Britain: The Symbolism and Politics of Remembrance* (Oxford: Berg, 1999), 242. Adrian Gregory makes a similar claim: "The discourse of memory was a national discourse." See Gregory, *Silence of Memory*, 6.

60. See King, *Memorials of the Great War*; Gregory, *Silence of Memory*; and Lloyd, *Battlefield Tourism*—all published as part of Berg's Legacy of the Great War Series, under Jay Winter's general editorship, and all bearing a poppy imprint on their covers. Catherine Moriarty has published a number of important articles on the subject, cited in later chapters. In addition, Ken Inglis has done pioneering work in the field, especially on Australian memorials.

61. Jay Winter and Emmanuel Sivan, "Setting the Framework," in *War and Remembrance in the Twentieth Century*, ed. Jay Winter and Emmanuel Sivan (Cambridge: Cambridge University Press, 1999), 39.

62. I borrow this formulation from Fran Brearton, who describes the poetic practice of writers like Ted Hughes and Michael Longley as "a remembering forwards as

200 NOTES TO PAGES 23–30

well as backwards." See Fran Brearton, "'But That Is Not New': Poetic Legacies of the First World War," in *The Cambridge Companion to the Poetry of the First World War*, ed. Santanu Das (Cambridge: Cambridge University Press, 2013), 231.

63. Sally Minogue and Andrew Palmer make a related point in their discussion of World War I poetry: "The desire to keep the dead alive was perhaps more acute and more sustained in the First World War precisely because of the numbers of dead." See Sally Minogue and Andrew Palmer, *The Remembered Dead: Poetry, Memory and the First World War* (Cambridge: Cambridge University Press, 2018), 23.

64. RG to Siegfried Sassoon, May 31, 1922, in Robert Graves, *In Broken Images: Selected Letters of Robert Graves, 1914–1916*, ed. Paul O'Prey (London: Hutchinson, 1982), 134.

65. Similar sentiments can be found, for example, in memoirs by Siegfried Sassoon, Edmund Blunden, and Vera Brittain. In what might stand as a trope for his entire memoir, Graves even testifies to the posthumous existence he enjoys after officially being declared dead. See Robert Graves, *Good-Bye to All That* (New York: Anchor Books, 1998), 219–228.

66. See, for example, Lecia Rosenthal, *Mourning Modernism: Literature, Catastrophe and the Politics of Consolation* (New York: Fordham University Press, 2011), and Erin E. Edwards, *The Modernist Corpse: Posthumanism and the Posthumous* (Minneapolis: University of Minnesota Press, 2018). See also Tambling, below. While the posthumous is frequently identified with a decisive rupture occurring sometime in the twentieth century, it is often linked to later occurrences in the century, most notably the Holocaust.

67. Jeremy Tambling, *Becoming Posthumous: Life and Death in Literary and Cultural Studies* (Edinburgh: Edinburgh University Press, 2001), 7.

68. Gregory, *Silence of Memory*, 119.

69. See Das, introduction, in *Race, Empire, and First World War Writing*, 7.

70. The *OED* lists as its first definition of "memory," now obsolete, "An act of commemoration, esp. of the dead." The latest example of this usage that it lists is from 1885.

71. Sarah Cole, *Modernism, Male Friendship, and the First World War* (Cambridge: Cambridge University Press, 2003), 212–213.

72. For significant exceptions, see Allyson Booth, *Postcards from the Trenches: Negotiating the Space between Modernism and the First World War* (New York: Oxford University Press, 1996), and Alice Kelly, *Commemorative Modernisms: Women Writers, Death, and the First World War* (Edinburgh: Edinburgh University Press, 2020). Kelley's book was published after my manuscript was completed and under review. More typically, studies linking twentieth-century literature with commemoration have focused on popular literature, as in Marzena Sokolowska-Paryz, *Reimagining the War Memorial, Reinterpreting the Great War: The Formats of British Commemorative Fiction* (Newcastle upon Tyne: Cambridge Scholars, 2012), or on war poetry, as in Minogue and Palmer, *Remembered Dead*.

73. Samuel Hynes coined the term "anti-monuments" to characterize the "paintings, poems, novels, histories, plays, music" that offered an "alternative version of the war's meaning" to the public monuments that extolled "value-bearing abstractions"; Hynes, *A War Imagined: The First World War and English Culture* (New York: Atheneum, 1991), 283. For resistant mourning, see Rae, *Modernism and Mourning*.

NOTES TO PAGES 30–35   201

74. Paul Fussell, *The Great War and Modern Memory*, 25th anniversary ed. (Oxford: Oxford University Press, 2000).

75. Leonard V. Smith, "Paul Fussell's *The Great War and Modern Memory*: Twenty-Five Years Later," *History and Theory* 40, no. 2 (May 2001): 242, https://www.jstor.org/stable/2678033.

76. Patricia Rae notes how the dissolution of "generic barriers" around the study of mourning, initiated by Jahan Ramazani in the coda to his book *Poetry of Mourning: The Modern Elegy from Hardy to Heaney* (Chicago: University of Chicago Press, 1994), allows us to perceive "the social significance of what might otherwise be seen only as nonconsequential expressions of private sentiment." Rae, "Introduction: Modernist Mourning," in *Modernism and Mourning*, 15.

77. Jahan Ramazani, "Afterword: 'When There Are So Many We Shall Have to Mourn,'" in Rae, *Modernism and Mourning*, 287.

78. Booth, *Postcards from the Trenches*, 17.

79. See, for example, Booth; Cole, *Modernism, Male Friendship*; Sarah Cole, *At the Violet Hour: Modernism and Violence in England and Ireland* (Oxford: Oxford University Press, 2012); Das, *Race, Empire, and First World War Writing*; Das, *The Cambridge Companion to the Poetry of the First World War*; Santanu Das and Kate McLoughlin, eds., *The First World War: Literature, Culture, Modernity* (Oxford: Oxford University Press, 2018); Christine Froula, *Virginia Woolf and the Bloomsbury Avant-Garde: War, Civilization, Modernity* (New York: Columbia University Press, 2005); Vincent Sherry, *The Great War and the Language of Modernism* (Oxford: Oxford University Press, 2003).

80. Andrew Frayn, "Introduction: Modernism and the First World War," *Modernist Cultures* 12, no. 1 (2017): 2, DOI: 10.3366/mod.2017.0153.

81. Barrett, "Great War and Post-modern Memory," 142.

82. Winter, *Sites of Memory*, 5.

83. Michael Kimmelman, "Out of Minimalism, Monuments to Memory," *New York Times*, January 13, 2002; quoted in Erika Doss, *Memorial Mania: Public Feeling in America* (Chicago: University of Chicago Press, 2010), 123.

1. Material Boys

1. Pamela Glenconner, *Edward Wyndham Tennant: A Memoir by His Mother* (London: John Lane, 1919), 312 (hereafter cited in text as *EWT*). Parts of this chapter, framed around memorial volumes produced by women, were published as "Writing Modern Deaths: Women, War, and the View from the Home Front," in *The History of British Women's Writing, 1880–1920*, vol. 7, ed. Holly A. Laird (London: Palgrave Macmillan, 2016), 284–297.

2. Dyer, *The Missing of the Somme*, 15, 32.

3. Hynes, *A War Imagined*, 212.

4. See Susan Stewart, *On Longing: Narratives of the Miniature, the Gigantic, the Souvenir, the Collection* (Durham, NC: Duke University Press, 1992), 132–150.

5. Vera Brittain, *Testament of Youth: An Autobiographical Study of the Years 1900–1925* (New York: Penguin Books, 2005), 252.

6. See, for example, Nicholas J. Saunders, *Trench Art: Materialities and Memories of War* (Oxford: Berg, 2003); Nicholas J. Saunders and Paul Cornish, eds., *Contested Objects:*

202   **NOTES TO PAGES 35–38**

Material Memories of the Great War (Abingdon, Oxon: Routledge, 2009); and Saunders, *Matters of Conflict.*

7. Kate McLoughlin, Lara Feigel, and Nancy Martin, "Writing War, Writing Lives," *Textual Practice* 29, no. 7 (2015): 1219, https://doi.org/DOI:10.1080/0950236X.2015.1095442.

8. Max Saunders has argued that "autobiography experienced a crisis in the later nineteenth century, partly because its project came to seem impossible." See Max Saunders, *Self Impression: Life-Writing, Autobiografiction, and the Forms of Modern Literature* (Oxford: Oxford University Press, 2010), 10.

9. Sir Sidney Lee, *Principles of Biography: The Leslie Stephen Lecture Delivered in the Senate House, Cambridge on 13 May 1911* (Cambridge: Cambridge University Press, 1911), 9.

10. Quoted in Michael Holroyd, *Lytton Strachey: The New Biography* (New York: Farrar, Straus and Giroux, 1995), 397.

11. According to Holroyd, "The war had acted as a catalyst on *Eminent Victorians* which began without a thesis but acquired a theme. Strachey had started his 'Victorian Silhouettes' in the spirit of detached irony, but was moved by circumstances to a moral conviction that gave his book its artistic cohesion." See Holroyd, *Lytton Strachey*, 421.

12. Lytton Strachey, *Eminent Victorians: The Definitive Edition* (London: Continuum, 2002), [3].

13. Holroyd, *Lytton Strachey*, 345, 421.

14. Laura Marcus, "The Newness of the 'New Biography': Biographical Theory and Practice in the Early Twentieth Century," in *Mapping Lives: The Uses of Biography*, ed. Peter France and William St. Clair (Oxford: British Academy/Oxford University Press, 2002), 195.

15. Lee, *Principles of Biography*, 9: "Character and exploits are for biographical purposes inseparable. Character which does not translate itself into exploit is for the biographer a mere phantasm."

16. "The Memory of the Brave," *Times*, May 26, 1915, 9. The editorial was reprinted as the lead item in the privately printed memorial, *Alec Rowan Herron* (Liverpool: Henry Young and Sons, 1915).

17. Paul Cornish, "'Sacred Relics': Objects in the Imperial War Museum 1917–39," in Saunders, *Matters of Conflict*, 39.

18. E. B. Osborn, *The New Elizabethans: A First Selection of the Lives of Young Men Who Have Fallen in the Great War* (London: John Lane, 1919). The extract from the *Sunday Times* was included in a two-page advertisement for *The New Elizabethans* that was printed at the end of Glenconner, *Edward Wyndham Tennant*, also published by John Lane.

19. Osborn, *New Elizabethans*, 1, 4. The closest contemporary work in this vein is A. St. John Adcock, *For Remembrance: Soldier Poets Who Have Fallen in the War* (London: Hodder and Stoughton, 1918). Almost half the figures Osborn highlights are also included in Adcock's volume.

20. Osborn, *New Elizabethans*, 1–4.

21. See Glenconner, *Edward Wyndham Tennant*, back material. The blurb is from the *Globe*.

NOTES TO PAGES 38–41   203

22. Osborn, *New Elizabethans*, xi. For the history of the *DNB*, see H. C. G. Matthew, *Leslie Stephen and the New Dictionary of National Biography* (Cambridge: Cambridge University Press, 1997), 7–8.

23. L. A. Clutterbuck, *The Bond of Sacrifice: A Biographical Record of All British Officers Who Fell in the Great War*, vol. 1, *Aug–Dec., 1914* (London: Anglo-African Publishing Contractors, [1916]). The second, and final, volume covered January to June 1915. The combined volumes include more than twenty-six hundred officer biographies, as compared with the twenty-five portraits in *The New Elizabethans*. Each entry generally contained a thumbnail photo of the officer and a stripped-down paragraph of biography.

24. Quoted in Matthew, *Leslie Stephen*, 9.

25. Sir Sidney Lee, *National Biography: A Lecture Delivered at the Royal Institution on the Evening of Friday, January 31, 1896* (London: Spottiswoode and Co., privately printed, 1896), 26–27.

26. Lee, 24.

27. Ramazani, *Poetry of Mourning*, 19. Ramazani quotes from Gary L. Long, "Organizations and Identity: Obituaries 1856–1972," *Social Forces* 65, no. 4 (June 1987): 964–1001, a sociological study of the American obituary.

28. Michèle Barrett, *Casualty Figures: How Five Men Survived the First World War* (London: Verso, 2007), xiii.

29. Hynes, *A War Imagined*, 209. Hynes adds that "in some cases," these works were also published "as testimonies against the war," but such instances seem exceptional. Hynes concentrates on works published for general circulation and not generally the privately published volumes that form a considerable part of my focus.

30. Victoria Stewart's "'War Memoirs of the Dead': Writing and Remembrance in the First World War," *Literature and History* 14, no. 2 (2005): 37–52, is a notable exception. I share with Stewart the sense that texts like these, despite generally being "consigned to the ranks of the ephemeral . . . can both shed light on memorial, and, specifically, auto/biographical practices, of the First World War" (39).

31. Brian Bond, *Survivors of a Kind: Memoirs of the Western Front* (London: Continuum, 2008). Bond adapted his title from the one Storm Jameson gave to her husband's posthumously published war memoir: Guy Chapman, *A Kind of Survivor: The Autobiography of Guy Chapman* (London: Gollancz, 1975).

32. H. M. Tomlinson, "Undertones," *New Adelphi* 2, no. 3 (March–May 1929): 258–260, quoted in Janet S. K. Watson, *Fighting Different Wars: Experience, Memory, and the First World War in Britain* (Cambridge: Cambridge University Press, 2004), 198.

33. Emily R. Wilson coins this term in her study of classical tragedy. See Emily R. Wilson, *Mocked with Death: Tragic Overliving from Sophocles to Milton* (Baltimore: Johns Hopkins University Press, 2004).

34. Diana Fuss, *Dying Modern: A Meditation on Elegy* (Durham, NC: Duke University Press, 2013).

35. For another discussion of this subject, see Carol Acton, *Grief in Wartime: Private Pain, Public Discourse* (Basingstoke: Palgrave Macmillan, 2007). In her treatment of World War I, "For Women Must Weep" (17–46), Acton focuses on the discourse produced for and by women.

36. Ramazani, *Poetry of Mourning*, 15.

204   **NOTES TO PAGES 42–46**

37. Geoffrey Batchen makes an analogous argument about nineteenth-century and early twentieth-century family photographs, embellished to enhance their memorial function and located in liminal spaces in the household like parlors and living rooms. See Geoffrey Batchen, *Forget Me Not: Photography and Remembrance* (Amsterdam: Van Gogh Museum; New York: Princeton Architectural Press, 2004), 96.

38. Edward Marsh, *Rupert Brooke: A Memoir* (New York: John Lane, 1918), would be the obvious exception. Others include [Marie Leighton], *Boy of My Heart* (London: Hodder and Stoughton, 1916), and Viola Meynell, *Julian Grenfell* (London: Burns and Oates, 1917).

39. George A. Smith and Hilda C. Miall Smith, *Two Brothers: Eric and Arnold Miall Smith* (London: Constable, printed for private circulation, 1918), 5–6.

40. A. Stodart-Walker, *James Logan Mackie* (Edinburgh: [T. & A. Constable], privately printed, 1919), 10.

41. *The Book of Bentley* (Burton-on-Trent: W. B. Darley, the Caxton Press, privately printed, 1918), 15, 19.

42. Evelyn C. Ewart, *Victor Alexander Ewart: A Memoir* (London: A. L. Humphreys, privately printed, 1921), 5–6, 10, 1.

43. Rae, "Introduction," 20. Rae comments on "the central place held by exclusionary consolatory fictions in national commemorative practices and rituals" in the work of Judith Butler and Marc Redfield.

44. Charles Hamilton Sorley, *The Letters of Charles Sorley, with a Chapter of Biography*, ed. W. R. Sorley (Cambridge: Cambridge University Press, 1919), vi.

45. Stodart-Walker, *James Logan Mackie*, [iii].

46. Marjorie Noble, *Marc Noble: A Memoir* (London: Country Life, printed for private circulation, 1918), 7.

47. See Lee, *Principles of Biography*, 12: "The second clause in this definition, which prescribes the need of completeness, offers no ambiguity. It excludes from the scope of biography careers of living men, careers which are incomplete, because death withholds the finishing touch. Death is a part of life and no man is fit subject for biography till he is dead."

48. Noble, *Marc Noble*, 8.

49. Virginia Woolf, "Rupert Brooke," in *The Essays of Virginia Woolf*, vol. 2, *1912–1918*, ed. Andrew McNeillie (San Diego: Harcourt, 1988), 278.

50. Woolf, 2:278.

51. Ivor Nicholson, ed., *Horace A. Link: A Memoir* (London: printed for private circulation, 1919).

52. Woolf, "Rupert Brooke," 2:278.

53. Virginia Woolf, "The Art of Biography," in *The Death of the Moth and Other Essays* (New York: Harcourt, 1942), 194–195.

54. Sir Oliver Lodge, *Christopher: A Study in Human Personality* (London: Cassell, 1918), 96–97.

55. Leighton's *Boy of My Heart* was published anonymously.

56. Guy Ridley, "Memoir," in *Poems by Ivar Campbell: With a Memoir by Guy Ridley* (London: A. L. Humphreys, 1917), 8, 9.

57. George Smith, ed., *George Buchanan Smith, 1890–1915* (Glasgow: James Maclehose and Sons, privately printed, 1916).

NOTES TO PAGES 46–52   205

58. Harold Parry, *In Memoriam: Harold Parry, Second Lieutenant, K.R.R.C.*, ed. Geoffrey P. Dennis (London: W. H. Smith, n.d. [1918?]).

59. Hynes identifies such features—"randomness of focus, shifting attitude towards the war, an abrupt, unfinished termination"—as "the qualities that you would expect in the records of a young life that came to a sudden end." See Hynes, *A War Imagined*, 209.

60. Batchen, *Forget Me Not*, 48.

61. Ethel Anne Priscilla Grenfell, Lady Desborough, *Pages from a Family Journal, 1888–1915* (Eton: Eton College, privately printed, 1916) (hereafter cited in text as *Pages*). Extant letters record the responses to the volume by a wide circle of family friends, while others not intimately acquainted with the family apparently received copies of the book after sending letters of condolence to the parents.

62. The volume includes more than twenty pages of such excerpts for each of the sons.

63. Quoted in Nicholas Mosley, *Julian Grenfell: His Life and the Times of His Death, 1888–1915* (London: Weidenfeld and Nicolson, 1976), 266.

64. Douglas A. Tollemache, ed., *The Career of a Second Lieutenant in the Year 1914* (Ipswich: printed for private circulation, 1915).

65. "WW1 Coldstream Officer Killed in Action Givenchy 1914—2nd Lieut. B. Tollemache," WorthPoint, https://www.worthpoint.com/worthopedia/ww1-coldstream-officer-killed-action-805298841, accessed June 30, 2021.

66. John Buchan, *These for Remembrance: Memoirs of 6 Friends Killed in the Great War* (London: Buchan and Enright, 1987; privately printed, 1919).

67. The publisher's note goes on to speculate about the number of copies originally published: "Quite how many copies were produced is not known, but it is unlikely to have been more than seven; one for John Buchan himself, and one each for the families of the six men whose lives he had commemorated. It is possible, however, that Buchan's was the only complete copy, and that each of his friends' families was given only the relevant section from the complete book. Hand-printing and -binding then, as now, were prohibitively expensive." Buchan, *These for Remembrance*, frontispiece. Evidence indicates, however, that a larger number of complete copies may have been printed than the publisher's note suggests. WorldCat lists nine libraries that currently own copies; one of these copies, in All Soul's College, Oxford, includes the letter Buchan sent offering the volume to the college, where Raymond Asquith, one of the men memorialized, had been a student.

68. John Buchan, *Francis and Riversdale Grenfell: A Memoir* (London: Thomas Nelson and Sons, 1920). The Grenfell memoir was written at the request of Field-Marshal Lord Grenfell, the uncle of Francis and Riversdale Grenfell, and was issued commercially. Although it was published after *These for Remembrance*, it was apparently written earlier.

69. Peter Vansittart, introduction to Buchan, *These for Remembrance*, [xxxiv].

70. See John Buchan, *Memory Hold-the-Door: The Autobiography of John Buchan* (London: Hodder and Stoughton, 1940). Buchan makes the somewhat disingenuous claim, "I have included one or two passages from a little book, *These for Remembrance*, of which a few copies were privately printed in 1919" (8).

71. Ivar Campbell, *The Prose Writings of Ivar Campbell* (London: privately printed, 1918), vi. *Poems by Ivar Campbell*, on the other hand, was published for general circulation,

206   **NOTES TO PAGES 52–57**

while a volume of *Letters of Ivar Campbell* was also published privately. In elaborating their thinking, the editors note "the difficulty of reconciling the wishes of those who will read the book with what they believe would have been the wishes of Ivar Campbell himself." Since "most of the prose works were either youthful—expressing opinions already deserted—or fragmentary, and would certainly not have satisfied any criterion laid down by the author," the editors explain that in order "to include in the volume several of the most attractive pieces, it has been decided to publish them privately" (*Prose Writings of Ivar Campbell*, v–vi).

72. Batchen, *Forget Me Not*, 93.

73. Nicholson, *Horace A. Link*, 7.

74. Jay Winter, "Forms of Kinship and Remembrance in the Aftermath of the Great War," in Winter and Sivan, *War and Remembrance in the Twentieth Century*, 40–60.

75. Harold Nicholson, *The Development of English Biography* (London: Hogarth Press, 1927), 17.

76. As "little books," these works might be understood, in part, through Susan Stewart's theorization of the miniature. See Stewart, *On Longing*, 37–69.

77. Cuthbert Morley Headlam, *George Roworth Parr, Prince Albert's Somerset Light Infantry: A Short Memoir* (Edinburgh: by T. & A. Constable, privately printed, 1915).

78. Buchan, *Francis and Riversdale Grenfell*, ix.

79. Lee, *National Biography*, 14–15.

80. The "Prefatory Note" to the 1921 supplement to the *DNB* explicitly acknowledges this contradiction: "A biographical dictionary which covers four years and a half of European war might be expected to abound in names taken from that glorious, heart-rending roll of honour which records the names of 946,000 citizens of the British Empire. But the loss which that list represents to the Empire at large, and to Great Britain and Ireland in particular . . . is not to be measured by those careers which a Dictionary of National Biography can chronicle." Instead, it settles for including a small handful of such biographies to "illustrate the richness and variety of the promise which sympathetic observers could perceive in that devoted generation." See *Dictionary of National Biography 1912–1921*, ed. H. W. C. Davis and J. R. H. Weaver (London: Oxford University Press, 1927), vi.

81. Sir Sidney Lee, *The Perspective of Biography*, The English Association, Pamphlet no. 41 (September 1918), 23.

82. Lee, *Principles of Biography*, 10.

83. Lee, *National Biography*, 13–14, 15.

84. Strachey, *Eminent Victorians*, 4.

85. Strachey, 4.

86. Woolf, "Rupert Brooke," 2:278, 277.

87. See Lorna C. Beckett, *The Second I Saw You: The True Love Story of Rupert Brooke and Phyllis Gardner* (London: British Library, 2015). Gardner left the manuscript of her unpublished memoir to the British Library after her death in 1939; the memoir, along with a cache of letters documenting the relationship, was unsealed in 2000 and subsequently published under the above title. For responses to the memoir's shocking revelations, see Nigel Jones, "Poetic Genius Who Despised Women: Celebrated as the Ultimate Romantic English Hero, a New Memoir Reveals Rupert Brooke Was a Vicious Sadist Who Thought All Women Were 'Beasts,'" *Daily Mail*, March 30, 2015, https://www.dailymail.co.uk/news/article-3018898/Poetic-genius-despised-women

-Celebrated-ultimate-romantic-English-hero-new-memoir-reveals-Rupert-Brooke
-vicious-sadist-thought-women-beasts.html.

88. Woolf, *Diary*, 2:79.

89. Virginia Woolf, "Maturity and Immaturity," in *The Essays of Virginia Woolf*, vol. 3, *1919–1924*, ed. Andrew McNeillie (San Diego: Harcourt, 1988), 127, 128.

90. Mildred Isemonger, ed., *Richard Vincent Sutton: A Record of His Life Together with Excerpts from His Private Papers* (London: G. W. Jones, 1922), [1].

91. Of Tennant, Woolf writes, "He seems condemned to remain a gifted and instinctive child," and as her title formulation, "Maturity and Immaturity," signals, she aligns him, throughout, with immaturity, as set against Joyce Kilmer's maturity. See Woolf, "Maturity and Immaturity," 3:128.

92. See London, "Writing Modern Deaths."

93. Marita Sturken, "Personal Stories and National Meanings: Memory, Reenactment, and the Image," in *The Seduction of Biography*, ed. Mary Rhiel and David Suchoff (New York: Routledge, 1996), 31.

94. Tollemache, *Career of a Second Lieutenant*, 13.

95. Tanya Dalziell, "Mourning and Jazz in the Poetry of Mina Loy," in Rae, *Modernism and Mourning*, 108.

96. Laqueur, *Work of the Dead*, 416.

97. This public-private fluidity also extended to publication practices, with a volume intended for one audience (private) sometimes repurposed, or even simply repackaged, for the other. It was not unusual for the same figure to be commemorated in both types of volumes or for public memorial volumes to mine privately published material.

98. Sturken, "Personal Stories," 31.

99. Hynes identifies this work as one of his prime examples of the "war memoirs of the dead" that are published "in some cases also as testimonies against the war." See Hynes, *A War Imagined*, 209.

100. See Dominic Hibberd, "Introduction," in *The Diary of a Dead Officer: Being the Posthumous Papers of Arthur Graeme West* (London: Imperial War Museum, 1991), vii–xxii. Hibberd offers a detailed analysis of the way C. M. Joad, "a committed pacifist, atheist, and revolutionary socialist," who edited the volume for its original publication, shaped the material to conform to his own political convictions. An appendix to the Imperial War Museum volume includes photos of letters from Edmund Blunden to West's sister from December 1932 and February 1933, responding to her complaints about Joad's editing of her brother's letters.

101. See Agnes J. Sanders, ed., *A Soldier of England: Memorials of Leslie Yorath Sanders* (Dumfries: J. Maxwell and Son, 1920); Ramazani, *Poetry of Mourning*, 71.

102. Fuss, *Dying Modern*, 108.

103. See Cathy Caruth, ed., *Trauma: Explorations in Memory* (Baltimore: Johns Hopkins University Press, 1995), 154, for the use of this term to characterize unresolved trauma.

104. Anita Helle, "'Blasé Sorrow': Ultramodernity's Mourning at the *Little Review*, 1917–20," in Rae, *Modernism and Mourning*, 121.

105. Isemonger, *Richard Vincent Sutton*, 193. The sentiments are those of Sir Frederick Carden, major, First Life Guards Reserve, and are the last to be included in the volume.

208   **NOTES TO PAGES 62–67**

106. Fuss, *Dying Modern*, 64, 58, 62.

107. Michael Heffernan, "For Ever England: The Western Front and the Politics of Remembrance in Britain," *Ecumene* 2, no. 3 (1995): 313.

108. Lee, *Perspective of Biography*, 12.

109. Buchan, *These for Remembrance*, 67. Buchan makes a similar argument about the letters of Basil Blackwood (44).

110. In what might appear a somewhat quixotic undertaking given the subject's disappearance from public consciousness, Nicholas Mosley published a biography of Julian Grenfell in 1976 to address precisely such missing elements, arguing that Grenfell has been misrepresented in the extant memoirs and notices of him and was in fact trying to resist the established attitudes of his time rather than embody them. Mosley bases his biography, in part, on a collection of essays that Grenfell wrote and tried to get published when he was twenty-one and that have not received any attention in coverage of him. He also addresses omissions and distortions in the use of his letters. See Mosley, *Julian Grenfell*, esp. 85–86.

111. The collection of poems, *Worple Flit and Other Poems*, was published posthumously by Blackwell's in 1916. An earlier collection of Tennant's poems, *Songs, Plays, and Ballads by E. W. T., 1897–1909*, was privately published by his family in 1909, when Tennant was twelve.

112. Alan Judd and David Crane, *First World War Poets* (London: National Portrait Gallery Publications, 2014), 5. For the frontispiece photograph, see https://www.npg.org.uk/collections/search/portrait/mw07848/Isaac-Rosenberg?LinkID=mp03867&role=sit&rNo=/.

113. Quoted in Devon Cox, *The Street of Wonderful Possibilities: Whistler, Wilde and Sargent in Tite Street* (London: Frances Lincoln, 2015).

114. These memoirs have generally been read as semifictional, with Sassoon representing himself as "George Sherston," a fictional character. Max Saunders, however, observes that such fictionalization was already occurring in Sassoon's wartime diaries, where he often referred to himself in the third person: "The diary extracts in the *Memoirs* have been rewritten—re-fictionalized—in order to make them sound more autobiographical; they have been translated into, or back into, the first person, and framed within a semi-fictionalized narrative." See Saunders, *Self Impression*, 6.

115. See Andrew J. Kunka, "The Evolution of Mourning in Siegfried Sassoon's War Writing," in Rae, *Modernism and Mourning*, 80–81.

116. Pamela Glenconner, *The Earthen Vessel: A Volume Dealing with Spirit-Communication Received in the Form of Book-Tests by Pamela Glenconner with a Preface by Sir Oliver Lodge* (London: John Lane, 1921), 81, 82.

117. Ramazani, *Poetry of Mourning*, ix.

118. Fuss, *Dying Modern*, 6–7.

119. Nicholson, *Horace A. Link*, 11.

120. See, for example, Fuss's discussion of "last-word" poems: "For the survivor, the poetic stewardship of last words is never uncompromised, even if one somehow manages to avoid the ever-present risks of simplification, totalization, calculation, and appropriation." See Fuss, *Dying Modern*, 41.

121. Noble, *Marc Noble*, 10.

NOTES TO PAGES 67–73   209

122. Parry, *In Memoriam*, v.

123. Batchen, *Forget Me Not*, 98.

124. Fussell, *The Great War and Modern Memory*, 316.

125. Brearton, "'But That Is Not New,'" 239.

126. Marcus, "The Newness of the 'New Biography,'" 193.

127. Winter, *Sites of Memory*, 5.

128. Ramazani, *Poetry of Mourning*, 28.

129. Saunders, *Self Impression*, 10.

130. Saunders, 456.

131. Virginia Woolf, "The Lives of the Obscure," in *The Common Reader* (London: Hogarth Press, 1925), 149. Woolf imagined this process occurring over centuries, while the works I discuss perform this operation in an extremely compressed time frame.

132. [Orlando Williams,] "Charles Sorley," *Times Literary Supplement*, December 11, 1919, 726; quoted in Watson, *Fighting Different Wars*, 185.

2. Sorley's Travels

1. RG to Edward Marsh, February 24, 1916, in Graves, *In Broken Images*, 39–40.

2. The first two quotes are from Graves's initial letter to Marsh, cited in the preceding note (Graves, 40); the third quote, "By the way, don't you love . . . ," occurs in a letter to Sassoon, June 23, 1916 (Graves, 53). Sorley, in fact, had a twin brother, Kenneth, who survived him by fifty-eight years, but Graves in effect (and in affect) turns Sorley into a posthumous twin for himself.

3. RG to Nichols, January 7, 1917, in Graves, 62. Nichols would also later "invent" or "solidify" a memory of seeing Sorley, claiming "to have caught a glimpse of him 'asleep in a dugout'" in Ploegsteert, where Sorley was stationed. See Harry Ricketts, *Strange Meetings: The Poets of the Great War* (London: Chatto and Windus, 2010), 114.

4. The second edition, first published in February 1916, was reprinted in February, April, and May 1916. A third edition was published in November 1916.

5. RG to SS, undated letter, early May 1916, in Graves, *In Broken Images*, 48. Graves's uncle, C. L. Graves, was an assistant editor of *Punch* and the *Spectator*.

6. In a letter dated June 30, 1917, Graves returns a poem Sassoon has sent him, "To Any Dead Officer," with a number of penciled-in editorial suggestions, noting, "I know you'll forgive these remarks, because you've patched up poems for me before now." See Graves, 72. In another letter, he notes, "There are two emendations I should love to put into Sorley. Perhaps I shall suggest them to his editor" (Graves, 48). For Graves's proposed emendation to "the 'millions of the mouthless dead' poem," see my discussion in the final section of this chapter. In the same letter, Graves also proposes a change to Sorley's "Odyssey" poem.

7. For a discussion of the triangulated relationship between Sassoon, Graves, and Sorley, see Patrick Campbell, *Siegfried Sassoon: A Study of the War Poetry* (Jefferson, NC: McFarland, 2007), esp. 67–68.

8. RG to SS, undated letter [early May 1916], in Graves, *In Broken Images*, 48. Sassoon, nine years older than Sorley, attended Marlborough College from 1902 to 1904; Sorley was there from 1908 to 1913. "So" was presumably a code word for homosexuality.

210   **NOTES TO PAGES 73–76**

9. RG to Nichols, January 7, 1917, in Graves, *In Broken Images*, 61. Graves concedes that Nichols's favorable review of Sorley in the *Westminster Gazette* is what convinces him that Nichols must be "a fellow of the right stuff" (62).

10. RG to Sassoon, June 30, 1917, in Graves, *In Broken Images*, 72. Sassoon apparently shared this assessment, telling Graves, "He's *not* as good as Sorley," adding, "— but one can't expect that." Quoted in Jean Moorcroft Wilson, *Siegfried Sassoon: The Making of a War Poet: A Biography (1886–1918)* (London: Duckworth, 1998), 421.

11. Siegfried Sassoon, *Siegfried Sassoon Diaries, 1915–1918*, ed. Rupert Hart-Davis (London: Faber and Faber, 1983), 94, 95; entry for July 16, 1916.

12. Sassoon, *Diaries*, 142; March 6, 1917.

13. RG to Marsh, August 7, 1916, in Graves, *In Broken Images*, 60.

14. RG to Nichols, January 7, 1917, in Graves, 62; Fuss, *Dying Modern*, 9.

15. Sassoon, *Diaries*, 106–107. The night before he observes, "Reading Sorley's letters has given me a cheer-up. He was so ready for all emergencies, so ready to accept the 'damnable circumstance of death'—or life" (106).

16. RG to Sassoon, July 13, 1917, in Graves, *In Broken Images*, 80.

17. I am drawing on Judith Butler's language here. See Butler, *Frames of War*, esp. the introduction, "Precarious Life, Grievable Life," 1–32.

18. Quoted in Thomas Burnett Swann, *The Ungirt Runner: Charles Hamilton Sorley, Poet of World War I* (Hamden, CT: Archon Books, 1965), 129. Sassoon paid a condolence call on Sorley's father in October 1916, and Graves corresponded with him about Sorely and sent him copies of his books; both received in return copies of *Letters from Germany*.

19. Cole, *Modernism, Male Friendship*, 148, 156. Cole calls attention to the use of the verb "to friend" in a poem by Robert Nichols, "Boy," in illuminating the way language performs this "urgent need" at the syntactic level,

20. Minogue and Palmer, *Remembered Dead*, 19; RG to Sassoon, January 13, 1918, in Graves, *In Broken Images*, 107. In his letter to Sassoon, Graves takes his fantasy one step further, speculating on a potential cosmopolitan community of recruits for their dining club of Sorley admirers: "Lenin and Trotsky . . . I wonder . . . Though perhaps Liebknecht."

21. On the last page of the manuscript of Owen's "Has Your Soul Slipped," written while he was at Craiglockhart, the words "Marlborough and Other Poems, Chas Sorley" are scrawled, suggesting Sassoon's note to Owen for recommended reading.

22. Robert Nichols, ed., *Anthology of War Poetry, 1914–1918* (London: Nicholson and Watson, 1943), 36.

23. Graves, *Good-Bye to All That*, 169.

24. A very similar articulation appears in *A Survey of Modernist Poetry* (1927), coauthored with Laura Riding, and it was republished in 1949 in Robert Graves, *The Common Asphodel: Collected Essays on Poetry, 1922–1949*.

25. Robert Graves, *Fairies and Fusiliers* (London: Heinemann, 1917), 23–24. Swann suggests that Graves sent Sorley's father a copy of this volume, writing, "I sent it to you as the father of the only great poet killed in this War" (Swann, *Ungirt Runner*, 129). In a letter to Sassoon from March 26, 1917, however, Graves identifies the book in question as *Goliath and David*; see Graves, *In Broken Images*, 67.

26. The publishing venture apparently never materialized. These letters are part of the Graves Letter Archive at Brigham Young University. The parcel consists of six

NOTES TO PAGES 76–78   211

letters, one typed, the others handwritten and signed. They are dated between January 8 and February 14, 1974. In one letter, Graves offers his most definitive account of meeting Sorley: "I met him only once which was at Christchurch, Oxford where we sat opposite each other sitting for scholarships. He got a scholarship, I got an exhibition." He also repeats, in substance, the claim he made to Sorley's father, "His death was my greatest grief of the war because he was the only poet for whom I had unqualified love & admiration," embellishing at the same time the substance of his putative meeting with Sorley, "We never talked together at length" (February 14, 1974), https://contentdm.lib.byu.edu/digital/collection/SCMisc/id/90.

27. See, for example, Dan Todman, *The Great War: Myth and Memory* (London: Continuum, 2007), 163: "The support of fellow wartime poets was crucial to the survival and revivification of Owen's work." The citation accompanying the 1985 Poets' Corner plaque to the Poets of the First World War offers a similar explanation for Sorley's inclusion: "Charles Sorley (1895–1915) was killed at the battle of Loos aged only 20 so left comparatively few complete poems but was well regarded by his contemporary poets."

28. J. Middleton Murry, "The Lost Legions," in *Aspects of Literature* (London: W. Collins Sons, 1920), 165, 163. The article originally appeared in the *Athenaeum*, January 30, 1920.

29. Murry, 160–161.

30. Murry, 161–162.

31. Katherine Mansfield, *Katherine Mansfield's Letters to John Middleton Murry, 1913–1922*, ed. John Middleton Murry (New York: Knopf, 1951), 532, 608. The first quote is from a note written to Murry in June 1920; the second is from a letter dated December 1, 1920.

32. Doris Dalglish, "Charles Sorley," *Friends' Quarterly Examiner* 71 (1937): 346. As Dalglish explains at the beginning of her essay, it was the death of Sorley's father that rendered this grief newly acute and occasioned her tribute.

33. J. B. Jones, "Sorleiana," *Swindon Review: A Local Miscellany of the Arts*, no. 4 (December 1948): 16–19. The article includes extracts from Jones's 1942 correspondence with Mrs. Sorley regarding this ad hoc monument.

34. See Martin Stephen, *The Price of Pity: Poetry, History and Myth in the Great War* (London: Leo Cooper, 1996), 176. Sorley is one of two dedicatees, the other being Mary Macpherson. Stephen is also the editor of *Never Such Innocence: A New Anthology of Great War Verse* (London: Buchan and Enright, 1988), which includes ten poems of Sorley's.

35. Peter Parker, *The Old Lie: The Great War and the Public-School Ethos* (London: Constable, 1987). Referencing G. E. Osborn's *The New Elizabethans*, he notes, "Even worse than Osborn's attempt to gather the poet into his fold is St John Adcock's *For Remembrance*" (155); "It is perhaps fortunate he did not live to see Adcock's volume" (157). Similarly, he derides the verse elegy of Sorley's schoolmaster John Bain as "a deplorable betrayal of Sorley's character and a travesty of his attitude to war and death" (217).

36. Jones, "Sorleiana," 19.

37. Bernard Bergonzi, *Heroes' Twilight: A Study of the Literature of the Great War*, 2nd ed. (London: Macmillan, 1980), 59, 55, 59.

38. Swann, *Ungirt Runner*, 144, 13. Swann concludes his preface with the acknowledgment, "The lives of many poets require apologies. . . . With Charles Sorley, however, the problem is quite reversed; it is hard not to sound idolatrous" (13–14).

212   **NOTES TO PAGES 79–82**

39. Swann, 104.

40. See, for example, T. Sturge Moore, *Some Soldier Poets* (New York: Harcourt, Brace and Howe, 1920), one of Swann's sources: "When we first admire a person after death we are apt to feel a kind of joy that he is now unalterable, not to be pottered over or finicked with or painted out for some supposed improvement" (56); "Death tempts us, nay forces us to overrate his actual production" (66). Like Swann, Moore romanticizes—even perhaps eroticizes—the figure of Sorley, going so far as to materialize Sorley's spirit in a ghostly encounter with Wordsworth, the elder poet welcoming wisdom from Sorley's "young rain-brightened lips" (67).

41. Review of *The Ungirt Runner* by Thomas Burnett Swann, *Choice* 2 (January 1966), 774.

42. Jean Moorcroft Wilson and Cecil Woolf, *Charles Hamilton Sorley: Exhibition Catalogue* (London: Cecil Woolf, 1985), 30. The biography referred to is Jean Moorcroft Wilson, *Charles Hamilton Sorley: A Biography* (London: Cecil Woolf, 1985).

43. While today that hit is generally taken today to be "When You See Millions of the Mouthless Dead," the poem was not always similarly valued; for some years after Sorley's death, "All the Hills and Vales Along" might have been a likelier candidate for this designation, or even "Expectans Expectavi," set to music by John Wood in 1919 and sung as an anthem in the Anglican service.

44. Jon Stallworthy, "Review of *Charles Hamilton Sorley: A Biography*, by Jean Moorcroft Wilson and *The Collected Letters of Charles Hamilton Sorley*, edited by Jean Moorcroft Wilson," *Review of English Studies*, n.s., 40, no. 159 (August 1989): 437.

45. Swann, *Ungirt Runner*, 13.

46. Stanley Plumley's *Posthumous Keats: A Personal Biography* (New York: W. W. Norton, 2008) offers one such model for an experimental biographical practice—one attentive to "certain connections and crossovers in the John Keats story" that do "not fit the profile of strict biographical narrative" (15).

47. Charles Hamilton Sorley, *The Collected Letters of Charles Hamilton Sorley*, ed. Jean Moorcroft Wilson (London: Cecil Woolf, 1990), 26 (hereafter cited in text as *CL*).

48. Ramazani, *Poetry of Mourning*, 80.

49. Michael Longley, "Pale Battalions," *Irish Times*, November 13, 2004, https://www.irishtimes.com/news/pale-battalions-1.1166330.

50. See Hirsch, *Generation of Postmemory*, 1–6, for a discussion of some of the key terms that have defined this discourse. The Holocaust, as Hirsch notes, has been considered "the limit case" for "memory studies," and while the specific operations of intergenerational memory cannot simply be transferred to another context, Hirsch's discussion, as I hope to demonstrate, remains resonant for thinking about the guardianship of traumatic memory in the World War I context.

51. Michael Longley, Andrew Motion, and Jon Stallworthy, "War Poetry: A Conversation," in Das, *Cambridge Companion to the Poetry of the First World War*, 257.

52. Brearton, "'But That Is Not New,'" 236. Brearton's larger argument addresses how Longley and other poets work through a similar familial legacy in their engagement with the war.

53. The word "amateur," it is worth remembering, has its etymological roots in the French and Latin for "one who loves."

NOTES TO PAGES 83–87   213

54. Frank Kermode, "Breeding," review of *The Diaries of Sylvia Warner Townsend*, ed. Claire Harman and *Sylvia and David: The Townsend Warner/Garnett Letters*, ed. Richard Garnett, *London Review of Books* 16, no. 14 (July 21 1994): 15–16.

55. Bernard Bergonzi, letter to the editor, *London Review of Books* 16, no. 17 (September 8, 1994, 178).

56. See John Bale, *Anti-sport Sentiments in Literature: Batting for the Opposition* (New York: Routledge, 2008), 54.

57. In a letter from Germany to the headmaster at Marlborough in July 2014, Sorley fantasized, "When I die (in sixty years) I am going to leave all my presumably enormous fortune to Marlborough on condition that a thorough knowledge of Richard Jefferies is ensured by the teaching there." Sorley, *Letters of Charles Sorley*, 201 (hereafter cited in text as *L*).

58. Frances G. Gay, "Charles Sorley's Poems," *Swindon Review: A Local Miscellany of the Arts*, no. 4 (December 1948): 7.

59. "Reports of Winter Meetings: 'Charles Sorley (1895–Oct. 1915): Poet and Disciple of Jefferies,'" *Richard Jefferies Society Newsletter*, Autumn Newsletter & Annual Report 2005–2006, 7–8.

60. Dominic Hibberd, "Who Were the War Poets, Anyway?," in *English Literature of the Great War Revisited: Proceedings of the Symposium on the British Literature of the First World War, University of Picardy 1986*, ed. Michel Roucoux (Amiens: Presses de l'U.E.R, Clerc Université, Picardy, 1986), 109.

61. See my discussion in the final section of this chapter.

62. RG to Sassoon, June 23, 1916, in Graves, *In Broken Images*, 53.

63. Brearton, "'But That Is Not New,'" 230.

64. The phrase appears on Bloomsbury's webpage advertising Wilson's *Edward Thomas: From Addlestrop to Arras, A Biography* (2015), https://www.bloomsbury.com/uk/edward-thomas-from-adlestrop-to-arras-9781408187135/.

65. The series is not limited to World War I poets, although they make up the majority of its offerings.

66. John Press, *Charles Hamilton Sorley*, War Poets Series (London: Cecil Woolf, 2006).

67. Winter makes this claim for the war poets themselves. "They are indeed among Assmann's 'figures of memory': the sentinels of the two-minute silence of Armistice Day. They seem to stand guard over the nation's acknowledgment, or active knowledge, its re-cognition, its eternal return to and remembrance of the catastrophe of 1914–18." See Jay Winter, "Beyond Glory: First World War Poetry and Cultural Memory," in Das, *Cambridge Companion to the Poetry of the First World War*, 251.

68. Wilson and Woolf, *Charles Hamilton Sorley*, title page.

69. Winter, "Beyond Glory," 243.

70. Santanu Das, preface to *Cambridge Companion to the Poetry of the First World War*, xix.

71. Dominic Hibberd laments this development, noting that the poets have achieved this position "on the basis of astonishingly little information"; he cites the Westminster Abbey monument as damning evidence of this tendency. See Hibberd, "Who Were the War Poets, Anyway?," 109.

214 **NOTES TO PAGES 87–91**

72. On the Westminster Abbey web page, a citation accompanies the announcement of the memorial, as it does at Poets' Corner, and Owen is credited as author in the entry under his name. His name, however, does not appear on the memorial itself as author of these sentiments. See http://www.westminster-abbey.org/our-history/people/poets-of-the-first-world-war.

73. Hibberd, "Who Were the War Poets, Anyway?," 109. While there are some other group memorials in Poets' Corner, these tend to be family units like the Brontë sisters. Hibberd is unsparing in his critique of the quality of the poets and the principles of their selection, noting that "at least half of the Abbey's 16 were second-rate poets or less, and one of them, Laurence Binyon, is remembered for precisely two lines" (115).

74. As Santanu Das notes, "War literature has an angular relationship to the categories of 'modernity' and 'modernism.'" World War I poetry, he argues, has been traditionally "cordoned off from the rest of early twentieth century poetry, where the category of 'modernism' has been dominant." See Das, "Reframing First World War Poetry: An Introduction," in Das, *Cambridge Companion to the Poetry of the First World War*, 21, 18.

75. For an overview of this phenomenon, see Bernard Bergonzi, "The First World War: Poetry, Scholarship, Myth," in Roucoux, *English Literature of the Great War Revisited*, 7–18.

76. Charles Hamilton Sorley, *The Poems and Selected Letters of Charles Hamilton Sorley*, ed. Hilda D. Spear (Dundee: Blackness Press, 1978).

77. To take just a few examples: Leeds University sponsored a Rosenberg exhibition in 1959; in 1974, the Imperial War Museum offered a *War Poets* exhibition featuring six war poets; in 1975, the National Book League sponsored a major Rosenberg retrospective, including paintings and manuscripts. These exhibitions might be seen as part of a larger shift in the war's representation from a military to a cultural experience.

78. Dyer, *The Missing of the Somme*, 110.

79. Todman, *The Great War*, 39, 157. During this time, and in the years after, Todman argues, "The poets were afforded special status amongst the commemoration of the war" (158).

80. Pierre Nora, "Between Memory and History: *Les Lieux de Mémoire*," *Representations* 26 (Spring 1989): 8.

81. Wilson and Woolf, *Charles Hamilton Sorley*, 31.

82. Dominiek Dendooven, "The Journey Back: On the Nature of Donations to the 'In Flanders Field Museum,'" in Saunders and Cornish, *Contested Objects*, 66.

83. Susanne Küchler, "The Place of Memory," in Forty and Küchler, *The Art of Forgetting*, 59. This idea is precisely the one Küchler is challenging in her essay, and that the volume in which the essay appears challenges more generally.

84. Letter to Susan Owen, December 31, 1917; quoted in Jon Stallworthy, *Wilfred Owen: A Biography* (Oxford: Oxford University Press, 1977), 253.

85. This sense of privilege is reinforced in the Cecil Woolf exhibition, which includes a display case dedicated to Marlborough College paraphernalia and ritual objects—items that themselves require explanatory notes for those not inculcated in public school culture.

NOTES TO PAGES 91–93 215

86. According to Martin Stephen, Sorley "is unique in terms of the letters and poems that have come down to us, and unique in that his father was a member of the syndicate which ran the Cambridge University Press, and which therefore published both his poems and letters." See Stephen, *The Price of Pity*, 84.

87. For some of the better-known poets, these institutions include the University of Cambridge (Brooke), University of Oxford and University of Texas (Owen), Cardiff University (Thomas), the Imperial War Museum (Rosenberg), the British Library, the National Library of Ireland, and the National Library of Wales, and the National Portrait Gallery.

88. See, for example, David Goldie, "Was There a Scottish War Literature? Scotland, Poetry, and the First World War," in *Oxford Handbook of British and Irish War Poetry*, ed. Tim Kendall (Oxford: Oxford University Press, 2007), 153–173.

89. Samuel Hynes, "Personal Narratives and Commemoration," in Winter and Sivan, *War and Remembrance in the Twentieth Century*, 207.

90. The biography, for example, draws on original material, including Wilson's personal interviews with the Sorley family.

91. Wilson and Woolf, *Charles Hamilton Sorley*, 5.

92. In this context, one might question the exhibition's claim to be launching "the first full-length biography" of Sorley, given the publication of Swann's biography, *The Ungirt Runner*, twenty years earlier, a work not mentioned in Wilson's biography. A copy of the book (which runs to 154 pages) was, however, included in the exhibition, which describes it as a "brief biography," raising the question of what counts as "full-length." Similarly, the fact that Hilda D. Spear's 1978 edition of *The Poems and Selected Letters of Charles Hamilton Sorley* is not mentioned in the *Collected Poems* although it too was displayed in the exhibition seems telling in emphasizing the gap Wilson's publications ostensibly fill.

93. Dominic Hibberd and John Onions, eds., *The Winter of the World: Poems of the Great War* (London: Constable, 2007), xxiii.

94. In recent years, there have been signs of increasing interest in Sorley. For example, in his introduction to *The Cambridge Companion to the Poetry of the First World War*, Santanu Das opens with a discussion of Sorley's "When You See Millions of the Mouthless Dead." See Das, "Reframing First World War Poetry," 3.

95. See, for example, Joseph Cohen, "In Memory of W. B. Yeats: And Wilfred Owen," *Journal of English and Germanic Philology* 58, no. 4 (1959): 638: "The reaction was immediate. John Hayward, the *Spectator*'s reviewer, wrote on November 20, 1936: 'The following omissions will probably be regretted, and perhaps resented in some quarters: Wilfred Owen, T. E. Hulme, Charles Sorley, Edwin Muir, Isaac Rosenberg, and Dylan Thomas.'" In contrast to Yeats, Sir Arthur Quiller Couch included "Song of the Ungirt Runners" in his *New Edition of the Oxford Book of English Verse* (1939).

96. Gardner argues that Sorley's poems "are in danger of being relegated to dusty shelves and, together with whizz-bangs, puttees and wire-cutters, to the memories of aging men." Brian Gardner, ed., *Up the Line to Death: The War Poets 1914–1918: An Anthology* (London: Methuen, 1964), xix. According to John Press, "By 1943 he was completely forgotten." John Press, "Charles Sorley," *Review of English Literature* 7, no. 3 (1966): 43. In 1958, Edmund Blunden laments, "Few mention Sorley now." Edmund

216   **NOTES TO PAGES 94–98**

Blunden, *War Poets 1914–1918* (London: Published for the British Council and the National Book League by Longmans, Green, 1958), 21.

97. Larry K. Uffelman, "Charles Hamilton Sorley: An Annotated Checklist," *Serif: The Magazine of Type and Typography* 10, no. 4 (1973): 4.

98. See Hibberd, "Who Were the War Poets, Anyway?," 115. While Hibberd does not mention specific names, Sorley would have been a likely candidate, at least when one gets to the upper limits of this count. As Stacy Gillis notes, this is precisely the position Sorley occupies in war poetry anthologies: "While the membership has fluctuated somewhat, at the centre are Owen, Rosenberg, Brooke, and Sassoon, with Charles Sorley, Julian Grenfell, Robert Graves, and Edmund Blunden slightly more subject to the vagaries of taste." Stacy Gillis, "'Many Sisters to Many Brothers': The Women Poets of the First World War," in Kendall, *Oxford Handbook of British and Irish War Poetry*, 102. In the United States, by contrast, Sorley's name would rarely be recognized.

99. *The Dictionary of National Biography: Missing Persons*, ed. C. S. Nicholls (Oxford: Oxford University Press, 1993), [v].

100. Das, "Reframing First World War Poetry," 13.

101. Winter, "Forms of Kinship," 40.

102. Charles Hamilton Sorley, *Letters from Germany and from the Army*, ed. W. R. Sorley (Cambridge: privately printed, 1916). Although the front matter of the volume indicates a print run of sixty copies, Robert Graves tells Sassoon that after sending "old Professor Sorley" a copy of *Goliath and David*, he received in return "the sixty-second copy (of a limited edition of sixty-six) of *Letters from Germany and the Army.*" RG to Siegfried Sassoon, March 26, 1917, in Graves, *In Broken Images*, 67. A presentation letter pasted into another copy of the volume suggests that Masefield was the recipient of the sixty-fifth copy.

103. Charles Hamilton Sorley, *Marlborough and Other Poems*, 2nd ed. (Cambridge: Cambridge University Press, 1916), viii.

104. *OED*, "Posthumous," *adj.*, def. 3. "Of a book or writing: published after the death of the author." This entry includes as its first example, "It is a Posthumous work, which never underwent the Hand or Pensil of the judicious Author," from 1668, M. Hale *Pref. Rolle's Abridgm.*

105. Early reviews picked up on this quality. The back matter to *Letters of Charles Sorley*, for example, includes the following excerpt from a review of *Marlborough*: "It is like some fragment of Greek statuary, perfect even in its incompleteness"—*Wilts County Paper. L*, [322].

106. E. B. Osborn confirms this desire on the part of readers, "I find myself regretting that his father has not given the many readers of his poems some such reasoned explanation of his career and character (both of which have a curious look of completeness) as that in which Lord Ribblesdale has dealt with the personality of his son, Charles Lister, in a spirit of almost scientific disinterestedness. Many others have felt the same regret." See Osborn, *New Elizabethans*, 55.

107. Charles Hamilton Sorley, *Marlborough and Other Poems*, 4th ed. (Cambridge: Cambridge University Press, 1919) (hereafter cited in text as *M*). The fifth edition of *Marlborough* (1922), on which the Cambridge Miscellany edition (1932) is based, is nearly identical to the fourth.

NOTES TO PAGES 98–100   217

108. The proposed small press run—Wilson alludes to a letter from Professor Sorley to Cambridge University Press, suggesting a modest run of one thousand copies—further reinforces the memorial element. See Sorley, *Collected Letters*, 9.

109. In *The Collected Letters* Wilson observes, "I understand that, following the publication of Charles Sorley's *Letters from Germany and from the Army* (1916) and *The Letters of Charles Sorley* (1919), Professor Sorley destroyed all his son's letters, that is, those in his possession" (*CL*, 32).

110. The same decision regarding chronological order informs Spear's earlier edition of the poems; Spear is more circumspect, however, in her assessment of Sorley's poetic accomplishment: "Dying at the age of twenty, Sorley had no chance to develop his poetic powers; his greatness remains in potential rather than in fulfillment. Few, if any, of his poems are perfect; in most of them the thought outstrips technique. Sorley was technically rather conventional." See Sorley, *Poems and Selected Letters*, 26.

111. Wilson, *Charles Hamilton Sorley*, 23, 35.

112. Charles Hamilton Sorley, *The Collected Poems of Charles Hamilton Sorley*, ed. Jean Moorcroft Wilson (London: Cecil Woolf, 1985), 36 (hereafter cited in text as *CP*).

113. Four of these seven poems, moreover, were previously printed in *Letters*. In his review of Wilson's biography of Sorley and her edition of *The Collected Poems*, Stallworthy points to discrepancies in the ways the poems are cited in the two publications and to the absence of attention to textual matters: "Purchasers and readers of such a *Collected Poems* in the 1980s expect—and are entitled to expect—information about the nature and status of copy-texts; also, incidentally, about their location" (Stallworthy, "Review," 438).

114. Stallworthy details the history of these additions in the introduction to his edition. See Wilfred Owen, *The Complete Poems and Fragments*, ed. Jon Stallworthy, 2 vols. (London: Chatto and Windus / Hogarth Press, 1983), xxi–xxv.

115. Bergonzi, "First World War," 10. Sorley wrote almost all of his poems before he saw active service, and the war did not necessarily figure explicitly in the remaining ones, raising a question about the aptness of the designation. With ever-increasing expansions of what counts as "war poetry," Stallworthy, among others, has questioned whether the term "war poet" has become too elastic to continue to be meaningful. See Longley, Motion, and Stallworthy, "War Poetry," 260.

116. See, for example, John H. Johnston, *English Poetry of the First World War: A Study in the Evolution of Lyric and Narrative Form* (Princeton, NJ: Princeton University Press, 1964), 55: "It is chiefly through his letters, however, that Sorley's personality and convictions are known to us; the poems are collateral manifestations of an intellectual force and clarity which never had the opportunity to express themselves fully in verse."

117. Wilson's introduction references "new letters [which] have come to light which are included here for the first time" (Wilson, *CL*, 14). Her edition, however, does not identify either the new letters or those taken from *Letters from Germany*. In the acknowledgments, she thanks Sorley's niece for making available "a previously unpublished letter" (Wilson, *CL*, 31); this is the only new letter specifically mentioned, and it is not identified in the text.

118. In this, the Sorley biography differs significantly from some of Wilson's other war poet biographies. In the case of Rosenberg, Wilson found enough new materials to revise *Isaac Rosenberg: Poet and Painter* (London: Cecil Woolf, 1975) and republish it

218   NOTES TO PAGES 100–105

as a new biography, *Isaac Rosenberg: The Making of a Great War Poet: A New Life* (Evanston, IL: Northwestern University Press, 2008). Sassoon lived long enough and accrued sufficient documentation to sustain two volumes: *Siegfried Sassoon: The Making of a War Poet* (1998) and *Siegfried Sassoon: The Journey from the Trenches: A Biography, 1918–1967* (New York: Routledge, 2003); Wilson subsequently published a one-volume biography, drawing on materials from the two earlier volumes, *Siegfried Sassoon: Soldier, Poet, Lover, Friend* (London: Duckworth, 2013).

119. Hirsch, *Generation of Postmemory*, 18. Where Hirsch focuses on works that self-consciously address the problematics of memory and attempt to shift the established terms and open up new networks of connection for thinking about the Holocaust, much of the postmemory work of World War I leaves the established tropes unexamined.

120. Hirsch, 39.

121. See, for example, Das, "Reframing First World War Poetry," 4: "Today, a hundred years after the war, the poetry of the soldier-poets has coalesced, beyond literary history and cultural memory, into a recognisable structure of feeling. Here lies an undeniable part of its power and some of the larger critical problems."

122. Hirsch, *Generation of Postmemory*, 36. Hirsch makes this point in relation to family photographs, but I believe the argument can be extended to address the objects I discuss here. "The key role that photographic images—and family photographs in particular—play as media of postmemory clarifies the connection between familial and affiliative postmemory, and the mechanisms by which public archives and institutions have been able both to re-embody and to re-individualize the more distant structures of cultural memory."

123. The new signpost was installed on October 3, 1976; it was dedicated by the bishop of Ely. According to John Press, the original signpost had been destroyed by this time, rendering a replacement necessary. It is unclear, then, whether the signpost at the IWM exhibition was the original or the copy. For a description of the dedication ceremony, see Press, *Charles Hamilton Sorley*, 22. See also James Runcie, "Sorley's Signpost," *Marlburian*, Michaelmas Term, 1976, which offers slightly different details of the event and the luncheon that preceded it and records a higher number of participants: sixty versus forty.

124. Sorley himself frequently referred to the bond he felt with the town and countryside of Marlborough. Writing to a school friend, A. E. Hutchinson, on December 15, 1914, he noted, "But if I must have an appellation to go through life with—and I suppose one must be labeled something—it is Marlburian: for Marlborough to me means the 'little red-capped town' (sorry for quoting from myself!) and the land that shelters it: not the school which has given it so much and so transient notoriety." See *L*, 249.

125. Sorley died four months after writing this letter, and commentators from Virginia Woolf to Jean Moorcroft Wilson have turned the words he wrote in this letter into a kind of epitaph, in particular his closing comments, "Details can wait—perhaps for ever. These are the plans" (*L*, 276). Woolf's 1919 signed review in the *Athenaeum* of Sorley's *Marlborough and Other Poems* takes "These Are the Plans" for its title (Woolf, *Essays* 2:73–77), while Wilson closes her biography on the words "Details can wait—perhaps for ever" (Wilson, *Charles Hamilton Sorley*, 215).

126. Stories of Sorley's legendary walks and runs were passed on to later generations of students, one of whom even researched his famous walk from Cambridge and pub-

NOTES TO PAGES 107–111   219

lished an article about it. See Mark Baker, "Charles Sorley's Long Walk to Marlborough and the Making of Three Poems," *Hatcher Review* 2, no. 16 (Autumn 1983): 285–291.

127. The poem was sent anonymously to John Bain, one of Sorley's schoolmasters, as a kind of puzzle poem, inviting the recipient to decode the author's identity. Bain's verse reply was published as a eulogy in the *Marlburian* on November 24, 1915, just over a month after Sorley's death. Professor Sorley prefaced the second edition of *Marlborough* with an excerpt from Bain's poem. Wilson, on the other hand, considers Sorley's poem so slight that she relegates it to the appendix of the *Collected Poems* and exempts it from her tally of Sorley's last writings.

128. Sorley supplies the specifics in the letter that accompanies the poem: "The place in question is the junction of the grass tracks on the Aldbourne down—to Ogbourne, Marlborough, Mildenhall and Aldbourne. It stands up quite alone. We could have gone there, had I been able to come down last Sunday." CHS to A. E. Hutchinson, December 15, 1914, *L*, 248.

129. In other poems such as "Barbury Camp" and "Stones," Sorley advances a similar argument about the traces of the dead that inhabit the landscape. The IWM exhibit misquotes this original title of the sonnet as "Death on the Downs," possibly following Wilson (*CP*, 27), an ascription that renders the association of the downs with death even more explicit. In a reissue of *Marlborough and Other Poems* with an introduction and added notes meant to introduce Sorley to American readers, Brett Rutherford retitles the work *Death and the Downs*. See Charles Hamilton Sorley, *Death and the Downs: The Poetry of Charles Hamilton Sorley*, ed. Brett Rutherford (Providence, RI: Yogh and Thorn, 2010).

130. In this poem, Sorley uses the unusual word "spook" to challenge mourners' desire to make personal connection with the dead. See my discussion of "When You See Millions of the Mouthless Dead" later in this chapter.

131. See Brendan Corcoran, "Keats's Death: Towards a Posthumous Poetics," *Studies in Romanticism* 48, no. 22 (Summer 2009): 321–348.

132. Fuss, *Dying Modern*, 13. Fuss suggests that such poems may represent "attempts to spiritually prepare for death" (13).

133. In 1983, only eight years after its installation, a pilgrim to the site reported, "The stone beside the sign post is now covered with lichen so that the inscription is difficult to read" (Baker, "Charles Sorley's Long Walk," 291n16). Recent photographs suggest further erosion, rendering the inscription practically unreadable. Local heritage and tourism websites provide information on the memorial, as does the National Trails website. Marlborough College records note the ritual laying of wreaths by students on anniversary occasions.

134. Brooke's most famous sonnet, "The Soldier," begins: "If I should die, think only this of me: / That there's some corner of a foreign field / That is for ever England." In a much-quoted letter to his mother, Sorley observed of Brooke, "That last sonnet-sequence of his . . . I find . . . overpraised. He is far too obsessed with his own sacrifice, regarding the going to war of himself (and others) as a highly intense, remarkable and sacrificial exploit, whereas it is merely the conduct demanded of him (and others) by the turn of circumstances, where non-compliance with this demand would have made life intolerable. . . . He has clothed his attitude in fine words: but he has taken the sentimental attitude." CHS to Mrs. Sorley, April 28, 1915, *L*, 263.

220   **NOTES TO PAGES 113–114**

135. See Elizabeth Vandiver, "Early Poets of the First World War," in Das, *Cambridge Companion to the Poetry of the First World War*, 76–77. This was the poem that Graves sent to Marsh in the letter in which he first declares his love for Sorley, and it is the Sorley poem recited at the Poets' Corner memorial dedication. During the centenary season, it was quoted on a 2015 commemorative stamp and was the title poem for James MacMillan's commissioned oratorio. In his introduction to *The Penguin Book of First World War Poetry*, 2nd ed. (London: Penguin, 1979), however, Jon Silkin marks it with an asterisk, one of five poems he includes not on the basis of his own taste or judgment of merit but because they represent "what he believes other people, a great many other people, have liked, even loved, as they responded to the horror and pity of war" (76).

136. I adopt this term from Robert Pogue Harrison's absorbing meditation on death and burial processes, and on the many places where the dead cohabit the world of the living. "The human returns to the humus," he writes, but "human culture, unlike nature, institutes a living memory, and not just a mineral retention, of the dead." See Robert Pogue Harrison, *The Dominion of the Dead* (Chicago: University of Chicago Press, 2003), 2. Sorley, here, seems to be dismissing even living memory.

137. Edna Longley, "The Great War, History, and the English Lyric," in *The Cambridge Companion to the Literature of the First World War*, ed. Vincent Sherry (Cambridge: Cambridge University Press, 2005), 63.

138. Das, "Reframing First World War Poetry," 3–4: "The eeriness of the image is enhanced by the poignant circumstances of the poem's posthumous discovery. Like John Keats's spookier and chilling fragment 'This Living Hand,' written a month before his death, Sorley's poem operates on that fine threshold where poetic form and personal tragedy meet."

139. In a letter to the master of Marlborough, November 28, 1914, Sorley claims that the line from *The Iliad* "should be read at the grave of every corpse in addition to the burial service, no saner and splendider comment on death has been made, especially, as here, where it seemed a cruel waste" (*L*, 245). The line appears in Greek in the letter where Sorley references it. Vandiver also identifies this moment as a pivot: "The poem's rejection of sentimentality pivots on the crucial words 'Yet many a better one has died before', a direct reference to *Iliad* 21.106–7" (Vandiver, "Early Poets of the First World War," 77).

140. Wilson, *Mocked with Death*, 21.

141. Responding to Roy Fuller's "Ghost Voice" (1980), Fuss comments on a recurring tendency in poems of this nature: "Mourning is the obligation of the living, not the dead; the modern dead are immune to the tears of the living"; "Through prosopopoeia, poets reanimate the dead to instruct the living not to reanimate them. These 'ghost voices' refuse reanimation *through* reanimation" (Fuss, *Dying Modern*, 69–70).

142. In a letter to Sassoon from early May 1916, Graves writes, "In the 'millions of the mouthless dead' poem the words 'It is a spook' have been changed in the second edition to 'It is a ghost' which is obviously wrong because, well, they were all ghosts. 'Spook' is an attempt, very unsuccessful, to avoid this truism. I'd like it to read 'It is a *lie*. None wears the face you knew'" (*In Broken Images*, 48). I have been unable to find any evidence of the change in wording Graves notes for the second edition; it does not appear in the February 1916 reprinting of the second edition I consulted or in any subsequent editions of the volume.

143. Elizabeth Vandiver, "'Millions of the Mouthless Dead': Charles Hamilton Sorley and Wilfred Owen in Homer's Hades," *International Journal of the Classical Tradition* 5, no. 3 (Winter 1999): 441.

144. "Life and Work of Aberdeen's Greatest War Poet Commemorated with Plaque," University of Aberdeen, News Details, November 5, 2018, https://www.abdn.ac.uk/news/12395/. The Sorley plaque was the first of five Historical Environment Scotland (HES) plaques unveiled in 2018 to honor Scottish poets of World War I.

145. CHS to Mrs. Sorley, June 13, 1915. Sorley offers several reasons for his reluctance, but it is the last of these that his mother cites in explaining the family's resistance to a memorial. "I'm afraid I think your proposal undesirable for many reasons. The proposal is premature: also I have at present neither the opportunity nor inclination for a careful revision and selection. Besides, this is no time for oliveyards and vineyards; more especially of the small-holdings type. For three years or the duration of the war, let be" (*L*, 273).

146. Prompted by a report of the placing of Wiltshire memorials to Richard Jefferies and Alfred Williams, Alan Fox Hutchinson, one of Sorley's schoolfellows (and the original recipient of his signpost poem "Lost"), wrote to the *Times* to propose that "a similar (though, perhaps smaller) memorial" be erected on the Downs "to the Marlburian poet Charles Sorley; 'Four-miler,' the fourth milestone from Marlborough, would be, as the goal of one of his favourite runs, an appropriate stone on which to fix a plaque; 1940, the twenty-fifth anniversary of his death, would be a suitable date" (*Times*, January 2, 1940, 4). Subsequent letters to the *Times* correct the position and designation of "Four-miler," explaining it is not a milestone but actually a clump of trees. In one of these letters, Sorley's mother, Janetta C. Sorley, weighs in on the controversy, mentioning in passing the earlier proposal for a similar memorial: "So nothing was done in that way then or since. Only his poems were published." *Times*, February 9, 1940, 6.

147. W. R. Sorley died in 1935; Mrs. Sorley died in 1957. Sorley's twin brother, Kenneth, died in 1973, and his sister, Jean, died in 1976.

148. Paola Filippucci's formulation, though articulated in relation to the construction of memory in Argonne, France, seems relevant here: "More specifically, however, the current focus on experience and immediacy in relation to the First World War can be interpreted as a bid to revitalize and repersonalize the social memory of the war, which is fading with the demise of survivors, but still 'alive' in terms of its many unresolved and unaddressed aspects." Paola Filippucci, "Postcards from the Past: War, Landscape and Place in Argonne, France," in Saunders and Cornish, *Contested Objects*, 227.

149. Andrew Motion, "Well Versed in the Legacy of Conflict: At the Imperial War Museum, Poet Laureate Andrew Motion Sifts Through Mementoes and Testimonies of Twelve Poets," *Times*, October 30, 2002.

150. Hirsch, *Generation of Postmemory*, 33.

151. Neil McPherson, *It Is Easy to Be Dead* (London: Oberon Books, 2016). The description of the play's sources appears on the title page. In Aberdeen, a headline for a local review read, "Requiem for Doomed Aberdeen War Poet" (*Press and Journal*, November 2, 2018), while the poster advertising the Scottish run of the play called it "The Forgotten Story of Charles Hamilton Sorley, Scotland's Greatest First World War Poet."

152. In the preface to the published version of the play, McPherson admits that his original idea for the play—conceived twenty-eight years earlier as a potential contribution

222 NOTES TO PAGES 118–121

to the seventieth anniversary Armistice Festival in London—was a one-man play about Wilfred Owen; informed at the time that Owen was already well-trodden territory, he was directed to Sorley as "one of the youngest and less well known of the war poets," a suggestion he remembered when he returned to the idea of writing a play about World War I under the influence of the centenary. See McPherson, *It Is Easy to Be Dead*, [6].

153. Laurence Binyon's poem "For the Fallen" (1914) has been adopted as the Ode of Remembrance and is regularly recited at Remembrance Day ceremonies. The lines "They shall grow not old, as we that are left grow old: / Age shall not weary them, nor the years condemn" are among the most quoted of all World War I literature.

154. McPherson also notes that his play was inspired by his own family history—in particular, the wrenching grief of his great-grandfather, minister of Scotland's Free Church and one of the book's dedicatees, over the death of his son at the Battle of the Somme. McPherson's play writes Sorley's Scots heritage into its very accents and idioms. Bréon Rydell, the play's producer, spearheaded a campaign to bring Sorley's memory home to Scotland—culminating in a commemorative event at the Scottish Poetry Library in Edinburgh in October 2018. He was also instrumental in having Sorley's childhood home recognized with a commemorative plaque, along with the homes of other forgotten Scottish soldiers.

155. Stanley Plumley uses these words to characterize Leigh Hunt's commemoration of Keats in his memoir *Brothers in Unity: Lord Byron and Some of His Contemporaries* (1828). For Hunt, Keats was "the great young poet who almost was"—a designation that echoes in the popular reception of the war poets. See Plumley, *Posthumous Keats*, 91, 94.

156. Hirsch, *Generation of Postmemory*, 16. Hirsch credits "feminism and other movements for social change" for leading the call for this type of interrogation.

3. Posthumous Was a Woman

1. Woolf first introduces "Shakespeare's sister" in chapter 3 of *A Room of One's Own* and returns to her in the concluding passage of the book, cited in this chapter's epigraph. See Virginia Woolf, *A Room of One's Own* (New York: Harcourt Brace Jovanovich, 1929), 117 (hereafter cited in text as *AROO*). An earlier version of the first half of this chapter was published as Bette London, "Posthumous Was a Woman: World War I Memorials and Woolf's Dead Poet's Society," *Woolf Studies Annual* 16 (2010): 45–69.

2. David Cannadine, "War and Death, Grief and Mourning in Modern Britain," in *Mirrors of Mortality: Studies in the Social History of Death*, ed. Joachim Whaley (New York: St. Martin's Press, 1982), 199. As discussed in chapter 1, the term "new Elizabethans" was coined by E. B. Osborn in 1919.

3. Cannadine, 224.

4. Karen L. Levenback, *Virginia Woolf and the Great War* (Syracuse, NY: Syracuse University Press, 1999), 31. For the full text of Woolf's remarks, see her diary entry for December 12, 1920, in Woolf, *Diary*, 2:79–80.

5. The prohibition on personal memorials in British battlefield graveyards was implemented in 1916 and continued with the establishment of the military cemeteries under the Imperial War Graves Commission.

NOTES TO PAGES 121–124   223

6. Mark Connelly, *The Great War, Memory and Ritual: Commemoration in the City and East London, 1916–1939* (Woodbridge, Suffolk: Royal Historical Society / Boydell Press, 2002), 143.

7. Lutyens designed more than fifty memorials in cities, towns, and villages in Britain and abroad, including the Memorial to the Missing of the Somme at Thiepval. His designs—especially the Cenotaph—were frequently copied and adapted by other war memorial designers in the United Kingdom and abroad. See Tim Skelton and Gerald Gliddon, *Lutyens and the Great War* (London: Frances Lincoln, 2008). See also King, *Memorials of the Great War*, for a discussion of Lutyens's influence on other memorial artists.

8. Dyer, *The Missing of the Somme*, 30–31.

9. Laqueur, *Work of the Dead*, 471.

10. Hugh Haughton, "Anthologizing War," in Kendall, *Oxford Handbook of British and Irish War Poetry*, 422.

11. Robert Wohl, *The Generation of 1914* (Cambridge, MA: Harvard University Press, 1979), 91. In making this point, Wohl cites Winston Churchill's eulogy: "Joyous, fearless, versatile, deeply instructed, with classical symmetry of mind and body . . . he was all that one would wish England's noblest sons to be in days when no sacrifice but the most precious is acceptable, and the most precious is that which is most freely proffered."

12. See Woolf, "These Are the Plans," in *Essays*, 3:74. Woolf distinguishes Sorley from other soldier-poets she reviews at the same time for his true poetic consciousness and for his great promise.

13. Wohl, *Generation of 1914*, 105.

14. Winter, *Sites of Memory*, 73.

15. Wohl, *Generation of 1914*, 106. For other discussions of this boom in war books, see Hynes, *A War Imagined*, 423–469. Hynes locates *A Room of One's Own* as part of this moment: "yet another product of the myth-making years" (268). As Hynes points out, the Hogarth Press was one of the first to take up works expressing these antiwar sentiments, with its publication in 1925 of Herbert Read's *In Retreat*—a text Read had been unable to publish in 1919 when for the world, in his words, "It was not yet time for the simple facts" (299).

16. S. P. Rosenbaum, introduction to Virginia Woolf, *Women & Fiction: The Manuscript Versions of* A Room of One's Own, ed. S. P. Rosenbaum (Oxford: Published for the Shakespeare Head Press by Blackwell Publishers, 1992), xxvi.

17. Cole, *At the Violet Hour*, 72.

18. Wohl, *Generation of 1914*, 112.

19. See, for example, this allusion to the scapegoating of the war: "<the war is made the scapegoat for / simply>," and this noting of the ubiquity of such sentiments, "<One has only to> / <read novels, newspaper; to hear people [say?]>" (Woolf, *Women & Fiction*, 20).

20. See Watson, *Fighting Different Wars*.

21. For an interesting reading of this passage along related lines, see Michèle Barrett, "Reason and Truth in *A Room of One's Own*," in *Virginia Woolf Out of Bounds: Selected Papers from the Tenth Annual Conference on Virginia Woolf*, eds. Jessica Berman and Jane Goldman (New York: Pace University Press, 2001), 125.

224   **NOTES TO PAGES 125–126**

22. Hynes, *A War Imagined*, 458. Hynes locates this phenomenon in the late 1920s.

23. Hynes has argued, "The War Book Controversy was a quarrel over history; but it was also a literary dispute." His point, however, is to emphasize the stylistic differences among the dispute's established participants—not as I argue here to consider it a dispute over (literary) history conducted by very different players and on modernist terms. See Hynes, *A War Imagined*, 455. Sharon Ouditt makes, in effect, the same argument in reverse, noting that Woolf's "on-going battle with Wells, Bennett and Galsworthy" in her modernist manifestos "can be seen as something greater than a clash of literary styles"; read in the context of the war propaganda all three men participated in producing, the question of what constitutes "reality" becomes an exposé of "the 'preposterous masculine fiction' of war." See Sharon Ouditt, *Fighting Forces, Writing Women: Identity and Ideology in the First World War* (London: Routledge, 1994), 174–175.

24. In a diary entry for October 9, 1917, Woolf observes with horror what must have been a not uncommon newspaper listing: "The K. Shuttleworths advertise the birth of a boy with the statement 'His Perfect Gift' a good title for an Academy picture, or a Mrs Ward novel, & rather a terrible testimony to the limelight now desired by the rich upon their sacrifices." Virginia Woolf, *The Diary of Virginia Woolf*, vol. 1, *1915–1919*, ed. Anne Olivier Bell (New York: Harcourt, 1977), 57.

25. For the centrality of the war to Woolf's lifework, see Mark Hussey, ed., *Virginia Woolf and War: Fiction, Reality, and Myth* (Syracuse, NY: Syracuse University Press, 1991). Levenback's *Virginia Woolf and the Great War* remains a landmark work in this area of Woolf studies. Christine Froula in *Virginia Woolf and the Bloomsbury Avant-Garde* has advanced the discussion in new directions, as has Sarah Cole in *At the Violet Hour*.

26. Teresa Winterhalter, "Guns and Big Guns in *A Room of One's Own*," in *Re: Reading, Re: Writing, Re: Teaching Virginia Woolf: Selected Papers from the Fourth Annual Conference on Virginia Woolf*, ed. Eileen Barrett and Patricia Cramer (New York: Pace University Press, 1995), 72–79. Scholars who have studied the manuscript versions of the text generally note the erasure or toning down of war references in the final published version. For a discussion of some of the ways *A Room of One's Own* calls attention to its war references, see Barrett, "Reason and Truth."

27. Jane Marcus, *Virginia Woolf, Cambridge and* A Room of One's Own: *"The Proper Upkeep of Names"* (London: Cecil Woolf, 1996), 48. Marcus's suggestive reading of Vanessa Bell's dust jacket is by no means typical. With her concern with the lack of proper upkeep of Woolf's name in her native country, and with "the rescue and resurrection of Virginia Woolf's reputation" (4), Marcus pursues her argument on very different lines from mine.

28. Cannadine, "War and Death," 224.

29. Lloyd, *Battlefield Tourism*, 84–85. According to Lloyd, "As a mystical figure, the Unknown Warrior ranked just behind Jesus Christ in the 1920s," and his appearance on the stage in C. Watson Mill's *The Eternal Flame* was seen by many as a desecration of a sacred national symbol.

30. In calling attention to these memorial tropes, I am also suggesting that *A Room of One's Own* bears certain resemblances to *Mrs. Dalloway*, where, as David Bradshaw has noted, "at one point or another, just about every aspect of the formal culture of remembrance is evoked." Like Bradshaw, I am interested in the way Woolf "not only opposes the official memorialization of the dead" but also "contributes to the culture

of remembrance" (118). See David Bradshaw, "'Vanished, Like Leaves': The Military, Elegy and Italy in *Mrs Dalloway*," *Woolf Studies Annual* 8 (2002): 107, 118.

31. Catherine W. Reilly, *English Poetry of the First World War: A Bibliography* (London: George Prior, 1978), xiii. Reilly identifies 2,225 English poets in her bibliography.

32. Osborn, *New Elizabethans*, 3. John Buchan references this rubric in *These for Remembrance*, his 1919 memoir to fallen friends: "It has become a fashion to talk of our dead as 'new Elizabethans' and to credit all with a certain zest in the business, as a romantic adventure" (46). Buchan prefaces both this and his other memoir of fallen soldiers, *Frances and Riversdale Grenfell* (1920), with an epigraph from Gabriel Harvey's 1592 poem, "Ah, That Sir Humphry Gilbert Should Be Dead," invoking the deaths of "old Elizabethans" as a frame for his works.

33. Between 1923 and 1926, the Hogarth Press published six of Robert Graves's books. In 1929, it published Edmund Blunden's *Nature in English Literature*. Woolf reviewed Siegfried Sassoon twice in the *Times Literary Supplement*.

34. Woolf, "These Are the Plans," in *Essays* 3:73. In "Two Soldier-Poets," Woolf opens by noting, "It is natural to feel an impulse of charity towards the poems written by young men who have fought or are still fighting"—an impulse only heightened when the soldiers in question are dead (*Essays*, 2:269).

35. Dyer, *The Missing of the Somme*, 29. There is some discrepancy in accounts of the number of poems Owen published in his lifetime. Dyer lists five poems, while many other sources note only four. Seven poems appeared in Edith Sitwell's 1919 edition of the anthology *Wheels*. Mark Rawlinson also notes the significance of "the posthumousness of his public literary career": "From this point of view, he is identical with his reception and publication histories, not differentiated from them and the uses to which he has been put (as in the case of Keats or Bob Dylan)." See Mark Rawlinson, "Wilfred Owen," in Kendall, *Oxford Handbook of British and Irish War Poetry*, 118.

36. Siegfried Sassoon, introduction to *Poems* by Wilfred Owen (London: Chatto and Windus, 1920), v. According to Edna Longley, "Elegy is arguably both a genre and the over-arching genre of war poetry. Indeed, the Great War may have made all lyric poetry more consciously elegiac and self-elegiac." See Longley, "The Great War," 78.

37. See George Spater and Ian Parsons, *A Marriage of True Minds: An Intimate Portrait of Leonard and Virginia Woolf* (New York: Harcourt Brace Jovanovich, 1977), 102, for a reproduction of the title page and dedication to the Hogarth volume, *Poems* by C. N. Sidney Woolf. Only five copies of this book are known to exist today. Cecil Woolf was killed in the Battle of Cambrai on November 29, 1917.

38. Review of *The Life and Last Words of Wilfrid Ewart* by Stephen Graham. Ironically, although Ewart had in fact served in the war as a captain in the Scots Guards, he did not die in the war; he was killed, in 1922, by a stray bullet while in Mexico. See Woolf, *Essays*, 3:409.

39. Winter, *Sites of Memory*, 62. By the time he published *Raymond*, Lodge's scientific scholarly work had earned him election to the Royal Society, a knighthood, and international recognition. From 1901 to 1903, he served as president of the Society for Psychical Research. Like other memorial volumes, *Raymond* contains a frontispiece photograph of the soldier in uniform. Divided into three parts, its first part, or "Normal Portion," follows the pattern of other memorial texts, including an "In Memoriam" section, transcripts of Raymond's letters from the front, and condolence letters from

226 NOTES TO PAGES 129–132

officers. See Sir Oliver Lodge, *Raymond; or Life and Death, with Examples of the Evidence for Survival of Memory and Affection after Death* (New York: George H. Doran, 1916).

40. For a discussion of the revival of spiritualism and its relationship to the culture of memorialization, see Winter, *Sites of Memory*, 54–77. For a further discussion of the rise of mediumship in this period, with an emphasis on how automatic writing functioned as a practice of authorship, see Bette London, *Writing Double: Women's Literary Partnerships* (Ithaca, NY: Cornell University Press, 1999).

41. Memorial volumes to women who died in the war are a rarity. The publisher Edward Arnold's publication, for private circulation, of his daughter's diary, *Peggy's Diary at No. 16 General Hospital* (1917), is the only one I have seen referenced.

42. Lodge, *Christopher*, 2 (hereafter cited in text as *C*).

43. Winter, *Sites of Memory*, 104.

44. This was also the logic of the Unknown Warrior, which invited each grieving family to identify the dead soldier as their own.

45. This, of course, is the gist of Woolf's parable of Shakespeare's sister: "But for my part, I agree with the deceased bishop, if such he was—it is unthinkable that any woman in Shakespeare's day should have had Shakespeare's genius. For genius like Shakespeare's is not born among labouring, uneducated, servile people. It was not born in England among the Saxons and the Britons. It is not born today among the working classes" (*AROO*, 50).

46. Sir Arthur Quiller-Couch may be Lodge's source here for the class-based analysis of genius, although he does not quote him expressly; Woolf, on the other hand, explicitly cites Quiller-Couch's *The Art of Writing* (1916) to legitimate her claim that "intellectual freedom depends upon material things": "Nobody could put the point more plainly. 'The poor poet has not in these days, nor has had for two hundred years, a dog's chance . . . a poor child in England has little more hope than had the son of an Athenian slave to be emancipated into that intellectual freedom of which great writings are born.'" From this, Woolf concludes, "Women, then, have not had a dog's chance of writing poetry" (*AROO*, 112). Hence her emphasis on "money and a room of one's own."

47. Here, as elsewhere, Woolf's language echoes the iconography of doomed youth and the conditions of trench warfare. She deploys similarly charged rhetoric in her discussion of Charlotte Brontë as her representative example of a nineteenth-century writer; Woolf insists "she will never get her genius expressed whole and entire. . . . How could she help but die young, cramped and thwarted?" (*AROO*, 72–73). For Woolf's public writings on the dilemma of the soldier-poet, see "Two Soldier-Poets" (*Essays*, 2:269–272); "Mr Sassoon's Poems" (*Essays*, 2:119–122); "Rupert Brooke" (*Essays*, 2:277–284); "These Are the Plans" (*Essays*, 3:73–77); and "Maturity and Immaturity" (*Essays*, 3:127–131).

48. Melba Cuddy-Keane, *Virginia Woolf, the Intellectual, and the Public Sphere* (Cambridge: Cambridge University Press, 2003), 49. Cuddy-Keane is discussing Woolf's essay "Abbeys and Cathedrals" (1932), but the context of memorials and monuments makes the example especially relevant: "The walk through London thus ends with a trope of substitution: the public garden in place of the public monument, the ordinary individual in place of the heroic statue. Furthermore, in this alternative democratic space, anonymity acquires a positive meaning; here finally is a place where 'the dead sleep in peace.'"

NOTES TO PAGES 132–134

49. See, for example, Santanu Das's comments on the centrality of sound to the soldier's experience: "'You couldn't; you can't communicate noise,' noted Robert Graves in an interview; 'Noise never stopped for one moment—ever'; and we have Sassoon's soldier 'going stark, staring mad because of the guns.'" See Santanu Das, "War Poetry and the Realm of the Senses: Owen and Rosenberg," in Kendall, *Oxford Handbook of British and Irish War Poetry*, 76.

50. Woolf, *Diary*, 1:34.

51. Woolf, 1:218. Desmond McCarthy served with the Red Cross, as an ambulance driver attached to the French army. Gerald Shove was a conscientious objector.

52. Woolf, *Diary*, 2:51.

53. Woolf, 2:72–73.

54. Woolf, 1:108–109.

55. Wohl, *Generation of 1914*, 114.

56. Edna Longley notes that "during the war 'soldier poet' was a tautology—'almost as familiar as a ration-card,' says Edmund Blunden) [*sic*]—rather than a problematic category." See Longley, "The Great War," 58.

57. Jay Winter, "Oxford and the First World War," in *The History of the University of Oxford*, vol. 8, *The Twentieth Century*, ed. Brian Harrison (Oxford: Clarendon Press, 1994), 19–20.

58. Patricia Utechin, *Sons of This Place: Commemoration of the War Dead in Oxford's Colleges and Institutions* (Oxford: Robert Dudgdale, 1998), 59.

59. Quoted in Brian Harrison, "College Life, 1918–1939," in Harrison, *History of the University of Oxford*, 81.

60. Woolf, "These Are the Plans," 3:73. In that same essay, however, she salutes another young man, Charles Sorley (see chapter 2), who found escape from Oxford a cause for celebration, even as she laments the tragic circumstances of his death.

61. For the history of Cambridge during the war, see Christopher N. L. Brooke, *A History of the University of Cambridge*, vol. 4, *1870–1990* (Cambridge: Cambridge University Press, 1993), 331–340. The occupation of Cambridge continued on a smaller scale even after the war: "After the armistice a number of American soldiers were settled in Cambridge awaiting transport home, and about 200 matriculated in the Easter Term 1919. Meanwhile arrangements were made from January 1919 till 1922 for short courses for naval officers, to give them a brief period of recovery from the stress of war and expose them a little to the academic and more to the social life of Cambridge" (334).

62. Levenback, *Virginia Woolf and the Great War*, 28–29.

63. K. S. Inglis, "The Homecoming: The War Memorial Movement in Cambridge England," *Journal of Contemporary History* 27 (1992): 583. The other major site was the memorial in Ely Cathedral. Inglis provides a fascinating account of the contradictory features of the Homecoming monument and the complex deliberations that went into its making.

64. The materialization of "J—H—" follows close on the narrator's extended meditation on the war ("Shall we lay the blame on the war?") and the ensuing swerve she takes, discussed earlier in this chapter. The J—H—sighting breaks off abruptly with the invocation of "youth," a culturally loaded term in the context of recent war losses: "For youth—/ Here was my soup." Ironically, Harrison would literally have been a

228   **NOTES TO PAGES 135–138**

ghost at the time of her presumed appearance, having died in April 1928, five months before the October day that serves as the departure point for Woolf's narrative.

65. Angela Ingram, "'The Sacred Edifices': Virginia Woolf and Some of the Sons of Culture," in *Virginia Woolf and Bloomsbury: A Centenary Celebration*, ed. Jane Marcus (Bloomington: Indiana University Press, 1987), 142n14.

66. Virginia Woolf, "Thoughts on Peace in an Air Raid," in *Death of the Moth*, 243.

67. Gail Braybon, introduction to Braybon, *Evidence, History and the Great War*, 5.

68. Gillis, "'Many Sisters to Many Brothers,'" 101.

69. "By contrast," Buck observes, "soldiers on active service wrote less than a fifth of the total output." See Claire Buck, "British Women's Writing of the Great War," in Sherry, *Cambridge Companion to the Literature of the First World War*, 88–89, 87. As Gillis notes, however, most of the women who wrote and published poetry during the war "resist the easy designation of 'war poet'" ("'Many Sisters to Many Brothers,'" 105).

70. Woolf, *Diary*, 1:124.

71. Woolf, "Two Solder-Poets," 2:271, 272.

72. Virginia Woolf, *The Letters of Virginia Woolf*, vol. 3, *1923–1928*, ed. Nigel Nicolson and Joanne Trautmann (New York: Harcourt Brace Jovanovich, 1977), 178.

73. Woolf, "Two Soldier-Poets," 2:269, 270.

74. Woolf, "These Are the Plans," 3:74.

75. Vincent Sherry, "The Great War and Modernist Poetry," in Kendall, *Oxford Handbook of British and Irish War Poetry*, 191.

76. Virginia Woolf, *The Diary of Virginia Woolf*, vol. 3, *1925–1930*, ed. Anne Olivier Bell (New York: Harcourt Brace Jovanovich, 1980), 223, 65. The first of these comments was written on April 29, 1929, six months before *A Room of One's Own* was published; the second was written three years earlier. From her first meeting with Eliot in November 1918, Woolf was sold on the importance of his poetry and his poetic credo—his belief, for example, in "'living phrases' & their difference from dead ones." She expressed more skepticism, however, about Ezra Pound and Wyndham Lewis, whom Eliot upheld as "great poets" (*Diary*, 3:218–219). In 1923, the Hogarth Press famously published *The Waste Land*.

77. John Lee, "Shakespeare and the Great War," in Kendall, *Oxford Handbook of British and Irish War Poetry*, 139, 140.

78. Froula, *Virginia Woolf and the Bloomsbury Avant-Garde*, 26–28. Froula offers a subtle, complex, and compelling reading of the path Woolf tracks to achieve the pronoun "one," and of the performative politics of her pronoun usage.

79. As Jeanette McVicker notes in her discussion of "Abbeys and Cathedrals" and "This Is the House of Commons," Whitehall is one of the locations through which Woolf articulates most overtly the theme of monumentalizing the past with its attendant exclusion of women. See Jeanette McVicker, "'Six Essays on London Life: A History of Dispersal," pt. 2, *Woolf Studies Annual* 10 (2004): 152.

80. See Bradshaw, "Vanished, Like Leaves," esp. 110–115.

81. Woolf, *Diary*, 3:23, 82.

82. Lloyd, *Battlefield Tourism*, 83–84.

83. Gregory, *Silence of Memory*, 136. For the 1920 response to the unveiling, see Laqueur, *Work of the Dead*, 482.

NOTES TO PAGES 138–140   229

84. Here, too, Woolf may have been drawing on the Cenotaph's popular history. According to Lloyd, "The people who visited the Cenotaph also drew upon a widely held belief that the spirit or even spirits of the war dead had not been extinguished by the war or by the Armistice. The Cenotaph provided the focal point for the widespread belief or wish to believe in the continuing presence of the dead." See Lloyd, *Battlefield Tourism*, 62.

85. James E. Young, *The Texture of Memory: Holocaust Memorials and Meaning* (New Haven, CT: Yale University Press, 1993), 30.

86. See Young, 45.

87. Booth, *Postcards from the Trenches*, 24, 33. Booth's reading of *Jacob's Room* is also relevant here: "*Jacob's Room* operates imagistically as an empty coffin—describing, at the end of the novel, not merely an approximation of his presence but also a silhouette of his absence" (46).

88. This statement was made by a civil servant in 1969, recalling his "exile" at Elephant and Castle. Since 1939, the civil service had increasingly branched out into other parts of London, with only the highest offices remaining in Whitehall. However anachronistic, the statement captures, I believe, the spirit of Woolf's gesture. See Brian Harrison, *The Transformation of British Politics, 1860–1995* (Oxford: Oxford University Press, 1996), 303–304.

89. For other readings of the countermemorial impulse in Woolf, see Tammy Clewell, "Consolation Refused: Virginia Woolf, the Great War, and Modernist Mourning," *Modern Fiction Studies* 50, no. 1 (Spring 2004): 197–223; Robert Reginio, "Virginia Woolf and the Technologies of Exploration: *Jacob's Room* as Counter-Monument," in *Woolf and the Art of Exploration: Selected Papers from the Fifteenth International Conference on Virginia Woof*, ed. Helen Southworth and Elisa Kay Sparks (Clemson, SC: Clemson University Digital Press, 2006).

90. See Hynes, *A War Imagined*, 283–310.

91. Laura Doyle, "The Body Unbound: A Phenomenological Reading of the Political in *A Room of One's Own*," in Berman and Goldman, *Virginia Woolf Out of Bounds*, 136.

92. For a discussion of "ephemeral monuments," see Forty and Küchler, *Art of Forgetting*, which devotes its entire part I to the subject.

93. As Sarah Cole notes, "The airplane had already, by the 1920s, established itself as a major technological legacy of war"; "By the mid-1920s, Woolf had come to see the airplane as a primary player in the whole dialectic of war, violence, commerce, and aesthetics." See Cole, *At the Violet Hour*, 249, 252.

94. My argument here echoes a point made by Laura Marcus in glossing this passage: "Woolf's point, presumably, is not that the human species will be extirpated, but that conceptions of 'man' and 'woman' are as relative and historically contingent as any other system of values and that the forms that gender and identity will take in the future are as yet unimaginable." See Laura Marcus, *Virginia Woolf* (Plymouth, UK: Northcote House, 1997), 51. In invoking Woolf's speculation as a supplement to her antimemorial memorialization, my argument adds a twist to Woolf's queering of commemoration.

95. Virginia Woolf, *The Years* (New York: Harcourt Brace Jovanovich, 1965), 336.

96. Although the official crime for which Cavell was tried was treason, from the beginning there were rumors of espionage, and Cavell's trial and execution have frequently

230   **NOTES TO PAGES 140–144**

been represented in these terms in literature and popular memory. Prior to the war, the hospital in Belgium was a training school for nurses headed by Cavell; Cavell was in England at the time war broke out, but she chose to return to Belgium to nurse soldiers from both sides under Red Cross auspices.

97. See Katie Pickles, *Transnational Outrage: The Death and Commemoration of Edith Cavell* (Basingstoke: Palgrave Macmillan, 2007).

98. *New Statesman*, April 10, 1920; quoted in Sue Malvern, "'For King and Country': Frampton's *Edith Cavell* (1915–20) and the Writing of Gender in Memorials to the Great War," in *Sculpture and the Pursuit of a Modern Ideal in Britain, c. 1880–1930*, ed. David J. Getsy (Aldershot: Ashgate, 2004), 224.

99. The annual observance was proposed by the National Liberal Club but was rejected by the government. See Anne-Marie Claire Hughes, "War, Gender and National Mourning: The Significance of the Death and Commemoration of Edith Cavell in Britain," *European Review of History: Revue européenne d'histoire* 12, no. 3 (2005): 435, http://dx.doi.org/10.1080/13507480500428938.

100. "Programme of Ceremony of the Unveiling of the Cavell Memorial, St. Martin's Place, on Wednesday, March 17th, at Noon, by Her Majesty Queen Alexandra" ([London], [1920]). Available at British Library, General Reference Collection 10825.g.25.

101. Malvern, "'For King and Country,'" 224.

102. According to Lord Gleichen, the half figure of the woman at top represents "Humanity protecting the Small States," while the "angry lion in relief" symbolizes "the feelings of the British peoples at the outrage." See Lord Edward Gleichen, *London's Open Air Statuary* (London: Longman's, 1928), 14. From the start, the monument was conceived as a national memorial, and the Office of Works for Westminster assumed responsibility for its upkeep; it is now one of six World War I memorials under the care of English Heritage.

103. King, *Memorials of the Great War*, 198–199. For a discussion of the place of women in the postwar commemorative landscape, see Alison S. Fell, *Women as Veterans in Britain and France after the First World War* (Cambridge: Cambridge University Press, 2018), 20–51.

104. Partly for these reasons, the Cavell memorial was upgraded to a Grade I heritage listing in 2014, putting it in company with the Cenotaph and with Jagger's Royal Artillery memorial at Hyde Park Corner, which was also upgraded at the same time.

105. Watson, *Fighting Different Wars*, 39, 288.

106. The families of women who died performing service to the nation, including work in munitions factories, did not receive the death plaque or a scroll or letter; only 655 British women were officially recognized as war deaths by the Commonwealth War Graves Commission. See Kim Philling, "Women Are 'Forgotten Victims of First World War,'" *Independent*, November 9, 2010, http://www.independent.co.uk/news/uk/home-news/women-are-forgotten-victims-of-first-world-war-2129167.html.

107. For a cogent discussion of the shrine, see Buck, *Conceiving Strangeness*, 185–189. Significantly, the IWM memorial emphasized the sacrifices of women munitions workers.

108. Vivien Newman, *We Also Served: The Forgotten Women of the First World War* (Barnsley: Pen and Sword, 2014), 161.

NOTES TO PAGES 144–147

109. Pickles, *Transnational Outrage*, 117.

110. Malvern, "'For King and Country,'" 222, 223. The erection of a memorial to Earl Haig in Whitehall in 1928, and of statues to World War I admirals Beatty and Jellico in Trafalgar Square in the 1940s, furthers Malvern's notion of an axis of commemoration.

111. Hughes, "War, Gender, and National Mourning," 438. The Unknown Warrior, of course, was the other significant exception to the ban on repatriation, but his case works from an opposite logic; where Cavell is singled out by name, his selection depends on his anonymity. As Hughes observes, "Ironically, her gender made her remarkable enough to be remembered as an individual on a scale that, had she been a man, she would not have been" (439).

112. Pickles, *Transnational Outrage*, 117.

113. In November 1923, for example, thirty thousand people participated in a pilgrimage to Cavell's grave in Norwich. See Lloyd, *Battlefield Tourism*, 39.

114. For discussions of the posthumous construction of Cavell's identity, see Malvern, "'For King and Country'"; Pickles, *Transnational Outrage*; and Hughes, "War, Gender, and National Mourning." See also Shane M. Barney, "The Mythic Matters of Edith Cavell: Propaganda, Legend, Myth and Memory," *Historical Reflections/Réflexions Historiques* 31, no. 2 (Summer 2005): 217–233.

115. In May 1915, for example, the French executed a woman for espionage, and soon after Cavell's death, they executed two nurses. By contrast, the British never executed any women, and in their accounts of Cavell's death and martyrdom they were at pains to deny any possible comparisons with their treatment of enemy civilians accused of comparable crimes, although the evidence tells a more complex story. The British, moreover, did not spare their own citizens. Under the Defence of the Realm Act, British journalists who transgressed regulations were threatened with execution, and thirty-four death sentences were passed on British conscientious objectors. Although none were carried out, several COs were transported to France, where they were subjected to mock executions.

116. Eleven foreign spies were eventually executed at the Tower of London. Although Cavell was not officially charged with espionage, the line between espionage and treason in her case was at best ambiguous.

117. Woolf, *The Years*, 336. Within the novel, Woolf leaves the issue at an impasse: "The cab remained fixed in the block." Here, as with Peggy's irreverent comment about "sanitary towels," the differences between Peggy and Eleanor reflect differing generational perspectives on the war.

118. Virginia Woolf, *Three Guineas*, ed. Jane Marcus and Mark Hussey (San Diego: Harcourt, 2006), 129 (hereafter cited in text as *TG*). Malvern suggests that Woolf's statement about women having no country "must owe something to Cavell," although there is no evidence of a direct influence; see Malvern, "'For King and Country,'" 234.

119. Virginia Woolf, *The Letters of Virginia Woolf*, vol. 4, *1929–1931*, ed. Nigel Nicolson and Joanne Trautman (New York: Harcourt Brace Jovanovich, 1978), 230.

120. The wording that appears on the memorial follows, in slightly abridged fashion, the typed version of the conversation that Stirling Gahan, the Anglican chaplain who met with Cavell on the eve of her execution, sent to the American legation in Brussels, which passed the typescript on to London; they were also the words Cavell's family agreed to when the inscription was being debated. Gahan's manuscript notes,

232   **NOTES TO PAGES 147–148**

however, record a slightly different iteration: "I know now that patriotism is not enough. It is not enough to love ones [*sic*] own people: one must love all men, and hate none'" (quoted in Pickles, *Transnational Outrage*, 40). In an article in the *Guardian*, Richard Norton-Taylor notes, "There is speculation among those concerned in the Cavell story that these words went too far and were too pacifist for the British government to accept" ("Edith Cavell, Shot by Germans during WWI, Celebrated 100 Years On," *Guardian*, October 12, 2015, https://www.theguardian.com/world/2015/oct/12/edith-cavell-nurse-shot-by-germans-wwi-celebrated). As I will discuss later, Cavell spoke other last words to Pastor Le Soeur on the following day, immediately before her execution. The words quoted above, moreover, were not the final words spoken in Cavell's conversation with Gahan, as Pickles documents. See Pickles, *Transnational Outrage*, 40.

121. For Pankhurst's words, see Hughes, "War, Gender and National Mourning," 432. For a discussion of the *Dreadnought* cartoon, see Angela K. Smith, "The Pankhursts and the War: Suffrage Magazines and First World War Propaganda," *Women's History Review* 12, no. 1 (2003): 103–118.

122. George Bernard Shaw, *Saint Joan: A Chronicle Play in Six Scenes and an Epilogue* (London: Constable, 1924), xxxii–xxxiii.

123. Gregory, *Silence of Memory*, 151. Of the more recent commentators, Jane Marcus has been especially influential in promoting Cavell as a proponent of "radical pacifism" and the victim of government censorship. See Jane Marcus, "The Asylums of Antaeus: Women, War, and Madness—Is There a Feminist Fetishism?," in *The New Historicism*, ed. H. Aram Veeser (New York: Routledge, 1989), 132–151.

124. Quentin Bell, *Virginia Woolf: A Biography*, 2 vols. (Orlando, FL: Harcourt, 1972), 2:258. The line appears in Woolf's unpublished memoir of Julian Bell, her nephew killed in the Spanish Civil War. Bell published excerpts from the manuscript as an appendix.

125. Holroyd, *Lytton Strachey*, 340.

126. As Pickles notes, "Newspaper coverage went so far as to report that Cavell's family considered the most appropriate memorial to her life was for men to enlist." See Pickles, *Transnational Outrage*, 69.

127. Michèle Barrett, "Virginia Woolf and Pacifism," in *Woolf in the Real World: Selected Papers from the Thirteenth International Conference on Virginia Woolf*, ed. Karen V. Kukil (Clemson, SC: Clemson University Digital Press, 2005), 37.

128. See Pickles, *Transnational Outrage*, 41. This second set of last words was recorded by Pastor Le Soeur, the chaplain appointed by the Germans to minister to the prisoners. Le Soeur accompanied Cavell to the execution site and was with her in the moments immediately preceding her execution when she purportedly spoke them. These last words were apparently recorded in French on a scrap of paper and subsequently were transcribed and translated for circulation.

129. Allegations of spying surrounded Cavell from the beginning, as did allegations that the British were deliberately suppressing relevant evidence. According to Pickles, "Previously top-secret documents released in 2002 reveal that in November 1918 MI5 was determined not to have Cavell's innocent image tarnished, and was desperate to shield her from accusations of being a spy" (Pickles, *Transnational Outrage*, 54). In September 2015, Dame Stella Rimington, the ex-head of MI5, told BBC radio that newly unearthed evidence provided definitive proof that Cavell's network was actively involved

in providing intelligence to the Allies, although the extent of Cavell's personal involvement in the sending of information remains undetermined; at the least, however, she would have been aware of her network's activities. See "Secrets and Spies: The Untold Story of Edith Cavell," *iPlayer Radio*, http://www.bbc.co.uk/programmes/b069wth6. Other allegations include the suggestion that under interrogation, Cavell betrayed several members of her network. See Hughes, "War, Gender, and National Mourning," 434.

130. See Pickles, *Transnational Outrage*, 111, 114, 106.

131. As Corinna Peniston-Bird notes, "Every aspect of this memorial was controversial" (263): from *who* would be honored (ex-servicewomen in the auxiliary forces vs. "all women of WWII," including civilians) to *how* they would be represented (figural sculptures of women in action, as originally planned vs. a symbolic invocation through representations of the women's discarded garments now hanging on pegs). The result was a monument that left almost everyone unsatisfied—a monument that figured no actual women. See Corinna Peniston-Bird, "War and Peace in the Cloakroom: The Controversy over the Memorial to the Women of World War II," in *Representations of Peace and Conflict*, ed. Stephen Gibson and Simon Mollan (Basingstoke: Palgrave Macmillan, 2012), 263–284. The possibility of also honoring servicewomen from World War I, advocated by some former ex-servicewomen, apparently dropped out early in the planning process.

132. Nicoletta F. Gullace, *"The Blood of Our Sons": Men, Women, and the Renegotiation of British Citizenship during the Great War* (New York: Palgrave Macmillan, 2002), 156.

133. Marcus, "Asylums of Antaeus," 134–135.

134. After her death, Cavell was showered with the kinds of honors Woolf urged women to reject: the King Albert Award Cross and Order of Leopold; the Crois Civique of the Belgian government; Chevalier of the French Legion of Honor. She was even given a memorial day in the Church of England Calendar of Saints.

135. Michael Hellyer, "Memories of the Two World Wars in the St Martin's Archives," *St Martin in the Fields*, News, 8 November 2013, https://web.archive.org/web/20150922072138/http://www.stmartin-in-the-fields.org/news/memories-of-the-two-world-wars-in-the-st-martins-archives/.

136. Hugh Richard Lawrie Sheppard, popularly known as Dick Sheppard, inaugurated the Peace Pledge movement with a postcard campaign in 1934, inviting all those willing to join him in a public demonstration renouncing war to send him a postcard; his effort officially became the Peace Pledge Union in 1935. The entry for the Edith Cavell Memorial on the PPU website credits Sheppard with being one of the people who exerted pressure on the government to get Cavell's "last words" added to her monument, although some have questioned whether stories to this effect are apocryphal.

137. When the IWM created its *Women's War Work* exhibition, with the intent of representing the full range of women's wartime occupations—and highlighting in particular women's work in munitions—Cavell was still called on to bolster the effort; a prominent bust of Cavell flanked one side of the entrance to the Women's War Shrine, with a bust of Dr. Elsie Inglis upholding the other.

138. During the war, "Tommy's sister" was sometimes used to describe "munitions girls." It could be extended to cover the range of war work performed by women, including participation in women's auxiliary services. I am, however, using the term here

234   **NOTES TO PAGES 151–153**

even more broadly to suggest all the sisters of fighting men, unable to contribute to the war in the same way as their brothers. Woolf, of course, would not have seen becoming a Tommy as a desirable aspiration for women. See Sharon Ouditt, "Tommy's Sisters: The Representations of Working Women's Experience," in *Facing Armageddon: The First World War Experienced*, ed. Hugh Cecil and Peter H. Liddle (London: Pen and Sword, 1996), 736–751.

139. Woolf also insisted that the "first duty" of members of the Outsiders' Society would be to bind themselves "not to fight with arms"—an option, she conceded, that was not open to them anyway (*TG*, 126).

140. See Smith, "Pankhursts and the War." For discussion of women's antiwar activism and resistance to supporting the war effort, see Laura E. Nym Mayhall, *The Militant Suffrage Movement: Citizenship and Resistance in Britain, 1860–1930* (Oxford: Oxford University Press, 2003), esp. 117–134; Jo Vellacott Newberry, "Anti-war Suffragists," *History* 62, no. 206 (1977): 411–425; Ouditt, *Fighting Forces*.

141. See Deborah Thom, "Making Spectaculars: Museums and How We Remember Gender in Wartime," in Braybon, *Evidence, History and the Great War*, 48–66.

142. These arguments have been now largely rejected by historians. Mayhall, for example, notes, "A consensus has emerged among historians that women's war work had little to do with the provisions of the bill that became law in 1918." See Mayhall, *Militant Suffrage Movement*, 185–186n17.

143. In dedicating the 1925 York Minster memorial to British women killed in World War I, the archbishop of York alluded to the Representation of the People Act of 1918 as another "great memorial" to women's "loyalty, efficiency and devotion"—a "gift to women of full citizenship of the Empire" in recognition of the service they performed for their nation. Quoted in Fell, *Women as Veterans*, 48–49.

144. Gullace, *"The Blood of Our Sons,"* 158.

145. "This raises the difficult question whether those who did not aid in the prosecution of the war, but did what they could to hinder the prosecution of the war, ought to use the vote to which they are entitled chiefly because others 'aided in the prosecution of the war'?" (*TG*, 175n12).

146. Gullace, *"The Blood of Our Sons,"* 178–179. Gullace puts the number of men in question at sixteen thousand.

147. I am drawing here on Jeanette McVicker's formulation of the shape of Woolf's career. See Jeanette McVicker, "'Six Essays on London Life': A History of Dispersal," pt. 1, *Woolf Studies Annual* 9 (2003): 145. I also borrow her term "pre-meditation" (151) in my discussion of the implications of shifting the way we read Shakespeare's sister.

148. Cuddy-Keane, *Virginia Woolf, the Intellectual*, 42.

149. Woolf, "Thoughts on Peace in an Air Raid," 243. See also Froula, *Virginia Woolf and the Bloomsbury Avant-Garde*, 87–128, for a provocative discussion of Woolf's interrogation of the possibilities of the elegiac genre to take on the daunting burden of collective mourning. Froula reads the elegiac work the novel performs, in part, through a meditation on the posthumous—in particular, through the novel's invocation of *Cymbeline's* character, Posthumus (see esp. 96–102).

150. According to James C. Robertson, *Dawn* "provoked at the time of its production the hardest-fought British censorship struggle of the entire inter-war period." The film was banned, if in some cases only temporarily, in Britain, Holland, Romania,

Australia, and India. James C. Robertson, "*Dawn* (1928): Edith Cavell and Anglo-German Relations," *Historical Journal of Film, Radio and Television* 4, no. 1 (1984): 15, DOI: 10.1080/01439688400260021.

151. Quoted in Liesbet Depauw, "Reframing the Past to Change the Future: Reflections on Herbert Wilcox's *Dawn* (1928) as a Historical Documentary and War Film," in *Perspectives on European Film and History*, ed. Leen Engelen and Roel Vande Winkel (Ghent: Academia Press, 2007), 169.

152. Depauw, 169.

153. In 1939, Wilcox remade the film for RKO with virtually the same reception. As his wife, Anna Neagle, who played the lead in the remake observed, "We intended this to be an *anti-war* film," but we "were often either accused of, or congratulated on, making war propaganda—the *last* thing we had in mind." See Andrew Kelly, *Cinema and the Great War* (London: Routledge, 1997), 64.

154. "Monuments: Edith Cavell Statue," London Remembers, http://www.london remembers.com/memorials/edith-cavell-statue.

155. Pickles, *Transnational Outrage*, 202.

156. Recent research now puts the number of deaths at more than one hundred.

157. When Hitler came to power in 1933, the plaque was removed from Berlin and erected at Peace House in south Denmark; it was hidden during the German occupation. In 1958, it was placed on permanent loan to the Peace Pledge Union, where it was unveiled in the PPU offices in London on January 3, 1959, by one of the COs who had been sentenced to be shot.

158. Among the more extreme responses, "An anonymous postcard, still on file in the Public Records Office, alleged that the women were impudent, cunning, pro-German and representatives of an international conspiracy of pacifism, to which women were particularly susceptible." As Malvern notes, the National Council of Women was hardly a radical organization; rather, it was, "a moderate, non-party reformist organization campaigning on issues such as prison conditions and women's education." See Malvern, "'For King and Country,'" 227.

159. The original bust, ironically enough, given Woolf's remarks in *A Room of One's Own* about the vast dome "so splendidly encircled by a band of famous names," all of them masculine, is now located in the British Museum (*AROO*, 26).

160. The organizers of the 2014 ceremony explicitly identify the event as part of a larger centenary campaign to publicize "this hidden history about conscientious objection and peace movement opposition to the First World War," noting, "It's an aspect of our British heritage and deserves to be remembered." *Opposing World War One: Courage and Conscience: An Information Briefing about Conscientious Objection and Peace Activism in the First World War* (2013), 1. The brochure was published by the five peace societies that formed the consortium: Fellowship of Reconciliation, Pax Christi, Peace Pledge Union, Quaker Peace and Social Witness, and Women's International League for Peace and Freedom.

4. Absent from Memory

1. Sir Frederick Kenyon, "War Graves: How the Cemeteries Will Be Designed." Kenyon warned that it was "clearly undesirable to allow free scope to the monumental

236 NOTES TO PAGES 158–164

mason, the sentimental versifier, or the crank." Quoted in Sonia Batten, "Exploring a Language of Grief in First World War Headstone Inscriptions," in Saunders and Cornish, *Contested Objects*, 168. An earlier version of this chapter was published as "The Names of the Dead: 'Shot at Dawn' and the Politics of Remembrance," in *The Great War: From Memory to History*, ed. Kellen Kurschinski et al. (Waterloo, ON: Wilfrid Laurier University Press, 2015), 171–192.

2. Michael Heffernan cites several examples of proposed inscriptions censored by the IWGC: "His loving parents curse the Hun"; "With every breath we draw, we curse the Germans more"; "Set out to help save England. Result: England permanently damned"; "He died just for the unjust"; "A victim of a cruel system." See Heffernan, "Forever England," 318n37.

3. It is not always clear whether families knew that a soldier was executed, as notification protocols were followed unevenly. In many instances, the IWGC was unable to reach a family member or received no response to the request for inscriptions. Consequently, there is no way of knowing whether the absence of inscription in these other cases is significant. We do know, though, that no other gravestone explicitly acknowledges the execution of a soldier.

4. The official policy at the time of Ingham's death was to notify the families as to the circumstances of the death, but the policy was not always followed. Because their executions were not common knowledge, Ingham and Longshaw were in fact memorialized in the St. Thomas Church Pendleton-Salford War Memorial and in stories in local newspapers.

5. Mark Hayhurst, *First Light* (London: Bloomsbury Methuen Drama, 2016).

6. Gerard Oram, *Worthless Men: Race, Eugenics and the Death Penalty in the British Army during the First World War* (London: Francis Boutle, 1998), 17.

7. Daniel J. Sherman, *The Construction of Memory in Interwar France* (Chicago: University of Chicago Press, 1999), 94.

8. The concept of posthumous harm has been the subject of considerable debate within the discipline of philosophy, where skepticism remains as to whether such an act is even possible. For a philosophical discussion of how the concept could be applied to World War I executed soldiers, see Floris Tomasini, *Remembering and Disremembering the Dead: Posthumous Punishment, Harm and Redemption over Time* (London: Palgrave Macmillan, 2017), esp. 42–64.

9. Thomas W. Laqueur, "Memory and Naming in the Great War," in *Commemorations: The Politics of National Identity*, ed. John R. Gillis (Princeton, NJ: Princeton University Press, 1994), 160, 155.

10. Anthony Babington, *For the Sake of Example: Capital Courts-Martial, 1914–1920* (New York: St. Martin's Press, 1983), xi, xii. Although Babington cites his own concern for the distress of the families as the reason for anonymity, Gerard Oram claims that "one of the conditions upon which Babington was granted access to the files was that he did not divulge the identities of any of the executed men." See Gerard Oram, *Military Executions during World War I* (Basingstoke: Palgrave Macmillan, 2003), 6.

11. Julian Putkowski and Julian Sykes, *Shot at Dawn: Executions in World War One by Authority of the British Army Act*, rev. ed. (London: Leo Cooper, 1992).

NOTES TO PAGES 164–167   237

12. Quoted in Cathryn Corns and John Hughes-Wilson, *Blindfold and Alone: British Military Executions in the Great War* (London: Cassell, 2001), 441.

13. Ernest Thurtle, *Shootings at Dawn: The Army Death Penalty at Work* (London: Victoria House Printing, n.d. [1924]), 3.

14. Laqueur, "Memory and Naming," 152; Thomas W. Laqueur, untitled, in *Grounds for Remembering*, eds. Maya Lin et al., Doreen B. Townsend Center Occasional Papers, no. 3 (Berkeley, CA: Townsend Center, 1995), 1.

15. See Derek Boorman, *At the Going Down of the Sun: British First World War Memorials* (York: Ebor Press, 1988), 13.

16. See "Shot at Dawn, Pardoned 90 Years On," *BBC News*, August 16, 2006, http://news.bbc.co.uk/2/hi/uk_news/england/4798025.stm. Sonia Batten documents another instance in Newport, South Wales, in 1921, when a group of returned soldiers insisted that the name of a man who had been shot as a deserter be included on a parish roll of honor while a number of parents whose sons were killed insisted that if that man's name was included on the memorial they would not permit their sons' names to go on it. See Batten, "Exploring a Language of Grief," 166–167. See also Jonathan Trigg, "'Shot at Dawn': Manipulating Remembrance and Forgetting," *Archaeological Review of Cambridge* 25, no. 1 (2010): 139–155, for a discussion of inconsistencies in memorialization practices.

17. Putkowski and Sykes note that fourteen of the men executed by firing squad appear in various volumes of *Soldiers Died in the Great War*, "with two regiments listing all men who were executed, suggesting that some regiments were either unaware of the exclusion directive, or that they preferred to ignore its existence" (*Shot at Dawn*, 26). *The British Jewry Book of Honour* (1922) also records the names of all the executed Jewish soldiers.

18. War Cabinet Meeting no. 279, 21 November 1917 (WO32/4575); quoted in Putkowski and Sykes, *Shot at Dawn*, 224.

19. In Canada, relatives did in fact receive memorial plaques, if they requested them. In New Zealand in 2005, war medals, certificates, and medallions were distributed to the families of the five executed soldiers formally pardoned in 2000.

20. Catherine Moriarty, "Private Grief and Public Remembrance: British First World War Memorials," in *War and Memory in the Twentieth Century*, ed. Martin Evans and Kenneth Lunn (Oxford: Berg, 1997), 126.

21. Although this policy was officially reversed late in the war, benefits continued to be distributed unevenly. A significant body of anecdotal evidence suggests many families never received them.

22. As Michèle Barrett points out, the converse was also true—with devastating effects for some ex-soldiers: if one is not dead, one cannot be remembered; see Barrett, *Casualty Figures*, 156.

23. Piet Chielens and Julian Putkowski, *Unquiet Graves Guide: Execution Sites of the First World War in Flanders* (London: Francis Boutle, 2000).

24. Hansard, HC Deb, October 19, 1993, vol. 230, col. 160, https://api.parliament.uk/historic-hansard/commons/1993/oct/19/pardon-for-solidiers-of-the-great-war.

25. According to Tomasini, "*First and Second order symbolic harms* are either harms to the interests of those who once existed (first order symbolic harms to ante-mortem

238   **NOTES TO PAGES 168–173**

persons), or they are biographical harms that occur after death and to a posthumous reputation (second order symbolic harms)"; these second-order symbolic harms "accrue to a living subject bearer, normally in the form of a relative or friend who is concerned that the memory of their dead is not misrepresented." See Tomasini, *Remembering and Disremembering the Dead*, 32.

26. Hansard, HC Deb, July 24, 1998, vol. 316, col. 1374, https://publications.parliament.uk/pa/cm199798/cmhansrd/vo980724/debtext/80724-07.htm#80724-07_head0.

27. Barrett, *Casualty Figures*, 158.

28. Janet Booth and James White document in detail the history of the campaign to win a pardon for Farr, including the central role played by Janet Booth, Gertie Harris's daughter. In the public relations campaign, it was Gertie's image, however, that had the most power and was given the most prominence. See *He Was No Coward: The Harry Farr Story* (self-published, 2017).

29. Boorman, *At the Going Down of the Sun*, 52.

30. According to Putkowski and Sykes, Burden was not previously commemorated in any grave or memorial to the missing, although this omission would not have been standard practice (*Shot at Dawn*, 49). His name now appears on Addenda Panel 60 at the Menin Gate Memorial to the Missing, and it is also a belated addition to local war memorials in Lewisham.

31. See Moriarty, "Private Grief and Public Remembrance," 135, 138.

32. In 1998, families and supporters of the executed soldiers were permitted a separate remembrance ceremony on the Saturday before Remembrance Day; in 2000, for the first time, they were included as part of the regular ceremony, but they were required to march with civilian groups. Jenny Edkins offers a cautionary note about how exactly this victory came about, noting that it was less a principled decision to include the families of the executed soldiers among the privileged mourners in the main remembrance ceremony at the Cenotaph than an accident of timing. See Edkins, *Trauma and the Memory of Politics*, 72. In 2003, advocates of the executed soldiers were allowed for the first time to march under the SAD banner.

33. Harris in fact lived until 2015, dying at the age of 101; she kept a framed copy of her father's posthumous pardon on the wall in her nursing home.

34. Maya Lin, untitled, in *Grounds for Remembering*, 8.

35. Laqueur, *Work of the Dead*, 449.

36. Laqueur, 449: "And the difficulties of building them were commensurate with their novelty; writing the dead in stone by the thousands and tens of thousands now seems so sadly commonplace that it is easy to forget what a prodigious epigraphic challenge this seemed a century ago."

37. Catherine Moriarty, "'The Returned Soldiers' Bug': Making the Shrine of Remembrance, Melbourne," in Saunders, *Contested Objects*, 156.

38. See, for example, Oram, *Worthless Men*.

39. Laqueur, untitled, in *Grounds for Remembering*, 5.

40. For an informative discussion of some of the complexities surrounding these issues, see Black, "'Thanks for the Memory.'" In his discussion of the deliberations over the Macclesfield war memorial in East Cheshire (135–137), Black recounts the unsuccessful efforts of the wife and brother of an ex-soldier who committed suicide in April 1921 to have the soldier's name recorded on the memorial.

NOTES TO PAGES 173–180   239

41. Marita Sturken, "The Wall, the Screen, and the Image: The Vietnam Veterans Memorial," *Representations* 35 (Summer 1991): 119.

42. Marita Sturken, *Tangled Memories: The Vietnam War, the AIDS Epidemic, and the Politics of Remembering* (Berkeley: University of California Press, 1997), 61.

43. Lin, untitled, in *Grounds for Remembering*, 9.

44. Bob Bushaway, "Name upon Name: The Great War and Remembrance," in *Myths of the English*, ed. Roy Porter (Cambridge: Polity Press, 1992), 139.

45. Tomasini has argued that "harms to the memory and biography of the dead are second order symbolic harms." See Tomasini, *Remembering and Disremembering the Dead*, 33. In the case of the shot-at-dawn soldiers, I am arguing, the posthumous harm was even more far-reaching, rendering biography impossible by foreclosing the construction or preservation of a biographical record. The invention of posthumous lives thus served as a biographical surrogate.

46. John Hughes-Wilson, "The New Contemptibles," *Spectator Archive*, June 3, 2000, http://archive.spectator.co.uk/article/3rd-june-2000/25/the-new-contemptibles. Many of the cases, including those listed above, displayed several of these "egregious" features.

47. Dyett's father, Commander W. H. R. Dyett, even launched a campaign to secure a pardon for his son; disillusioned by the failures of his efforts, he and his family eventually left the United Kingdom, and he renounced his British citizenship. See Leonard Sellers, *Death for Desertion: The Story of the Court Martial and Execution of Sub Lt. Edwin Leopold Dyett* (Barnsley: Pen and Sword, 2003).

48. Stephen Moss, "End of Shame," *Guardian*, August 18, 2006, 27, https://www.theguardian.com/commentisfree/2006/aug/19/comment.military.

49. See Matt Roper, "Heroes Not Cowards: Pardons for Men Shot in WWI," *Daily Mirror*, June 22, 2006, https://www.mirror.co.uk/news/uk-news/heroes-not-cowards-pardons-for-men-630385, for the first four examples; see "Heroes Not Deserters: True Stories of the Shot-at-Dawn Soldiers," *Daily Mirror*, August 17, 2006, for the remaining three.

50. Dismissal of these stories as merely "sob stuff" can be traced back almost to the first publicizing of them. Ernest Thurtle, for example, relays an anecdote, dating to the early 1920s, of being assailed in the House of Commons for subjecting its members to "more sob stuff." Thurtle, *Shootings at Dawn*, 3.

51. Sturken, *Tangled Memories*, 5.

52. Winston Churchill, introduction to *The Secret Battle* by A. P. Herbert (London: Methuen, 1929), v. The novel was ostensibly modeled on the Sub-lieutenant Edwin Dyett case.

53. Between 1928 and 1935, during the war book boom, *The Secret Battle* was issued five times; it was republished eight times, by eight different publishers, between 1963 and 2001.

54. See Sokolowska-Paryz, *Reimagining the War Memorial*, esp. 68–87, for a detailed and insightful discussion of the way the original meaning of the Hamp case was altered in subsequent retellings.

55. William Moore's *The Thin Yellow Line* (London: Leo Cooper, 1974), a work of investigative journalism produced by an author with no access to military records or to the names of victims, has been credited with being the "first book to raise publicly

240 **NOTES TO PAGES 181–189**

the issue of capital courts martial" (Corns and Hughes-Wilson, *Blindfold and Alone*, 21). Moore himself mentions a *Times* story from 1972 that brought these shocking stories to the attention of the public. Babington's *For the Sake of Example* was published in 1983; Putkowski and Sykes's *Shot at Dawn* was originally published in 1989. Before this, the subject was pursued by some academics, but it did not garner a large audience.

56. Corns and Hughes-Wilson, *Blindfold and Alone*, 20–21.

57. The Web is filled with examples of *Private Peaceful* lesson plans, essay assignments, and ideas for class projects. A film version of *Private Peaceful* (dir. Pat O' Connor) was released in 2012.

58. After reading the novel, the relatives of Thomas Peacefull (the original spelling of the family name), discovered a great-uncle previously unknown to them. Morpurgo promised to include information about the "real" Private Peaceful in the foreword to a new edition of the book. "I know it is fiction," reported one of the relatives, "but I don't want a member of my family to be thought of as a coward. I asked Mr Morpurgo if he could arrange some sort of acknowledgment and he said he would include it in the next edition of the book." Angela Levine, "Great War Hero who was the Real Private Peaceful," *Mail Online*, June 30, 2012, http://www.dailymail.co.uk/news/article-2166881/Great-War-hero-real-Private-Peaceful.html.

59. Nora High, quoted in Roper, "Heroes Not Cowards."

60. "Why Do We Let This Man Cast a Shadow over Our War Dead?," *Daily Express*, November 6, 1988, 1.

61. Hansard, HC Deb, October 19, 1993, vol. 230, col. 160.

62. Revisionist historians also promoted a parallel argument about the posthumous harm that the pardons would perform on soldiers who did not desert but withstood the war's pressures.

63. See, for example, Joan M. Pilkington, *They Shall Grow Not Old: The Barton, Bilsborrow and Myerscough War Memorial Project 2003–2004* (Barton, UK: Barton, Bilsborrow and Myerscough War Memorial Trustees, 2005), for an example of a local effort to remedy this situation. The project entailed sending primary school students out to research the biographies of the villages' twentieth-century war dead, the names that appeared on the war memorial.

64. See King, *Memorials of The Great War*, for a history and analysis of the negotiations and debates surrounding both national and local war memorials.

65. Barrett, *Casualty Figures*, 156.

66. Dyer, *The Missing of the Somme*, 11.

67. Sokolowska-Paryz, *Reimagining the War Memorial*, 55.

68. See, for example, "The Tuesday Poem," *Northern Echo*, September 12, 2006, for a reprint of Yorkshire poet, Tom Ward's, "A Pardon for Harry." The MySpace page (myspace.com/privateharryfarr), no longer active, included lyrics and a link to a performance of Reg Meuross's folk ballad about Farr, ". . . And Jesus Wept."

69. Jenny Edkins, "Missing Migrants and the Politics of Naming: Names without Bodies, Bodies without Names," *Social Research* 83, no. 2 (Summer 2016): 361, 362.

70. Edkins, 361–362.

71. Edkins, 362.

72. See Briggs, "D. H. Lawrence," 203. Lawrence unmasks these shameful aspects of war in a series of postwar commentaries, most notably in his essay "Democracy"

(1919), but they continue to have relevance in thinking about a collective reckoning with the war and its devastating consequences.

73. Sturken, "The Wall, the Screen, and the Image," 132.

74. See, for example, Mackinlay's plea to fellow members of Parliament in advancing a Private Member's Bill in 1993: "We could draw a line under the unhappy events of the first world war, do all we can to repair the damage done to the reputation of those men, to heal the wounds of the families and to allow the veterans of the great war who are still alive to go to sleep tonight content in the knowledge that their comrades are now deemed to be brave soldiers." Hansard, HC Deb, October 19, 1993, vol. 230, col. 160. Those who opposed pardons were, if anything, even more invested in drawing a line under the subject.

75. Hansard, HC Deb, September 18, 2006, vol. 449, col. 135WS, https://publications .parliament.uk/pa/cm200506/cmhansrd/vo060918/wmstext/60918m0001.htm#06 091914000012.

76. In this, they had some scholarly backup. Gerard Oram, who compared statistics for death sentences across various constituencies, argues, "What emerges from these comparisons is the inescapable fact that Irish soldiers were four times more likely to be sentenced to death by courts martial than were most other soldiers serving in the British Army" (Oram, *Worthless Men*, 59). Newspapers in Ireland ran sensational stories with headlines like "Shot for Being Irish."

77. Oram, 104.

78. Santanu Das, introduction to Das, *Race, Empire, and First World War Writing*, 1.

79. Oram notes, for example, that fourteen Chinese laborers were sentenced to death, and ten executions were carried out. See Oram, *Worthless Men*, 108.

80. See Julian Putkowski and Mark Dunning, *Murderous Tommies: The Courts Martial of Thirteen British Soldiers Executed for Murder during the First World War* (Barnsley: Pen and Sword, 2016).

81. By considering death sentences passed and not just carried out, Oram argues, this pattern emerges more clearly. See Oram, *Worthless Men*, 15–16.

82. Hansard, July 1919; quoted in Corns and Hughes-Wilson, *Blindfold and Alone*, 463.

83. Dyer, *The Missing of the Somme*, 54. Dyer's book was originally published in 1994 during the early years of the pardons campaign, more than a decade before pardons were granted.

84. Dyer, 54, 53.

85. Edkins, "Missing Migrants," 362.

86. In 2004, the National Union of Journalists wreath read: "The Captains and Kings depart . . . / We remain to speak for the 306 shot at dawn."

87. Hansard, HC Deb, July 24, 1998, vol. 316, col. 1374, https://publications .parliament.uk/pa/cm199798/cmhansrd/vo980724/debtext/80724-07.htm#80724 -07_head0.

88. These are precisely the questions, as mentioned in the introduction, that Adrian Gregory identifies as "the crucial questions" for thinking about memory in Britain. See Gregory, *Silence of Memory*, 119.

89. Laqueur, *Work of the Dead*, 424.

Bibliography

Acton, Carol. *Grief in Wartime: Private Pain, Public Discourse.* Basingstoke: Palgrave Macmillan, 2007.

Adcock, A. St. John. *For Remembrance: Soldier Poets Who Have Fallen in the War.* London: Hodder & Stoughton, 1918.

Babington, Anthony. *For the Sake of Example: Capital Courts-Martial, 1914–1920.* New York: St. Martin's Press, 1983.

Baker, Mark. "Charles Sorley's Long Walk to Marlborough and the Making of Three Poems." *Hatcher Review* 2, no. 16 (Autumn 1983): 285–291.

Bale, John. *Anti-sport Sentiments in Literature: Batting for the Opposition.* New York: Routledge, 2008.

Barney, Shane M. "The Mythic Matters of Edith Cavell: Propaganda, Legend, Myth and Memory." *Historical Reflections/Réflexions Historiques* 31, no. 2 (Summer 2005): 217–233.

Barrett, Michèle. "Afterword: Death and the Afterlife: Britain's Colonies and Dominions." In Das, *Race, Empire, and First World War Writing,* 301–320.

——. *Casualty Figures: How Five Men Survived the First World War.* London: Verso, 2007.

——. "The Great War and Post-modern Memory." *New Formations* 41 (Autumn 2000): 138–157.

——. "Reason and Truth in *A Room of One's Own.*" In Berman and Goldman, *Virginia Woolf Out of Bounds,* 120–129.

——. "Virginia Woolf and Pacifism." In *Woolf in the Real World: Selected Papers from the Thirteenth International Conference on Virginia Woolf,* edited by Karen V. Kukil, 37–41. Clemson, SC: Clemson University Digital Press, 2005.

——. "'White Graves' and Natives: The Imperial War Graves Commission in East and West Africa, 1918–1939." In *Bodies in Conflict: Corporeality, Materiality and Transformation,* edited by Paul Cornish and Nicholas J. Saunders, 80–90. London: Routledge, 2014.

Batchen, Geoffrey. *Forget Me Not: Photography and Remembrance.* Amsterdam: Van Gogh Museum; New York: Princeton Architectural Press, 2004.

Batten, Sonia. "Exploring a Language of Grief in First World War Headstone Inscriptions." In Saunders and Cornish, *Contested Objects,* 163–177.

Becker, Annette. "Museums, Architects and Artists on the Western Front: New Commemoration for a New History?" In *Remembering the First World War,* edited by Bart Ziino, 90–109. Abingdon, Oxon: Routledge, 2015.

Beckett, Lorna C. *The Second I Saw You: The True Love Story of Rupert Brooke and Phyllis Gardner.* London: British Library, 2015.

244 BIBLIOGRAPHY

Bell, Quentin. *Virginia Woolf: A Biography*. 2 vols. Orlando, FL: Harcourt, 1972.

Bergonzi, Bernard. "The First World War: Poetry, Scholarship, Myth." In Roucoux, *English Literature of the Great War Revisited*, 7–18.

——. *Heroes' Twilight: A Study of the Literature of the Great War*. 2nd ed. London: Macmillan, 1980.

Berman, Jessica, and Jane Goldman, eds. *Virginia Woolf Out of Bounds: Selected Papers from the Tenth Annual Conference on Virginia Woolf*. New York: Pace University Press, 2001.

Black, Jonathan. "'Thanks for the Memory': War Memorials, Spectatorship and the Trajectories of Commemoration 1919–2001." In Saunders, *Matters of Conflict*, 134–148.

Blunden, Edmund. *War Poets 1914–1918*. London: Published for the British Council and the National Book League by Longmans, Green, 1958.

Bond, Brian. *Survivors of a Kind: Memoirs of the Western Front*. London: Continuum, 2008.

The Book of Bentley. Burton-on-Trent: W. B. Darley, the Caxton Press, privately printed, 1918.

Boorman, Derek. *At the Going Down of the Sun: British First World War Memorials*. York: Ebor Press, 1988.

Booth, Allyson. *Postcards from the Trenches: Negotiating the Space between Modernism and the First World War*. New York: Oxford University Press, 1996.

Booth, Janet, and James White. *He Was No Coward: The Harry Farr Story*. Self-published, 2017.

Bradshaw, David. "'Vanished, Like Leaves': The Military, Elegy and Italy in *Mrs Dalloway*." *Woolf Studies Annual* 8 (2002): 107–125.

Braybon, Gail. Introduction to *Evidence, History and the Great War: Historians and the Impact of 1914–18*, edited by Gail Braybon, 1–29. New York: Berghahn Books, 2003.

Brearton, Fran. "'But That Is Not New': Poetic Legacies of the First World War." In Das, *Cambridge Companion to the Poetry of the First World War*, 229–241.

Briggs, Marlene A. "D. H. Lawrence, Collective Mourning, and Cultural Reconstruction after World War I." In Rae, *Modernism and Mourning*, 198–212.

Brittain, Vera. *Testament of Youth: An Autobiographical Study of the Years 1900–1925*. New York: Penguin Books, 2005.

Brooke, Christopher N. L. *A History of the University of Cambridge*. Vol. 4, *1870–1990*. Cambridge: Cambridge University Press, 1993.

Buchan, John. *Francis and Riversdale Grenfell: A Memoir*. London: Thomas Nelson and Sons, 1920.

——. *Memory Hold-the-Door: The Autobiography of John Buchan*. London: Hodder and Stoughton, 1940.

——. *These for Remembrance: Memoirs of 6 Friends Killed in the Great War*. London: Buchan and Enright, 1987; privately printed, 1919.

Buck, Claire. "British Women's Writing of the Great War." In Sherry, *Cambridge Companion to the Literature of the First World War*, 85–112.

——. *Conceiving Strangeness in British First World War Writing*. London: Palgrave Macmillan, 2015.

BIBLIOGRAPHY 245

Bushaway, Bob. "Name upon Name: The Great War and Remembrance." In *Myths of the English*, edited by Roy Porter, 136–167. Cambridge: Polity Press, 1992.

Butler, Judith. *Frames of War: When Is Life Grievable?* London: Verso, 2009.

Campbell, Ivar. *Poems by Ivar Campbell: With a Memoir by Guy Ridley*. London: A. L. Humphreys, 1917.

———. *The Prose Writings of Ivar Campbell*. London: privately printed, 1918.

Campbell, Patrick. *Siegfried Sassoon: A Study of the War Poetry*. Jefferson, NC: McFarland, 2007.

Cannadine, David. "War and Death, Grief and Mourning in Modern Britain." In *Mirrors of Mortality: Studies in the Social History of Death*, edited by Joachim Whaley, 187–242. New York: St. Martin's Press, 1982.

Caruth, Cathy, ed. *Trauma: Explorations in Memory*. Baltimore: Johns Hopkins University Press, 1995.

Chapman, Guy. *A Kind of Survivor: The Autobiography of Guy Chapman*. London: Gollancz, 1975.

Chielens, Piet, and Julian Putkowski. *Unquiet Graves Guide: Execution Sites of the First World War in Flanders*. London: Francis Boutle, 2000.

Churchill, Winston. Introduction to *The Secret Battle* by A. P. Herbert, v–viii. London: Methuen, 1929.

Clewell, Tammy. "Consolation Refused: Virginia Woolf, the Great War, and Modernist Mourning." *Modern Fiction Studies* 50, no. 1 (Spring 2004): 197–223.

Clutterbuck, L. A. *The Bond of Sacrifice: A Biographical Record of All British Officers Who Fell in the Great War*. Vol. 1, *Aug–Dec., 1914*. London: Anglo-African Publishing Contractors, [1916].

Cohen, Joseph. "In Memory of W. B. Yeats: And Wilfred Owen." *Journal of English and Germanic Philology* 58, no. 4 (1959): 637–649.

Cole, Sarah. *At the Violet Hour: Modernism and Violence in England and Ireland*. Oxford: Oxford University Press, 2012.

———. *Modernism, Male Friendship, and the First World War*. Cambridge: Cambridge University Press, 2003.

Connelly, Mark. *The Great War, Memory and Ritual: Commemoration in the City and East London, 1916–1939*. Woodbridge, Suffolk: Royal Historical Society/Boydell Press, 2002.

Corcoran, Brendan. "Keats's Death: Towards a Posthumous Poetics." *Studies in Romanticism* 48, no. 2 (Summer 2009): 321–348.

Cornish, Paul. "'Sacred Relics': Objects in the Imperial War Museum 1917–39." In Saunders, *Matters of Conflict*, 35–50.

Corns, Cathryn, and John Hughes-Wilson. *Blindfold and Alone: British Military Executions in the Great War*. London: Cassell, 2001.

Cox, Devon. *The Street of Wonderful Possibilities: Whistler, Wilde and Sargent in Tite Street*. London: Frances Lincoln, 2015.

Cuddy-Keane, Melba. *Virginia Woolf, the Intellectual, and the Public Sphere*. Cambridge: Cambridge University Press, 2003.

Dalglish, Doris. "Charles Sorley." *Friends' Quarterly Examiner* 71 (1937): 346–359.

Dalziell, Tanya. "Mourning and Jazz in the Poetry of Mina Loy." In Rae, *Modernism and Mourning*, 102–117.

246   **BIBLIOGRAPHY**

Das, Santanu, ed. *The Cambridge Companion to the Poetry of the First World War.* Cambridge: Cambridge University Press, 2013.

——. "Indians at Home, Mesopotamia and France, 1914–1918: Towards an Intimate History." In Das, *Race, Empire, and First World War Writing,* 70–89.

——, ed. *Race, Empire, and First World War Writing.* Cambridge: Cambridge University Press, 2011.

——. "Reframing First World War Poetry: An Introduction." In Das, *Cambridge Companion to the Poetry of the First World War,* 3–34.

——. "War Poetry and the Realm of the Senses: Owen and Rosenberg." In Kendall, *Oxford Handbook of British and Irish War Poetry,* 73–99.

Das, Santanu, and Kate McLoughlin, eds. *The First World War: Literature, Culture, Modernity.* Oxford: Oxford University Press, 2018.

Dendooven, Dominiek. "The Journey Back: On the Nature of Donations to the 'In Flanders Field Museum.'" In Saunders and Cornish, *Contested Objects,* 60–72.

Depauw, Liesbet. "Reframing the Past to Change the Future: Reflections on Herbert Wilcox's *Dawn* (1928) as a Historical Documentary and War Film." In *Perspectives on European Film and History,* edited by Leen Engelen and Roel Vande Winkel, 157–182. Ghent: Academia Press, 2007.

Dictionary of National Biography: Missing Persons. Edited by C. S. Nicholls. Oxford: Oxford University Press, 1993.

Dictionary of National Biography 1912–1921. Edited by H. W. C. Davis and J. R. H. Weaver. London: Oxford University Press, 1927.

Doss, Erika. *Memorial Mania: Public Feeling in America.* Chicago: University of Chicago Press, 2010.

Doyle, Laura. "The Body Unbound: A Phenomenological Reading of the Political in *A Room of One's Own.*" In Berman and Goldman, *Virginia Woolf Out of Bounds,* 129–140.

Dyer, Geoff. "Dead Time." In Mathews et al., *Shot at Dawn,* n.p.

——. *The Missing of the Somme.* New York: Vintage, 2011.

Edkins, Jenny. "Missing Migrants and the Politics of Naming: Names without Bodies, Bodies without Names." *Social Research* 83, no. 2 (Summer 2016): 359–389.

——. *Trauma and the Memory of Politics.* Cambridge: Cambridge University Press, 2003.

Edwards, Erin E. *The Modernist Corpse: Posthumanism and the Posthumous.* Minneapolis: University of Minnesota Press, 2018.

English, James F. *The Economy of Prestige: Prizes, Awards, and the Circulation of Cultural Value.* Cambridge, MA: Harvard University Press, 2008.

Ewart, Evelyn C. *Victor Alexander Ewart: A Memoir.* London: A. L. Humphreys, privately printed, 1921.

Fell, Alison S. *Women as Veterans in Britain and France after the First World War.* Cambridge: Cambridge University Press, 2018.

Filippucci, Paola. "Postcards from the Past: War, Landscape and Place in Argonne, France." In Saunders and Cornish, *Contested Objects,* 220–236.

Forty, Adrian, and Susanne Küchler, eds. *The Art of Forgetting.* London: Bloomsbury, 2001.

Frayn, Andrew. "Introduction: Modernism and the First World War." *Modernist Cultures* 12, no. 1 (2017): 1–15. DOI: 10.3366/mod.2017.0153.

Froula, Christine. *Virginia Woolf and the Bloomsbury Avant-Garde: War, Civilization, Modernity*. New York: Columbia University Press, 2005.

Fuss, Diana. *Dying Modern: A Meditation on Elegy*. Durham, NC: Duke University Press, 2013.

Fussell, Paul. *The Great War and Modern Memory*. 25th anniversary ed. Oxford: Oxford University Press, 2000.

Gardner, Brian, ed. *Up the Line to Death: The War Poets 1914–1918: An Anthology*. London: Methuen, 1964.

Gay, Frances G. "Charles Sorley's Poems." *Swindon Review: A Local Miscellany of the Arts*, no. 4 (December 1948): 5–9.

Gillis, Stacy. "'Many Sisters to Many Brothers': The Women Poets of the First World War." In Kendall, *Oxford Handbook of British and Irish War Poetry*, 100–113.

Glenconner, Pamela. *The Earthen Vessel: A Volume Dealing with Spirit-Communication Received in the Form of Book-Tests by Pamela Glenconner with a Preface by Sir Oliver Lodge*. London: John Lane, 1921.

———. *Edward Wyndham Tennant: A Memoir by His Mother*. London: John Lane, 1919.

Goldie, David. "Was There a Scottish War Literature? Scotland, Poetry, and the First World War." In Kendall, *Oxford Handbook of British and Irish War Poetry*, 153–173.

Graves, Robert. *Fairies and Fusiliers*. London: Heinemann, 1917.

———. *Good-Bye to All That*. New York: Anchor Books, 1998.

———. *In Broken Images: Selected Letters of Robert Graves, 1914–1916*, edited by Paul O'Prey. London: Hutchinson, 1982.

Gregory, Adrian. *The Silence of Memory: Armistice Day 1919–1946*. Oxford: Berg, 1994.

Grenfell, Ethel Anne Priscilla, Lady Desborough. *Pages from a Family Journal, 1888–1915*. Eton: Eton College, privately printed, 1916.

Gullace, Nicoletta F. *"The Blood of Our Sons": Men, Women, and the Renegotiation of British Citizenship during the Great War*. New York: Palgrave Macmillan, 2002.

Harrison, Brian. "College Life, 1918–1939." In Harrison, *History of the University of Oxford*, 81–108.

———, ed. *The History of the University of Oxford*. Vol. 8, *The Twentieth Century*. Oxford: Clarendon Press, 1994.

———. *The Transformation of British Politics, 1860–1995*. Oxford: Oxford University Press, 1996.

Harrison, Robert Pogue. *The Dominion of the Dead*. Chicago: University of Chicago Press, 2003.

Haughton, Hugh. "Anthologizing War." In Kendall, *Oxford Handbook of British and Irish War Poetry*, 421–444.

Hayhurst, Mark. *First Light*. London: Bloomsbury Methuen Drama, 2016.

Headlam, Cuthbert Morley. *George Roworth Parr, Prince Albert's Somerset Light Infantry: A Short Memoir*. Edinburgh: T. & A. Constable, privately printed, 1915.

Heffernan, Michael. "For Ever England: The Western Front and the Politics of Remembrance in Britain." *Ecumene* 2, no. 3 (1995): 293–323.

248 **BIBLIOGRAPHY**

Helle, Anita. "'Blasé Sorrow': Ultramodernity's Mourning at the *Little Review*, 1917–20." In Rae, *Modernism and Mourning*, 118–135.

Hibberd, Dominic. "Introduction." In *The Diary of a Dead Officer: Being the Posthumous Papers of Arthur Graeme West*, vii–xxii. London: Imperial War Museum, 1991.

———. "Who Were the War Poets, Anyway?" In Roucoux, *English Literature of the Great War Revisited*, 108–120.

Hibberd, Dominic, and John Onions, eds. *The Winter of the World: Poems of the Great War*. London: Constable, 2007.

Hirsch, Marianne. *The Generation of Postmemory: Writing and Visual Culture after the Holocaust*. New York: Columbia University Press, 2012.

Holroyd, Michael. *Lytton Strachey: The New Biography*. New York: Farrar, Straus and Giroux, 1995.

Hughes, Anne-Marie Claire. "War, Gender and National Mourning: The Significance of the Death and Commemoration of Edith Cavell in Britain." *European Review of History: Revue européenne d'histoire* 12, no. 3 (2005): 425–444. http://dx.doi.org/10.1080/13507480500428938.

Hughes-Wilson, John. "The New Contemptibles." *Spectator Archive*, June 3, 2000. http://archive.spectator.co.uk/article/3rd-june-2000/25/the-new -contemptibles.

Hussey, Mark, ed. *Virginia Woolf and War: Fiction, Reality, and Myth*. Syracuse, NY: Syracuse University Press, 1991.

Hynes, Samuel. "Personal Narratives and Commemoration." In Winter and Sivan, *War and Remembrance in the Twentieth Century*, 205–220.

———. *A War Imagined: The First World War and English Culture*. New York: Atheneum, 1991.

Imperial War Museums [IWM]. *Poppies: Blood Swept Lands and Seas of Red*. London: IWM, 2018.

Inglis, K. S. "The Homecoming: The War Memorial Movement in Cambridge England." *Journal of Contemporary History* 27 (1992): 583–605.

Ingram, Angela. "'The Sacred Edifices': Virginia Woolf and Some of the Sons of Culture." In *Virginia Woolf and Bloomsbury: A Centenary Celebration*, edited by Jane Marcus, 125–145. Bloomington: Indiana University Press, 1987.

Isemonger, Mildred, ed. *Richard Vincent Sutton: A Record of His Life Together with Excerpts from His Private Papers*. London: G. W. Jones, 1922.

Johnston, John H. *English Poetry of the First World War: A Study in the Evolution of Lyric and Narrative Form*. Princeton, NJ: Princeton University Press, 1964.

Jones, J. B. "Sorleiana." *Swindon Review: A Local Miscellany of the Arts*, no. 4 (December 1948): 16–19.

Judd, Alan, and David Crane. *First World War Poets*. London: National Portrait Gallery Publications, 2014.

Kapp, Paul Hardin, and Cele C. Otnes. "The Poppies Exhibit: Producing and Consuming Commemoration of World War I in Britain." In *Heritage of Death: Landscapes of Emotion, Memory and Practice*, edited by Mattias Frihammar and Helaine Silverman, 107–122. New York: Routledge, 2018.

BIBLIOGRAPHY 249

Kelly, Alice. *Commemorative Modernisms: Women Writers, Death, and the First World War*. Edinburgh: Edinburgh University Press, 2020.

Kelly, Andrew. *Cinema and the Great War*. London: Routledge, 1997.

Kendall, Tim, ed. *The Oxford Handbook of British and Irish War Poetry*. Oxford: Oxford University Press, 2007.

Kermode, Frank. "Breeding." Review of *The Diaries of Sylvia Warner Townsend*, ed. Claire Harman and *Sylvia and David: The Townsend Warner/Garnett Letters*, ed. Richard Garnett. *London Review of Books* 16, no. 14 (July 21 1994), 15–16.

Kidd, Jenny, and Joanne Sayner. "Unthinking Remembrance? Blood Swept Lands and Seas of Red and the Significance of Centenaries." *Cultural Trends* 27, no. 2 (2018): 68–82. https://doi.org/10.1080/09548963.2018.1453448.

King, Alex. *Memorials of the Great War in Britain: The Symbolism and Politics of Remembrance*. Oxford: Berg, 1998.

——. "Remembering and Forgetting in the Public Memorials of the Great War." In Forty and Küchler, *Art of Forgetting*, 147–169.

Küchler, Susanne. "The Place of Memory." In Forty and Küchler, *Art of Forgetting*, 53–72.

Kunka, Andrew J. "The Evolution of Mourning in Siegfried Sassoon's War Writing." In Rae, *Modernism and Mourning*, 69–84.

Laqueur, Thomas W. "Memory and Naming in the Great War." In *Commemorations: The Politics of National Identity*, edited by John R. Gillis, 150–167. Princeton, NJ: Princeton University Press, 1994.

——. Untitled. In Lin et al., *Grounds for Remembering*, 1–7.

——. *The Work of the Dead: A Cultural History of Mortal Remains*. Princeton, NJ: Princeton University Press, 2015.

Lee, John. "Shakespeare and the Great War." In Kendall, *Oxford Handbook of British and Irish War Poetry*, 134–152.

Lee, Sir Sidney. *National Biography: A Lecture Delivered at the Royal Institution on the Evening of Friday, January 31, 1896*. London: Spottiswoode and Co., privately printed, 1896.

——. *The Perspective of Biography*. The English Association, Pamphlet no. 41. September 1918.

——. *Principles of Biography: The Leslie Stephen Lecture Delivered in the Senate House, Cambridge on 13 May 1911*. Cambridge: Cambridge University Press, 1911.

[Leighton, Marie]. *Boy of My Heart*. London: Hodder and Stoughton, 1916.

Levenback, Karen L. *Virginia Woolf and the Great War*. Syracuse, NY: Syracuse University Press, 1999.

Lin, Maya. Untitled. In Lin et al., *Grounds for Remembering*, 8–14.

Lin, Maya, Andrew Barshay, Stephen Greenblatt, Thomas Laqueur, and Stanley Saitowitz. *Grounds for Remembering*. Doreen B. Townsend Center Occasional Papers, no. 3. Berkeley, CA: Townsend Center, 1995.

Lloyd, David W. *Battlefield Tourism: Pilgrimage and the Commemoration of the Great War in Britain, Australia and Canada, 1919–1939*. Oxford: Berg, 1998.

Lodge, Sir Oliver. *Christopher: A Study in Human Personality*. London: Cassell, 1918.

250 BIBLIOGRAPHY

——. *Raymond; or Life and Death, with Examples of the Evidence for Survival of Memory and Affection after Death*. New York: George H. Doran, 1916.

London, Bette. "The Names of the Dead: 'Shot at Dawn' and the Politics of Remembrance." In *The Great War: From Memory to History*, edited by Kellen Kurschinski, Steve Marti, Alicia Robinet, Matt Symes, and Jonathan F. Vance, 171–192. Waterloo, ON: Wilfrid Laurier University Press, 2015.

——. "Posthumous Was a Woman: World War I Memorials and Woolf's Dead Poet's Society." *Woolf Studies Annual* 16 (2010): 45–69.

——. *Writing Double: Women's Literary Partnerships*. Ithaca, NY: Cornell University Press, 1999.

——. "Writing Modern Deaths: Women, War, and the View from the Home Front." In *The History of British Women's Writing, 1880–1920*. Vol. 7, edited by Holly A. Laird, 284–297. London: Palgrave Macmillan, 2016.

Long, Gary L. "Organizations and Identity: Obituaries 1856–1972." *Social Forces* 65, no. 4 (June 1987): 964–1001.

Longley, Edna. "The Great War, History, and the English Lyric." In Sherry, *Cambridge Companion to the Literature of the First World War*, 57–84.

Longley, Michael, Andrew Motion, and Jon Stallworthy. "War Poetry: A Conversation." In Das, *Cambridge Companion to the Poetry of the First World War*, 257–267.

Malvern, Sue. "'For King and Country': Frampton's *Edith Cavell* (1915–20) and the Writing of Gender in Memorials to the Great War." In *Sculpture and the Pursuit of a Modern Ideal in Britain, c. 1880–1930*, edited by David J. Getsy, 219–238. Aldershot: Ashgate, 2004.

Mansfield, Katherine. *Katherine Mansfield's Letters to John Middleton Murry, 1913–1922*. Edited by John Middleton Murry. New York: Knopf, 1951.

Marcus, Jane. "The Asylums of Antaeus: Women, War, and Madness—Is There a Feminist Fetishism?" In *The New Historicism*, edited by H. Aram Veeser, 132–151. New York: Routledge, 1989.

——. *Virginia Woolf, Cambridge and* A Room of One's Own: *"The Proper Upkeep of Names."* London: Cecil Woolf, 1996.

Marcus, Laura. "The Newness of the 'New Biography': Biographical Theory and Practice in the Early Twentieth Century." In *Mapping Lives: The Uses of Biography*, edited by Peter France and William St. Clair, 193–218. Oxford: British Academy / Oxford University Press, 2002.

——. *Virginia Woolf*. Plymouth, UK: Northcote House, 1997.

Marsh, Edward. *Rupert Brooke: A Memoir*. New York: John Lane, 1918.

Mathews, Chloe Dewe, Geoff Dyer, Hew Strachan, and Helen McCarthy. *Shot at Dawn*. Madrid: Ivory Press, 2014.

Matthew, H. C. G. *Leslie Stephen and the New Dictionary of National Biography*. Cambridge: Cambridge University Press, 1997.

Mayhall, Laura E. Nym. *The Militant Suffrage Movement: Citizenship and Resistance in Britain, 1860–1930*. Oxford: Oxford University Press, 2003.

McLoughlin, Kate, Lara Feigel and Nancy Martin. "Writing War, Writing Lives." *Textual Practice* 29, no. 7 (2015): 1219–1223. https://doi.org/10.1080/0950236X.2015.1095442.

McPherson, Neil. *It Is Easy to Be Dead*. London: Oberon Books, 2016.

BIBLIOGRAPHY 251

McVicker, Jeanette. "'Six Essays on London Life': A History of Dispersal." Pt. 1. *Woolf Studies Annual* 9 (2003): 143–165.

——. "'Six Essays on London Life': A History of Dispersal." Pt. 2. *Woolf Studies Annual* 10 (2004): 141–172.

Meynell, Viola. *Julian Grenfell.* London: Burns and Oates, 1917.

Minogue, Sally, and Andrew Palmer. *The Remembered Dead: Poetry, Memory and the First World War.* Cambridge: Cambridge University Press, 2018.

Moore, T. Sturge. *Some Soldier Poets.* New York: Harcourt, Brace and Howe, 1920.

Moore, William. *The Thin Yellow Line.* London: Leo Cooper, 1974.

Moriarty, Catherine. "Private Grief and Public Remembrance: British First World War Memorials." In *War and Memory in the Twentieth Century*, edited by Martin Evans and Kenneth Lunn, 125–142. Oxford: Berg, 1997.

——. "'The Returned Soldiers' Bug': Making the Shrine of Remembrance, Melbourne." In Saunders and Cornish, *Contested Objects*, 144–162.

Morpurgo, Michael. *Private Peaceful.* London: HarperCollins, 2003.

Mosley, Nicholas. *Julian Grenfell: His Life and the Times of His Death, 1888–1915.* London: Weidenfeld and Nicolson, 1976.

Murry, J. Middleton. "The Lost Legions." In *Aspects of Literature*, 157–166. London: W. Collins Sons, 1920.

Newberry, Jo Vellacott. "Anti-war Suffragists." *History* 62, no. 206 (1977): 411–425.

Newman, Vivien. *We Also Served: The Forgotten Women of the First World War.* Barnsley: Pen and Sword, 2014.

Nichols, Robert, ed. *Anthology of War Poetry, 1914–1918.* London: Nicholson and Watson, 1943.

Nicholson, Harold. *The Development of English Biography.* London: Hogarth Press, 1927.

Nicholson, Ivor, ed. *Horace A. Link: A Memoir.* London: printed for private circulation, 1919.

Noble, Marjorie. *Marc Noble: A Memoir.* London: Country Life, printed for private circulation, 1918.

Nora, Pierre. "Between Memory and History: *Les Lieux de Mémoire.*" *Representations* 26 (Spring 1989): 7–24.

Oram, Gerard. *Military Executions during World War I.* Basingstoke: Palgrave Macmillan, 2003.

——. *Worthless Men: Race, Eugenics and the Death Penalty in the British Army during the First World War.* London: Francis Boutle, 1998.

Osborn, E. B. *The New Elizabethans: A First Selection of the Lives of Young Men Who Have Fallen in the Great War.* London: John Lane, 1919.

Ouditt, Sharon. *Fighting Forces, Writing Women: Identity and Ideology in the First World War.* London: Routledge, 1994.

——. "Tommy's Sisters: The Representations of Working Women's Experience." In *Facing Armageddon: The First World War Experienced*, edited by Hugh Cecil and Peter H. Liddle, 736–751. London: Pen and Sword, 1996.

Owen, Wilfred. *The Complete Poems and Fragments.* Edited by Jon Stallworthy. 2 vols. London: Chatto and Windus/Hogarth Press, 1983.

Parker, Peter. *The Old Lie: The Great War and the Public-School Ethos.* London: Constable, 1987.

BIBLIOGRAPHY

Parry, Harold. *In Memoriam: Harold Parry, Second Lieutenant, K.R.R.C.* Edited by Geoffrey P. Dennis. London: W. H. Smith, n.d. [1918?].

Peniston-Bird, Corinna. "War and Peace in the Cloakroom: The Controversy over the Memorial to the Women of World War II." In *Representations of Peace and Conflict*, edited by Stephen Gibson and Simon Mollan, 263–284. Basingstoke: Palgrave Macmillan, 2012.

Pickles, Katie. *Transnational Outrage: The Death and Commemoration of Edith Cavell.* Basingstoke: Palgrave Macmillan, 2007.

Pilkington, Joan M. *They Shall Grow Not Old: The Barton, Bilsborrow and Myerscough War Memorial Project 2003–2004.* Barton, UK: Barton, Bilsborrow and Myerscough War Memorial Trustees, 2005.

Plumley, Stanley. *Posthumous Keats: A Personal Biography.* New York: W. W. Norton, 2008.

Press, John. *Charles Hamilton Sorley.* War Poets Series. London: Cecil Woolf, 2006.

——. "Charles Sorley." *Review of English Literature* 7, no. 3 (1966): 43–60.

Putkowski, Julian, and Mark Dunning. *Murderous Tommies: The Courts Martial of Thirteen British Soldiers Executed for Murder during the First World War.* Barnsley: Pen and Sword, 2016.

Putkowski, Julian, and Julian Sykes. *Shot at Dawn: Executions in World War One by Authority of the British Army Act.* Rev. ed. London: Leo Cooper, 1992.

Rae, Patricia. "Introduction: Modernist Mourning." In Rae, *Modernism and Mourning*, 13–49.

——, ed. *Modernism and Mourning.* Lewisburg, PA: Bucknell University Press, 2007.

Ramazani, Jahan. "Afterword: 'When There Are So Many We Shall Have to Mourn.'" In Rae, *Modernism and Mourning*, 286–295.

——. *Poetry of Mourning: The Modern Elegy from Hardy to Heaney.* Chicago: University of Chicago Press, 1994.

Rawlinson, Mark. "Wilfred Owen." In Kendall, *Oxford Handbook of British and Irish War Poetry*, 114–133.

Reginio, Robert. "Virginia Woolf and the Technologies of Exploration: *Jacob's Room* as Counter-Monument." In *Woolf and the Art of Exploration: Selected Papers from the Fifteenth International Conference on Virginia Woof*, edited by Helen Southworth and Elisa Kay Sparks, 86–94. Clemson, SC: Clemson University Digital Press, 2006.

Reilly, Catherine W. *English Poetry of the First World War: A Bibliography.* London: George Prior, 1978.

Ricketts, Harry. *Strange Meetings: The Poets of the Great War.* London: Chatto and Windus, 2010.

Ridley, Guy. "Memoir." In Campbell, *Poems by Ivar Campbell*, 7–28.

Robertson, James C. "*Dawn* (1928): Edith Cavell and Anglo-German Relations." *Historical Journal of Film, Radio and Television* 4, no. 1 (1984): 15–28. DOI: 10.1080/01439688400260021.

Rosenthal, Lecia. *Mourning Modernism: Literature, Catastrophe and the Politics of Consolation.* New York: Fordham University Press, 2011.

Roucoux, Michel, ed. *English Literature of the Great War Revisited: Proceedings of the Symposium on the British Literature of the First World War, University of Picardy 1986.* Amiens: Presses de l'U.E.R, Clerc Université, Picardy, 1986.

BIBLIOGRAPHY   253

Runcie, James. "Sorley's Signpost." *Marlburian*, Michaelmas Term, 1976.

Sanders, Agnes J., ed. *A Soldier of England: Memorials of Leslie Yorath Sanders*. Dumfries: J. Maxwell and Son, 1920.

Sassoon, Siegfried. Introduction to *Poems* by Wilfred Owen, v–vi. London: Chatto and Windus, 1920.

———. *Siegfried Sassoon Diaries, 1915–1918*. Edited by Rupert Hart-Davis. London: Faber and Faber, 1983.

Saunders, Max. *Self Impression: Life-Writing, Autobiografiction, and the Forms of Modern Literature*. Oxford: Oxford University Press, 2010.

Saunders, Nicholas J., ed. *Matters of Conflict: Material Culture, Memory and the First World War*. Abingdon, Oxon: Routledge, 2004.

———. *The Poppy: A Cultural History from Ancient Egypt to Flanders Fields to Afghanistan*. London: Oneworld, 2013.

———. *Trench Art: Materialities and Memories of War*. Oxford: Berg, 2003.

Saunders, Nicholas J., and Paul Cornish, eds. *Contested Objects: Material Memories of the Great War*. Abingdon, Oxon: Routledge, 2009.

Sellers, Leonard. *Death for Desertion: The Story of the Court Martial and Execution of Sub Lt. Edwin Leopold Dyett*. Barnsley: Pen and Sword, 2003.

Shaw, George Bernard. *Saint Joan: A Chronicle Play in Six Scenes and an Epilogue*. London: Constable, 1924.

Sherman, Daniel J. *The Construction of Memory in Interwar France*. Chicago: University of Chicago Press, 1999.

Sherry, Vincent, ed. *The Cambridge Companion to the Literature of the First World War*. Cambridge: Cambridge University Press, 2005.

———. "The Great War and Modernist Poetry." In Kendall, *Oxford Handbook of British and Irish War Poetry*, 190–207.

———. *The Great War and the Language of Modernism*. Oxford: Oxford University Press, 2003.

Silkin, Jon, ed. Introduction to *The Penguin Book of First World War Poetry*, 2nd ed., 15–77. London: Penguin Books, 1979.

Skelton, Tim, and Gerald Gliddon. *Lutyens and the Great War*. London: Frances Lincoln, 2008.

Smith, Angela K. "The Pankhursts and the War: Suffrage Magazines and First World War Propaganda." *Women's History Review* 12, no. 1 (2003): 103–118.

Smith, George, ed. *George Buchanan Smith, 1890–1915*. Glasgow: James Maclehose and Sons, privately printed, 1916.

Smith, George A., and Hilda C. Miall Smith. *Two Brothers: Eric and Arnold Miall Smith*. London: Constable, printed for private circulation, 1918.

Smith, Leonard V. "Paul Fussell's *The Great War and Modern Memory*: Twenty-Five Years Later." *History and Theory* 40, no. 2 (May 2001): 241–260. https://www.jstor.org/stable/2678033.

Sokolowska-Paryz, Marzena. *Reimagining the War Memorial, Reinterpreting the Great War: The Formats of British Commemorative Fiction*. Newcastle upon Tyne: Cambridge Scholars, 2012.

Sorley, Charles Hamilton. *The Collected Letters of Charles Hamilton Sorley*. Edited by Jean Moorcroft Wilson. London: Cecil Woolf, 1990.

254 **BIBLIOGRAPHY**

——. *The Collected Poems of Charles Hamilton Sorley*. Edited by Jean Moorcroft Wilson. London: Cecil Woolf, 1985.

——. *Death and the Downs: The Poetry of Charles Hamilton Sorley*. Edited by Brett Rutherford. Providence, RI: Yogh and Thorn, 2010.

——. *Letters from Germany and from the Army*. Edited by W. R. Sorley. Cambridge: privately printed, 1916.

——. *The Letters of Charles Sorley, with a Chapter of Biography*. Edited by W. R. Sorley. Cambridge: Cambridge University Press, 1919.

——. *Marlborough and Other Poems*. 2nd ed. Cambridge: Cambridge University Press, 1916.

——. *Marlborough and Other Poems*. 4th ed. Cambridge: Cambridge University Press, 1919.

——. *The Poems and Selected Letters of Charles Hamilton Sorley*. Edited by Hilda D. Spear. Dundee: Blackness Press, 1978.

Spater, George, and Ian Parsons. *A Marriage of True Minds: An Intimate Portrait of Leonard and Virginia Woolf*. New York: Harcourt Brace Jovanovich, 1977.

Stallworthy, Jon. "Review of *Charles Hamilton Sorley: A Biography*, by Jean Moorcroft Wilson and *The Collected Letters of Charles Hamilton Sorley*, edited by Jean Moorcroft Wilson." *Review of English Studies*, n.s., 40, no. 159 (August 1989): 436–438. http://www.jstor.org/stable/516017.

——. *Wilfred Owen: A Biography*. Oxford: Oxford University Press, 1977.

Stephen, Martin, ed. *Never Such Innocence: A New Anthology of Great War Verse*. London: Buchan and Enright, 1988.

——. *The Price of Pity: Poetry, History and Myth in the Great War*. London: Leo Cooper, 1996.

Stewart, Susan. *On Longing: Narratives of the Miniature, the Gigantic, the Souvenir, the Collection*. Durham, NC: Duke University Press, 1992.

Stewart, Victoria. "'War Memoirs of the Dead': Writing and Remembrance in the First World War." *Literature and History* 14, no. 2 (2005): 37–52.

Stodart-Walker, A. *James Logan Mackie*. Edinburgh: [T. & A. Constable], privately printed, 1919.

Strachey, Lytton. *Eminent Victorians: The Definitive Edition*. London: Continuum, 2002.

Sturken, Marita. "Personal Stories and National Meanings: Memory, Reenactment, and the Image." In *The Seduction of Biography*, edited by Mary Rhiel and David Suchoff, 31–42. New York: Routledge, 1996.

——. *Tangled Memories: The Vietnam War, the AIDS Epidemic, and the Politics of Remembering*. Berkeley: University of California Press, 1997.

——. "The Wall, the Screen, and the Image: The Vietnam Veterans Memorial." *Representations* 35 (Summer 1991): 118–142.

Swann, Thomas Burnett. *The Ungirt Runner: Charles Hamilton Sorley, Poet of World War I*. Hamden, CT: Archon Books, 1965.

Tambling, Jeremy. *Becoming Posthumous: Life and Death in Literary and Cultural Studies*. Edinburgh: Edinburgh University Press, 2001.

Thom, Deborah. "Making Spectaculars: Museums and How We Remember Gender in Wartime." In Braybon, *Evidence, History and the Great War*, 48–66.

BIBLIOGRAPHY 255

Thurtle, Ernest. *Shootings at Dawn: The Army Death Penalty at Work.* London: Victoria House Printing, n.d. [1924].

Todman, Dan. *The Great War: Myth and Memory.* London: Continuum, 2007.

——. "The Ninetieth Anniversary of the Battle of the Somme." In *War Memory and Popular Culture: Essays on Modes of Remembrance and Commemoration,* edited by Michael Keren and Holger H. Herwig, 23–40. Jefferson, NC: McFarland, 2009.

Tollemache, Douglas A., ed. *The Career of a Second Lieutenant in the Year 1914.* Ipswich: printed for private circulation, 1915.

Tomasini, Floris. *Remembering and Disremembering the Dead: Posthumous Punishment, Harm and Redemption over Time.* London: Palgrave Macmillan, 2017.

Tomlinson, H. M. "Undertones." *New Adelphi* 2, no. 3 (March–May 1929): 258–260.

Trigg, Jonathan. "'Shot at Dawn': Manipulating Remembrance and Forgetting." *Archaeological Review of Cambridge* 25, no. 1 (2010): 139–155.

Uffelman, Larry K. "Charles Hamilton Sorley: An Annotated Checklist." *Serif: The Magazine of Type and Typography* 10, no. 4 (1973): 3–17.

Utechin, Patricia. *Sons of This Place: Commemoration of the War Dead in Oxford's Colleges and Institutions.* Oxford: Robert Dudgdale, 1998.

Vandiver, Elizabeth. "Early Poets of the First World War." In Das, *Cambridge Companion to the Poetry of the First World War,* 69–80.

——. "'Millions of the Mouthless Dead': Charles Hamilton Sorley and Wilfred Owen in Homer's Hades." *International Journal of the Classical Tradition* 5, no. 3 (Winter 1999): 432–455.

Vansittart, Peter. "Introduction." In Buchan, *These for Remembrance,* [vii–xxxiv].

Watson, Janet S. K. *Fighting Different Wars: Experience, Memory, and the First World War in Britain.* Cambridge: Cambridge University Press, 2004.

Wellings, Ben, Shanti Sumartojo, and Matthew Graves. "Commemorating Race and Empire in the First World War Centenary." In *Commemorating Race and Empire in the First World War Centenary,* edited by Ben Wellings and Shanti Sumartojo, 7–20. Liverpool: Liverpool University Press, 2018.

Wilson, Emily R. *Mocked with Death: Tragic Overliving from Sophocles to Milton.* Baltimore: Johns Hopkins University Press, 2004.

Wilson, Jean Moorcroft. *Charles Hamilton Sorley: A Biography.* London: Cecil Woolf, 1985.

——. *Isaac Rosenberg: The Making of a Great War Poet: A New Life.* Evanston, IL: Northwestern University Press, 2008.

——. *Isaac Rosenberg: Poet and Painter.* London: Cecil Woolf, 1975.

——. *Siegfried Sassoon: The Journey from the Trenches: A Biography, 1918–1967.* New York: Routledge, 2003.

——. *Siegfried Sassoon: The Making of a War Poet: A Biography (1886–1918).* London: Duckworth, 1998.

——. *Siegfried Sassoon: Soldier, Poet, Lover, Friend.* London: Duckworth, 2013.

Wilson, Jean Moorcroft, and Cecil Woolf. *Charles Hamilton Sorley: Exhibition Catalogue.* London: Cecil Woolf, 1985.

Winter, Jay. "Beyond Glory: First World War Poetry and Cultural Memory." In Das, *Cambridge Companion to the Poetry of the First World War,* 242–255.

BIBLIOGRAPHY

——. "Forms of Kinship and Remembrance in the Aftermath of the Great War." In Winter and Sivan, *War and Remembrance in the Twentieth Century*, 40–60.

——. "Oxford and the First World War." In Harrison, *History of the University of Oxford*, 3–26.

——. *Sites of Memory, Sites of Mourning: The Great War in European Cultural History*. Cambridge: Cambridge University Press, 1995.

Winter, Jay, and Emmanuel Sivan. "Setting the Framework." In Winter and Sivan, *War and Remembrance in the Twentieth Century*, 6–39.

——, eds. *War and Remembrance in the Twentieth Century*. Cambridge: Cambridge University Press, 1999.

Winterhalter, Teresa. "Guns and Big Guns in *A Room of One's Own*." In *Re: Reading, Re: Writing, Re: Teaching Virginia Woolf: Selected Papers from the Fourth Annual Conference on Virginia Woolf*, edited by Eileen Barrett and Patricia Cramer, 72–79. New York: Pace University Press, 1995.

Wohl, Robert. *The Generation of 1914*. Cambridge, MA: Harvard University Press, 1979.

Woolf, Virginia. *The Common Reader*. London: Hogarth Press, 1925.

——. *The Death of the Moth and Other Essays*. New York: Harcourt, 1942.

——. *The Diary of Virginia Woolf*. Vol. 1, *1915–1919*. Edited by Anne Olivier Bell. New York: Harcourt, 1977.

——. *The Diary of Virginia Woolf*. Vol. 2, *1920–1924*. Edited by Anne Olivier Bell. New York: Harcourt, 1978.

——. *The Diary of Virginia Woolf*. Vol. 3, *1925–1930*. Edited by Anne Olivier Bell. New York: Harcourt Brace Jovanovich, 1980.

——. *The Essays of Virginia Woolf*. Vol. 2, *1912–1918*. Edited by Andrew McNeillie. San Diego: Harcourt, 1988.

——. *The Essays of Virginia Woolf*. Vol. 3, *1919–1924*. Edited by Andrew McNeillie. San Diego: Harcourt, 1988.

——. *The Letters of Virginia Woolf*. Vol. 3, *1923–1928*. Edited by Nigel Nicolson and Joanne Trautmann. New York: Harcourt Brace Jovanovich, 1977.

——. *The Letters of Virginia Woolf*. Vol. 4, *1929–1931*. Edited by Nigel Nicolson and Joanne Trautman. New York: Harcourt Brace Jovanovich, 1978.

——. *A Room of One's Own*. New York: Harcourt Brace Jovanovich, 1929.

——. *Three Guineas*. Edited by Jane Marcus and Mark Hussey. San Diego: Harcourt, 2006.

——. *Women & Fiction: The Manuscript Versions of* A Room of One's Own. Edited by S. P. Rosenbaum. Oxford: Published for the Shakespeare Head Press by Blackwell Publishers, 1992.

——. *The Years*. New York: Harcourt Brace Jovanovich, 1965.

Young, James E. *The Texture of Memory: Holocaust Memorials and Meaning*. New Haven, CT: Yale University Press, 1993.

Index

Page numbers in *italics* indicate illustrations. Titles of works by known authors are most easily found under the author's name, unless otherwise indicated.

Adcock, A. St. John, 202n19, 211n35
Afghanistan war, xiii
afterlife of WWI, 1–32; British experience, focus on, 21–22; citizenship, commemoration as act of, 9; commemoration of commemoration, 1, 13, 29; contestation, remembrance as ongoing process of, 22, 28, 29; culture of memory and, 20–25, 28–32; familiarity of tropes and images, 11–12, 20, 87, 89, 102–3; literary and memorial practices, dialogue between, 21–22; modern reflections of, xii–xiii; modernism and memorial practices, 30–32; poppy wearing, distribution, and symbolism, 10–11; postmemory, concept of, 4–5, 8, 22, 81, 100–101, 116, 178, 218n119, 218n122; remembrance *versus* memory, 29, 32, 95–96; *Shot at Dawn* photographic exhibition (2014–2016), 13–20, *15*, *18*; uniformity of memorialization masking other differences, 9–12; the unmemorialized, 9–12, 26–27, 155–57, 184; in US *versus* UK, xi–xii. *See also* centenary commemoration; commemorative volumes; executed soldiers; Poppies installation; posthumous life; Sorley, Charles Hamilton; Woolf, Virginia
Aldington, Richard, 123
amateur biographies of dead soldiers. *See* commemorative volumes
ambivalent mourning, 61
Anthem for Doomed Youth exhibition (IWM, 2002), 101–4, 106, 110–11, 116–18, 214n77, 219n129
antimonuments, countermonuments, and ephemeral monuments, 7, 13, 27, 55, 116, 138, *139*, 200n73, 229n92

antiwar movements. *See* pacifism and antiwar sentiments
Arnold, Edward and Peggy, 226n41
art world, critiques of memorialization in, 6–9
Ashmore, Bob, *Rough Justice*, 176
Asquith, Herbert, 152
Asquith, Raymond, 63, 133
Australia and New Zealand, 9, 172, 237n19
autobiographical fragments, 33–35, 44, 63–64

Babington, Anthony, *For the Sake of Example*, 163, 236n10, 239–40n55
Bailleulmont Communal Cemetery, Pas-de-Calais, 160, *161*, 162, 192
Bain, John, 211n34, 219n127
Barrett, Michèle, 10, 32, 148, 168, 184, 237n22; *Casualty Figures*, 39–40
Batchen, Geoffrey, *Forget Me Not*, 47, 52, 67, 204n37
Batten, Sonia, 237n16
battlefield tourism, 18, 182, 198n43
Becker, Annette, 12, 18, 19
Behn, Aphra, 126, 153
Bell, Julian, 232n124
Bell, Vanessa, 126, 224n27
Bergonzi, Bernard, 78, 83
Berkeley, Reginald, 154
Binyon, Laurence, 214n73; "For the Fallen," 222n153
biography: amateur (*see* commemorative volumes); commemorative impulse in, 52, 54–55; as genre, 35–36, 39, 68, 69; and modernism, 68–69; "new biography," 25, 35–36, 38, 39, 44, 54, 55. *See also*, Lee, Sir Sidney; Strachey, Lytton
Birkenhead, Lord, 154

258 INDEX

Black, Jonathan, 238n40
Black Lives Matter movement, xiii
Blackadder Goes Forth (TV show), 11, 181
Blair, Tony, 167
"Blood Swept Lands and Seas of Red."
 See Poppies installation
Blunden, Edmund, 40, 76, 93, 123, 127, 180,
 200n65, 207n100, 215–16n96, 216n98,
 225n33, 227n56
Bond, Brian, *Survivors of a Kind*, 40, 203n31
The Book of Bentley, 42, 48–49, *53*
Boorman, Derek, *At the Going Down of the
 Sun*, 169
Booth, Allyson, 31, 138, 229n87
Booth, Janet (daughter of Gertie Harris),
 169, 170, 238n28
Bradshaw, David, 137, 224–25n30
Braybon, Gail, xi, 135
Brearton, Fran, 68, 82, 84, 199–200n62
Briggs, Marlene, 9, 189, 240n72
Brittain, Vera, 35, 45, 134, 200n65
Brontë, Charlotte, 226n47
Brooke, Rupert: in *Anthem for Doomed Youth*
 exhibition, 102, 117; in canon of war poets,
 93, 216n98; commemorative volumes
 and, 43, 44, 56–57, 204n38, 206–7n87;
 eulogization of, 80, 122, 223n11; Gardner's
 memoir of affair with, 56–57, 206–7n87;
 Marsh's memoir of, 44, 56, 80; "The
 Soldier," 219n134; Sorley and, 73, 80, 88,
 93, 102, 111, 113, 219n134; Woolf on, 43,
 44, 56, 122, 123, 136
Browne, Des, 179, 190
Buchan, John, 44, 54, 63; *Memory Hold-the-
 Door*, 51, 205n68; *These for Remembrance*,
 50–51, 205nn67–68, 225n32
Buck, Claire, 9–10, 135, 228n69
Burden, Herbert Francis, 169, 174, *178*,
 238n30
Bushaway, Bob, 173
Butler, Judith, 10, 165, 210n17

*The Cambridge Companion to the Poetry of the
 First World War*, 81, 215n94
Cambridge Homecoming monument, 134,
 227n63
Cambridge University, 56, 92, 130, 132–34,
 215n87, 227n61
Cambridge University Press, 91, 93, 94, 96,
 215n86
Cameron, David, 6, 8, 198n40
Campbell, Ivar, 45–46, 51–52, 205–6n71
Canada, 165, 237n19

*The Career of a Second Lieutenant in the Year
 1914*, 49–50
Cavell, Edith, 27, 140–56; abundance of
 memorials to, 140–45, 149–51, 193,
 233n134; Edith Cavell Memorial,
 St. Martin's Place, London, 140–50, *141*,
 155, 156, 230n102, 230n104, 231–32n120,
 233n136; embalmed dog of, 149; executions
 conducted by British compared, 145–46;
 exhumation and reburial in Norwich,
 142, *143*, 145; films about, 140, 145,
 153–54, 234–35n150; German trial
 and execution of, 140, 145, 229–30n96,
 232–33nn128–129; last words of, 146–49,
 154, 155, 211–12n120, 232n128; over-
 shadowing other women's narratives,
 150–51; pacifism and antiwar sentiments,
 association with, 147–49, 154, 232n123; on
 recruitment posters, 145, *146*; Royal Mint
 commemorative coin, 155; traditional
 feminine values and, 145, 149, 151;
 women's suffrage movement and, 152;
 Woolf and, 140–42, 146–54, 231n1
Cecil Woolf Publishers, 84–88, *86*, 94, 98, 99,
 103–4
Cenotaph, London, 2–4; belief in presence
 of the dead at, 229n84; commemorative
 volumes and, 57, 64, 198n43; Edith Cavell
 memorial and, 143, 144; executed soldiers
 and, 168–69, 170, 193, 238n32; as Grade I
 heritage listing, 230n104; Lutyens's design
 of, 121, 223n7; modernism of, 2–4, *3*, 8;
 photo of, *3*; Poppies exhibition and, 2–4,
 6, 8, 9; unemployed ex-servicemen, as site
 of protest for, 9; Woolf and, 27, 57,
 120–21, 130, 137–39, 229n84
centenary commemoration, xi, 1, 6, 7,
 10–13, 13–15, 84, 94, 115, 118, 156, 181,
 196–97n18, 198n34, 235n160. *See also*
 Poppies installation
Chamberlain, Sir Austen, 154
Chapman, Guy, 203n31
Charteris, Evan, 48
Childs, David, 177
Churchill, Winston, 178, 223n11
citizenship, commemoration as act of, 9
class. *See* social class
Clutterbuck, L. A., *The Bond of Sacrifice*, 38,
 203n23
Cole, Herbert, 147
Cole, Sarah, 29, 74, 123, 229n93
collective remembrance/memory, 52, 85,
 93, 94, 96, 177, 188, 190, 191

colonial soldiers and laborers in WWI, 9–10, 12, 184, 190–91, 241n76, 241n79

commemorative volumes, 21, 25–26, 33–71; as alternative/supplement to public structures of commemoration, 60–63, 70; as amateur productions, 23, 25, 46, 52, 55; autobiographical fragments in, 33–35, 44, 63–64; chapter headings and narrative arc of, 44–46; contemporary public reception of, 70; eclectic aesthetic of, 46–47, 56, 60; ephemeral nature of, 25, 55, 67–68, 70, 203n30; genre, emergence as, 39–47; hybridity of, 41, 54–60, 66; inherent contradictions of, 65–67; as material objects, 41–42, 47–64; modernism and, 41, 61, 66, 67, 68–71; ordinariness and shortness of subjects' lives, problem of, 39, 42–44, 55–56; portraiture in, 64–65; public/private boundaries, blurring, 56–60, *58*, 62, 207n97; readability of, 47, 51; resistance to demands of biographical genre in, 59; self-deprecating presentation of, 53–54; similarities between subjects of, 63–64; social class and, 38, 43, 44; to women, 226n41; Virginia Woolf on, 43, 44, 56–58, 70, 128–31, 207n91, 209n131. *See also specific volumes, authors, and subjects*

Concannon, Don, 164

Confederate monuments controversy, xiii

Connelly, Mark, 121

conscientious objectors, 27, 155–57, *157*, 184, 192, 227n51, 231n115, 235n160

Conviction (TV documentary), 179

Corcoran, Brendan, 110

Corns, Cathryn, and John Hughes-Wilson, *Blindfold and Alone*, 180–81

countermonuments, antimonuments, and ephemeral monuments, 7, 13, 27, 55, 116, 138, 139, 200n73, 229n92

cowardice, execution for. *See* executed soldiers

Cuddy-Keane, Melba, 132, 153, 226n48

culture and heritage industries in UK, 6–7, 18, 85, 198n43

culture of memory, 20–25, 28–32

Cummins, Paul, 1, 7, 9, 11, 12, 197n23, 197n29

Curzon, Lord, 4

Dalby Forest, Yorkshire, Nissen Hut memorial in, 7

Dalglish, Doris, 77, 211n32

Dalziell, Tanya, 59

Das, Santanu, 9, 12, 94, 214n74, 215n94, 218n121, 220n138, 227n49; *Race, Empire, and First World War Writing*, 190–91

Davis, H. W. C., 38

Dawn (film), 153–54, 234–35n150, 235n153

Dearmer, Geoffrey, 136

DeComyn, Andy, 15, 17, 19

Defense of the Realm Act, 231n115

Deller, Jeremy, 6, 14; *We're Here Because We're Here*, 198n44

Derby, Lord, 165

Desborough, Ethel Anne Priscilla Grenfell, Lady, *Pages from a Family Journal*, 47–59, *49*, *53*, 205n61

deserters, execution of. *See* executed soldiers

The Diary of a Dead Officer, 60, 207n100

Dictionary of National Biography (DNB), 25, 38–39, 54–55, 56; *Missing Persons* supplement, 38–39, 94

Doss, Erika, 121

Downton Abbey (TV show), 181

Drake, Peter, *The Prisoner's Friend*, 176, 177

Dunning, Mark, 191

Dyer, Geoff, 17, 19; *The Missing of the Somme*, xi–xii, 33, 17, 19, 33, 88, 121, 127, 184, 192, 195n3, 225n35, 241n83

Dyett, Edwin Leopold, 174–75, 239n47, 239n52

Edkins, Jenny, 8, 187–89, 192, 238n32

Eliot, T. S., 69, 87, 132, 136, 228n76; *Poems 1909–1925* and *Prufrock*, 123

Emanuel, Oliver, and Gareth Williams, *The 306*, 15, 199n46

ephemeral monuments, antimonuments, and countermonuments, 7, 13, 27, 55, 116, 138, 139, 200n73, 229n92

Equal Franchise Act (1928), 125

Ewart, Evelyn and Victor Alexander, 42–43

executed soldiers, 27–28; Edith Cavell compared to, 145–46; Cenotaph ceremonies and, 168–69, 170, 193, 238n32; closure, memorialization as, 187, 189–94; dying off of surviving WWI veterans and, 168; colonial soldiers and laborers as, 184, 190–91; families of, 160–61, 162, 165–66, 168–70, 177, 179, 188, 236n3, 236n10, 237n21, 238n32; Irish as, 190, 241n76; Haig memorial controversy and, 182–83; Albert Ingham, gravestone of, 158–61, *159*, 192, 236nn3–4; memorializations of, 162, 169–76, 182–85, 188; naming of,

260   **INDEX**

executed soldiers (*continued*)
163–67, 170–71, 184, 185, 187–88;
newspaper accounts of, 174–75, 177;
pardons, opposition to, 182, 183, 240n62;
paucity of information on, 175; poppies
with white centers commemorating, 11;
public response to stories of, 174–79, 187;
SAD (Shot at Dawn) movement and
pardons campaign, 16, 19, 21, 28, 160–61,
167–71, 173–76, 178–81, 183, 185, 187,
190–91, 194; Shot at Dawn Memorial,
National Arboretum, Staffordshire,
15–17, 16, 19, 145, 146, 169, 174, 176–78,
178, 185–87, 186; Shot at Dawn photographic exhibition (2014–2016), 13–20, 15,
18; social class and, 166, 175; as subjects
of literature, film, and television, 15, 161,
176–77, 179–82, 199n46; as unmemorial-
ized/missing, 161–66, 187–89; as WWI
phenomenon, 161
executions: of Edith Cavell by Germans,
140, 145, 229–30n96, 232–33nn128–129;
of enemy civilians by British, 145–46,
231nn115–16; French executions of
women for espionage, 231n115

Farage, Nigel, 6
Farr, Harry, 162, 166, 169, 174, 176, 178,
238n28, 240n68
Feigel, Laura, 35, 202n7
feminist theory and scholarship, 125,
135–36, 153, 222n156
Filippucci, Paola, 221n148
First World War Peace, 156
For King and Country (film), 180
14-18 NOW: WWI Centenary Art
Commissions, 14–15, 19, 118
Frampton, Sir George, 142, 149
Frayn, Andrew, 31
Freeman, John Bentley, 42, 48–49, 53
Froula, Christine, 137, 228n78
Fuller, Roy, "Ghost Voice," 220n141
Fuss, Diana, 41, 61, 62, 74, 110, 208n120,
219n132, 220n141
Fussell, Paul, *The Great War and Modern
Memory*, 30, 67–68

Gahan, Sterling, 231–32
Gardner, Brian, 93, 215n96
Gardner, Phyllis (lover of Rupert Brooke),
56–57, 206–7n87
Garnett, David, 36, 82–83
Gay, Frances J., 83

gender. *See* women and gender issues
Gillis, Stacy, 135, 216n98
Gleichen, Lord Edward, 230n102
Glenconner, Pamela, 33–34, 34, 45, 46, 57,
58, 64, 65–66, 202n18
Goll, Yvan, "Requiem for the Dead of
Europe," xi
Gollancz, Israel, *A Book of Homage to
Shakespeare*, 137
Graves, Robert, 23–24, in canon of war
poets, 216n98; commemorative volumes
and, 40, 200n65; *Fairies and Fusiliers*, 24,
210n25; *Good-Bye to All That*, 24, 76;
Hogarth Press publishing, 225n33; on
noise in war, 227n49; *Over the Brazier*, 24;
Sassoon and, 72–75, 209n6; Sorley and,
72–77, 85, 88, 90, 93, 97, 114, 118–19,
209n2, 209n6, 210–11nn25–26, 210n18,
210n20, 216n98, 220n135, 220n142;
"Sorley's Weather," 76; truth-telling in
war books, 125; Woolf's ambivalence
about, 127
Gregory, Adrian, 21, 25, 138, 148, 199nn59–60,
241n88
Grenfell, Billy, 47–49, 49
Grenfell, Field-Marshal Lord, 53, 205n68
Grenfell, Francis and Riversdale, 44, 51, 54,
205n68, 225n32
Grenfell, Julian, 47–49, 49, 93, 102, 133,
204n38, 208n110, 216n98
Gullace, Nicoletta, 149, 152
Gurney, Ivor, 88, 94

Haig, Field Marshal Earl, 182–83, 231n110
Haldane, Lord, 152
Harris, Gertrude ("Gertie"), 162, 163, 168–70,
176, 238n28, 238n33
Harrison, Jane, 134, 227–28n64
Harrison, Robert Pogue, 220n136
Hayhurst, Mark, *First Light*, 161
Hayward, John, 215n95
Heffernan, Michael, 62, 236n2
Helle, Anita, 61
Herbert, A. P., *The Secret Battle*, 179–80,
239n52
heritage industries in UK, 6–7, 18–19, 85,
198n43
Hibberd, Dominic, 83, 87, 94, 207n100,
213n71, 214n73, 216n98; *The Winter of the
World* (with John Onions), 93
High, Nora, 176
Highgate, Thomas, 171
Hill, Reginald, *The Wood Beyond*, 180

Hipkin, John, 168
Hirsch, Marianne, 4, 12, 22, 81, 100–101, 116, 117, 118, 198n39, 212n50, 218n119, 218n122, 222n156
Hodson, J. L., *Return to the Wood*, 180
Hogarth Press, 84, 126, 127, 223n15, 225n33
Holocaust, xii, 4, 7, 8, 22, 81, 138, 200n66, 212n50, 218n119
Holroyd, Michael, 36, 202n11
homosociality and homoeroticism, 73, 74, 75, 119, 209n8
Hughes, Ann-Marie Claire, 144, 231n111
Hughes, Christopher, 104
Hughes, Ted, 87, 199–200n62
Hughes-Wilson, John, 174; *Blindfold and Alone* (with Cathryn Corns), 180–81
Hunt, Leigh, 222n155
Hutchinson, Alan Fox, 108, 218n124, 221n146
Hynes, Samuel, 33, 40, 92, 139, 200n73, 203n29, 205n59, 207n99, 223n15, 224n23

Iddon, Brian, 172
The Iliad, 114, 220n139
Imperial War Graves Commission (IWGC), 121, 158–60, 222n5, 236nn2–3
Imperial War Museum (IWM): *Anthem for Doomed Youth* exhibition (2002), 101–4, 106, 110–11, 116–18, 214n77, 219n129; Cecil Woolf Publishers War Poets series and, 85; commemorative volumes and, 70, 198n40, 198n43; embalmed dog of Edith Cavell held by, 149; Poppies exhibition at, 13; Rosenberg and, 215n87; Women's War Shrine, 143, 144, 230n107; women's war work, commemoration of, 151–52, 233n137
Ingham, Albert and George, 158–62, *159*, 177, 192, 235nn3–4
Inglis, Ken S., 134, 199n60, 227n63
Ingram, Angela, 135
Iraq war, xiii
Ireland and Irish soldiers, 9, 11, 81–82, 180, 190, 241n76

Jameson, Cecil, 89, 104, 106
Jameson, Storm, 203n31
Jefferies, Richard, 83, 111–12, 213n57; *Life of the Field*, 83
Jewish service in WWI, xii, 237n17
Joad, C. M., 207n100
Johnston, Jennifer, *How Many Miles to Babylon*, 180

Jones, Hilda Coombes, 169, 170
Jones, J. B., 77–78, 211n33
Jones, Jonathan, 6
Judenplatz Holocaust Memorial, Vienna, 7, 8

Kapp, Paul Hardin, 196n11
Keats, John, 74, 84, 100, 110, 118, 212n46, 222n155; *Endymion*, 102; "This Living Hand," 220n138
Kelly, Alice, 200n72
Kenyon, Sir Frederick, 158, 235–36n1
Kermode, Frank, 82–83
Kidd, Jenny, 198n34
King, Alex, 1, 21, 199n60
King, Laurie, *Justice Hall*, 180
Kipling, Rudyard, 164
Kitchener, Lord, statue of, 121
Küchler, Susanne, 89, 214n83
Kunka, Andrew J., 65

landscape as memorial, 16, 17–19, *18*
Laqueur, Thomas W., 28, 60, 194, 122, 163, 164, 171, 172, 197n27, 238n36
last words, 34, 146–49, 231–32n120, 232n128, 233n136, 218n125; last-word poems, 110, 208n120
Lawrence, D. H., 9, 87, 240–41n72
Le Soeur, Pastor, 231–32n120, 232n128
League of War Resisters, 155
Ledwidge, Francis, 103
Lee, John, 137
Lee, Sir Sidney, 36, 38–39, 43, 54–55, 56, 62, 202n15, 204n47
Leighton, Marie, *Boy of My Heart*, 45, 204n38, 204n55
Leighton, Roland, 45
Levenback, Karen L., 121, 134
Lin, Maya, 170–71, 173
Link, Horace A., 44, 52, 58, 66–67
Lister, Charles, 133, 216n106
Lloyd, David W., 21, 126, 138, 224n29
Lloyd George, David, 148
Lodge, Raymond, 128, 225–26n39
Lodge, Sir Oliver J., 44, *45*, 46, 128–31, 225–26n39, 226n46
London, WWI memorials in, 121, 155
Long, Gary L., 39
Longley, Edna, 113, 225n36, 227n56
Longley, Michael, 81–82, 199–200n62; "In Memoriam," 82
Longshaw, Alfred, 160, 177
Loos, Battle of, 76, 81, 111, 211n27
Loos Memorial to the Missing, 81, 111

262   **INDEX**

Losey, Joseph, 180
lost generation, concept of, 27, 123–24, 131–40
Lutyens, Sir Edwin, 121, 223n7
Lynch, Martin, *Holding Hands at Paschendale*, 176, 177

Mackie, James Logan, 42, 43
Mackinlay, Andrew, 166, 167, 183, 241n74
Macmillan, Harold, 133
MacMillan, James, *All the Hills and Vales Along*, 118, 220n135
Major, John, 194
Malvern, Sue, 141–42, 144, 231n110, 231n118
Mansfield, Katherine, 77
Marcus, Jane, 126, 149, 224n27, 232n123
Marcus, Laura, 36, 68, 69, 229n94
Marlborough College, 42, 86, 89–92, 98, 100, 102, 104–6, 209n8, 213n57, 214n85, 219n133
Marlborough downs memorial to Sorley. *See* Sorley's Signpost
Marsh, Edward, 44, 56, 72, 75, 80, 204n38, 209n2
Martin, Nancy, 35, 202n7
Masefield, John, 75, 77
material culture of remembrance, 34–35, 41–42, 47–64, 89–91, 102, 103–4, 116. *See also* memorials
Mathews, Chloe Dewe, 14, 16–19
McLoughlin, Kate, 35, 201n79, 202n7
McPherson, Neil, *It Is Easy to Be Dead*, 117–18, 221–22nn151–152, 222n154
McVicker, Jeanette, 228n79
Melbourne Shrine of Remembrance, 172
memoirs of the dead. *See* commemorative volumes
memoirs of the living, 40–41. *See also* war books/War Book Controversy
memorials: antimonuments, countermonuments and ephemeral monuments, 7, 13, 27, 55, 116, 138, 139, 200n73, 229n92; commemorative volumes as alternative/supplement to, 60–63, 70; landscape as, *16*, 17–19, *18*; military cemeteries, 5, 121, 122, 144, 158, 164, 182, 185, 187, 191–92, 222n5; modernism and, 2–4, *3*, 8, 138–39, 173; naming the dead on, 28, 55, 197n27; at Oxford and Cambridge Universities, 133, 134, 135; postwar phenomenon of, 5, 121, 172–73, 223n7, 238n36; London Remembers website, 155; to women,

143–44, 149, 230n107, 233n131. *See also* executed soldiers; *specific memorials by name*
memory, culture of, 20–25, 28–32
memory *versus* remembrance, 29, 32, 95–96
Menin Gate Memorial to the Missing, Ypres, 64, 166, 173, 238n30
Meynell, Viola, 204n38
Miall Smith, Eric and Arnold, 42
military cemeteries, 5, 121, 122, 144, 158–62, *159*, 164, 182, 185, 187, 191–92, 222n5
military offenses, execution for. *See* executed soldiers
Mill, C. Watson, *The Eternal Flame*, 224n29
Minogue, Sally, 75, 200n63
modernism: biography and, 68–69; of Cenotaph, London, 2–4, *3*, 8; commemorative volumes and, 41, 61, 66, 67, 68–71; facticity and, 125; memorial practices and, 30–32; memorials and, 2–4, *3*, 8, 138–39, 173; New Modernist Studies, 31–32, 69; postwar antimodernist debates, 7–8; war poets and, 88, 136, 214n74; of Woolf, 125, 138–39, 224n23
The Monocled Mutineer (TV show), 181
Montague, C. E., *Rough Justice*, 180
monuments. *See* memorials
Moore, T. Sturge, 212n40
Moore, William, *The Thin Yellow Line*, 239–40n55
Moriarty, Catherine, 21, 165, 170, 172, 199n60
Morpurgo, Michael: *Private Peaceful*, 181–82, 240nn57–58; *War Horse*, 181
Morrell, Lady Ottoline, 64, 65
Mosley, Nicholas, 208n110
Motion, Andrew, 116, 117
Mukherji, Kalyan, 12
Murry, John Middleton, 77

naming the dead, 28, 55, 163–67, 170–71, 184, 185, 187–88, 197n27
National Council of Women, 147, 155, 235n158
National Union of Journalists, 193, 241n86
National Union of Women's Suffrage Societies, 151
Neagle, Anna, 235n153
Nelson, William ("Billy"), 176, 177
"new biography." *See* biography
"new Elizabethans," war dead as, 120, 225n32. *See also* Osborn, E. B.
New Modernist Studies, 31–32, 69

INDEX 263

New Zealand and Australia, 9, 172, 237n19
Newman, Vivien, 144
Nichols, Robert, 72, 73, 209n3, 210n9, 210n19; *Anthology of War Poetry, 1914–1918*, 75
Nicholson, Harold, 52
9/11 and 9/11 Memorial, xiii, 22, 187
No More War Movement, 10
Noble, Marjorie and Marc, 43, 67
No-Conscription League, 149
Nora, Pierre, 89, 96

Onions, John, *The Winter of the World* (with Dominic Hibberd), 93
Oram, Gerard, 161, 190, 191, 236n10, 241n76, 241n79, 241n81
Osborn, E. B., *The New Elizabethans*, 37–38, 120, 127, 202nn18–19, 203n23, 211n34, 216n106, 225n32
Otnes, Cele C., 196n11
Ouditt, Sharon, 224n23
Owen, Wilfred: alternate war story in poems of, 123; in canon of war poets, 216n98; commemorative volumes and, 60–61; McPherson's *It Is Easy to Be Dead* and, 221–22n152; Poet's Corner memorial, Westminster Abbey, 214n71; posthumous publication of most work of, 127, 225n35; Sorley and, 76, 81, 87, 90, 94, 99, 102, 117, 210n21
The Oxford Book of Modern Verse (ed. Yeats), 93, 215n95
Oxford University, 14, 72, 90, 92, 132–34, 215n87

pacifism and antiwar sentiments, 10, 11; commemorative volumes and, 60, 207n100; poppy symbolism and, 10–11; Sorley/war poets and, 74; women, war resistance by, 151–52, 157, 234n140, 234n145, 235n158; Woolf/Cavell and, 123–24, 147–49, 150–52, 154, 155–57, 157, 223n15, 232n123, 233n136, 235n153. *See also* conscientious objectors; *specific organizations*
Palmer, Andrew, 75, 200n63
Pankhurst, Emmeline and Christabel, 151
Pankhurst, Sylvia, 147
Parker, Peter, *The Old Lie*, 78, 211n24
Parr, George Roworth, 53
Parry, Harold, 46, 67
patriotism, 6, 9, 12, 60–62, 122–24, 139, 145–48, 151–52, 155, 192, 231–32n120

Peace Pledge Union (PPU), 148, 156, 233n136, 235n157
Peniston-Bird, Corinna, 233n131
Philpot, Glyn Warren, 64
photography: commemorative volumes, portraiture in, 64–65; postmemory and, 218n122; as practice of remembrance, 47, 52, 204n37; *Shot at Dawn* photographic exhibition (2014–2016), 13–20, *15*, *18*; Sorley, photos and drawings of, *79*, 89, 104, 106, *108*
Pickles, Katie, 140, 144, 149, 155, 232n126
Piper, Tom, 1, 5, 6, 11
Plumley, Stanley, 212n46, 222n155
Poets' Corner memorial, Westminster Abbey, 87–88, 92–93, 103, 211n27, 213–14nn71–73
politics of commemoration and memory, 6, 10, 16, 59, 60, 62, 179, 188–89
Poppies installation (2014): afterlife of, 11, 12–13, *13*, 196n11, 198n40; "Blood Swept Lands and Seas of Red" as official title of, 1, 9, 11–12; popular and critical responses to, 1–9, 21; *Shot at Dawn* photographic exhibition compared, 13–15, 19–20; at Tower of London, 1–6, *2*, *5*; uniformity masking other differences, 9–12; *Wave*, 12, 13, 196n11; *Weeping Widow*, *5*, 12–13, *13*, 196n11
poppy wearing, distribution, and symbolism, 10–11
posthumous birth, postwar phenomenon of, 23, 125, 224n24
posthumous harm, 28, 160, 163, 167, 169, 174, 176, 182, 183, 236n8, 237–38n25, 239n45, 240n62
posthumous life: of Achilles, after death of Patroclus, 114; in commemorative volumes, 129 (*see also* commemorative volumes); concept of, 22–25, 65; naming, constituted in, 164; Sorley's "When You See Millions of the Mouthless Dead" and, 113–14; in spiritualism, 129; war survivors' experience of themselves as dead, 23–24, 40–41, 65, 123, 200n65; Woolf on challenges of, 126–31
posthumous publication: as wartime and postwar phenomenon, 23, 126–28; as memorial (*see* commemorative volumes); of Owen, 99, 123, 127; of Sorley, 72, 90, 96–97; of Philip Woolf, 128; spirit communication as, 127–29. *See also* memorials; commemorative volumes

264   INDEX

posthumous redemption/restitution, 28, 163, 176, 182

postmemory, 4–5, 8, 22, 81, 100–101, 116, 178, 218n119, 218n122

Pound, Ezra, 69, 136, 228n76

Powell, Enoch, 12

Press, John, 85, 86, 93, 215n96, 218n123

prosthetic memory, 89

public monuments. *See* memorials

Putkowski, Julian, 183, 191; *Shot at Dawn* (with Julian Sykes), 164, 167, 168, 174, 237n17, 239–40n55

"queering" and queer theory, 118–19, 122, 229n94

Quiller Couch, Sir Arthur, 215n95, 226n46

Rae, Patricia, 31, 201n76, 204n43

Ramazani, Jahan, 39, 60–61, 66, 69, 81, 201n76; on *Modernism and Mourning*, 31

Rawlinson, Mark, 225n35

Read, Herbert, *In Retreat*, 223n15

Reid, John, 168, 193

remembrance *versus* memory, 29, 32, 95–96

Representation of the People Act (1918), 152, 234nn142–43

resistant mourning, 30, 61, 200n73

Ridley, Guy, *Poems by Ivar Campbell*, 45–46, 205–6n71

Rimington, Dame Stella, 232–33n129

Robertson, James C., 234–35n150

A Room of One's Own (Woolf), 21, 27, 120–57; alternative histories of WWI and, 135–36, 139; as countermonument, 138–39; on Charlotte Brontë, 226n47; Edith Cavell and, 142, 144–54; on gender as constructed and contingent, 139–40, 220n94; lectures serving as basis for, 123, 153; "lost generation," Woolf's awareness of, 123–24, 131–40; modernism of, 30; on money and a room of one's own as prerequisite for women writers, 132, 226n46; *Mrs. Dalloway* and, 224–25n30; "Oxbridge" as opening setting of, 132–35; posthumous and commemorative literature, sensitivity of Woolf about, 126–31; postwar context of, 120–26, 131, 153, 157, 223n15, 224n26; Shakespeare's sister in, 27, 120, 123, 125–28, 130–32, 136–40, 142, 145, 149, 150–54, 156–57, 193, 222n1, 226n45, 234n147; *Three Guineas* and, 153; on truth, 124–25

Rosenbaum, S. P., 123

Rosenberg, Isaac, 64, 88, 90, 94, 117, 123, 214n77, 215n87, 216n98, 217–18n118

Russell, Bertram, 36

Rydell, Bréon, 222n154

Sanders, Agnes J. and Leslie Yorath, 60–61, 61

Sassoon, Siegfried, 23; in *Anthem for Doomed Youth* exhibition, 117; in canon of war poets, 216n98; commemorative volumes and, 40, 64–65, 66, 200n65, 208n114; Graves and, 72–75, 209n6; "On Passing the New Menin Gate," 173; on Wilfred Owen, 127; portrait of, 64; "Sherston" trilogy, 65, 208n114; *Siegfried's Journey, 1916–1920*, 64–65; "A Soldier's Declaration," 74; Sorley and, 72–77, 85, 90, 102, 210n15, 210n18, 210nn20–21, 216n98; Wilson biography, 217–18n118; Woolf on, 127, 136, 225n33

Saunders, Max, *Self Impression*, 69, 202n7

Sayner, Joanne, 198n34

Scottish National War Memorial, Castle Rock, Edinburgh, 165

Scottish poet, Sorley viewed as, 84, 88, 91–92, 105, 118, 222n154

Shakespeare, Judith (in Woolf's *A Room of One's Own*), 27, 120, 123, 125–28, 130–32, 136–40, 142, 145, 149, 150–54, 156–57, 193, 222n1, 226n45, 234n147

Shakespeare, William, 136–37

Shaw, George Bernard, *Saint Joan*, 147

shell shock, 167, 174, 180, 183, 187

Sheppard, Hugh Richard (Dick), 150, 233n136

Sherman, Daniel J., 163

Sherry, Vincent, 136, 201n79

Shot at Dawn (TV documentary), 179

Shot at Dawn Memorial, National Arboretum, Staffordshire, 15–17, 16, 19, 145, 146, 169, 174, 176–78, 178, 185–87, 186

Shot at Dawn (SAD) movement, 16, 19, 21, 28, 160–61, 167–71, 173–76, 178–81, 183, 185, 187, 190–91, 194

Shot at Dawn photographic exhibition (2014–2016), 13–20, 15, 18

shot-at-dawn soldiers. *See* executed soldiers

Silkin, Jon, 220n135

Sitwell, Edith, 127, 225n35

Smith, George Buchanan, 46

Smith, James, 172, 176

Smith, Leonard V., 30

INDEX 265

Smith, Les, *Early One Morning*, 176, 177
social class: afterlife of WWI, different responses to, 9–10; commemorative volumes and, 38, 43, 44; executed soldiers and, 166, 175; Sorley on, 90; of war poets, 90, 91, 132–35; Woolf on, 132–33
Sokolowska-Paryz, Marzena, 185, 200n72
Somme Memorial to the Missing at Thiepval, 121, 192, 223n7
Sorley, Charles Hamilton, 26, 72–119; Aberdeen memorial plaque, *115*, 222n154; affective response to, 74–75; 80–82, 114–15, 117–19; in *Anthem for Doomed Youth* exhibition (IWM, 2002), 101–4, 106, 110–11, 116–18, 219n129; attachment to Marlborough town and countryside, 79, 102, 104–6, 108–9, 111–12, 218n124, 221n146; Brooke and, 73, 80, 88, 93, 102, 111, 113, 219n134; Cecil Woolf Publishers and, 84–88, *86*, 94, 98, 99, 103–4; *Charles Hamilton Sorley* exhibition (1985), 80, 86–93, 94, 101, 103–4, 214n85; critical stature of, 83–84, *93–95*, 215–16n96, 215n94, 216n98; Graves and, 72–77, 85, 88, 90, 93, 97, 114, 118–19, 209n2, 209n6, 210–11nn25–26, 210n18, 210n20, 216n98, 220n135, 220n142; later popular responses to, 80–84; Loos, death at Battle of, 76, 81, 111, 211n27; Marlborough downs memorial to (*see* Sorley's Signpost); personality, sense of, 63, 105–6, 217n116; photos and drawings of, 89, 104; on Poets' Corner memorial, 87–88; posthumous cult of, 74–80; rethinking approach to, 117–19; Sassoon and, 72–77, 85, 90, 102, 210n15, 210n18, 210nn20–21, 216n98; as Scottish poet, 84, 88, 91–92, 105, 118, 222n154; signpost as insignia for, 104–6, *107*, *108*; signpost poems, 106–11; sites of memory/remembrance and, 91–96; surviving documentation for, 89–91; as war poet, 99, 217n115; Woolf on, 122–23, 136, 218n125, 223n12, 227n60
Sorley, Charles Hamilton, works about: MacMillan's *All the Hills and Vales Along* (oratorio), 118, 220n135; McPherson's *It Is Easy to Be Dead*, 117–18, 221–22nn151–152, 222n154; *The Ungirt Runner* and *The Goat Without Horns* (Swann), 78–80, 215n92; Wilson's biography and editions, 80, 81, 83, 84, 86, 88, 98–101, 103, 106, *108*, 215n92, 217–18nn117–118, 217n113, 218n125, 219n127

Sorley, Charles Hamilton, works by: "All the Hills and Vales Along," 83, 94, *95*, 112–13, 212n43, 220n135; "Barbury Camp," 83, 219n129; *Collected Letters of Charles Hamilton Sorley* (ed. Wilson), 81, 98, 100, 101, 217n117; *Collected Poems of Charles Hamilton Sorley* (ed. Wilson), 86, 99, 106, *108*, 215n92, 217n113, 219n127; "Expectans Expectavi," 212n43; "I Have Not Brought My Odyssey," 106–7, 219n127; *Letters from Germany and from the Army*, 96, 97, 98, 100, 210n18, 216n102, 217n117, 217nn108–9; *The Letters of Charles Sorley, with a Chapter of Biography*, 43, 70, 77, 79, 96, 97, 98, 216n105, 217n109, 217n113; "Lost," 106–10, 219n128, 221n146; "Marlborough," 105; *Marlborough and Other Poems*, 72, 89, 93, 94, 96–99, 105, 106, 216nn105–7, 219n127; *The Poems and Selected Letters of Charles Hamilton Sorley* (ed. Spear), 88, 106, *107*, 215n92, 217n110; "The Song of the Ungirt Runners," 78, 83, 215n95; "Stones," 219n129; "Two Sonnets," 109–11; *Verses from Marlborough: Charles Hamilton Sorley*, 92; "When You See Millions of the Mouthless Dead," 74, 110, 113–15, 209n6, 212n43, 215n94, 219n130, 220n138, 220n142
Sorley, Janetta C. (mother), 116, 211n33, 221nn145–47
Sorley, Kenneth and Jean (siblings), 93, 209n2, 221n147
Sorley, W. R. (father and Cambridge professor), 43, 74, 91, 96–100, 105, 114, 210n18, 210n25, 211n32, 215n86, 216n102, 216n106, 217nn108–9, 219n127, 221n147
Sorley's Signpost, 92, 102, *103*, 111–12, *112*, 115–16, 218n123; memorial stone, 102, 111, 219n133
Spear, Hilda D., ed., *The Poems and Selected Letters of Charles Hamilton Sorley*, 88, 106, *107*, 215n92, 217n110
spiritualism and psychical research, xii, 65–66, 129, 226n40, 229n84
Stallworthy, Jon, 80, 217n113, 217n115; Wilfred Owen, *The Complete Poems and Fragments*, 88, 99
Stephen, Martin, 211n34, 215n86; *Never Such Innocence*, 118; *The Price of Pity*, 78
Stevens, Dorothy, plaque to conscientious objectors, 155
Stewart, Susan, 34
Stewart, Victoria, 203n30

266   **INDEX**

Stodart-Walker, A., 43
Stones, Tom and Joseph William ("Willie"), 170, 176, 177
Strachan, Hew, 11
Strachey, Lytton, 35–36, 38, 55, 56, 148, 202n11; *Eminent Victorians*, 35–36, 202n11
Sturken, Marita, 59, 60, 173, 189
Survivors: formal recognition, lack of, 184, 237n22; "posthumous life" experienced by, 23–24, 40–41, 65, 123, 200n65; war memoirs of, 40–41
Sutton, Richard Vincent, 57, 62
Swann, Thomas Burnett, 210n25, 211n38, 212n40; *The Goat Without Horns*, 78–79; *The Ungirt Runner*, 78–80, 215n92
Sykes, Julian, *Shot at Dawn* (with Julian Putkowski), 164, 167, 168, 174, 237n17, 239–40n55

Tambling, Jeremy, *Becoming Posthumous*, 23
Tavistock Square, London, memorials in, 155–57, *157*
Taylor, Rex, 76
Tennant, Christopher Coombe, 44–45, *45*, 46, 129–31
Tennant, Edward Wyndham, 33–34, *34*, 45, 46, 57, *58*, 63–66, 207n91
Tennyson, Julian, 75
Thomas, Edward, 88, 102, 215n87
Thurtle, Ernest, *Shootings at Dawn*, 164, 239n50
Todd, Charles, 180
Todman, Dan, xi, 88, 195n3, 211n27, 214n79
Tollemache, Bevil, 49–50, 59–60
Tomb of the Unknown Warrior, 2, 5, 6, 8, 9, 120–21, 126, 137, 139, 142, 144, 145, 198n43, 224n29, 226n44, 231n111
Tomlin, Stephen, 156
Tomlinson, H. M., 40
"Tommy's sister," 151, 233–34n138
Tower of London: execution of enemy civilians in, 145–46, 231n116; Poppies installation at (2014), 1–6, *2*, *5*; violent history of, 19, 199n57
Toynbee, Arnold, 133
Treitell, Lady Phyllis, 83
Turner Prize, 6–7

United Kingdom: culture and heritage industries in, 6–7, 18, 85, 198n43; memory of WWI in, compared to US, xi–xii; textual focus on, 21–22. *See also* afterlife of WWI

United States: Confederate monuments controversy, xiii; Iraq/Afghanistan wars, xiii; National World War I Memorial, Washington, DC, xi; 9/11 and 9/11 Memorial, xiii, 22, 187; Vietnam Veterans Memorial, Washington, DC, 8, 170, 173, 189; WWI as "forgotten war" in, xi–xii
Unknown Warrior, Tomb of. *See* Tomb of the Unknown Warrior
the unmemorialized, 9–12, 26–27, 155–57, 161–66, 184. *See also* executed soldiers; *A Room of One's Own*
Unquiet Graves, guidebook, conference, and tour, 166–67, 177, 182

Vandiver, Elizabeth, 113, 114, 220n139
Vansittart, Peter, 51
Verdenal, Jean, 123
Verity, Simon, 104
Vietnam Veterans Memorial, Washington, DC, 8, 170, 173, 189

war books, boom in, and War Book Controversy, 123–25, 223n15, 224n23
war memorials. *See* memorials; *specific memorials by name*
war poets: affective response, ability to generate, 80, 81, 121, 218n121; *Anthem for Doomed Youth* exhibition (IWM, 2002), 101–4, 106, 110–11, 116–18, 214n77, 219n129; canonical members of, 94, 216n98; Cecil Woolf Publishers' War Poets Series, 84–85; executed soldiers compared to, 161; modernism and, 88, 136, 214n74; overremembrance and cultural canonization of, 25, 70, 87; Poets' Corner memorial, Westminster Abbey, 87–88, 93, 103, 211n27; public familiarity with, 11–12, 26; resurgence of interest in, 87–89, 214n77; rethinking approach to, 117–19; social and gender privilege of, 90, 91, 132–35; symbolism of, 117, 122, 213n67; Woolf's critiques of, 120–23, 127, 133, 136, 225n34. *See also* Sorley, Charles Hamilton, *and other specific war poets*
War Poets Association, 85
war resistance. *See* pacifism and antiwar sentiments
War Resisters International, 155
Ward, Lambert, 191–92
Warner, Sylvia Townsend, 82–83
Watson, Janet, 70, 124, 144
West, Arthur Graeme, 60, 207n100

INDEX 267

Westminster Abbey: Cavell, funeral service for, 142, *143*; Poets' Corner memorial, 87–88, *93*, 103, 211n27, 213–14nn71–73; tomb of Aphra Behn in, 126. *See also* Tomb of the Unknown Warrior

white poppies, 10–11

Whitehall, Woolf on, 137–38, *139*, 228n79

Whiteread, Rachel, 6, 7, 14

Wiesenthal, Simon, 7

Wilcox, Herbert, 153–54, 235n153

Williams, Gareth, and Oliver Emanuel, *The 306*, 15, 199n46

Wilson, Emily R., 40–41, 114, 203n33

Wilson, Jean Moorcroft, 80, 81, 83, 84, 86, 88, 98–101, 103, 106, *108*, 215n92, 217–18nn117–118, 217n109, 217n113, 218n125, 219n127

Wilson, John, *Hamp*, 180

Winter, Jay, 9, 20–21, 29, 32, 52, 87, 95–96, 123, 126, 130, 199n60, 213n67; *Sites of Memory, Sites of Mourning*, 7–8, 20, 32, 126

Wohl, Robert, 122, 124, 133, 223n11

women and gender issues, 27; careers and professions, 125, 145, 150; commemorative volumes authored by, 59; commemorative volumes to women, 226n41; erasure of women from public war narrative, 144, 149, 151–53, 162; gender as constructed and contingent, Woolf on, 139–40, 220n94; poets, women as, 122, 135–36, 228n69; traditional feminine values and portrayals of Cavell, 145, 149, 151; war memorials to women, 143–44, 149, 230n107, 233n131; war poets, social and gender privilege of, 90, 132–35; war resistance by, 151–52, 157, 234n140, 234n145, 235n158; war work by, 150–52, 233–34n138, 234nn142–43; women dying in service in WWI, 9, 144, 230n106. *See also* Cavell, Edith; Woolf, Virginia; women's suffrage movement

Women in Black, 148

Women's Co-operative Guild, 10

Women's International League for Peace and Freedom, 149

Women's Social and Political Union, 151

women's suffrage movement, 151, 152, 234n145, 234nn142–43

Wood, John, 212n43

Woolf, Cecil (publisher and nephew of Leonard), 84–88, *86*, 94, 98, 99, 101, 103–4

Woolf, Cecil (war poet and brother of Leonard), 84, 128, 132, 136, 225n37

Woolf, Leonard, 84, 128, 132, 137

Woolf, Philip (brother of Leonard), 84, 128, 132

Woolf, Virginia: on Rupert Brooke, 43, 44, 56, 122, 123, 136; Edith Cavell and, 140–42, 146–54, 231n118; Cenotaph and, 27, 57, 120–21, 130, 137–39, 229n84; on commemorative volumes, 43, 44, 56–58, 70, 128–31, 207n91, 209n131; on "lives of the obscure," 70, 209n131; memorial bust, Tavistock Square, London, 156, 235n159; modernism of, 125, 138–39, 224n23; posthumous and commemorative literature, sensitivity about, 126–31; on Sassoon, 127, 136, 225n33; on Sorley, 122–23, 136, 218n125, 223n12, 227n60; war poets critiqued by, 120–23, 127, 133, 136, 225n34; Cecil Woolf (brother-in-law), publication of war poetry of, 128, 136

Woolf, Virginia, works by: "Abbeys and Cathedrals," 226n48, 228n79; *Jacob's Room*, 229n87; "Lives of the Obscure," 70, 209n131; "Maturity and Immaturity," 207n91, 226n47; *Mrs. Dalloway*, 137, 224–25n30; "These Are the Plans," 134, 218n125, 226n47, 227n60; "Thoughts on Peace in an Air Raid," 135, 234n149; *Three Guineas*, 150, 151, 152, 153, 231n118, 234n139; "Two Soldier Poets," 225n34, 226n47; "Women and Fiction," 124, 126, 140, 223n19; *The Years*, 140, 141, 142, 146–47, 153, 231n117. *See also A Room of One's Own*

World War I. *See* afterlife of WWI

Yeats, W. B., 93, 136, 215n95

York Minster Women of Empire war memorial, 143–44, 234n143

Young, James E., 51, 138, 139

Lightning Source UK Ltd.
Milton Keynes UK
UKHW010635161222
413998UK00004B/123/J